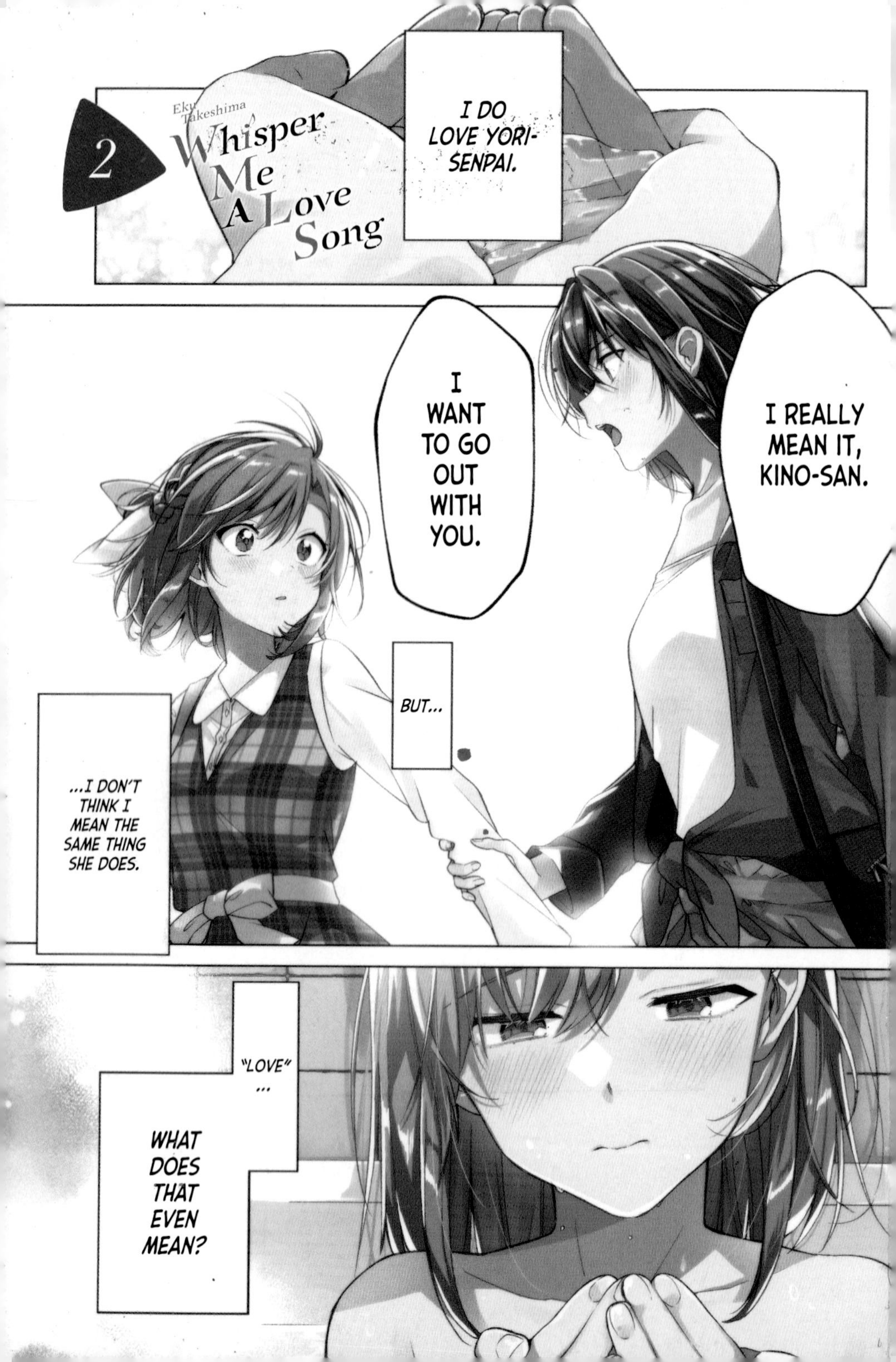

I DO LOVE YORI-SENPAI.
2
Eku Takeshima
Whisper Me A Love Song
I REALLY MEAN IT, KINO-SAN.
I WANT TO GO OUT WITH YOU.
BUT...
...I DON'T THINK I MEAN THE SAME THING SHE DOES.
"LOVE"...
WHAT DOES THAT EVEN MEAN?

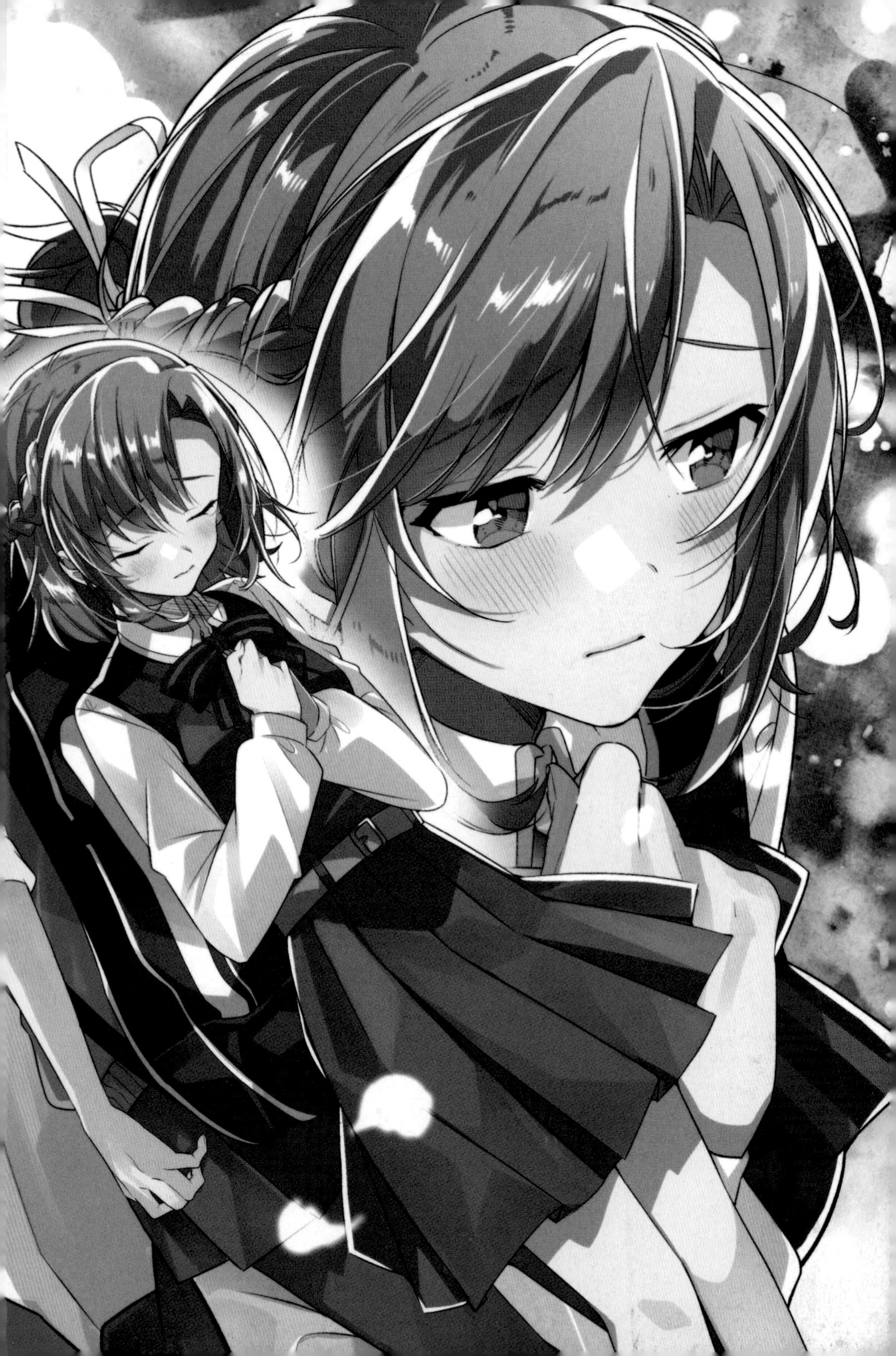

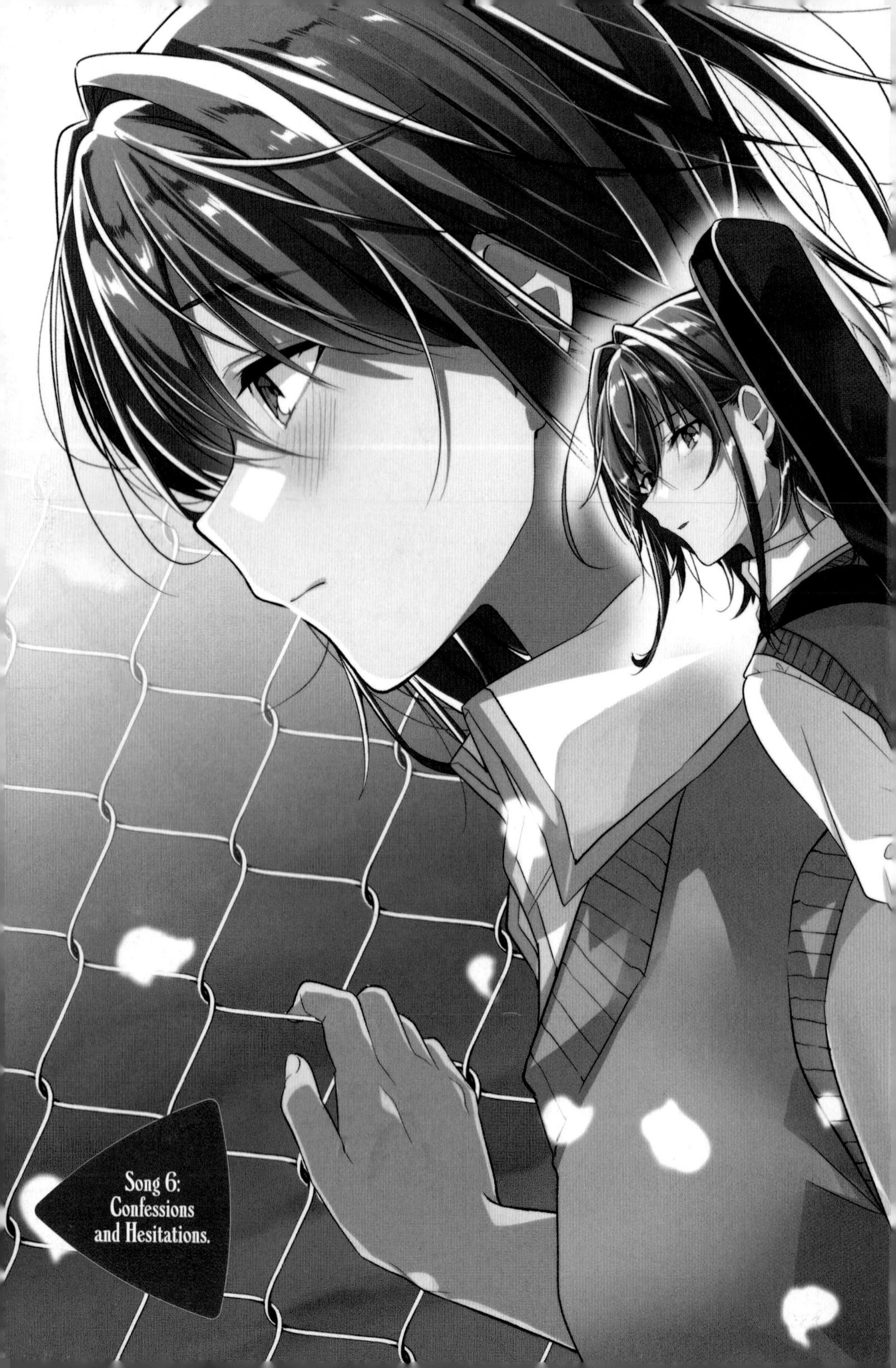
Song 6:
Confessions
and Hesitations.

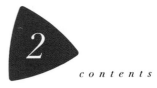

contents

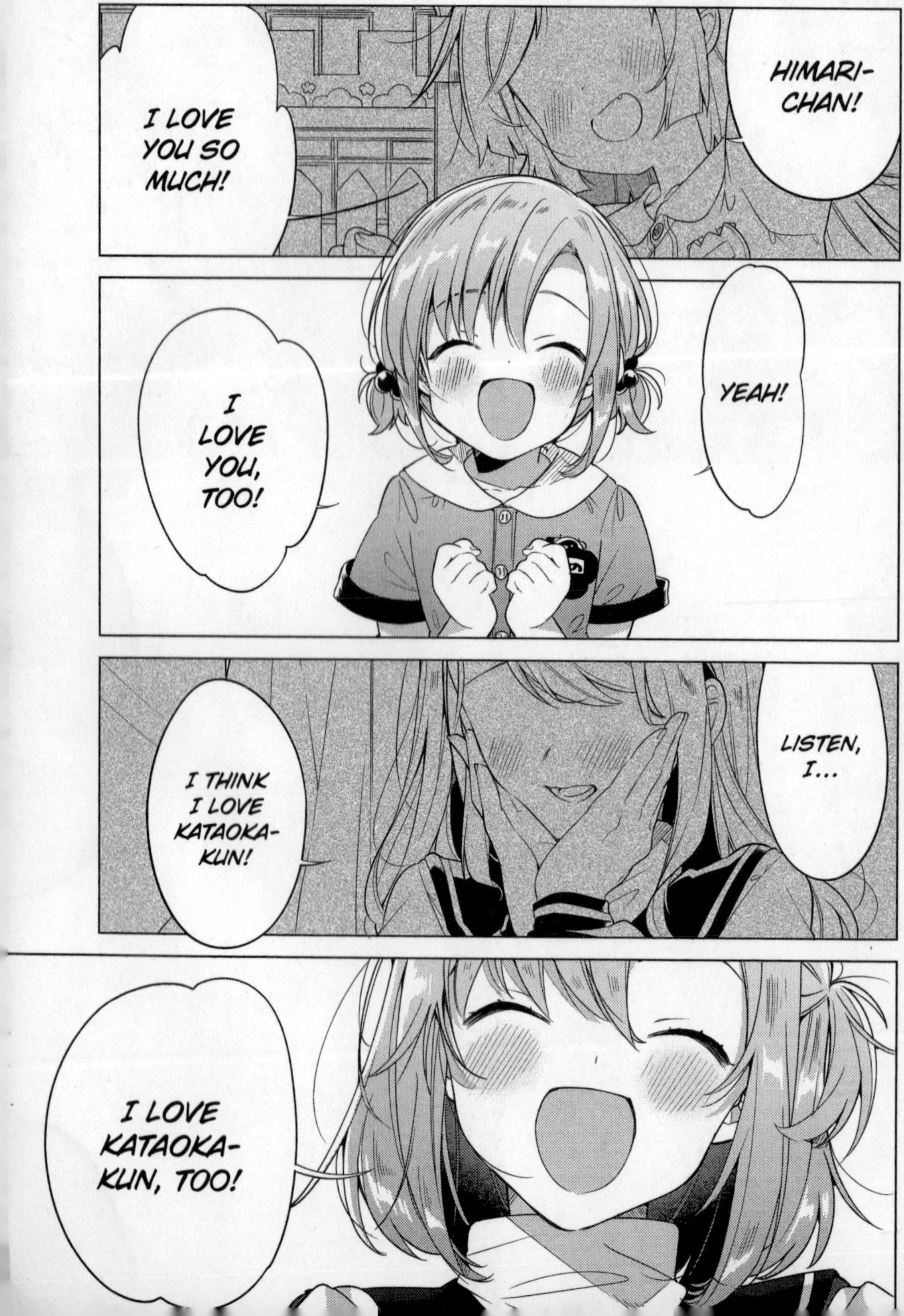
HIMARI-CHAN!
I LOVE YOU SO MUCH!
YEAH!
I LOVE YOU, TOO!
LISTEN, I...
I THINK I LOVE KATAOKA-KUN!
I LOVE KATAOKA-KUN, TOO!

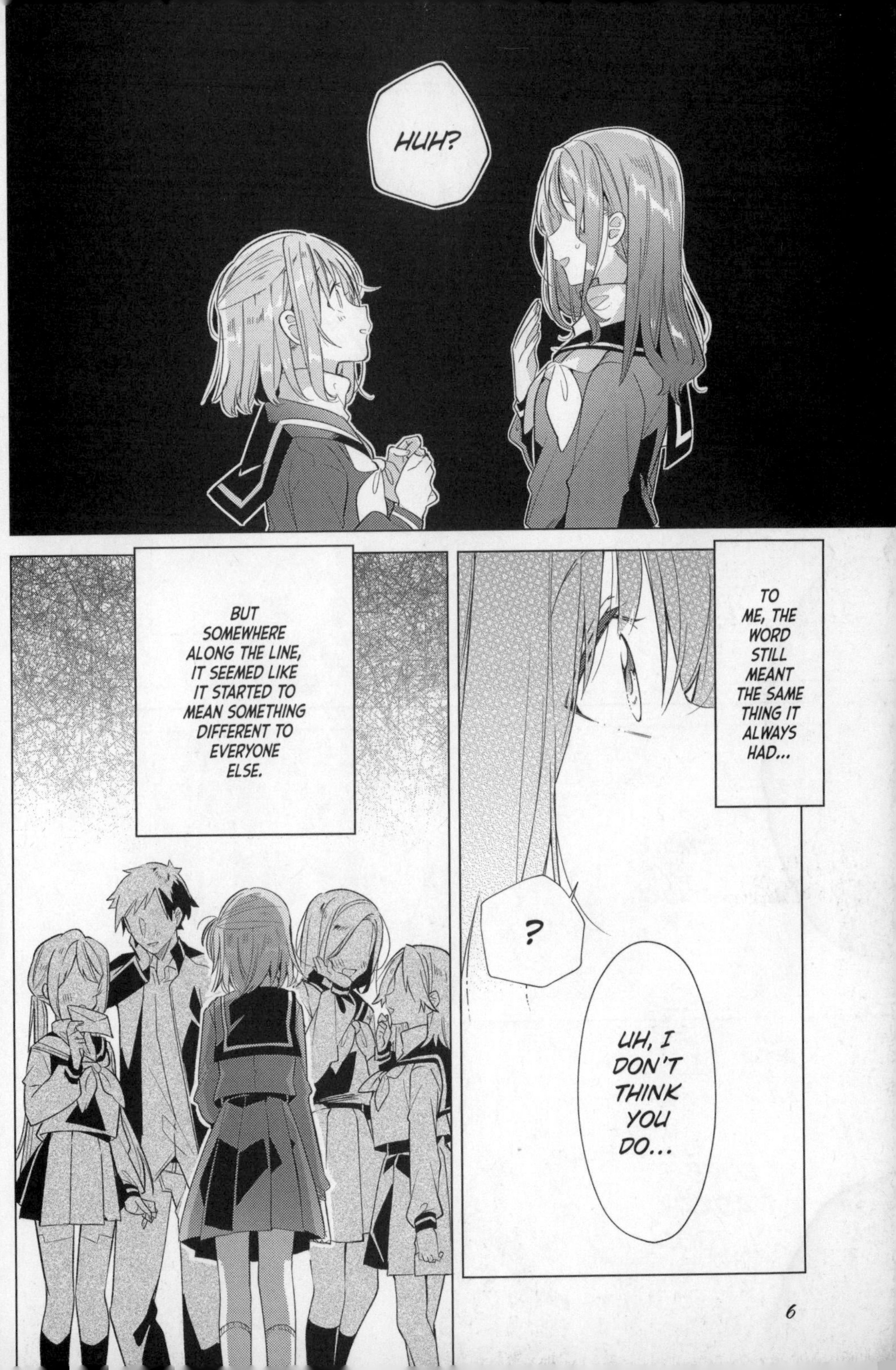
HUH?
TO ME, THE WORD STILL MEANT THE SAME THING IT ALWAYS HAD...
?
UH, I DON'T THINK YOU DO...
BUT SOMEWHERE ALONG THE LINE, IT SEEMED LIKE IT STARTED TO MEAN SOMETHING DIFFERENT TO EVERYONE ELSE.

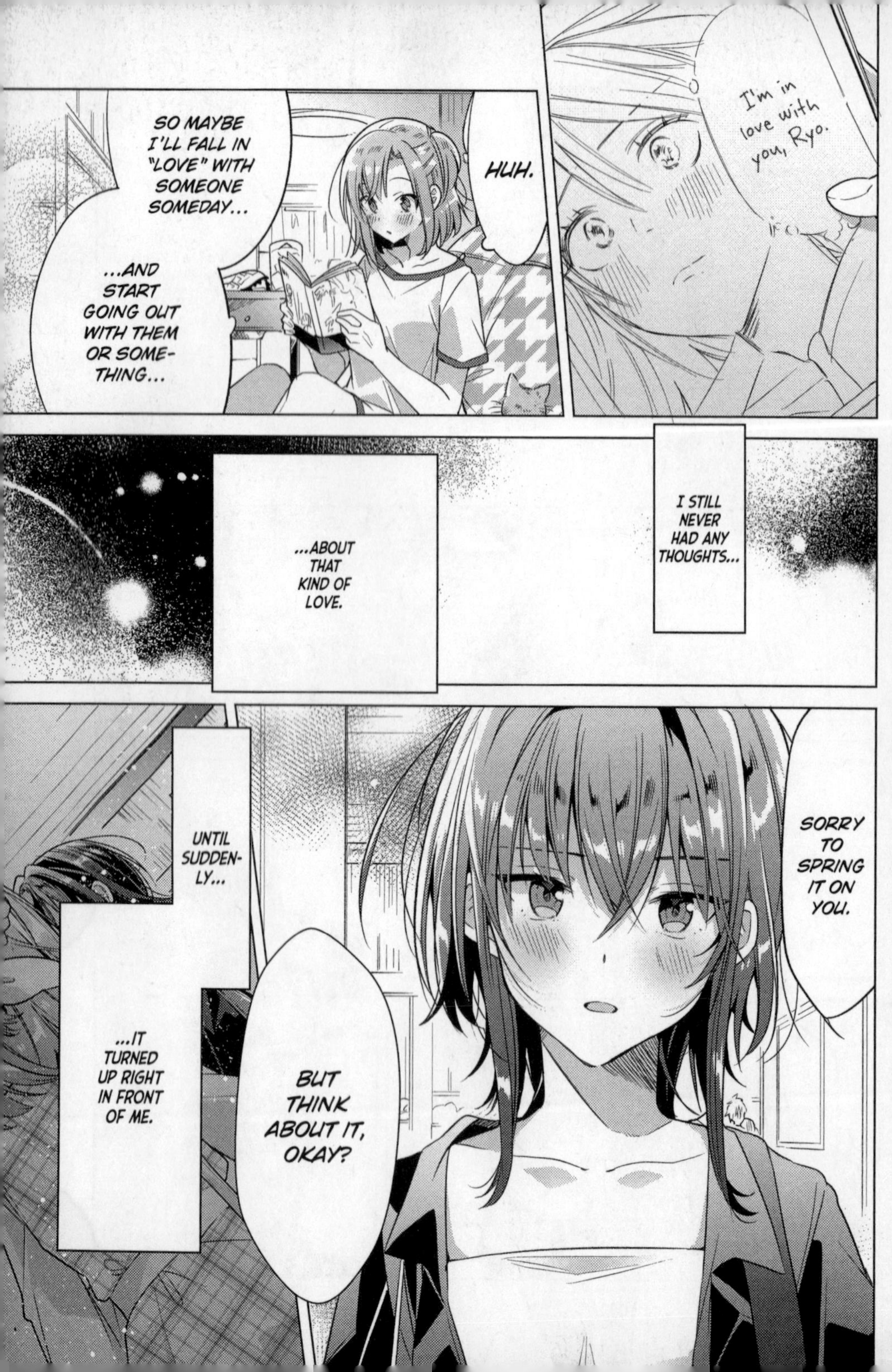
I'm in love with you, Ryo.
HUH.
SO MAYBE I'LL FALL IN "LOVE" WITH SOMEONE SOMEDAY...
...AND START GOING OUT WITH THEM OR SOME-THING...
I STILL NEVER HAD ANY THOUGHTS...
...ABOUT THAT KIND OF LOVE.
SORRY TO SPRING IT ON YOU.
UNTIL SUDDEN-LY...
BUT THINK ABOUT IT, OKAY?
...IT TURNED UP RIGHT IN FRONT OF ME.

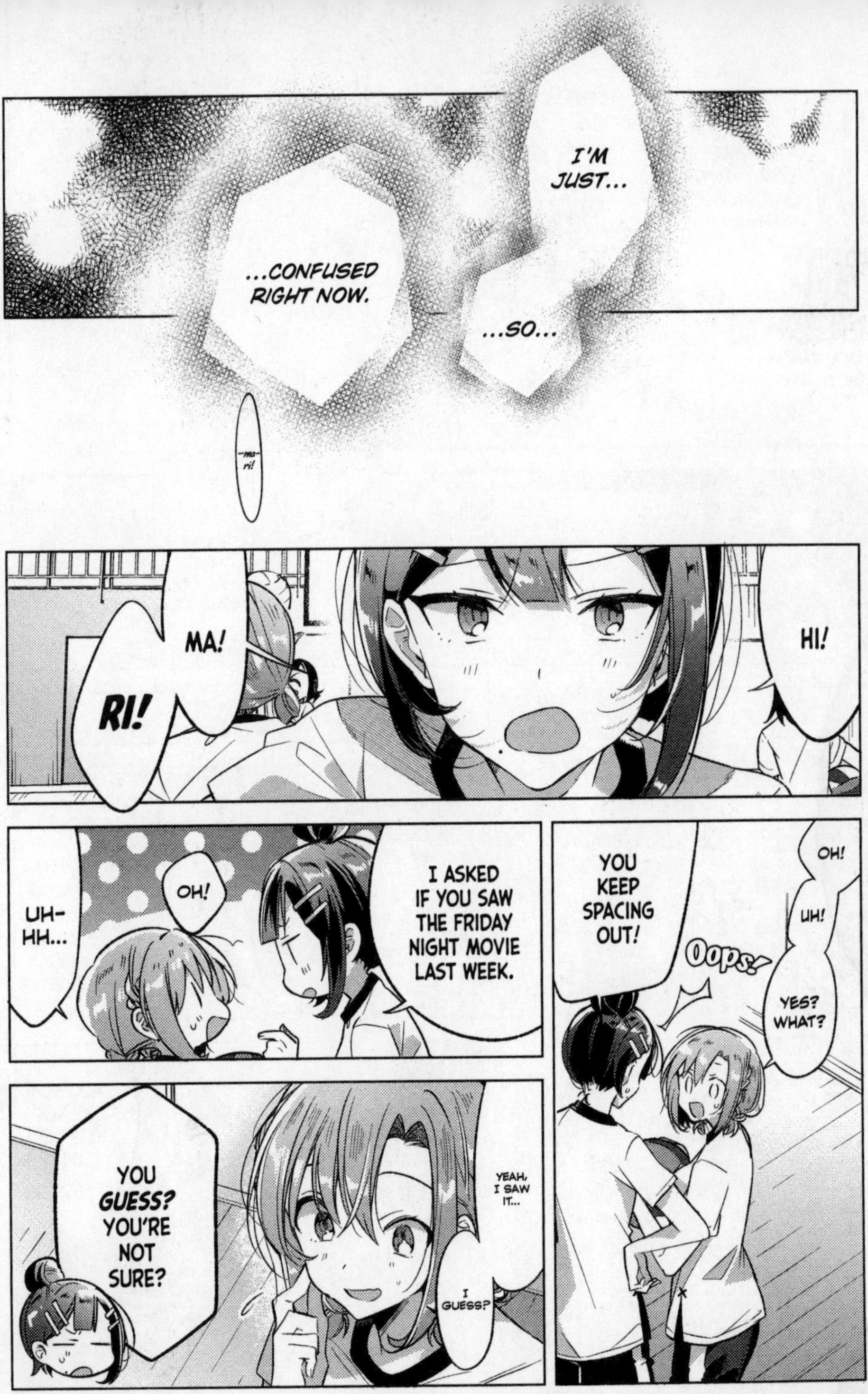
I'M JUST...
...CONFUSED RIGHT NOW.
...SO...
—ma-ri!
HI!
MA!
RI!
OH!
UH!
YES? WHAT?
Oops!
YOU KEEP SPACING OUT!
I ASKED IF YOU SAW THE FRIDAY NIGHT MOVIE LAST WEEK.
OH!
UH-HH...
YEAH, I SAW IT...
I GUESS?
YOU GUESS? YOU'RE NOT SURE?

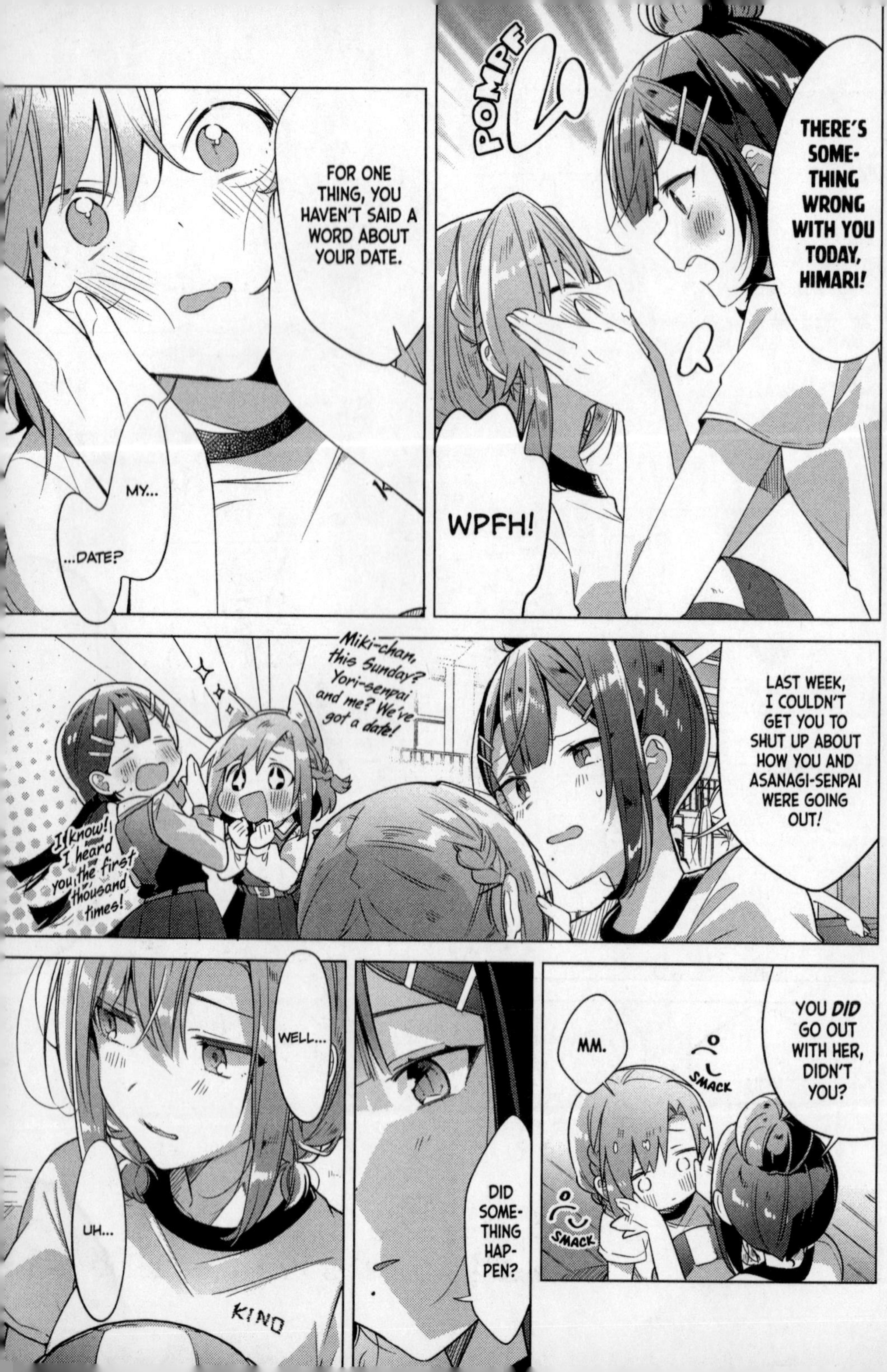
POMPF
THERE'S SOMETHING WRONG WITH YOU TODAY, HIMARI!
WPFH!
FOR ONE THING, YOU HAVEN'T SAID A WORD ABOUT YOUR DATE.
MY...
...DATE?
LAST WEEK, I COULDN'T GET YOU TO SHUT UP ABOUT HOW YOU AND ASANAGI-SENPAI WERE GOING OUT!
Miki-chan, this Sunday? Yori-senpai and me? We've got a date!
I know! I heard you the first thousand times!
YOU *DID* GO OUT WITH HER, DIDN'T YOU?
SMACK
MM.
SMACK
DID SOMETHING HAPPEN?
WELL...
UH...
KINO

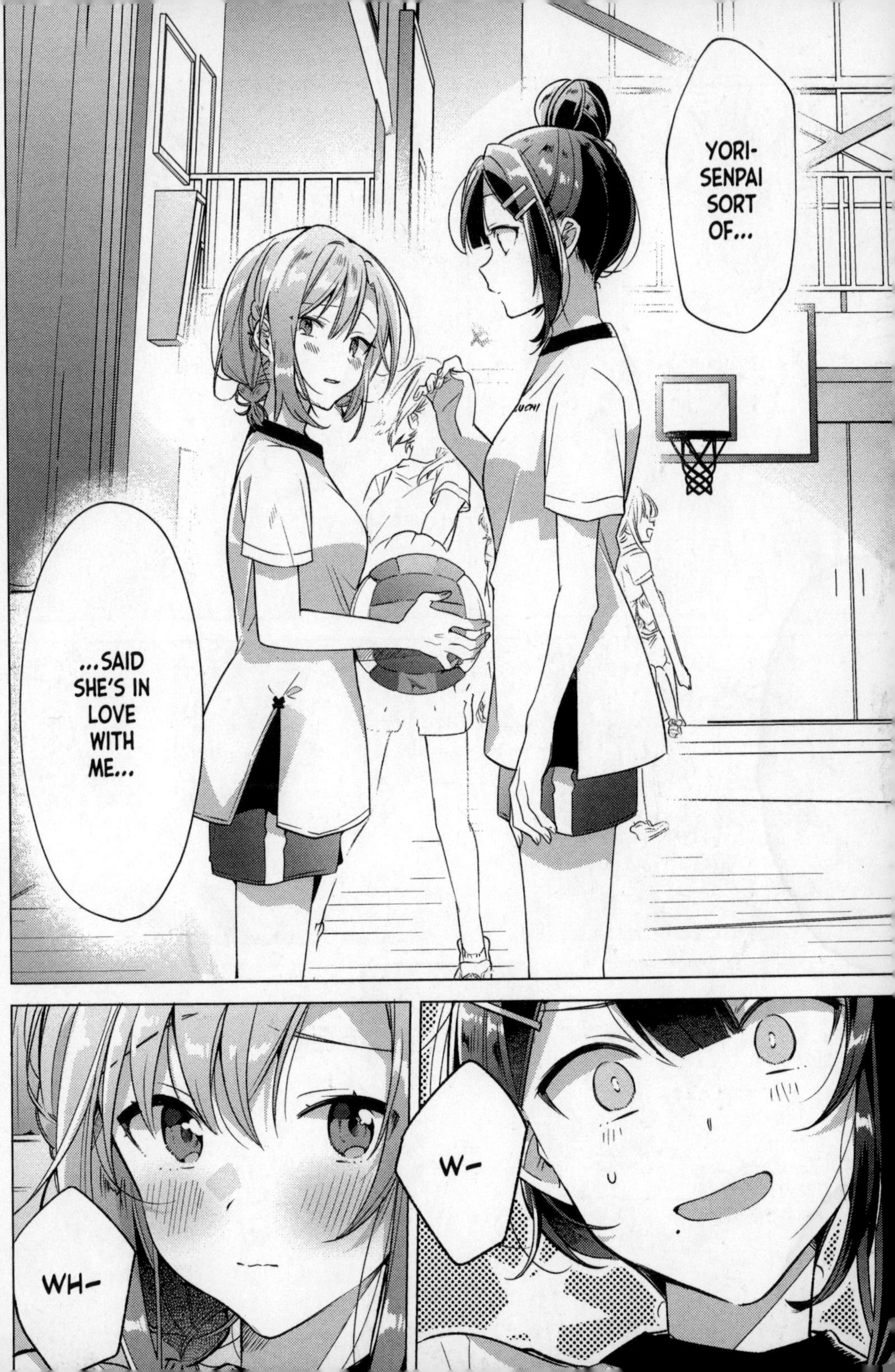
YORI-SENPAI SORT OF...
...SAID SHE'S IN LOVE WITH ME...
W-
WH-

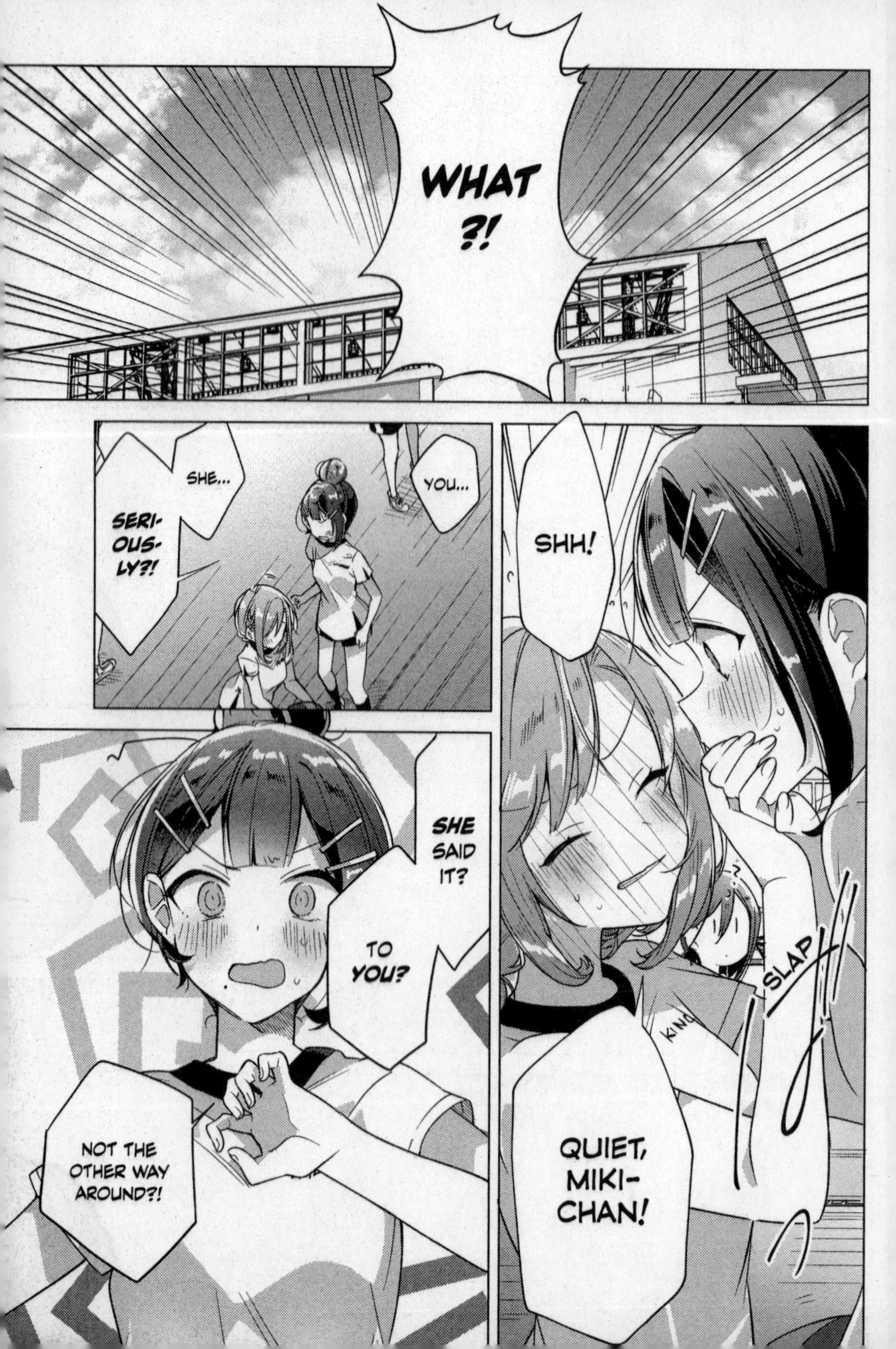
WHAT ?!
SHH!
SLAP
QUIET, MIKI-CHAN!
YOU...
SHE...
SERIOUSLY?!
SHE SAID IT?
TO YOU?
NOT THE OTHER WAY AROUND?!

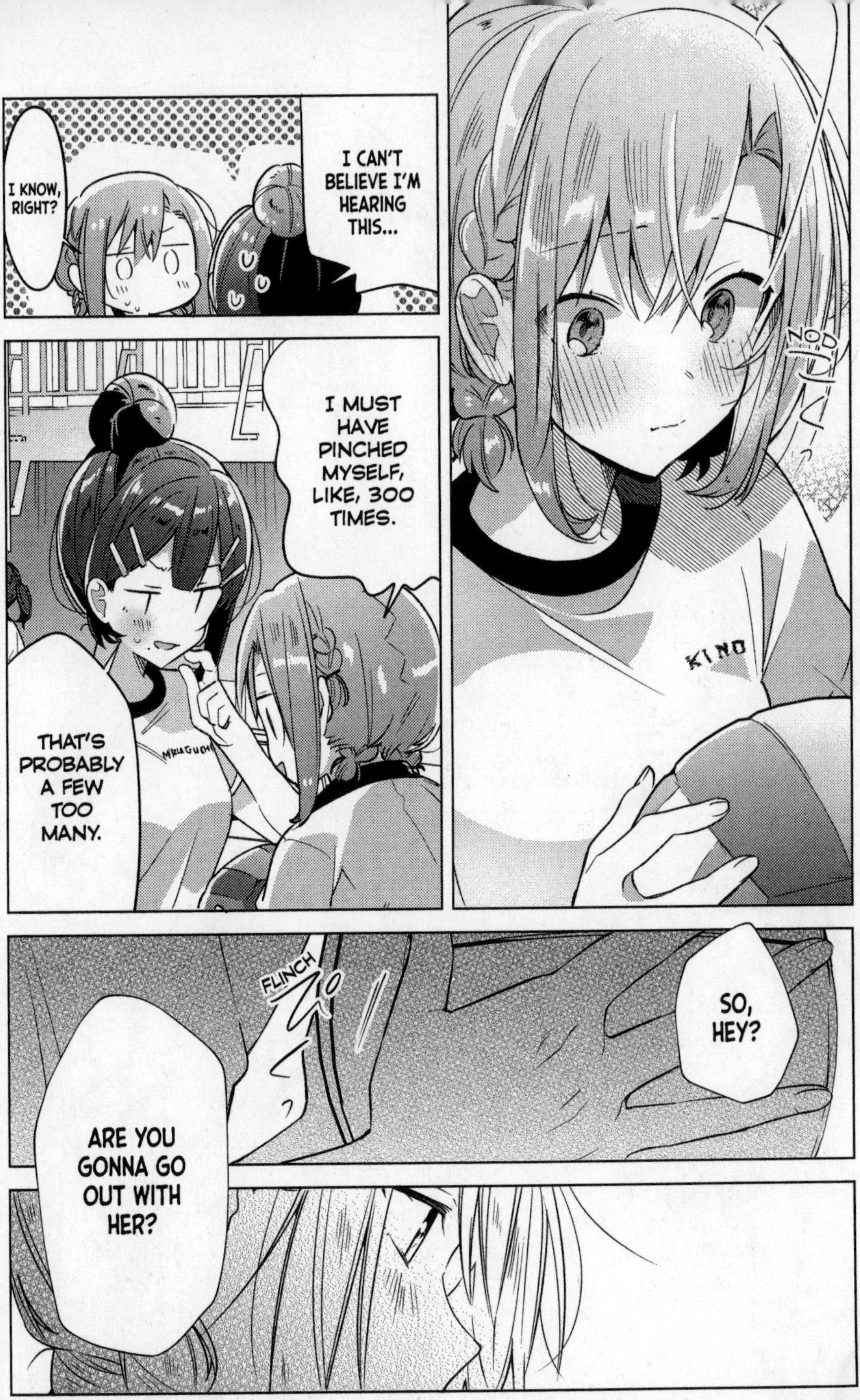
NOD
KINO
I CAN'T BELIEVE I'M HEARING THIS...
I KNOW, RIGHT?
I MUST HAVE PINCHED MYSELF, LIKE, 300 TIMES.
THAT'S PROBABLY A FEW TOO MANY.
SO, HEY?
FLINCH
ARE YOU GONNA GO OUT WITH HER?

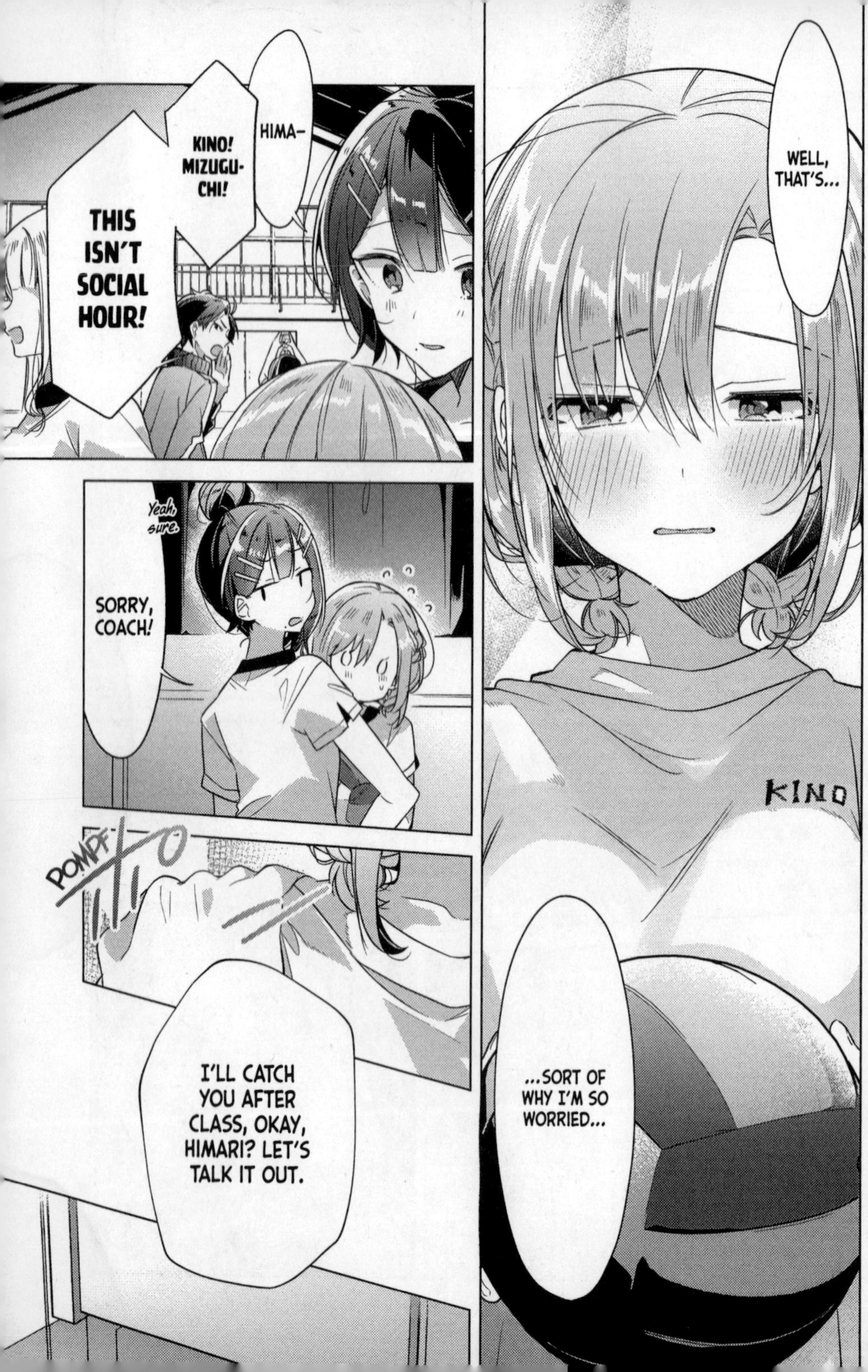
WELL, THAT'S...
KINO
...SORT OF WHY I'M SO WORRIED...
HIMA–
KINO! MIZUGU-CHI!
THIS ISN'T SOCIAL HOUR!
Yeah, sure.
SORRY, COACH!
POMPF
I'LL CATCH YOU AFTER CLASS, OKAY, HIMARI? LET'S TALK IT OUT.

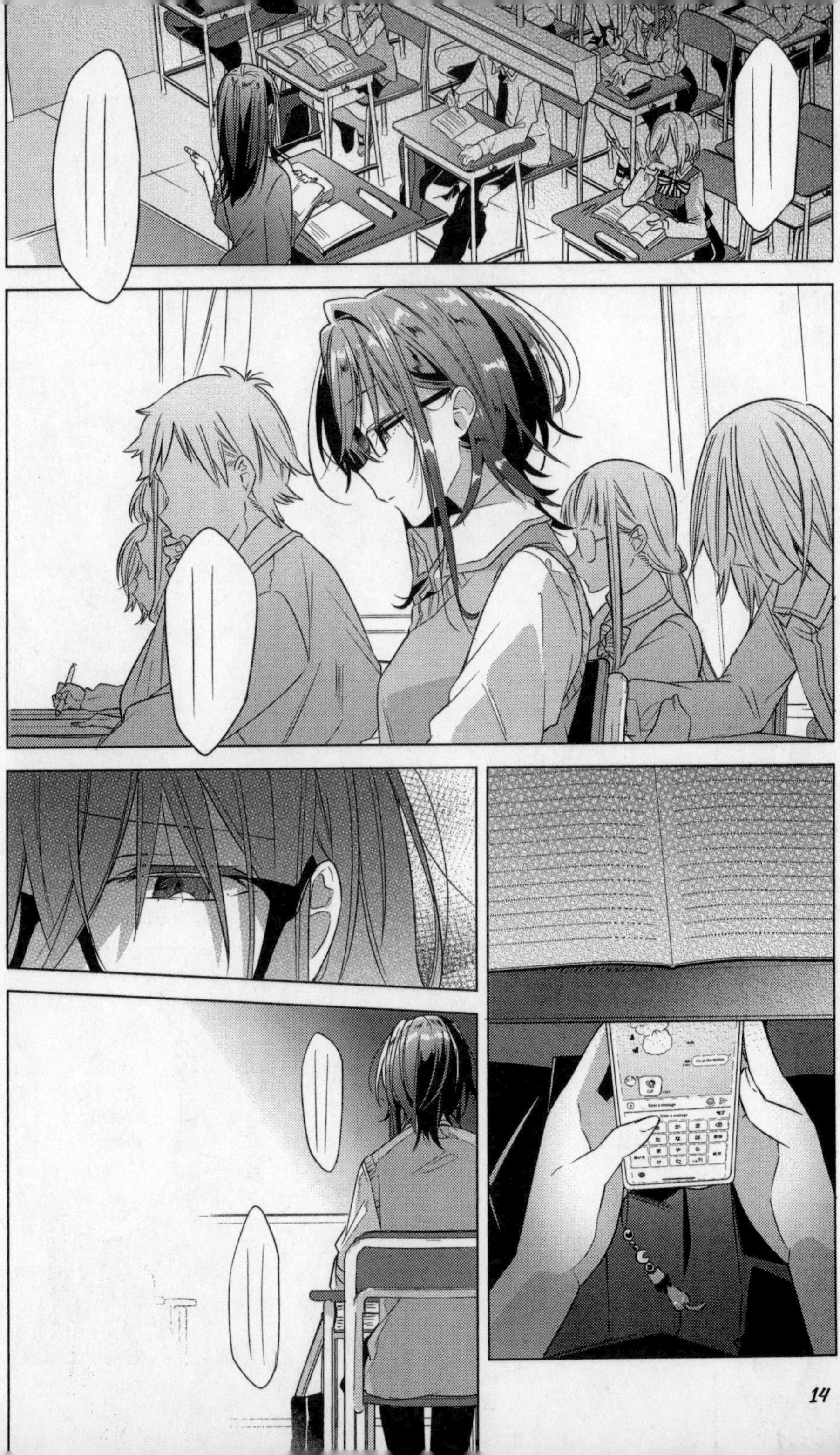
I'm at the station.
Call
Enter a message

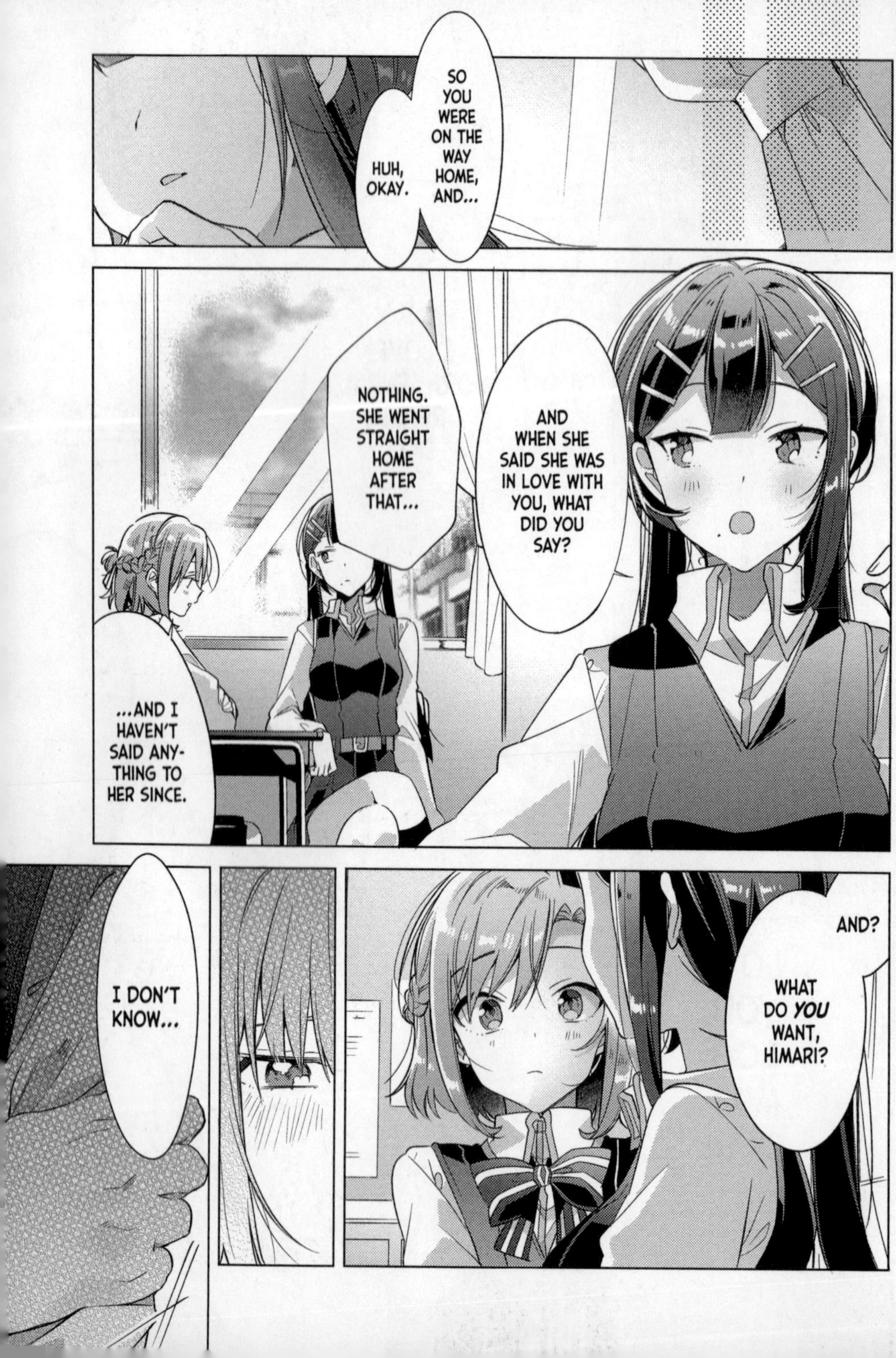
SO YOU WERE ON THE WAY HOME, AND...
HUH, OKAY.
AND WHEN SHE SAID SHE WAS IN LOVE WITH YOU, WHAT DID YOU SAY?
NOTHING. SHE WENT STRAIGHT HOME AFTER THAT...
...AND I HAVEN'T SAID ANY-THING TO HER SINCE.
AND?
WHAT DO *YOU* WANT, HIMARI?
I DON'T KNOW...

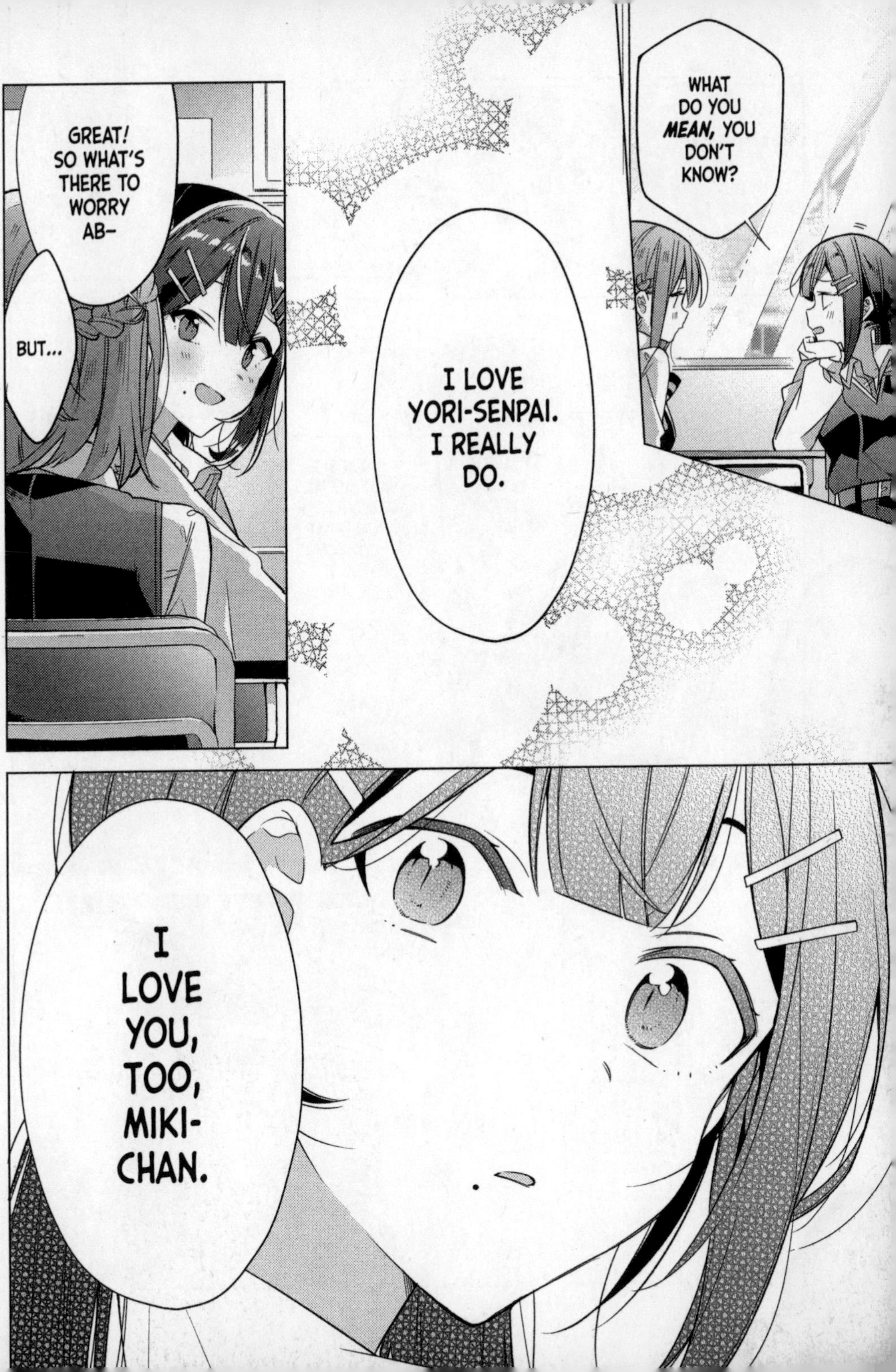
WHAT DO YOU MEAN, YOU DON'T KNOW?
I LOVE YORI-SENPAI. I REALLY DO.
GREAT! SO WHAT'S THERE TO WORRY AB–
BUT...
I LOVE YOU, TOO, MIKI-CHAN.

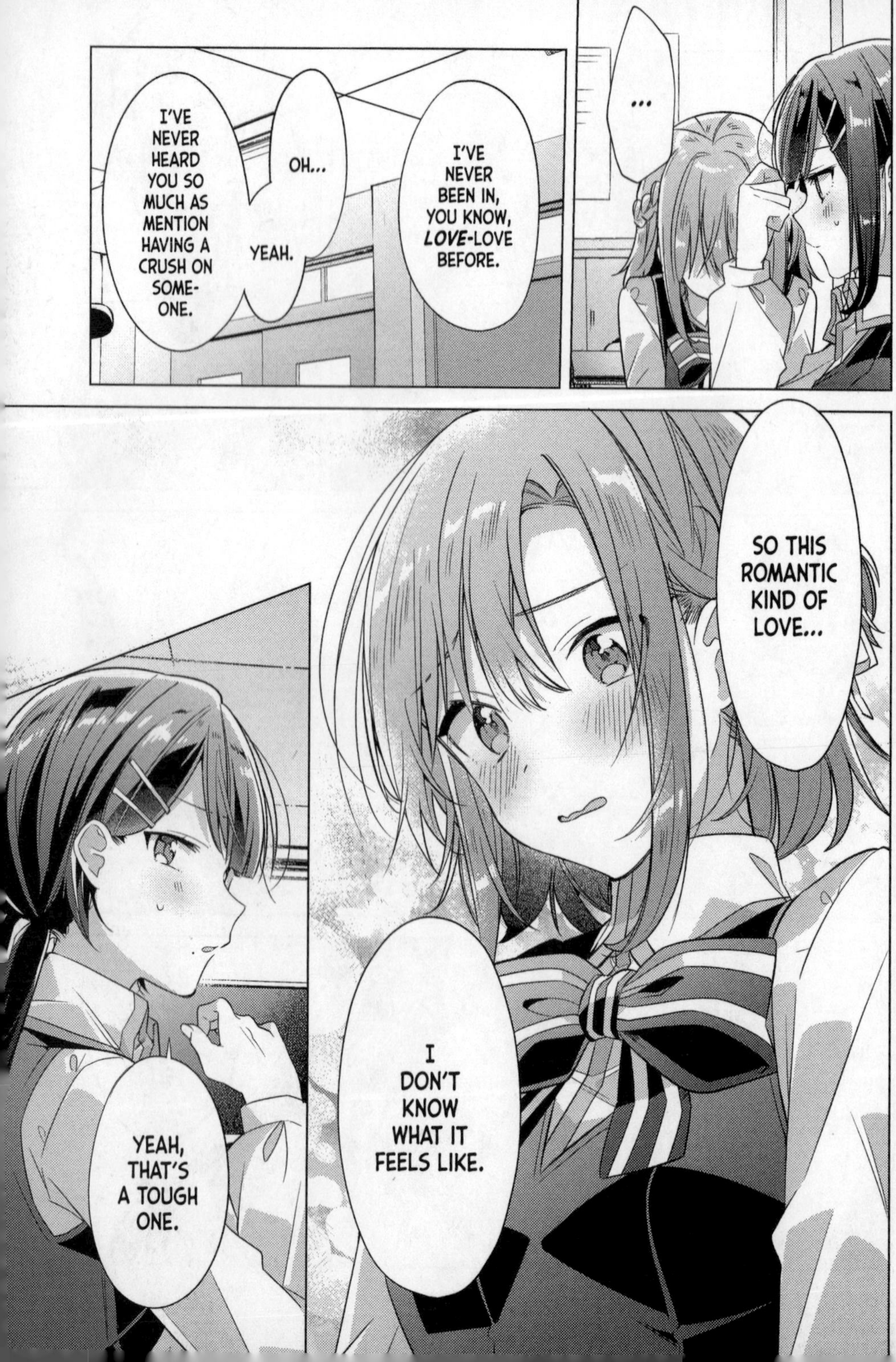
...
I'VE NEVER BEEN IN, YOU KNOW, *LOVE*-LOVE BEFORE.
OH... YEAH.
I'VE NEVER HEARD YOU SO MUCH AS MENTION HAVING A CRUSH ON SOME-ONE.
SO THIS ROMANTIC KIND OF LOVE...
I DON'T KNOW WHAT IT FEELS LIKE.
YEAH, THAT'S A TOUGH ONE.

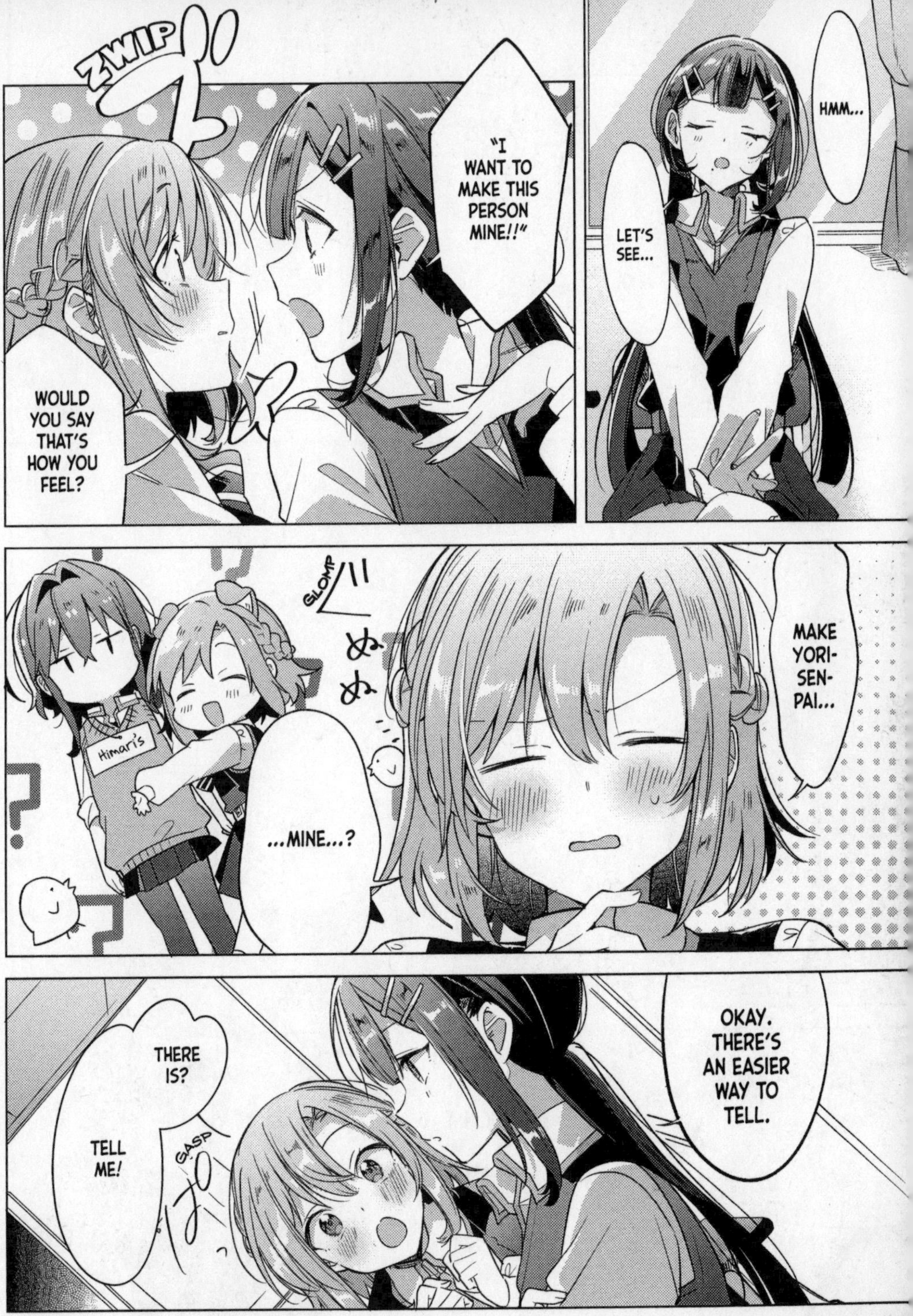
HMM...
LET'S SEE...
ZWIP
"I WANT TO MAKE THIS PERSON MINE!!"
WOULD YOU SAY THAT'S HOW YOU FEEL?
MAKE YORI-SENPAI...
...MINE...?
GLOMP
Himari's
OKAY. THERE'S AN EASIER WAY TO TELL.
GASP
THERE IS?
TELL ME!

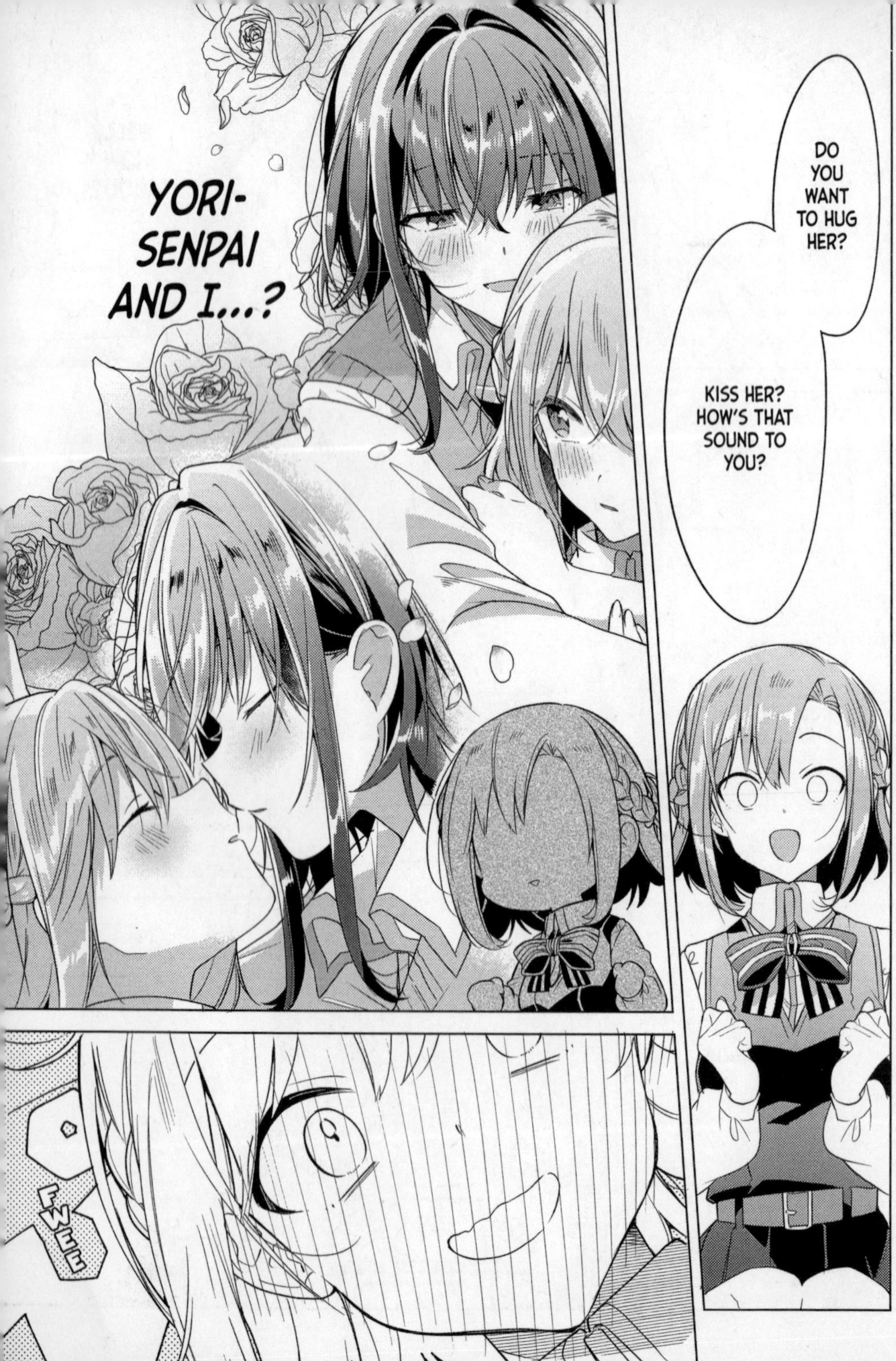
DO YOU WANT TO HUG HER?
KISS HER? HOW'S THAT SOUND TO YOU?
YORI-SENPAI AND I...?
FWEE

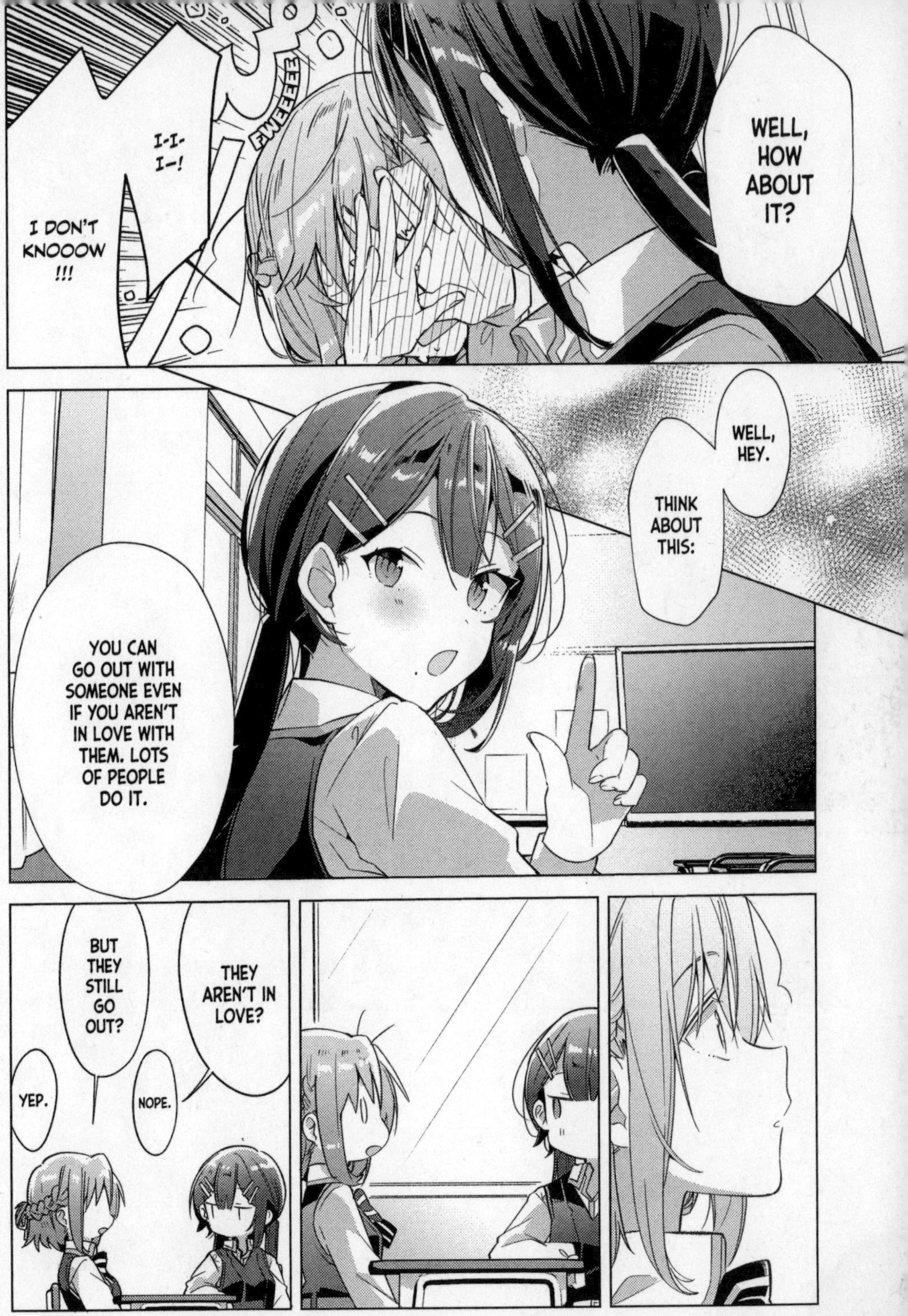
WELL, HOW ABOUT IT?
I-I-I–!
FWEEEEEE
I DON'T KNOOOW!!!
WELL, HEY.
THINK ABOUT THIS:
YOU CAN GO OUT WITH SOMEONE EVEN IF YOU AREN'T IN LOVE WITH THEM. LOTS OF PEOPLE DO IT.
THEY AREN'T IN LOVE?
BUT THEY STILL GO OUT?
NOPE.
YEP.

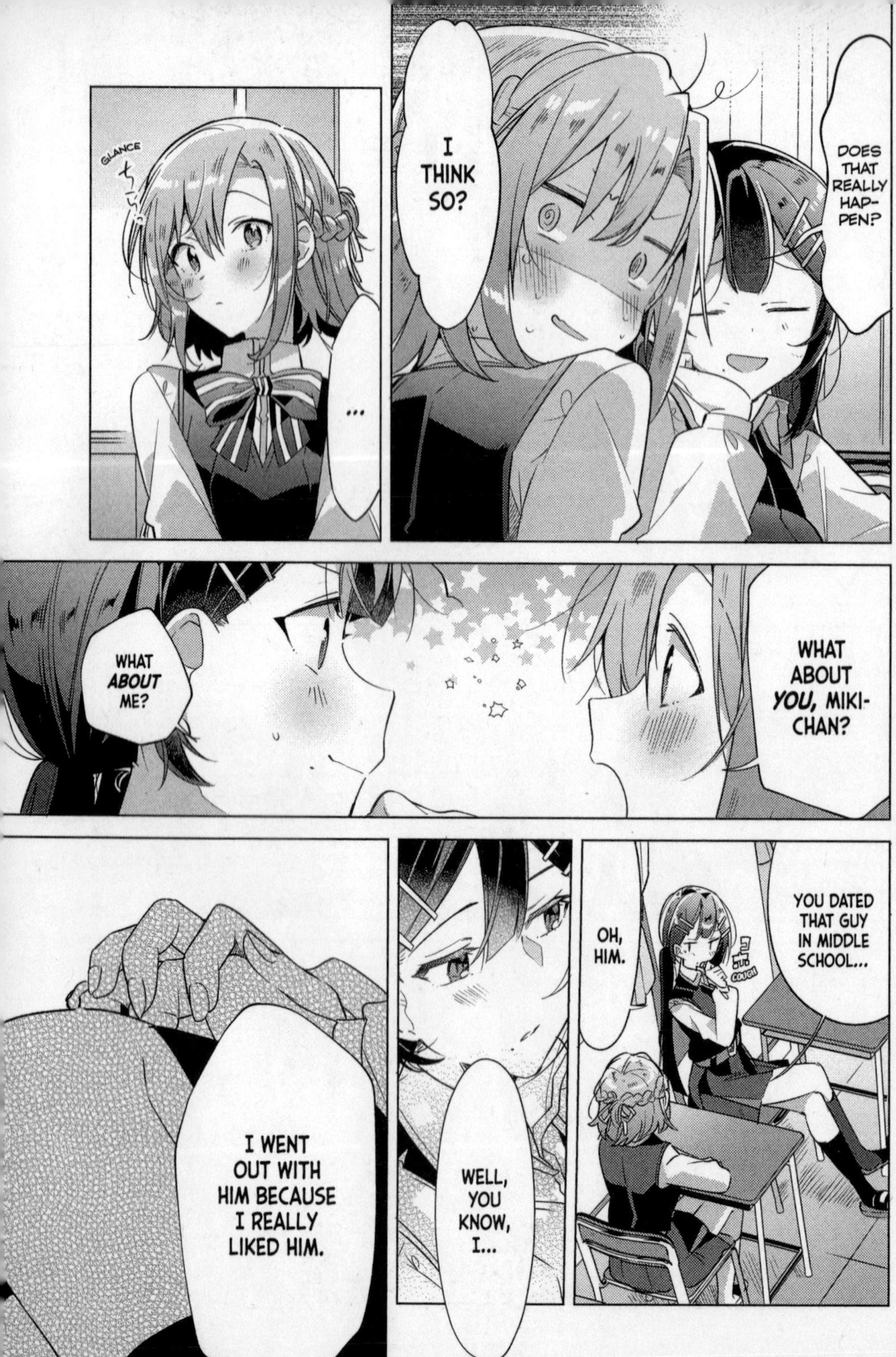
DOES THAT REALLY HAP-PEN?
I THINK SO?
GLANCE
...
WHAT ABOUT *YOU,* MIKI-CHAN?
WHAT *ABOUT* ME?
YOU DATED THAT GUY IN MIDDLE SCHOOL...
OH, HIM.
COUGH
WELL, YOU KNOW, I...
I WENT OUT WITH HIM BECAUSE I REALLY LIKED HIM.

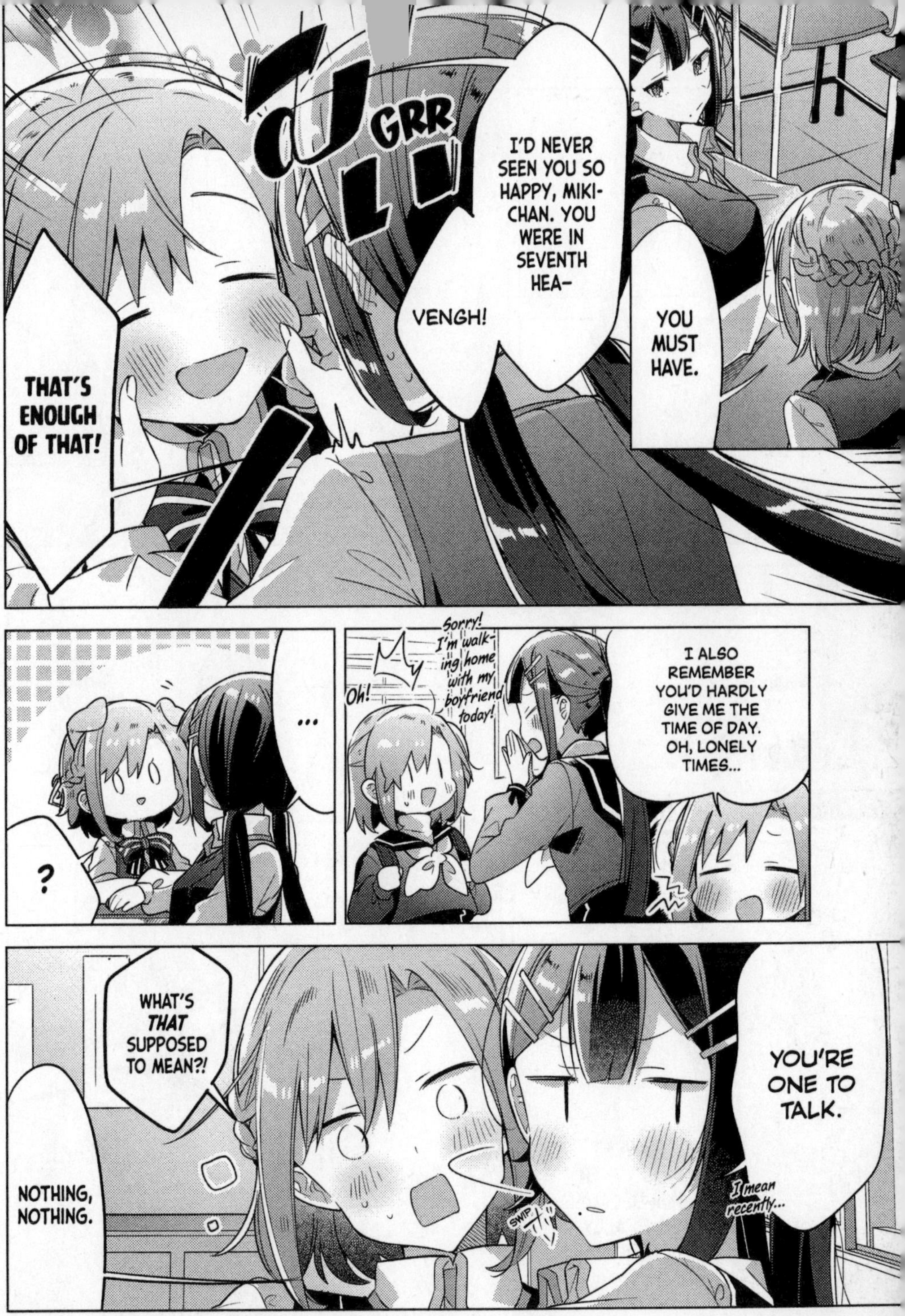
YOU MUST HAVE.
I'D NEVER SEEN YOU SO HAPPY, MIKI-CHAN. YOU WERE IN SEVENTH HEA-
VENGH!
GRR
THAT'S ENOUGH OF THAT!
I ALSO REMEMBER YOU'D HARDLY GIVE ME THE TIME OF DAY. OH, LONELY TIMES...
Sorry! I'm walking home with my boyfriend today!
Oh!
...
?
YOU'RE ONE TO TALK.
I mean recently...
SWIP
WHAT'S *THAT* SUPPOSED TO MEAN?!
NOTHING, NOTHING.

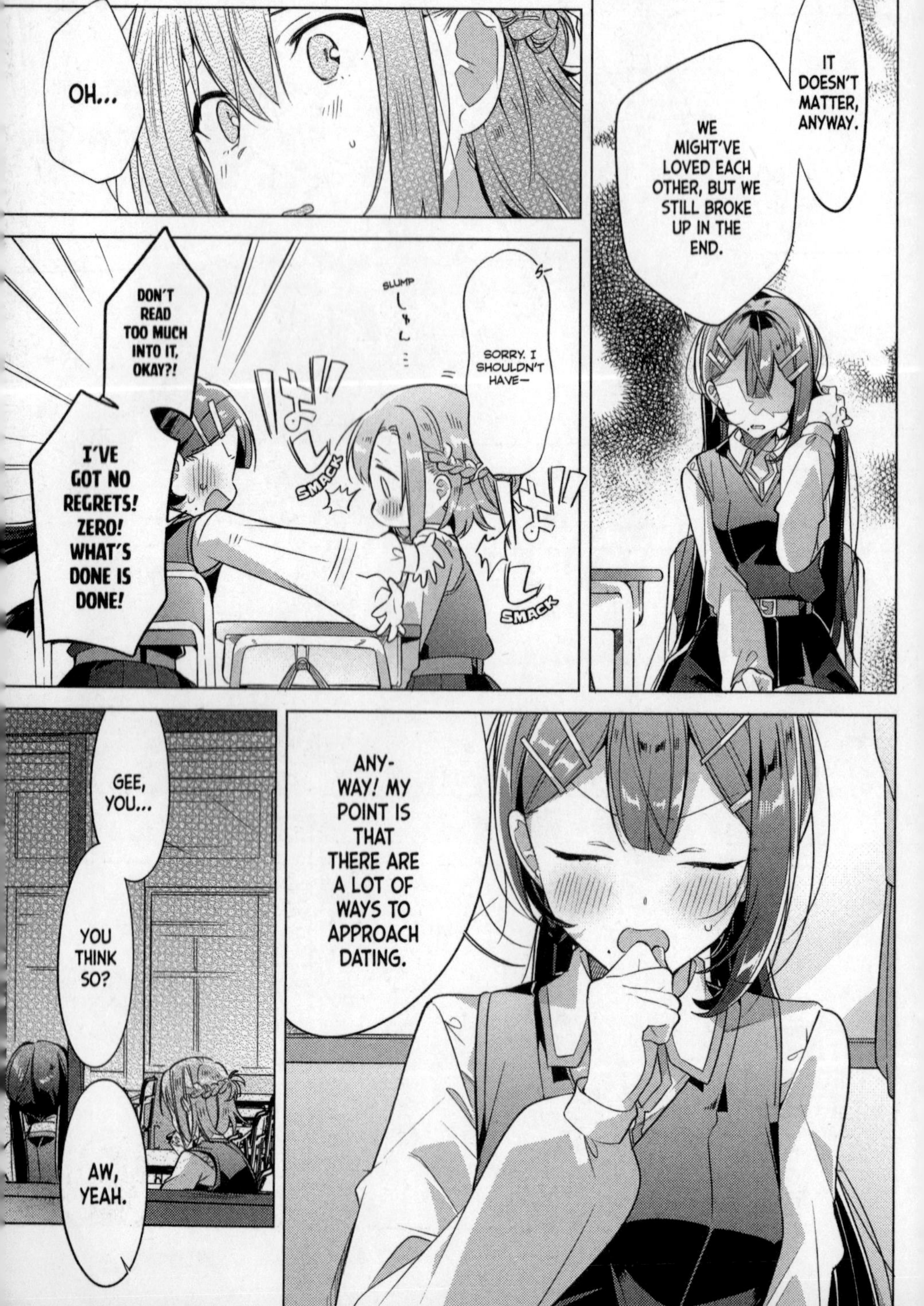
IT DOESN'T MATTER, ANYWAY.
WE MIGHT'VE LOVED EACH OTHER, BUT WE STILL BROKE UP IN THE END.
OH...
S—
SORRY. I SHOULDN'T HAVE—
SLUMP
SMACK
SMACK
DON'T READ TOO MUCH INTO IT, OKAY?!
I'VE GOT NO REGRETS! ZERO! WHAT'S DONE IS DONE!
ANY-WAY! MY POINT IS THAT THERE ARE A LOT OF WAYS TO APPROACH DATING.
GEE, YOU...
YOU THINK SO?
AW, YEAH.

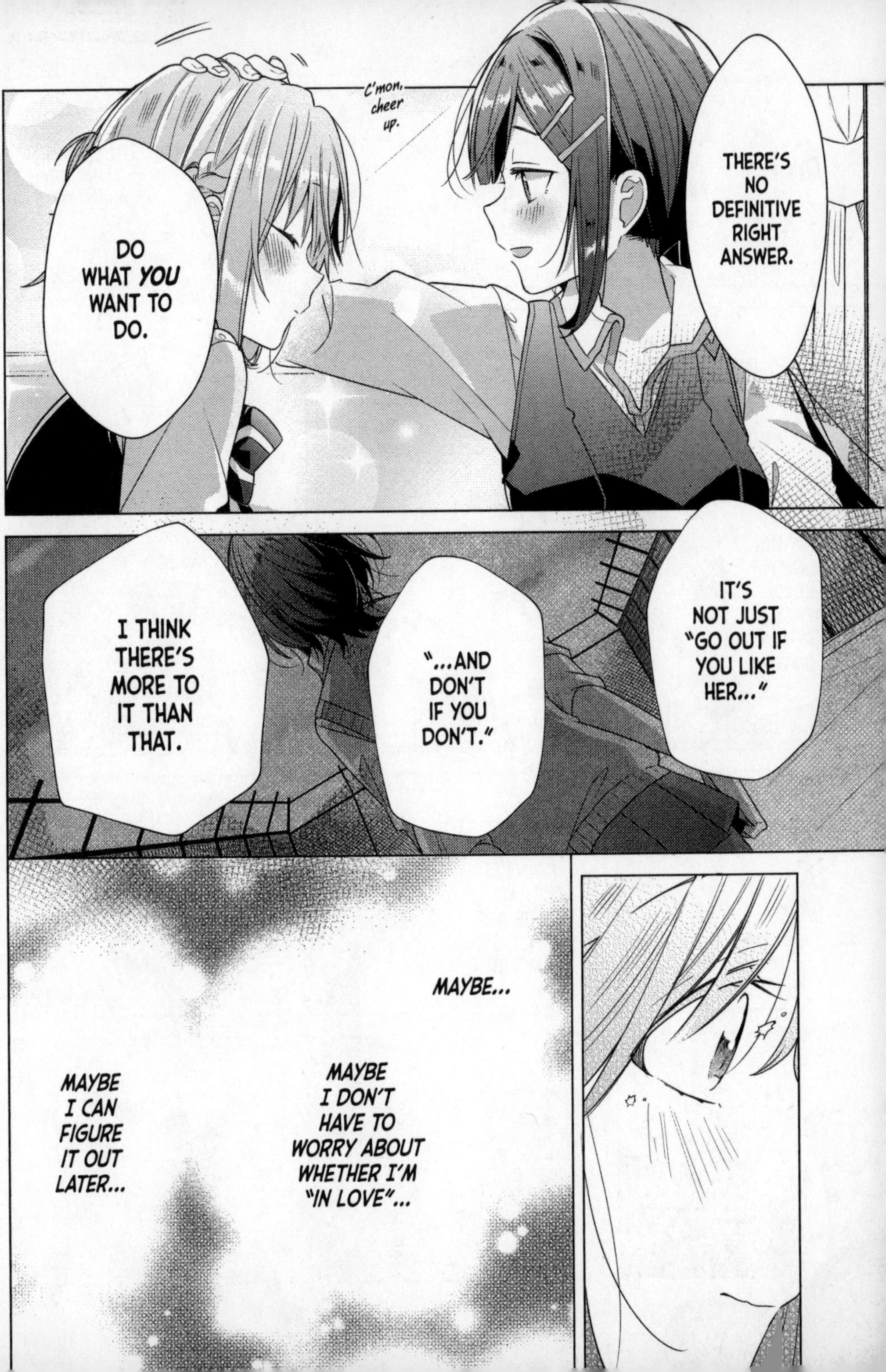
THERE'S NO DEFINITIVE RIGHT ANSWER.
C'mon, cheer up.
DO WHAT *YOU* WANT TO DO.
IT'S NOT JUST "GO OUT IF YOU LIKE HER..."
"...AND DON'T IF YOU DON'T."
I THINK THERE'S MORE TO IT THAN THAT.
MAYBE...
MAYBE I DON'T HAVE TO WORRY ABOUT WHETHER I'M "IN LOVE"...
MAYBE I CAN FIGURE IT OUT LATER...

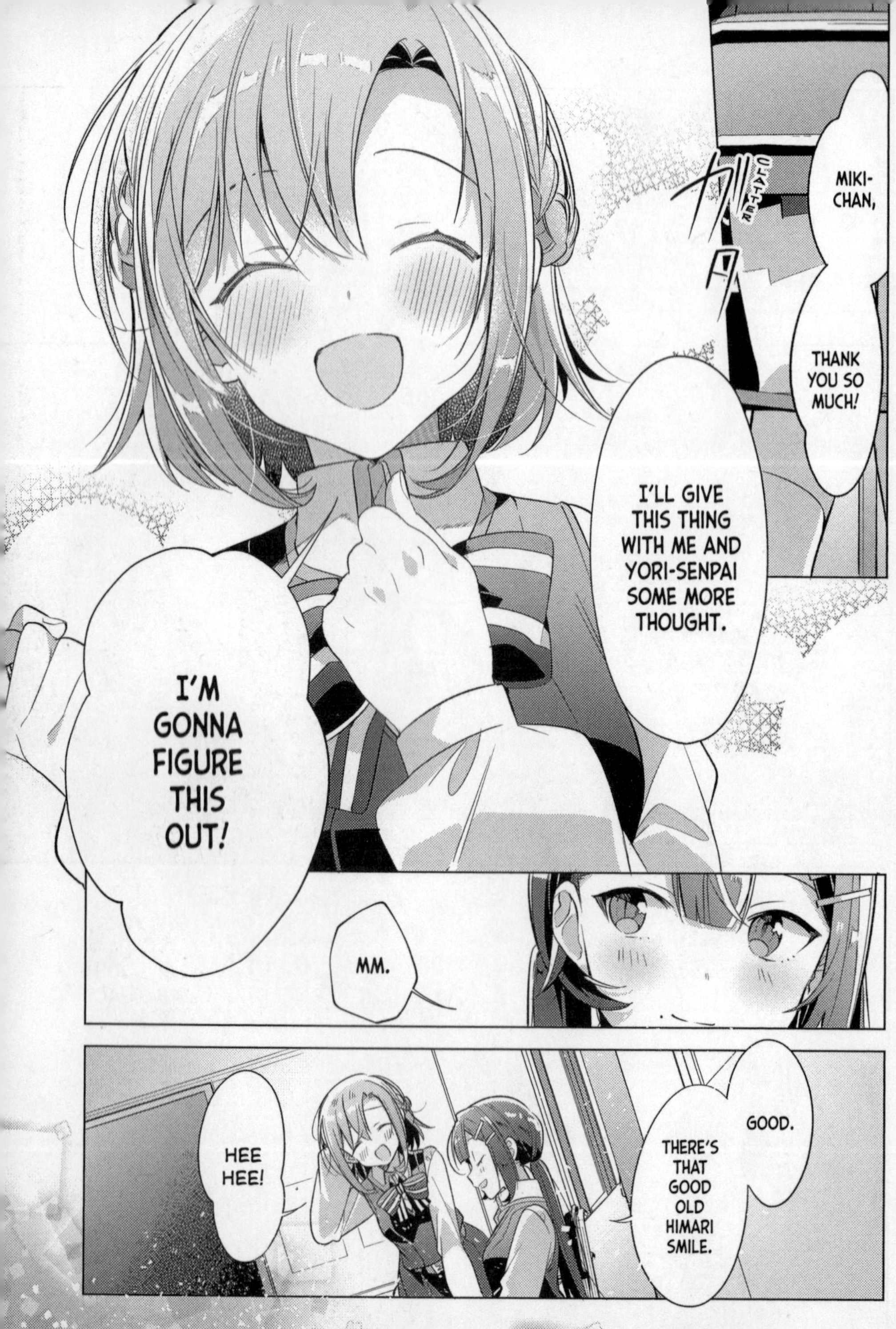
CLATTER
MIKI-CHAN,
THANK YOU SO MUCH!
I'LL GIVE THIS THING WITH ME AND YORI-SENPAI SOME MORE THOUGHT.
I'M GONNA FIGURE THIS OUT!
MM.
GOOD.
THERE'S THAT GOOD OLD HIMARI SMILE.
HEE HEE!

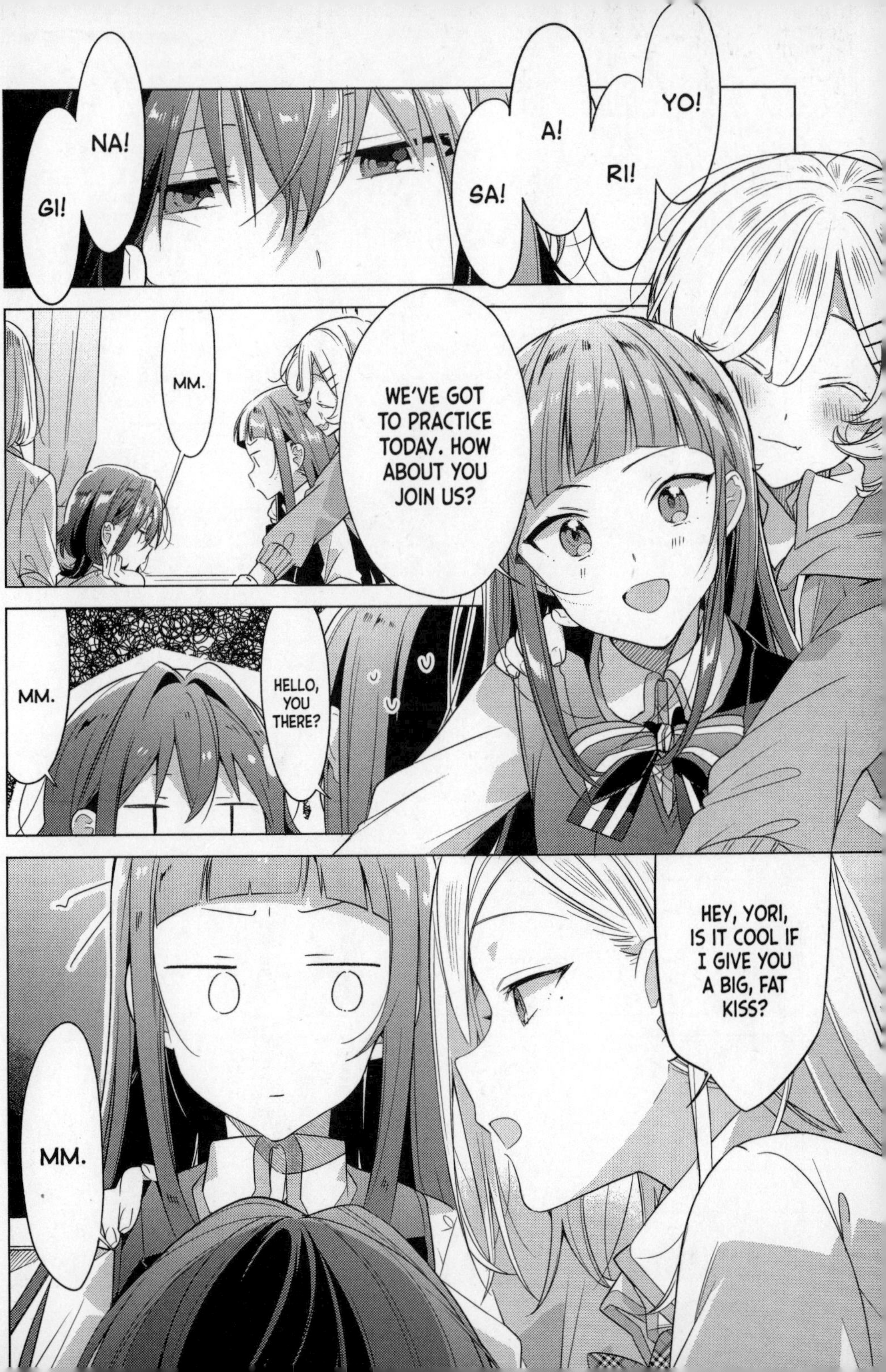
YO!
A!
RI!
SA!
NA!
GI!
WE'VE GOT TO PRACTICE TODAY. HOW ABOUT YOU JOIN US?
MM.
HELLO, YOU THERE?
MM.
HEY, YORI, IS IT COOL IF I GIVE YOU A BIG, FAT KISS?
MM.

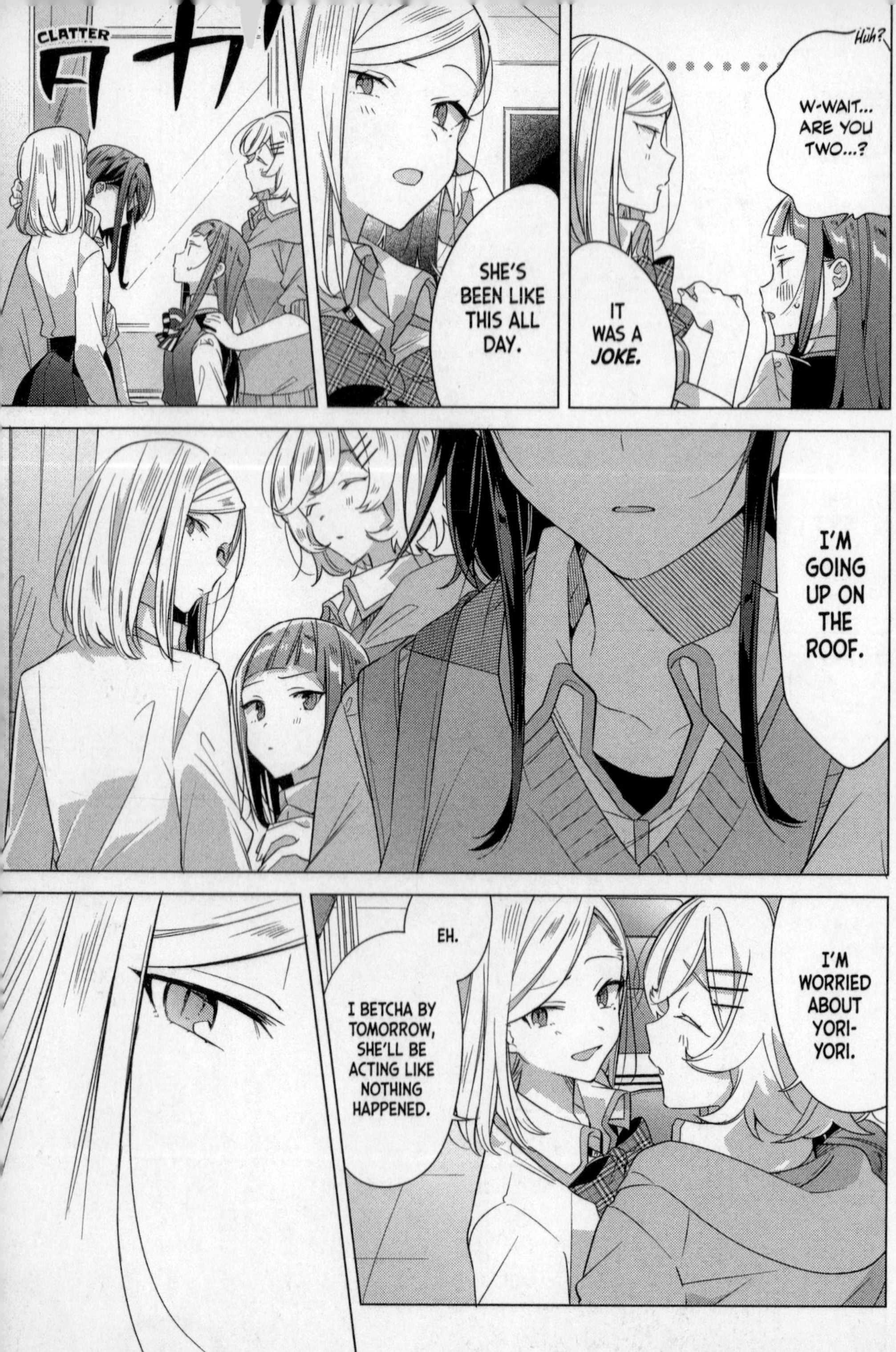
Huh?
• • • • • •
W-WAIT... ARE YOU TWO...?
IT WAS A JOKE.
SHE'S BEEN LIKE THIS ALL DAY.
CLATTER
I'M GOING UP ON THE ROOF.
I'M WORRIED ABOUT YORI-YORI.
EH.
I BETCHA BY TOMORROW, SHE'LL BE ACTING LIKE NOTHING HAPPENED.

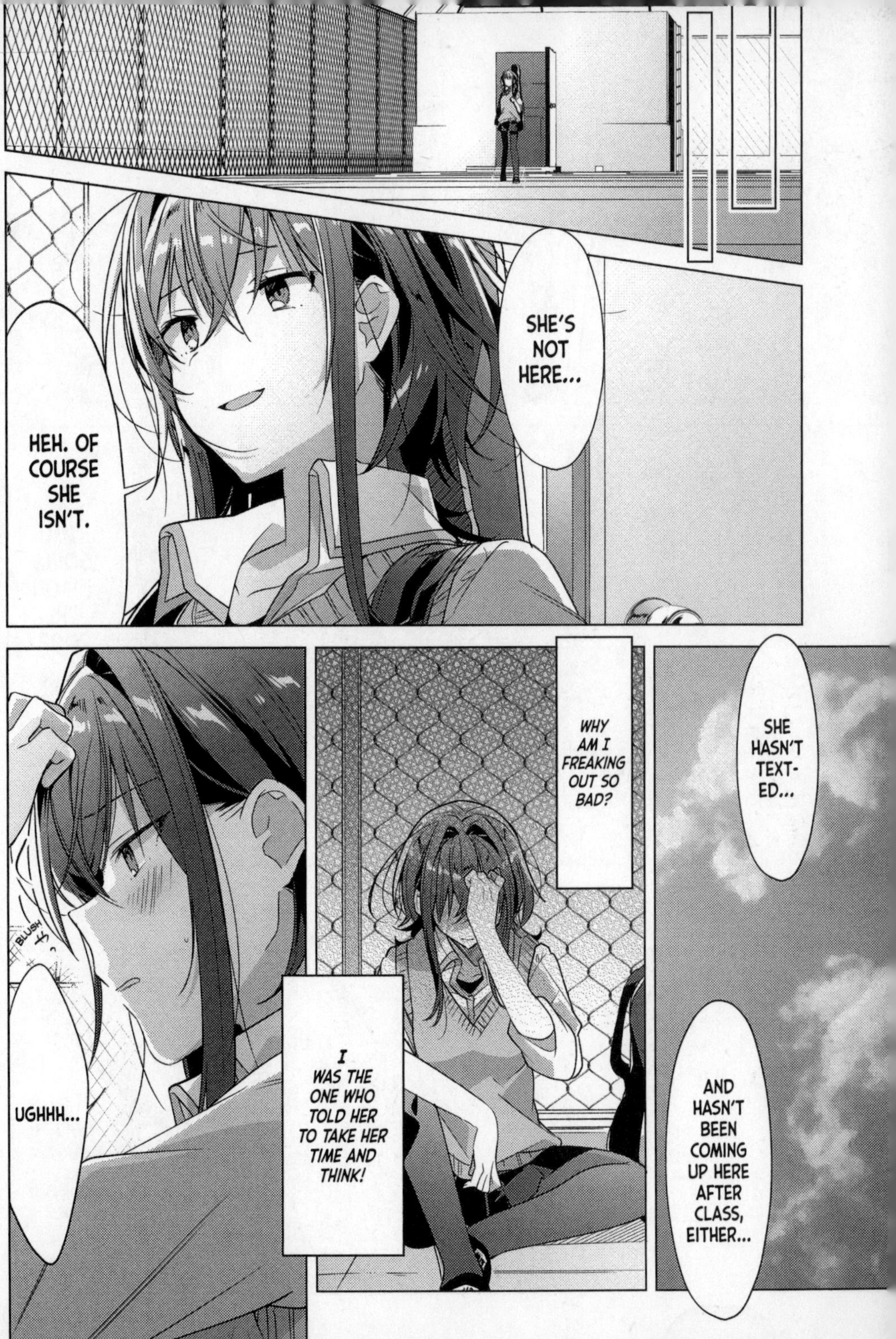
SHE'S NOT HERE...
HEH. OF COURSE SHE ISN'T.
SHE HASN'T TEXTED...
AND HASN'T BEEN COMING UP HERE AFTER CLASS, EITHER...
WHY AM I FREAKING OUT SO BAD?
I WAS THE ONE WHO TOLD HER TO TAKE HER TIME AND THINK!
BLUSH
UGHHH...

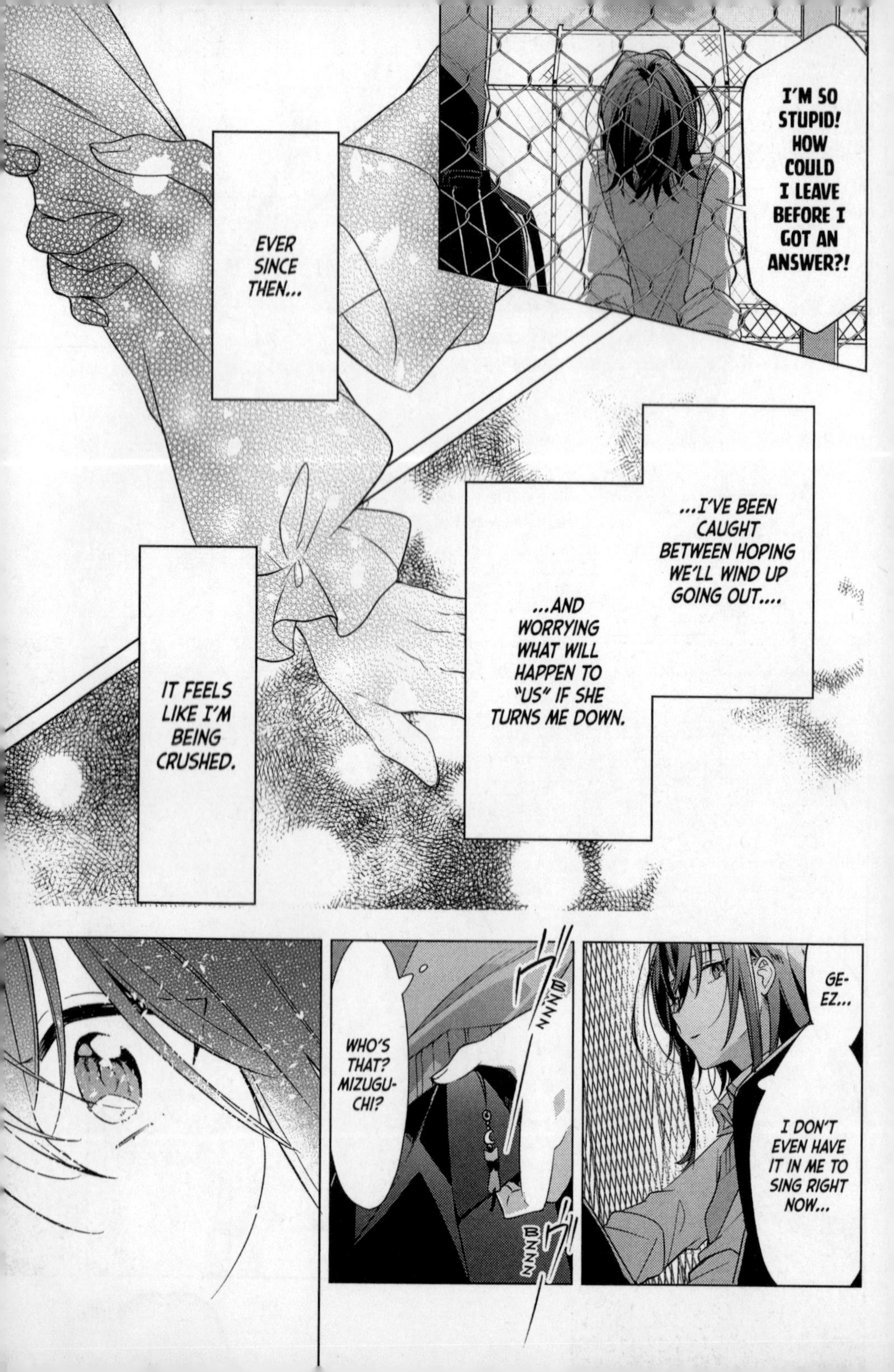
I'M SO STUPID! HOW COULD I LEAVE BEFORE I GOT AN ANSWER?!
EVER SINCE THEN...
...I'VE BEEN CAUGHT BETWEEN HOPING WE'LL WIND UP GOING OUT....
...AND WORRYING WHAT WILL HAPPEN TO "US" IF SHE TURNS ME DOWN.
IT FEELS LIKE I'M BEING CRUSHED.
GE-EZ...
I DON'T EVEN HAVE IT IN ME TO SING RIGHT NOW...
BZZZ
WHO'S THAT? MIZUGU-CHI?
BZZZ

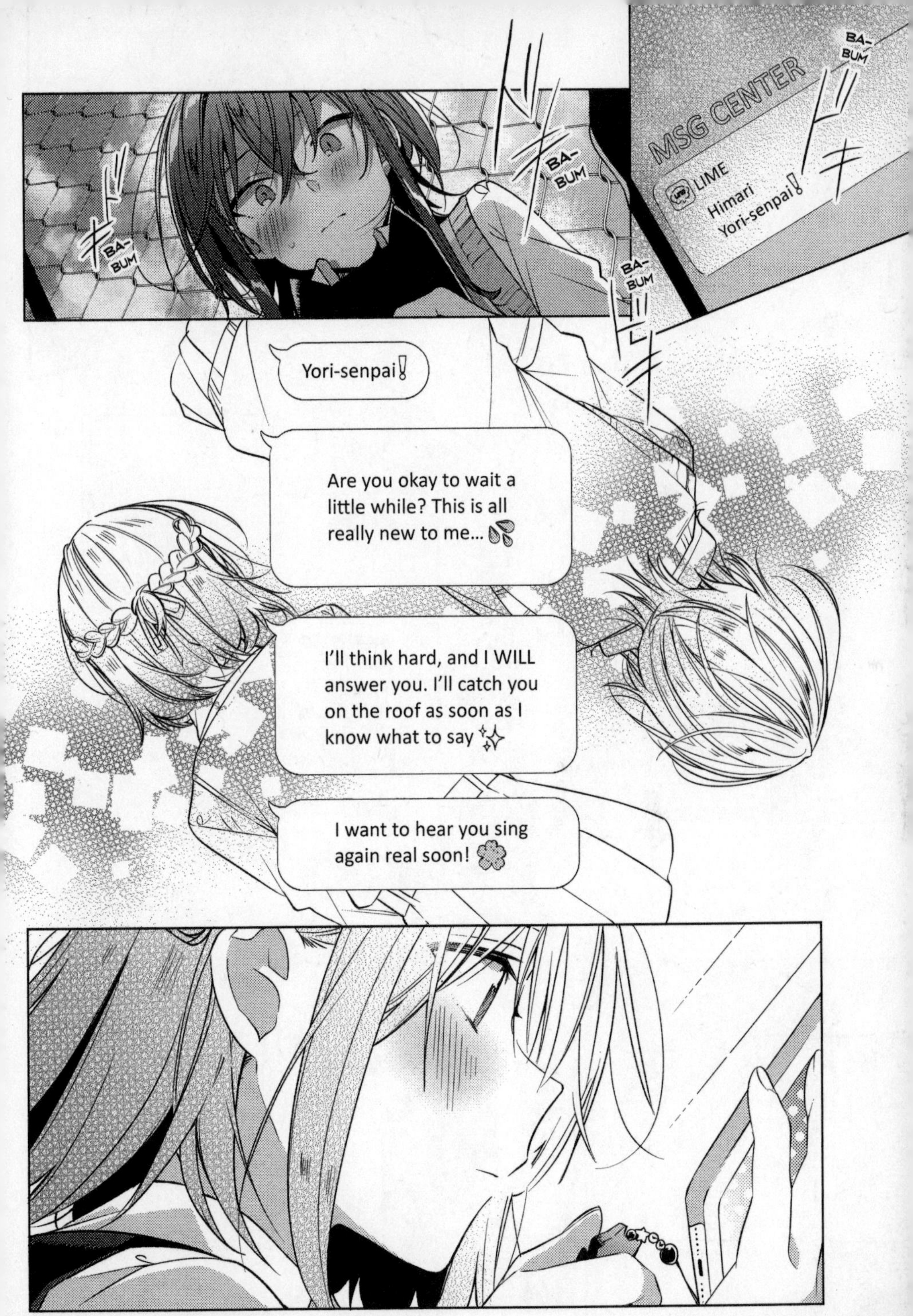
BA-BUM
MSG CENTER
LIME
Himari
Yori-senpai!
BA-BUM
BA-BUM
BA-BUM
Yori-senpai!
Are you okay to wait a little while? This is all really new to me...
I'll think hard, and I WILL answer you. I'll catch you on the roof as soon as I know what to say
I want to hear you sing again real soon!

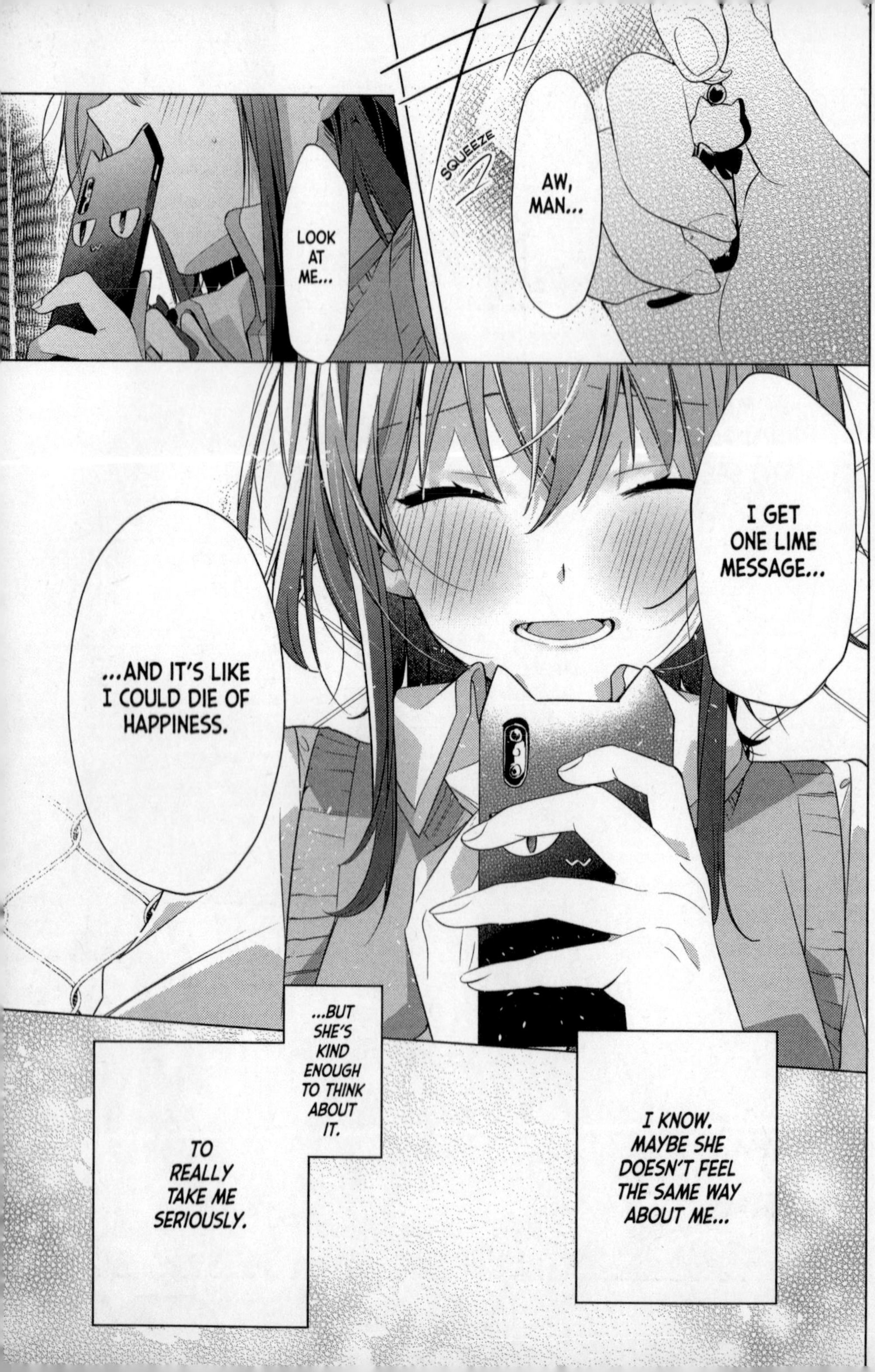
SQUEEZE
AW, MAN...
LOOK AT ME...
I GET ONE LIME MESSAGE...
...AND IT'S LIKE I COULD DIE OF HAPPINESS.
I KNOW. MAYBE SHE DOESN'T FEEL THE SAME WAY ABOUT ME...
...BUT SHE'S KIND ENOUGH TO THINK ABOUT IT.
TO REALLY TAKE ME SERIOUSLY.

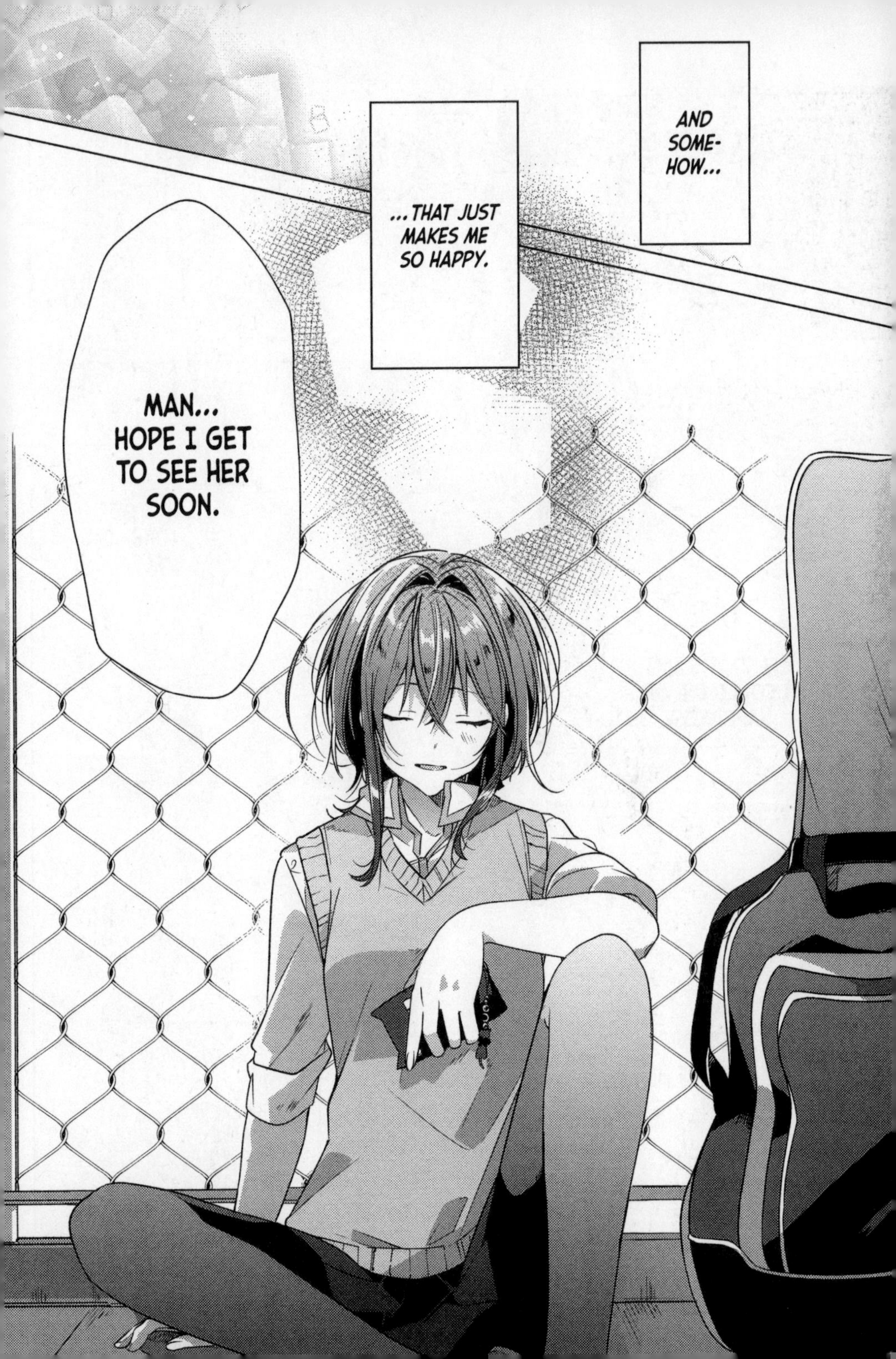
AND SOME-HOW...
...THAT JUST MAKES ME SO HAPPY.
MAN... HOPE I GET TO SEE HER SOON.

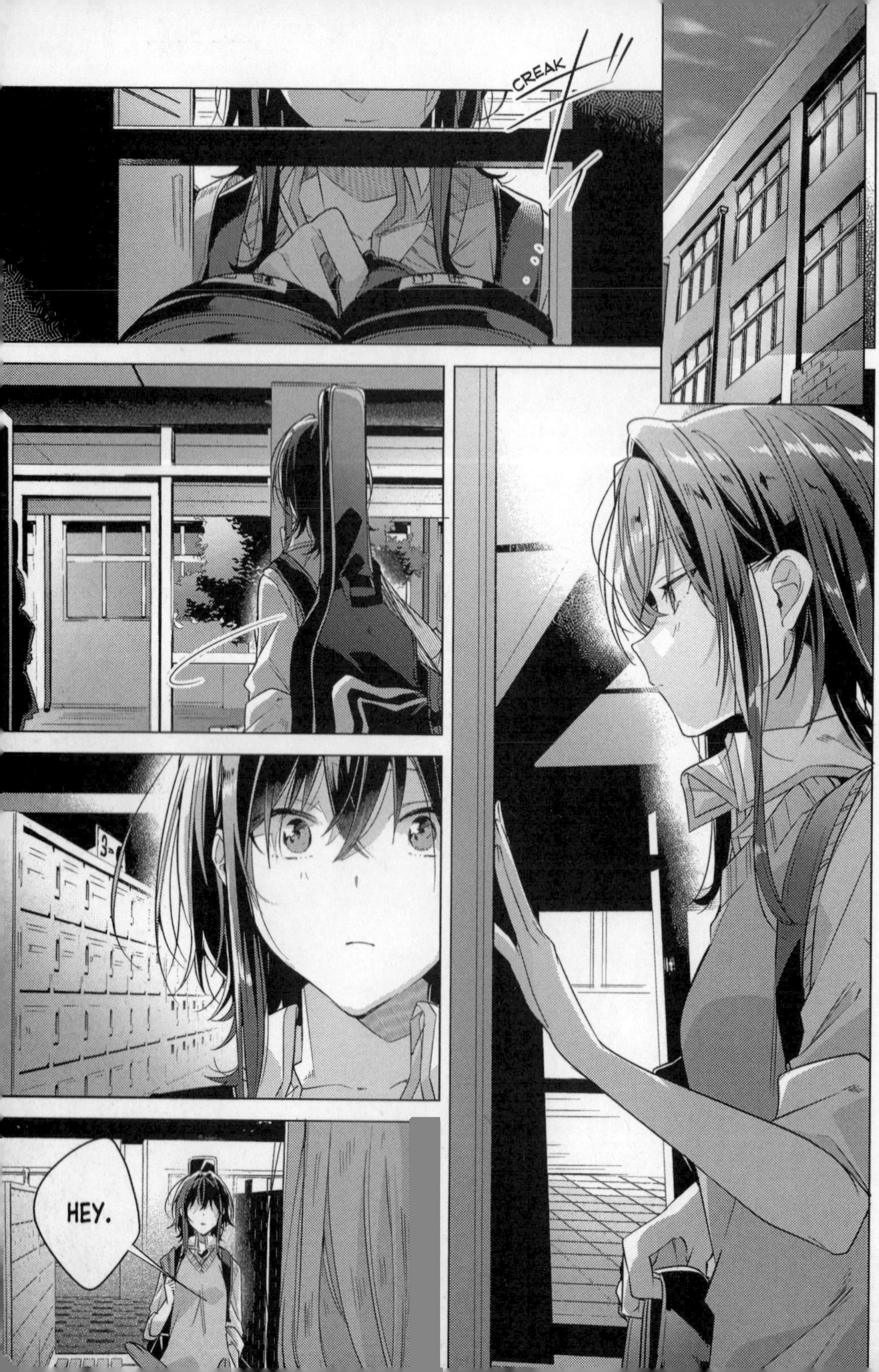
CREAK
HEY.

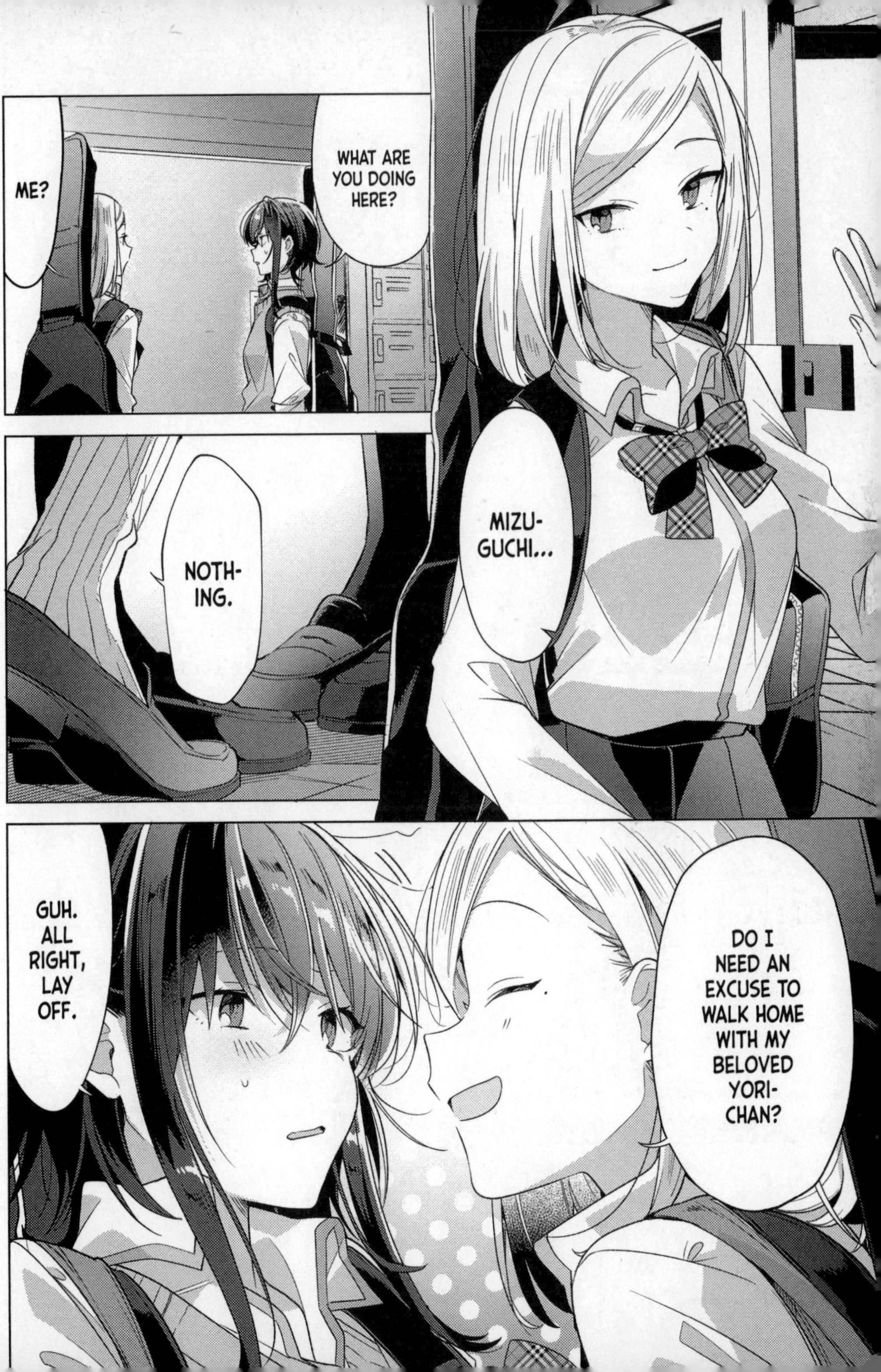
MIZU-GUCHI...
WHAT ARE YOU DOING HERE?
ME?
NOTH-ING.
DO I NEED AN EXCUSE TO WALK HOME WITH MY BELOVED YORI-CHAN?
GUH. ALL RIGHT, LAY OFF.

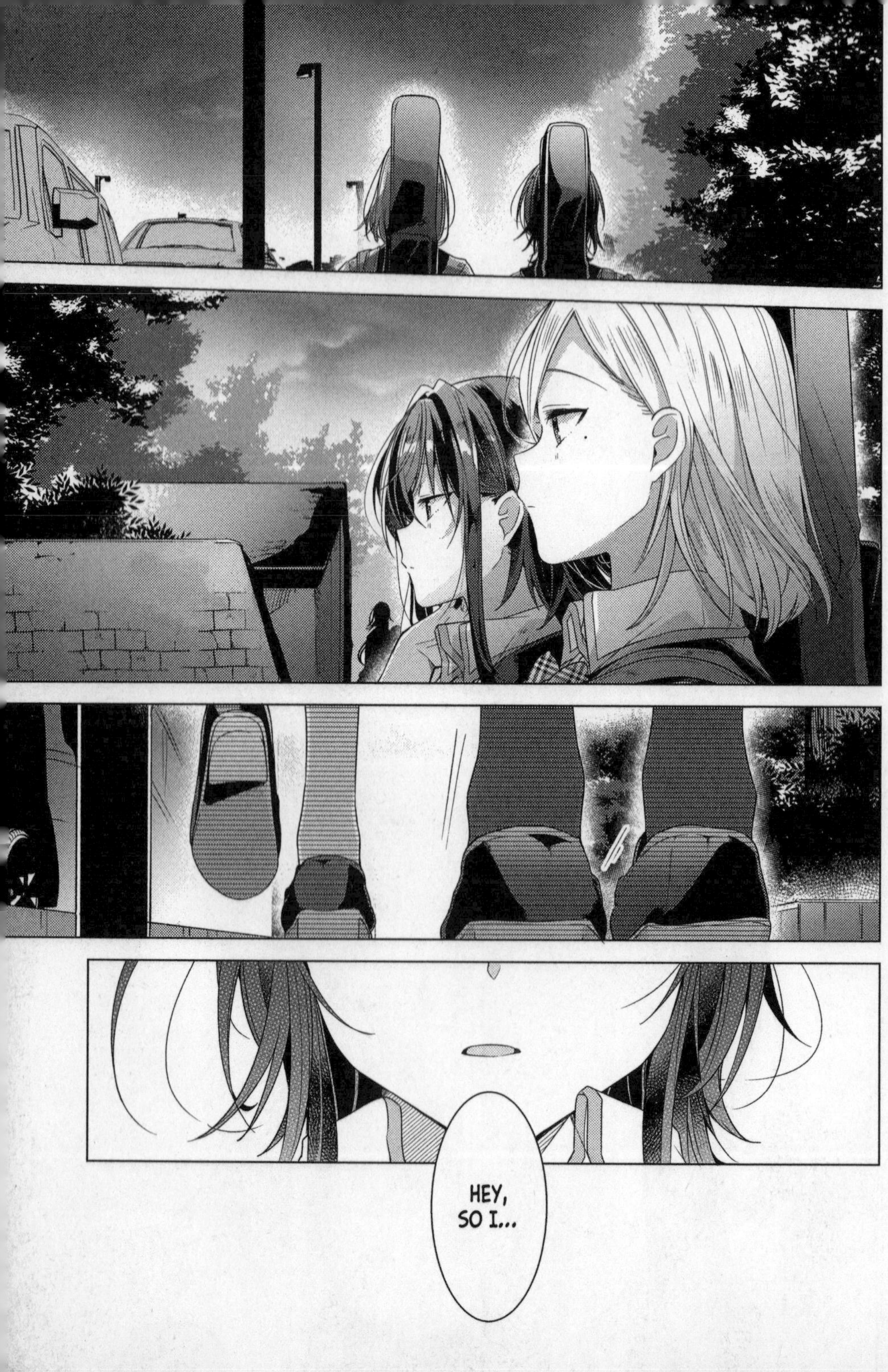
HEY, SO I...

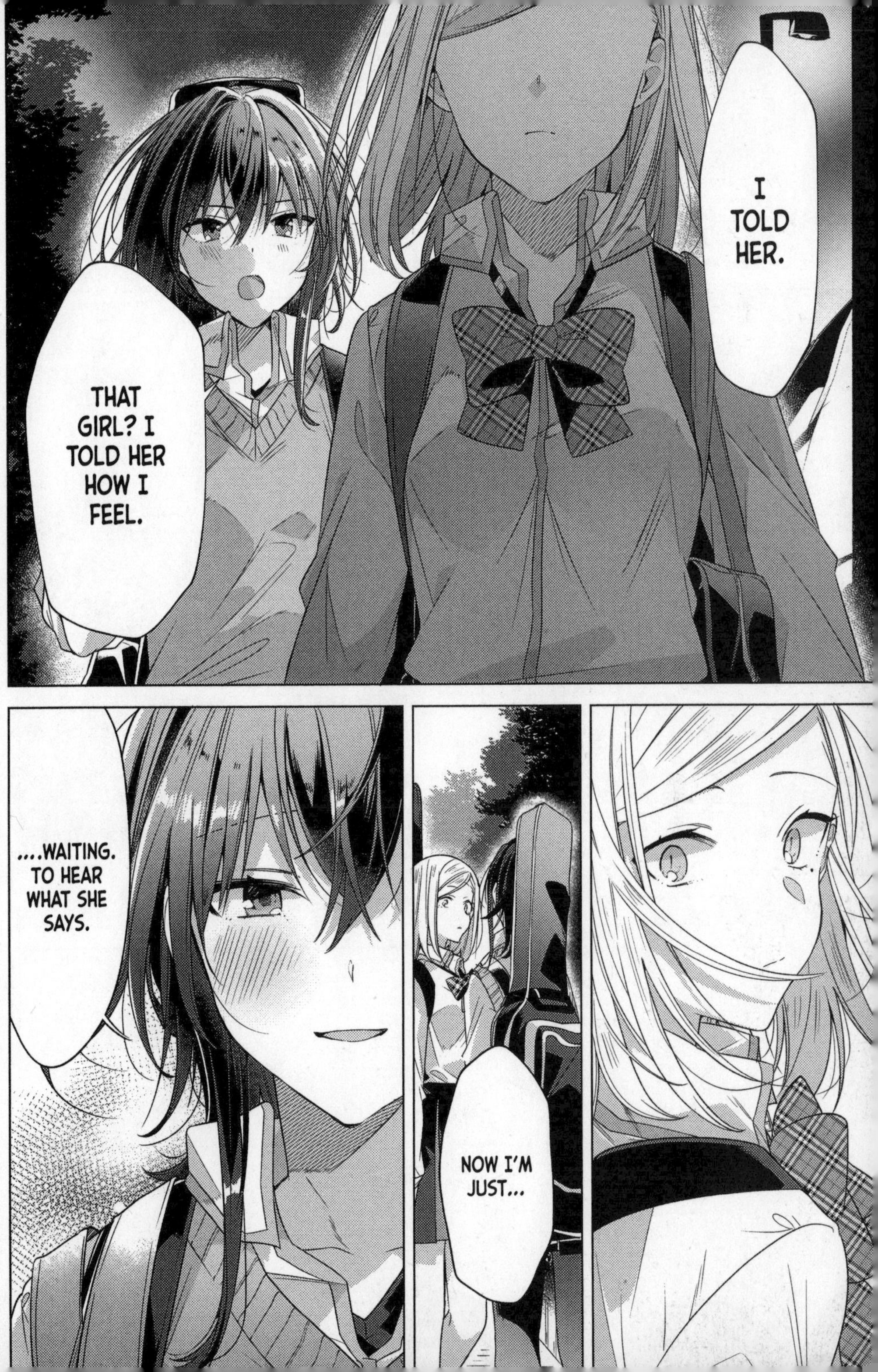
I TOLD HER.
THAT GIRL? I TOLD HER HOW I FEEL.
NOW I'M JUST...
....WAITING. TO HEAR WHAT SHE SAYS.

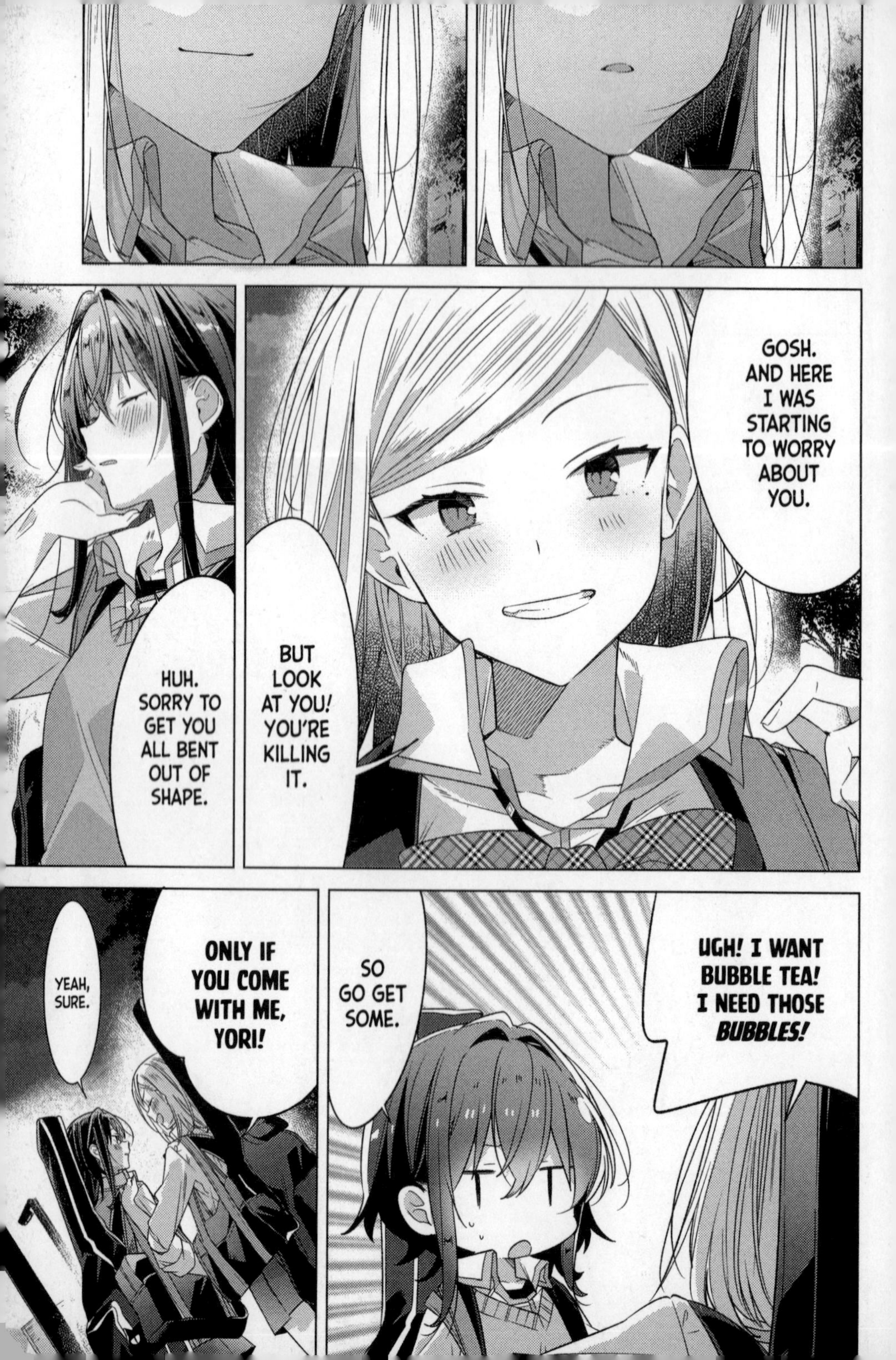
GOSH. AND HERE I WAS STARTING TO WORRY ABOUT YOU.
BUT LOOK AT YOU! YOU'RE KILLING IT.
HUH. SORRY TO GET YOU ALL BENT OUT OF SHAPE.
UGH! I WANT BUBBLE TEA! I NEED THOSE *BUBBLES!*
SO GO GET SOME.
ONLY IF YOU COME WITH ME, YORI!
YEAH, SURE.

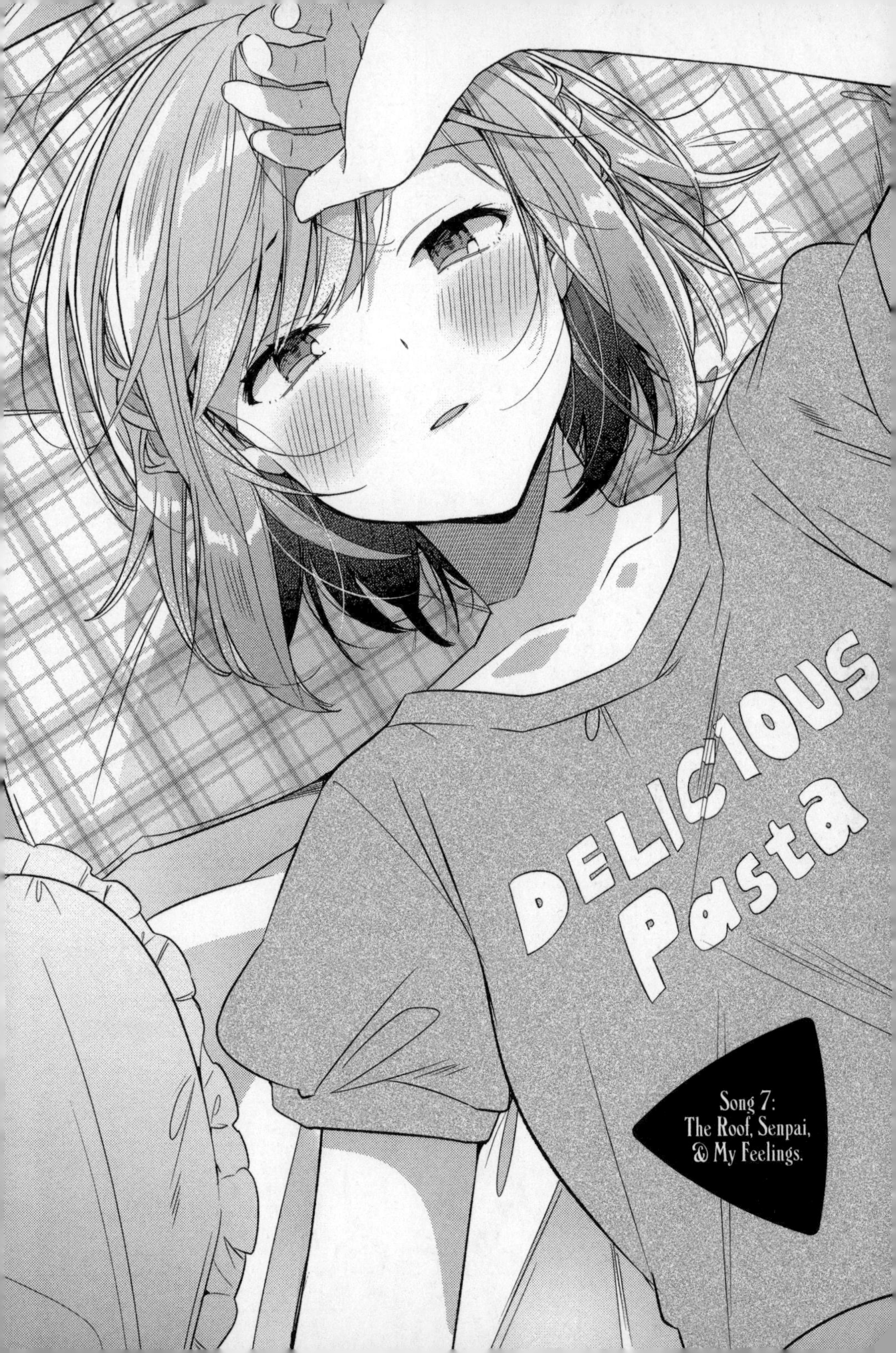
DELICIOUS
Pasta
Song 7:
The Roof, Senpai,
& My Feelings.

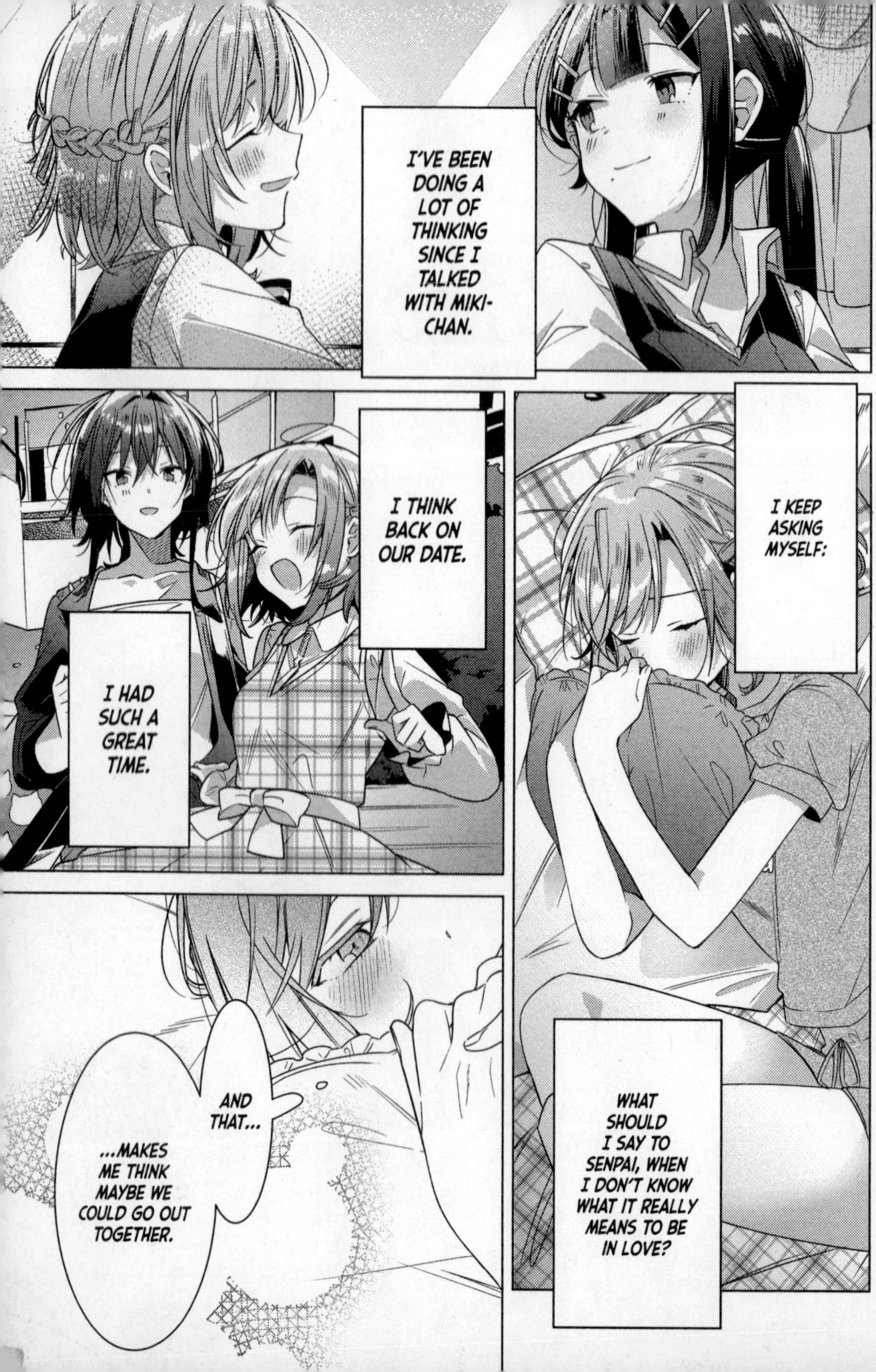
I'VE BEEN DOING A LOT OF THINKING SINCE I TALKED WITH MIKI-CHAN.
I KEEP ASKING MYSELF:
WHAT SHOULD I SAY TO SENPAI, WHEN I DON'T KNOW WHAT IT REALLY MEANS TO BE IN LOVE?
I THINK BACK ON OUR DATE.
I HAD SUCH A GREAT TIME.
AND THAT...
...MAKES ME THINK MAYBE WE COULD GO OUT TOGETHER.

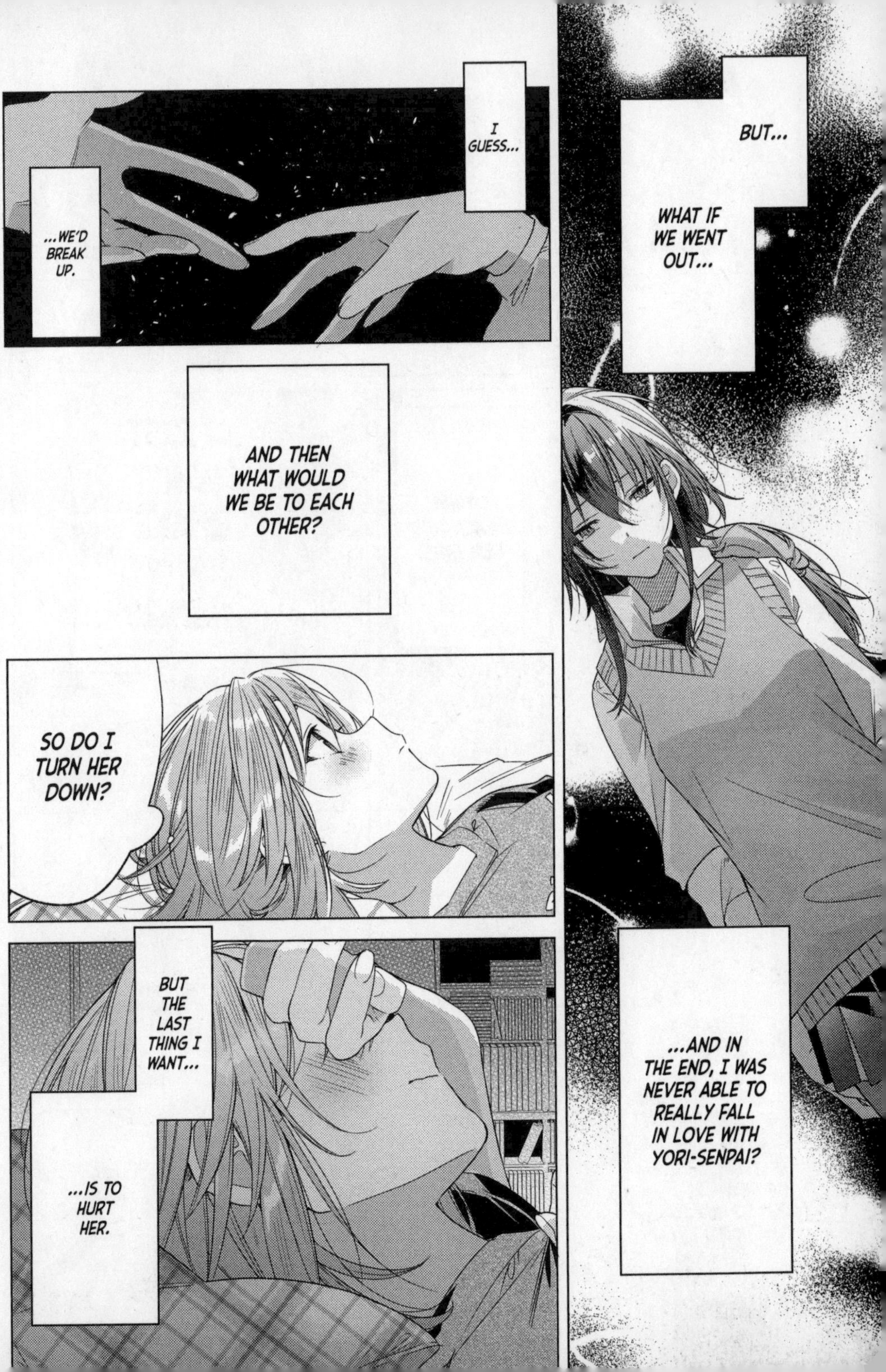
BUT...
WHAT IF WE WENT OUT...
...AND IN THE END, I WAS NEVER ABLE TO REALLY FALL IN LOVE WITH YORI-SENPAI?
I GUESS...
...WE'D BREAK UP.
AND THEN WHAT WOULD WE BE TO EACH OTHER?
SO DO I TURN HER DOWN?
BUT THE LAST THING I WANT...
...IS TO HURT HER.

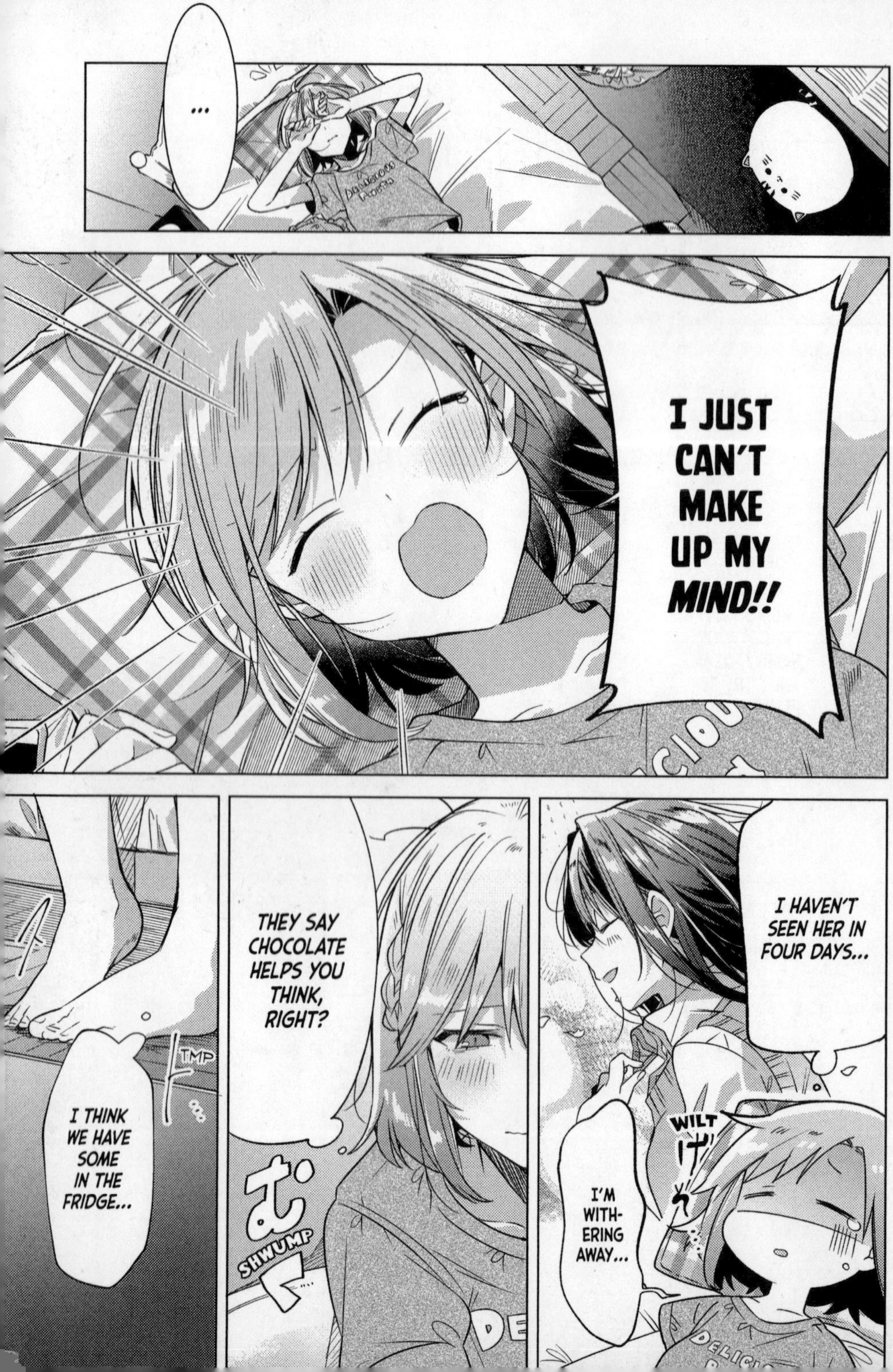
...
I JUST CAN'T MAKE UP MY MIND!!
I HAVEN'T SEEN HER IN FOUR DAYS...
WILT
I'M WITH-ERING AWAY...
THEY SAY CHOCOLATE HELPS YOU THINK, RIGHT?
SHWUMP
TMP
I THINK WE HAVE SOME IN THE FRIDGE...

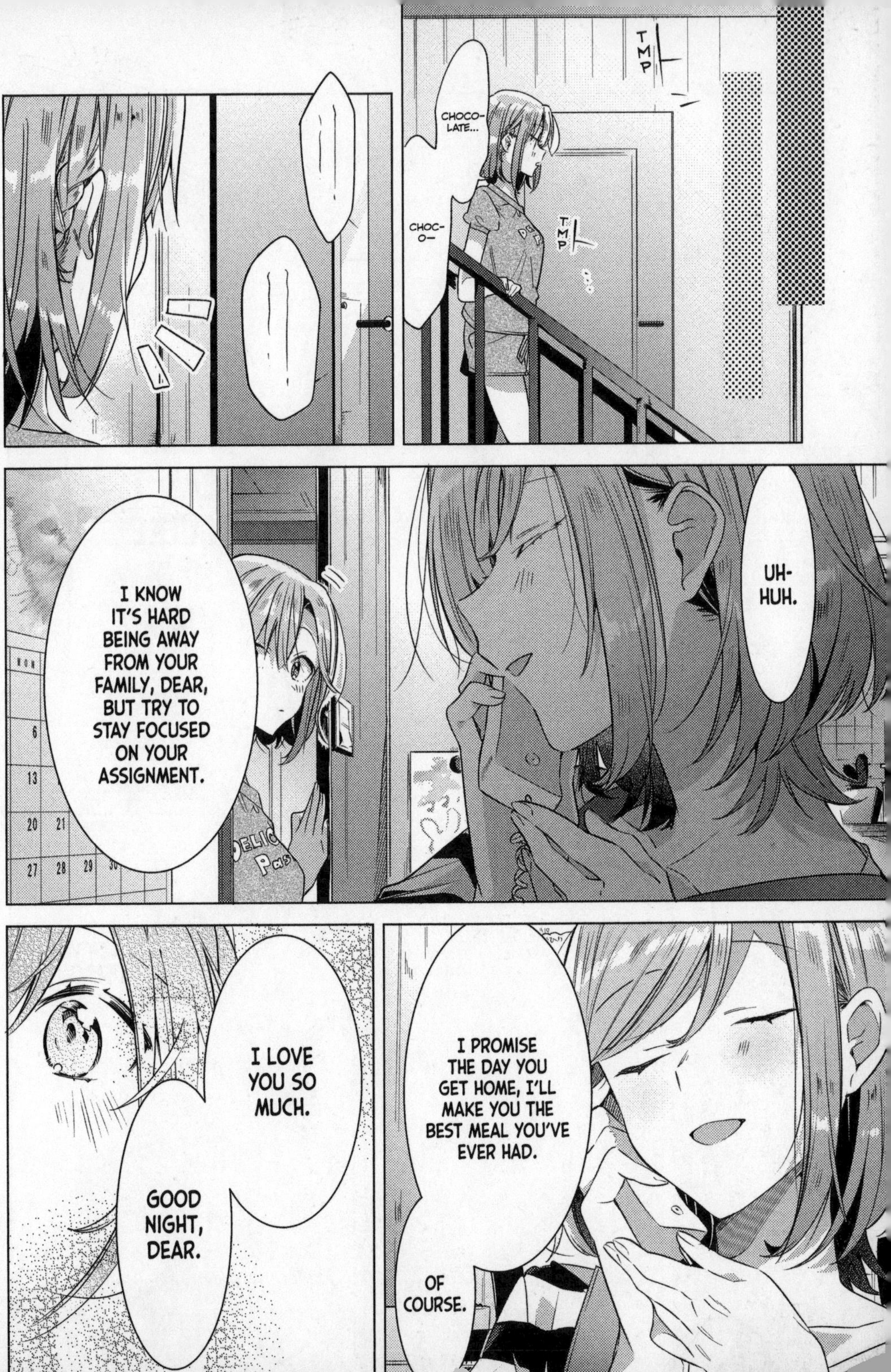
TMP
CHOCO-LATE...
CHOCO-O—
TMP
UH-HUH.
I KNOW IT'S HARD BEING AWAY FROM YOUR FAMILY, DEAR, BUT TRY TO STAY FOCUSED ON YOUR ASSIGNMENT.
I PROMISE THE DAY YOU GET HOME, I'LL MAKE YOU THE BEST MEAL YOU'VE EVER HAD.
OF COURSE.
I LOVE YOU SO MUCH.
GOOD NIGHT, DEAR.

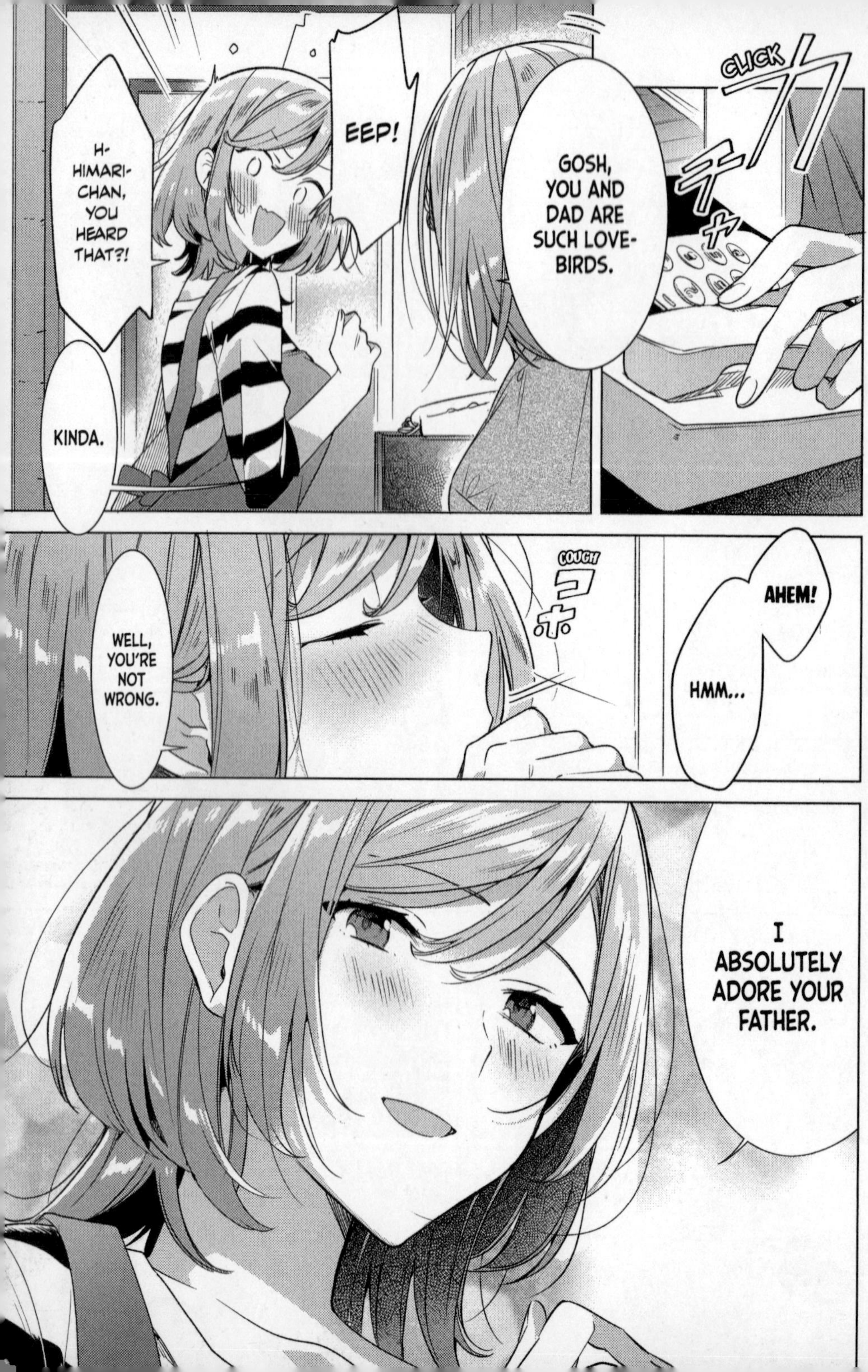
CLICK
GOSH, YOU AND DAD ARE SUCH LOVE-BIRDS.
EEP!
H-HIMARI-CHAN, YOU HEARD THAT?!
KINDA.
AHEM!
HMM...
COUGH
WELL, YOU'RE NOT WRONG.
I ABSOLUTELY ADORE YOUR FATHER.

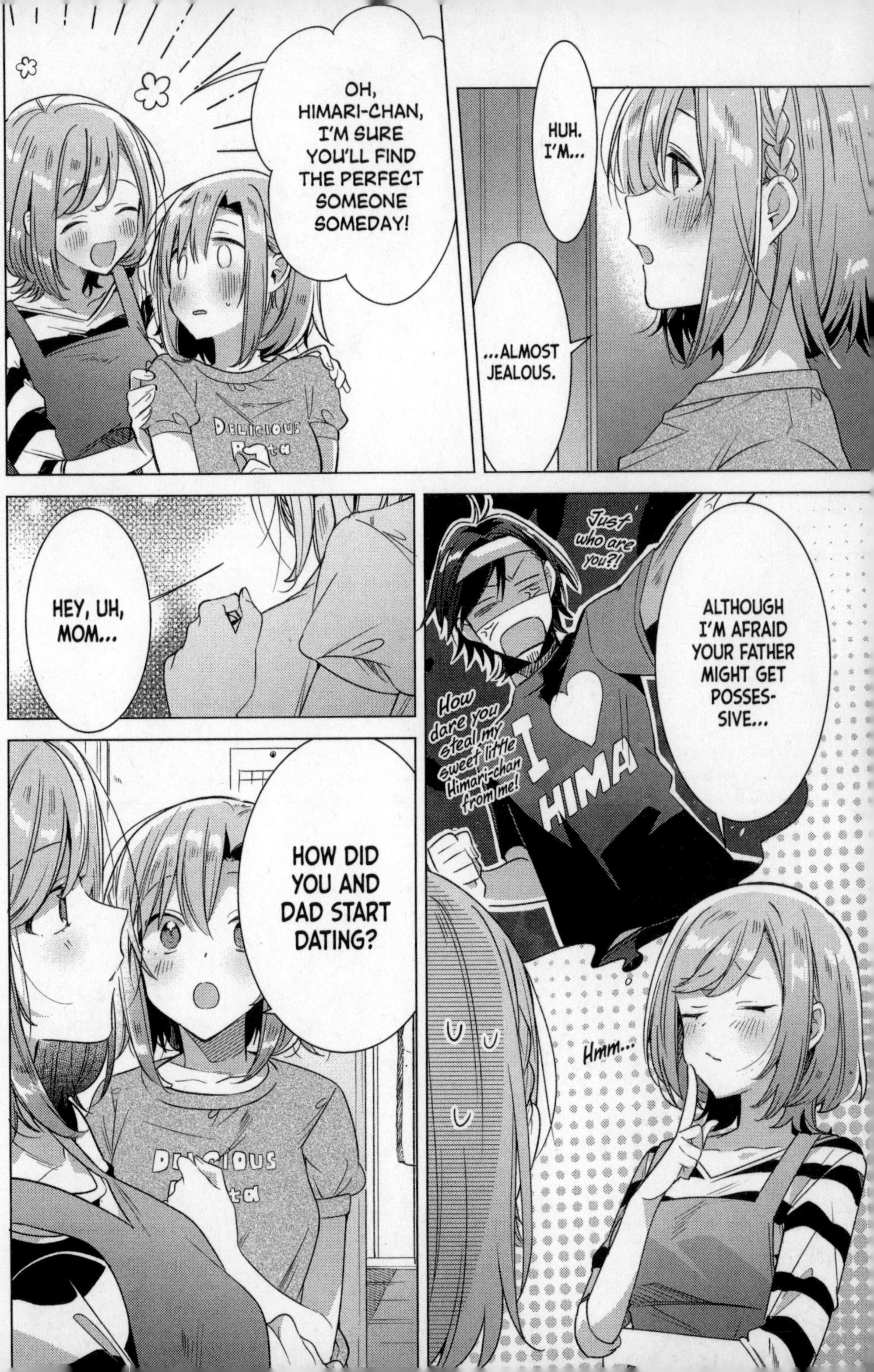
HUH. I'M...
...ALMOST JEALOUS.
OH, HIMARI-CHAN, I'M SURE YOU'LL FIND THE PERFECT SOMEONE SOMEDAY!
DELICIOUS
ALTHOUGH I'M AFRAID YOUR FATHER MIGHT GET POSSES-SIVE...
Just who are you?!
How dare you steal my sweet little Himari-chan from me!
I ♥ HIMA
Hmm...
HEY, UH, MOM...
HOW DID YOU AND DAD START DATING?
DELICIOUS

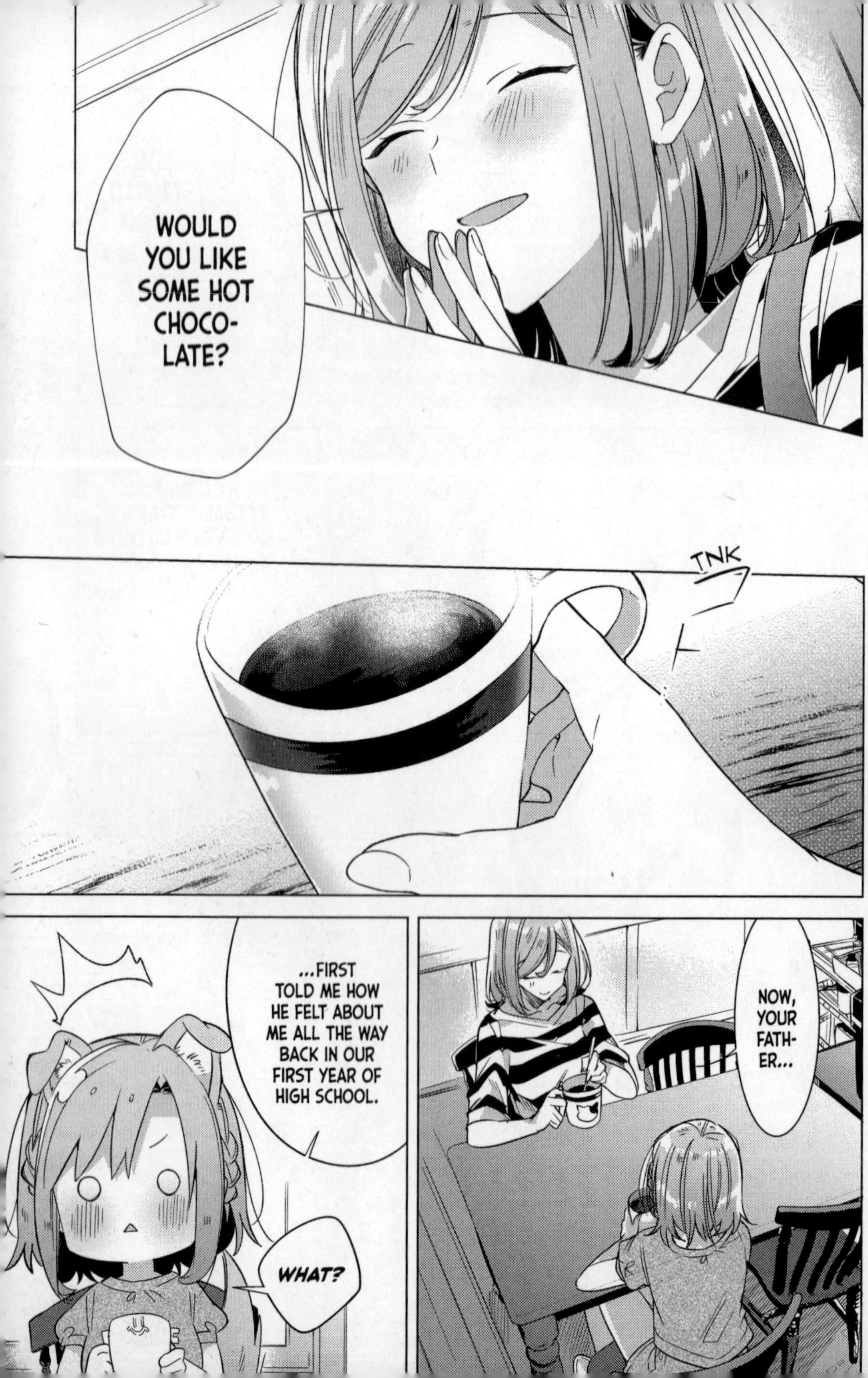
WOULD YOU LIKE SOME HOT CHOCO-LATE?
TNK
NOW, YOUR FATH-ER...
...FIRST TOLD ME HOW HE FELT ABOUT ME ALL THE WAY BACK IN OUR FIRST YEAR OF HIGH SCHOOL.
WHAT?

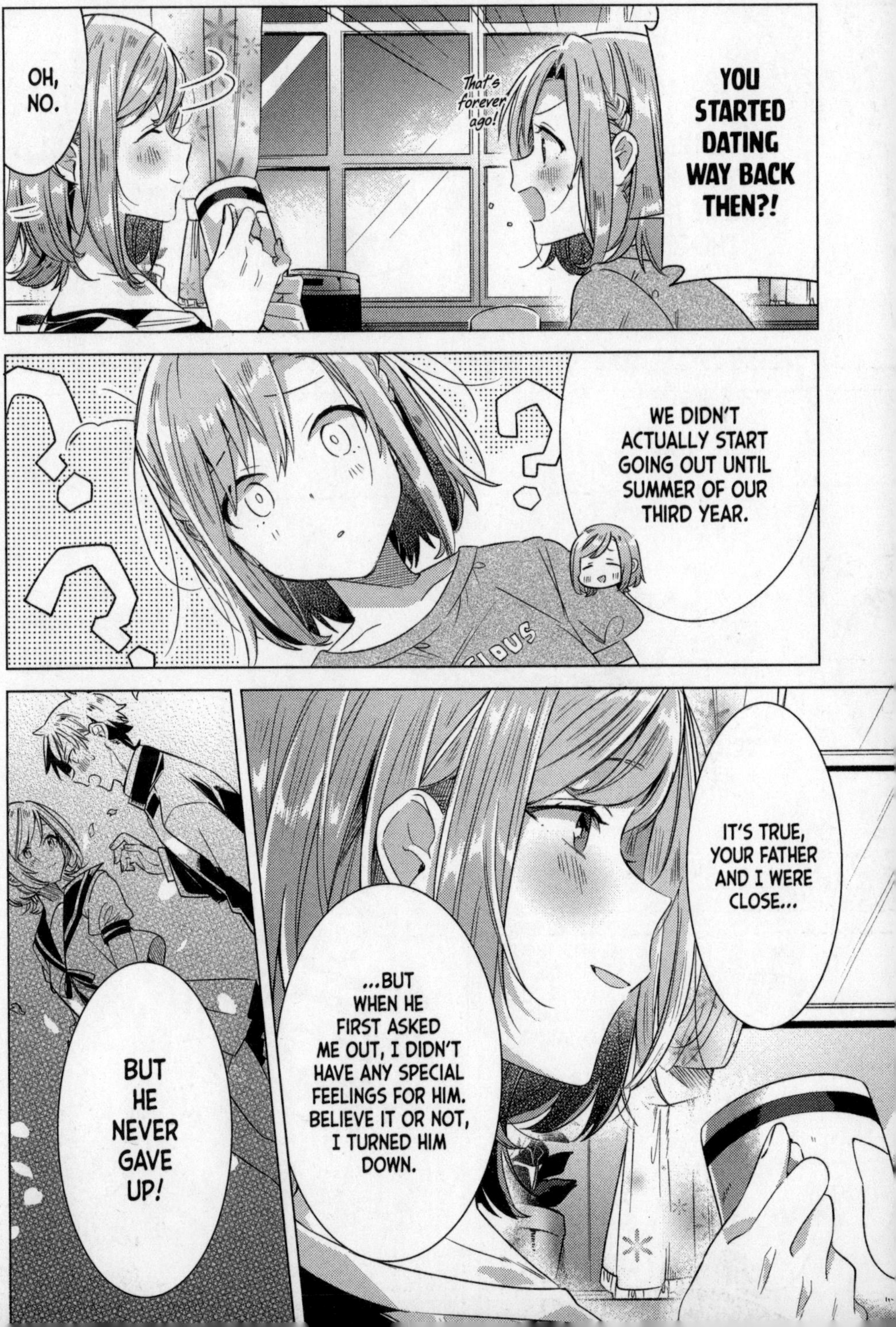
YOU STARTED DATING WAY BACK THEN?!
That's forever ago!
OH, NO.
WE DIDN'T ACTUALLY START GOING OUT UNTIL SUMMER OF OUR THIRD YEAR.
IT'S TRUE, YOUR FATHER AND I WERE CLOSE...
...BUT WHEN HE FIRST ASKED ME OUT, I DIDN'T HAVE ANY SPECIAL FEELINGS FOR HIM. BELIEVE IT OR NOT, I TURNED HIM DOWN.
BUT HE NEVER GAVE UP!

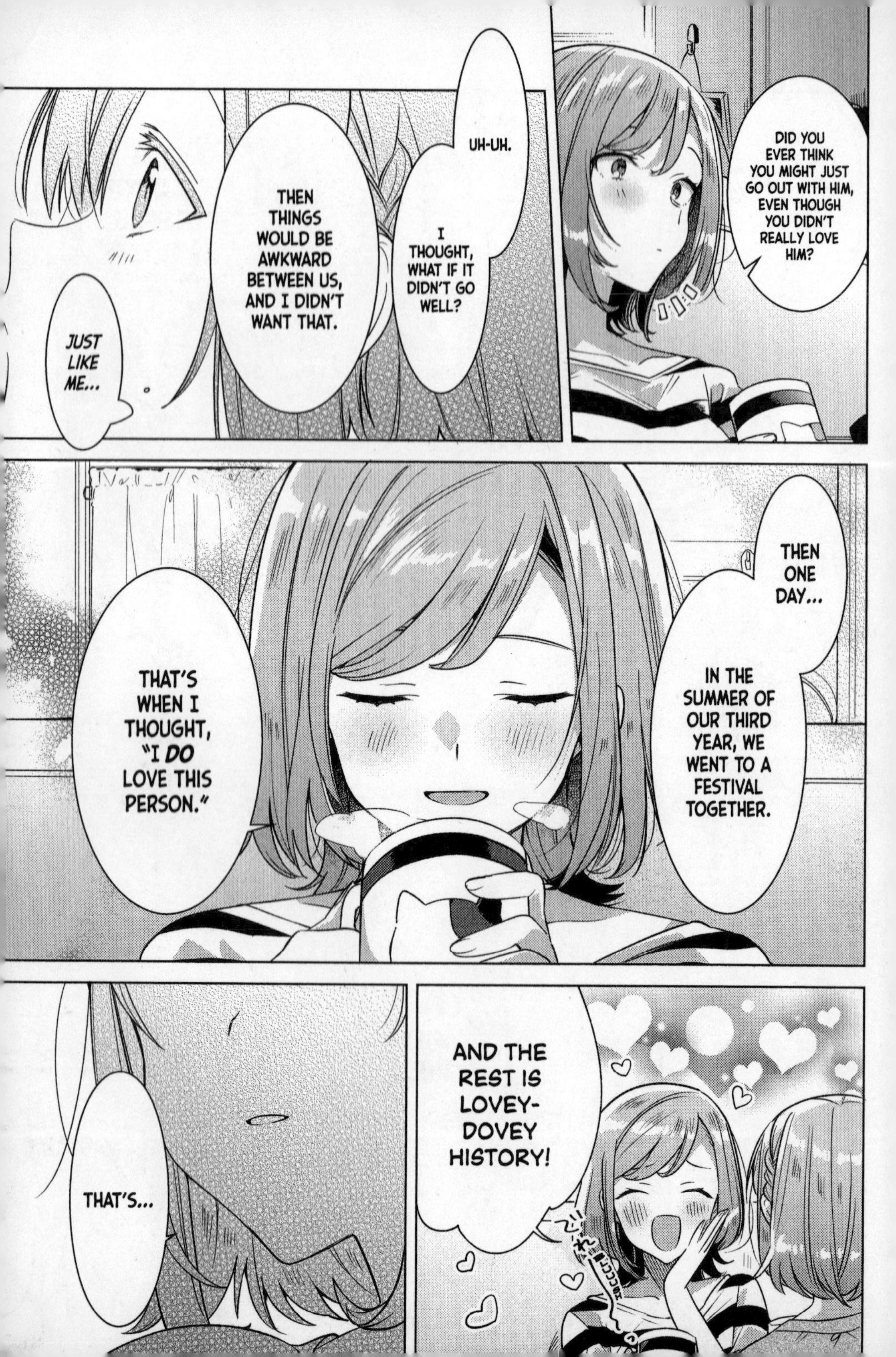
DID YOU EVER THINK YOU MIGHT JUST GO OUT WITH HIM, EVEN THOUGH YOU DIDN'T REALLY LOVE HIM?
UH-UH.
I THOUGHT, WHAT IF IT DIDN'T GO WELL?
THEN THINGS WOULD BE AWKWARD BETWEEN US, AND I DIDN'T WANT THAT.
JUST LIKE ME...
THEN ONE DAY...
IN THE SUMMER OF OUR THIRD YEAR, WE WENT TO A FESTIVAL TOGETHER.
THAT'S WHEN I THOUGHT, "I *DO* LOVE THIS PERSON."
AND THE REST IS LOVEY-DOVEY HISTORY!
THAT'S...

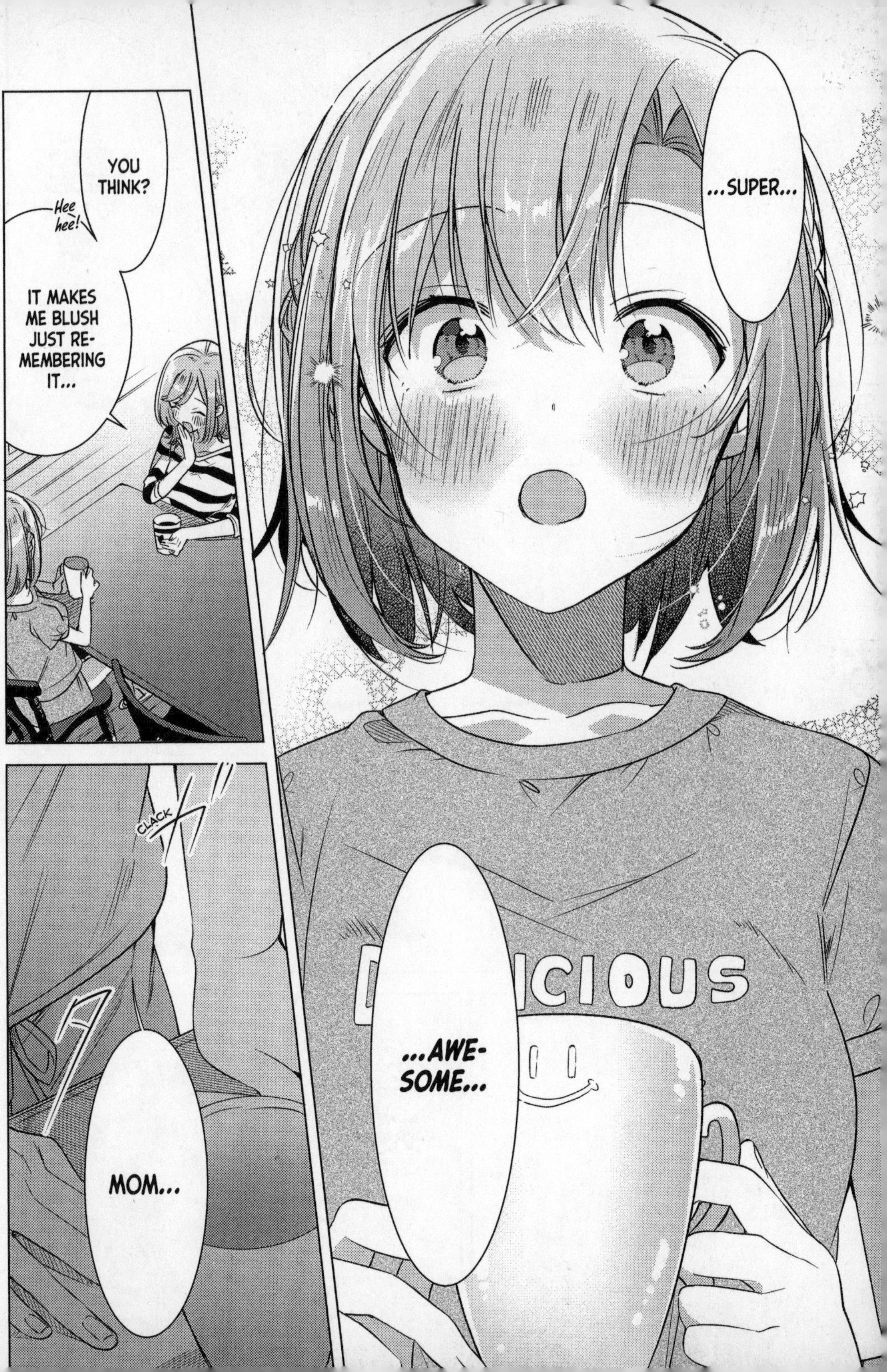
...SUPER...
...AWE-SOME...
YOU THINK?
Hee hee!
IT MAKES ME BLUSH JUST RE-MEMBERING IT...
CLACK
MOM...

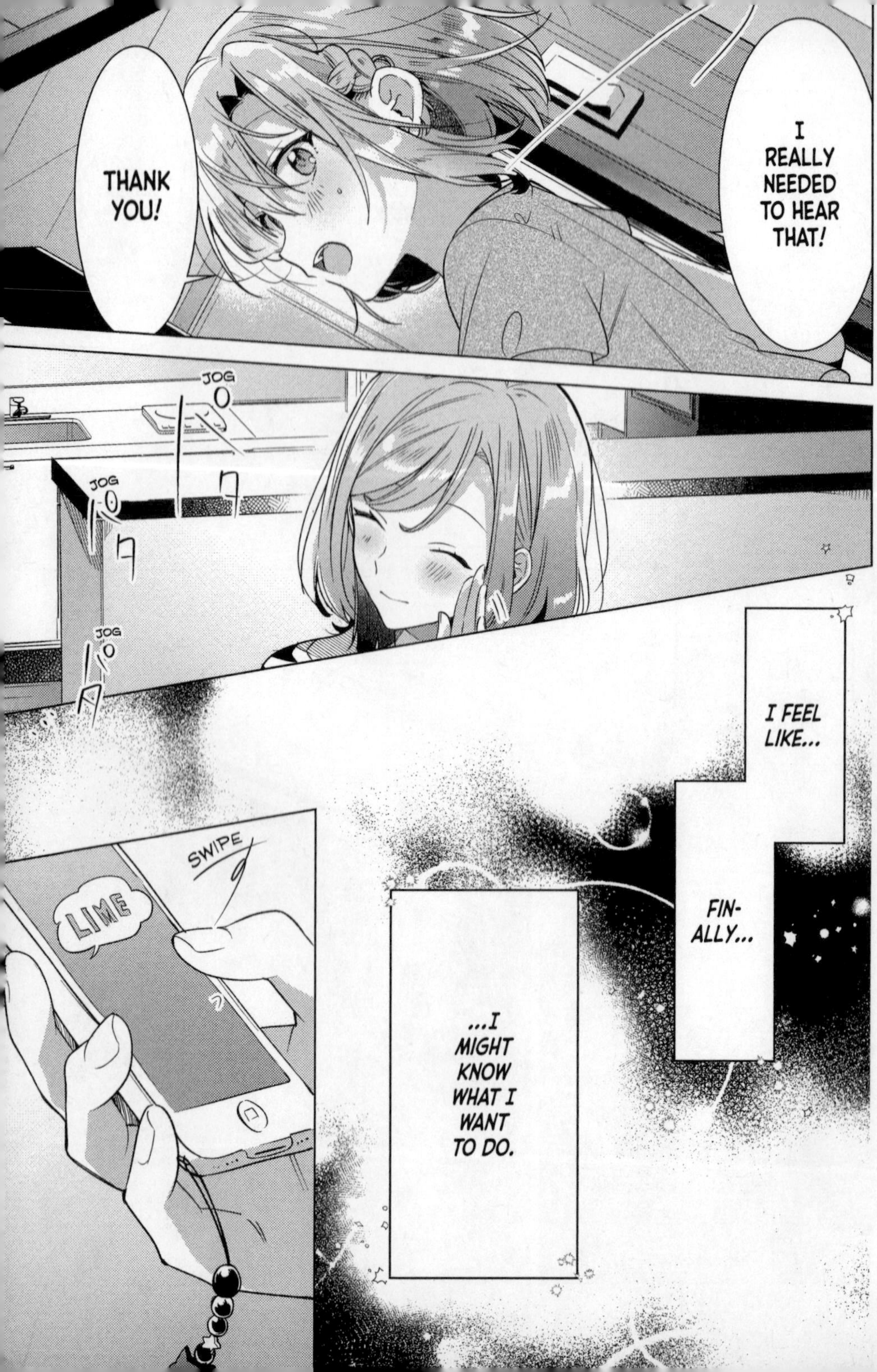
I REALLY NEEDED TO HEAR THAT!
THANK YOU!
JOG
JOG
JOG
I FEEL LIKE...
FIN-ALLY...
...I MIGHT KNOW WHAT I WANT TO DO.
SWIPE
LIME

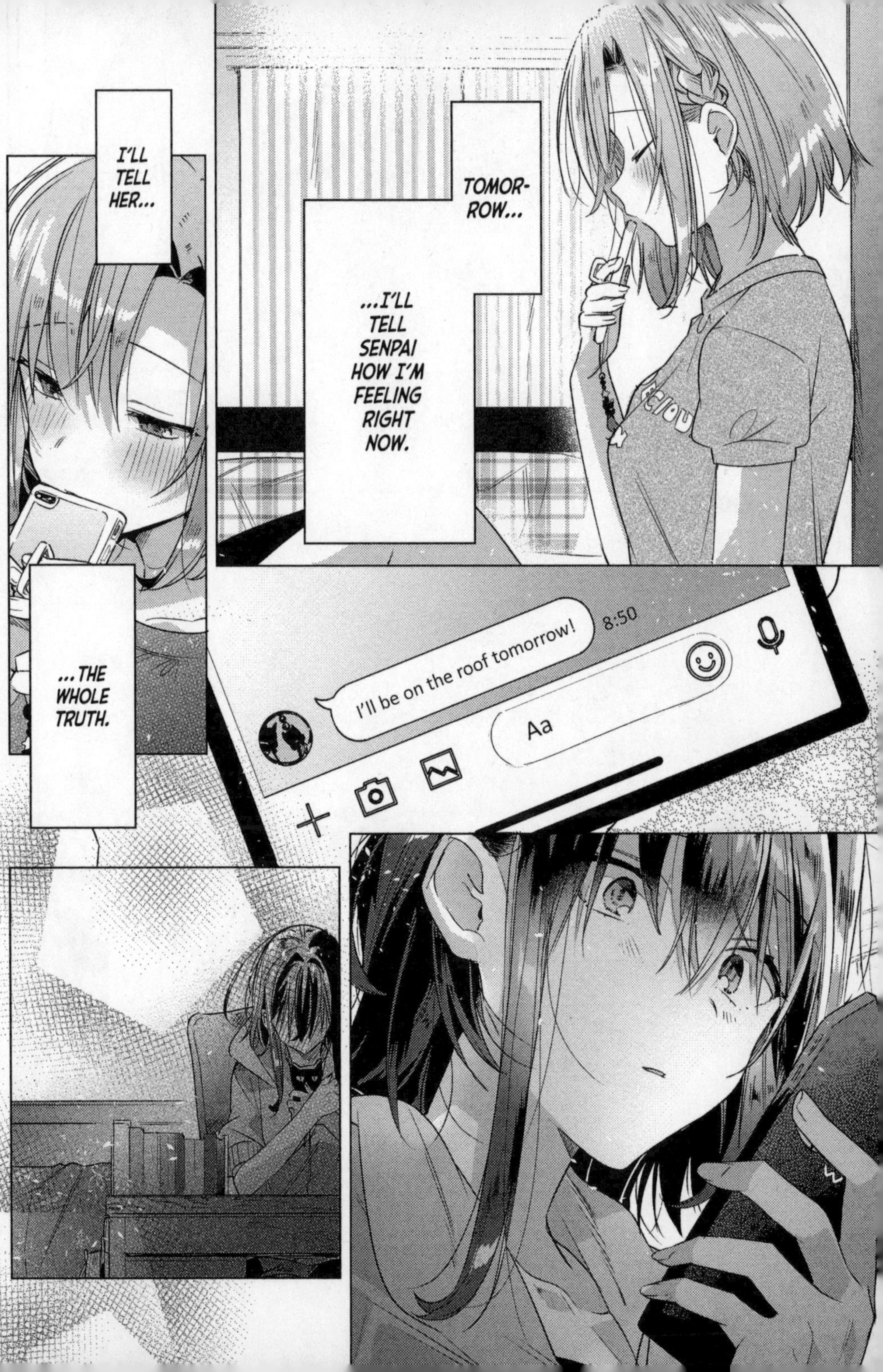
TOMOR-
ROW...
...I'LL TELL SENPAI HOW I'M FEELING RIGHT NOW.
I'LL TELL HER...
...THE WHOLE TRUTH.
8:50
I'll be on the roof tomorrow!
Aa

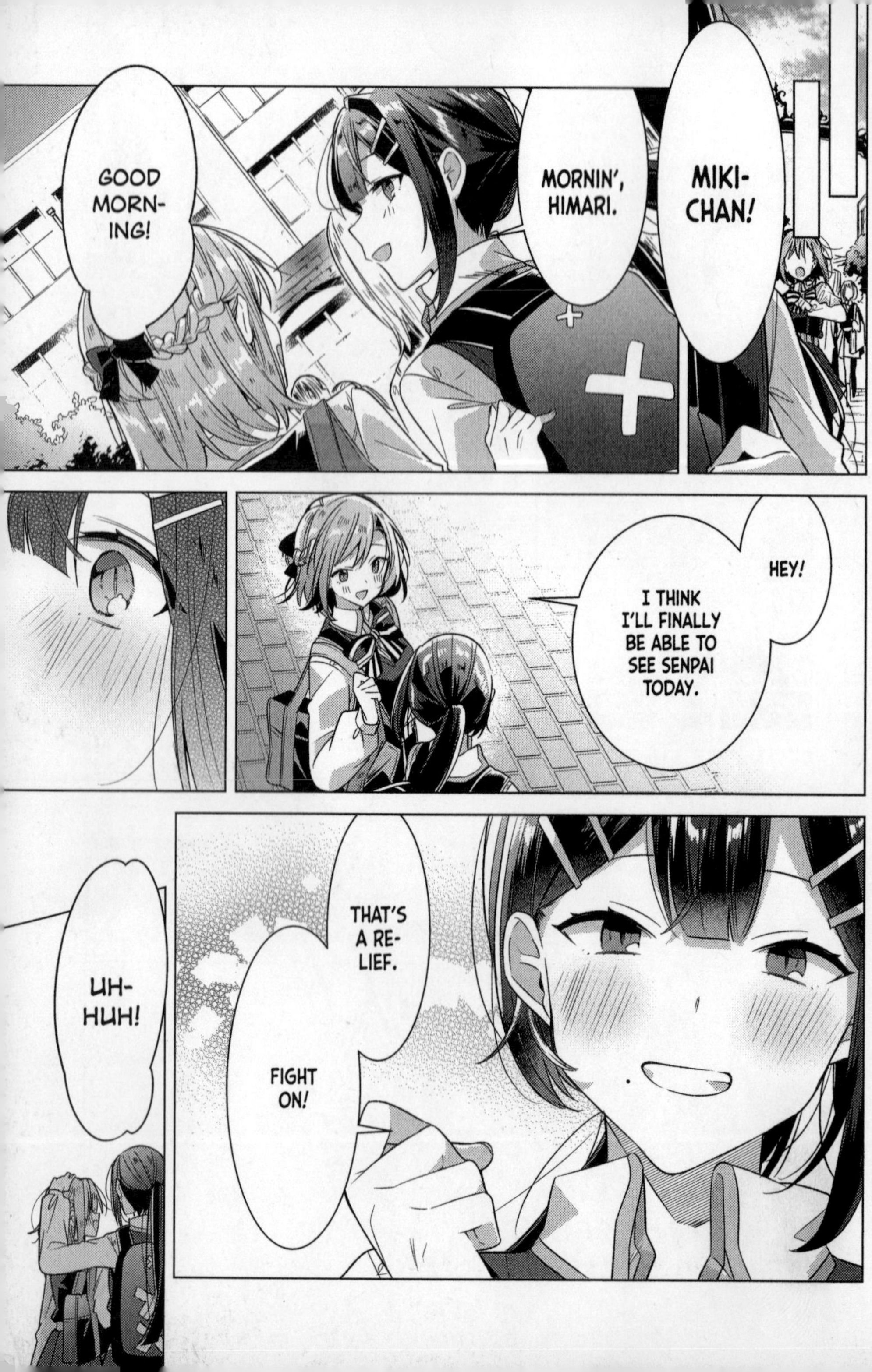
MIKI-CHAN!
MORNIN', HIMARI.
GOOD MORN-ING!
HEY!
I THINK I'LL FINALLY BE ABLE TO SEE SENPAI TODAY.
THAT'S A RE-LIEF.
FIGHT ON!
UH-HUH!

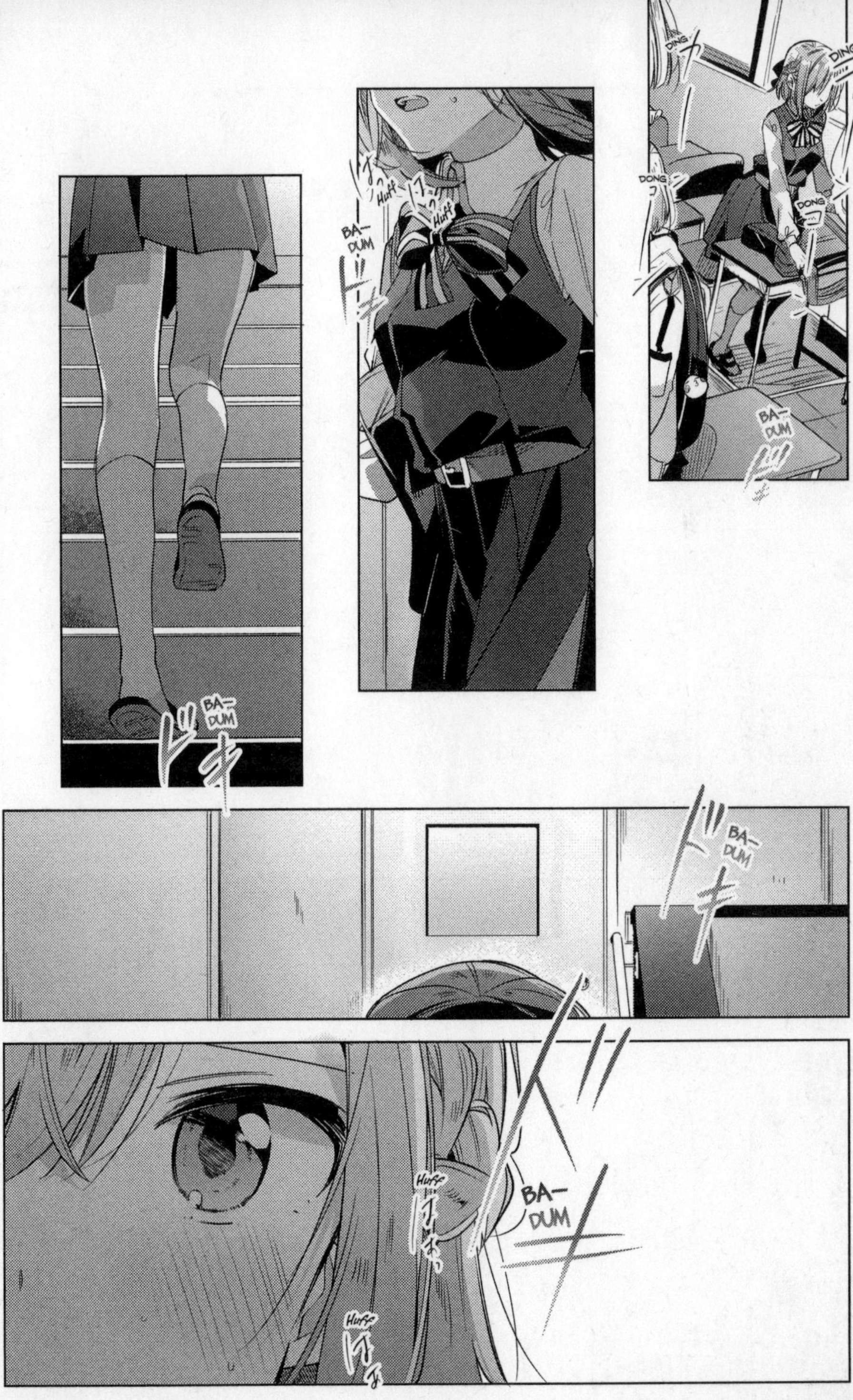

DING
DING
DONG
DONG
BA-DUM
Huff
Huff
BA-DUM
BA-DUM
BA-DUM
Huff
BA-DUM
Huff

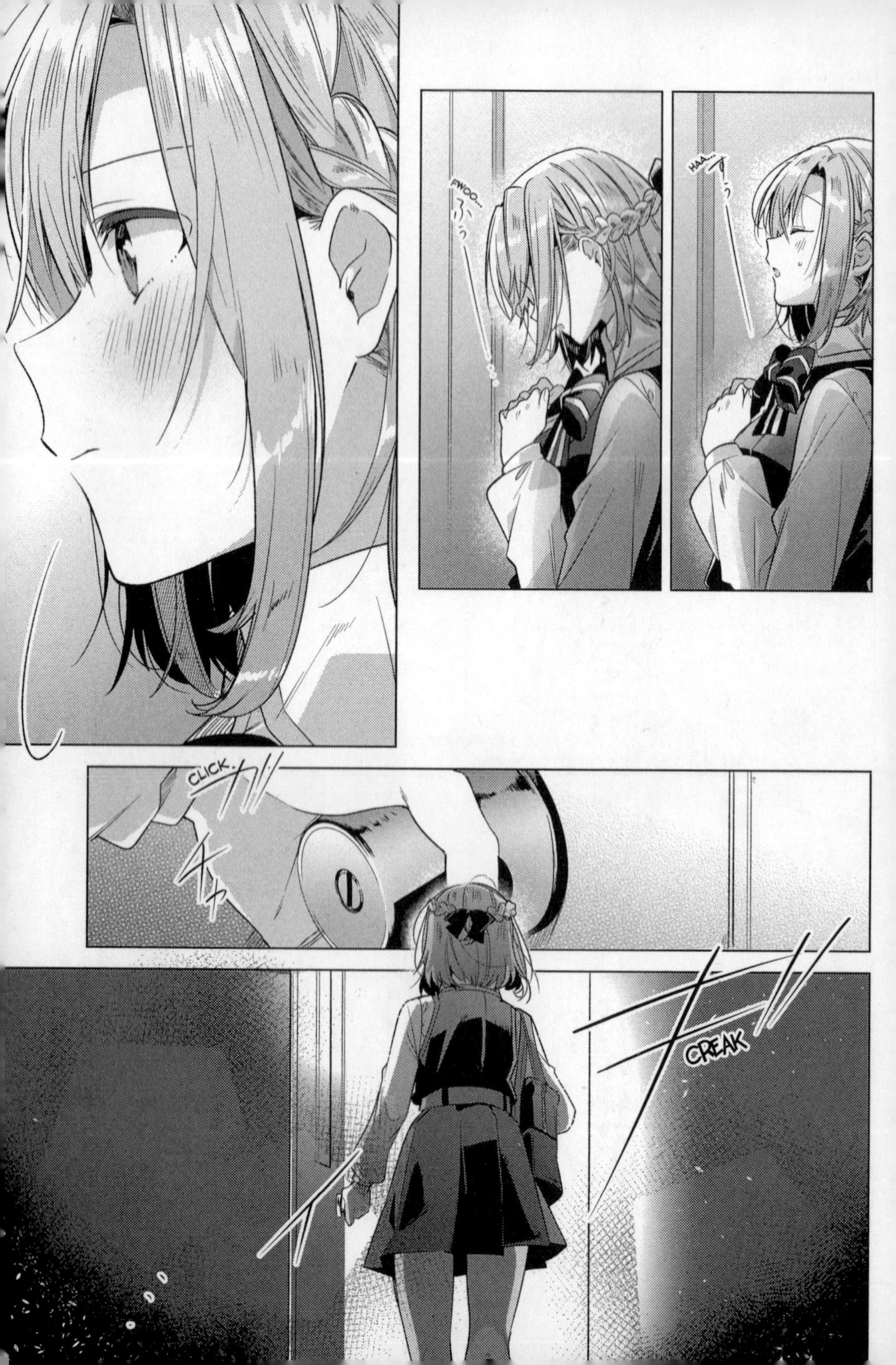
HAA...
FWOO...
CLICK.
CREAK

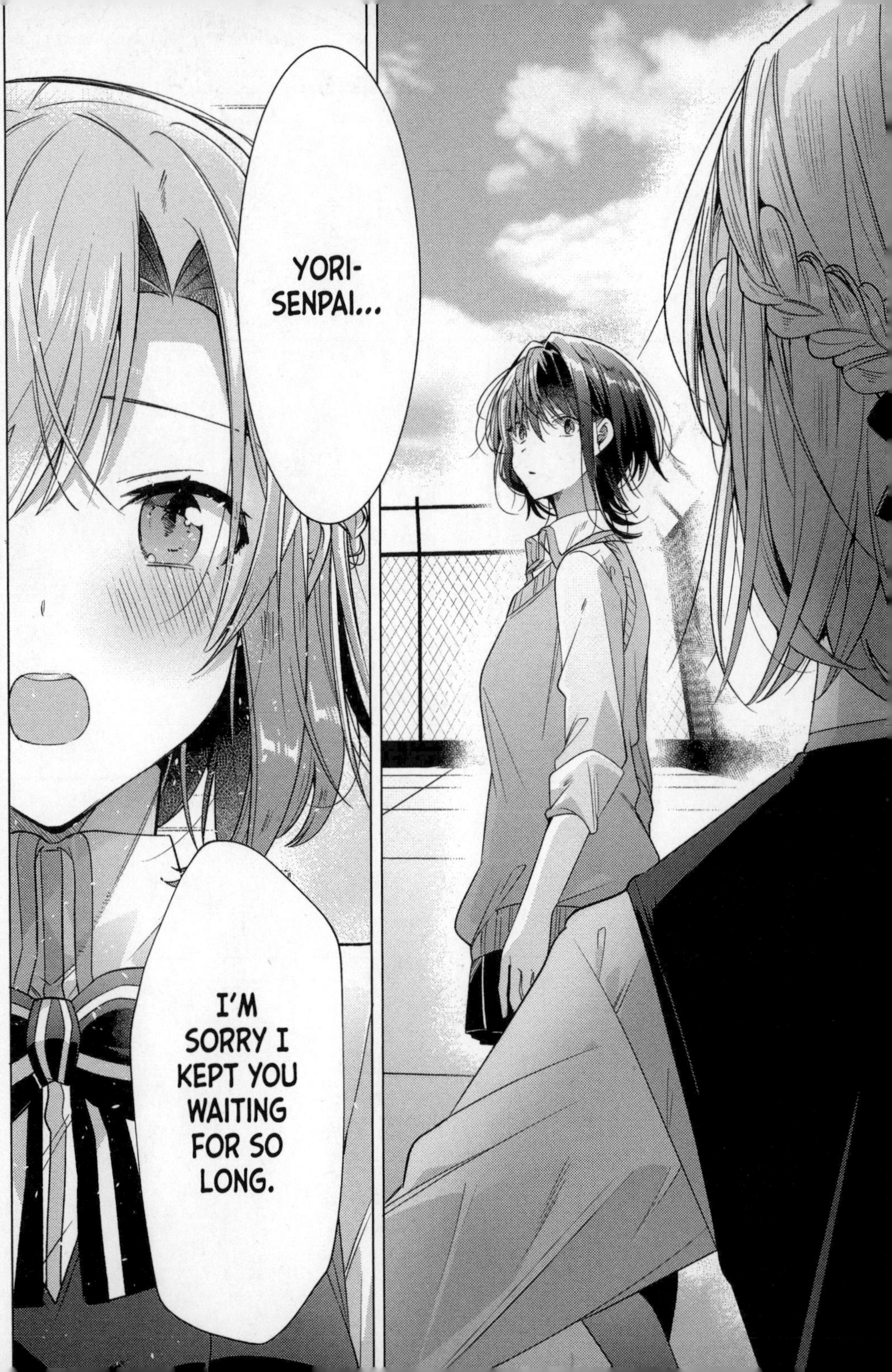
YORI-
SENPAI...
I'M SORRY I KEPT YOU WAITING FOR SO LONG.

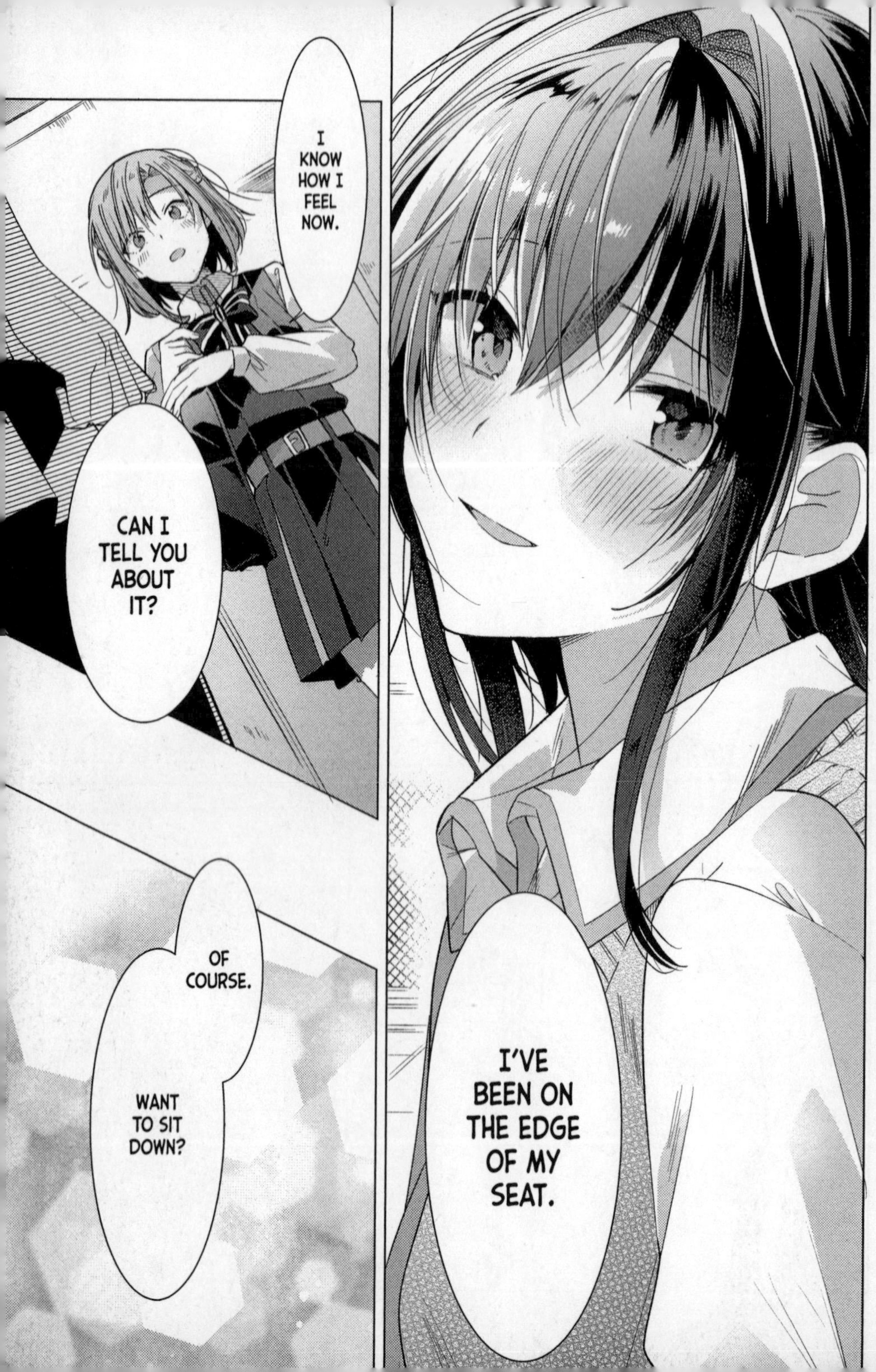
I'VE BEEN ON THE EDGE OF MY SEAT.
I KNOW HOW I FEEL NOW.
CAN I TELL YOU ABOUT IT?
OF COURSE.
WANT TO SIT DOWN?

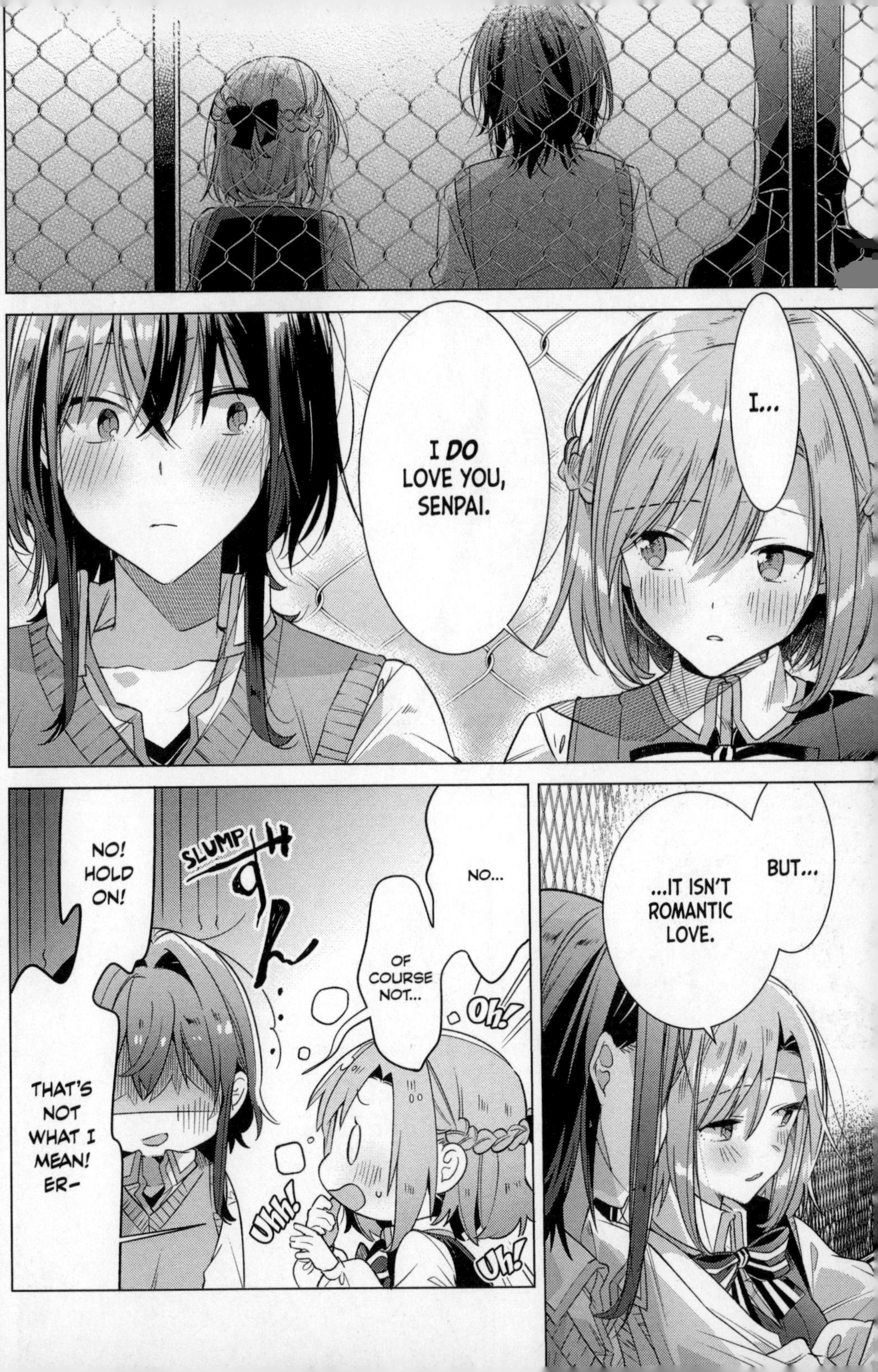
I...
I DO LOVE YOU, SENPAI.
BUT...
...IT ISN'T ROMANTIC LOVE.
NO...
OF COURSE NOT...
Oh!
SLUMP
Uhh!
Uh!
NO! HOLD ON!
THAT'S NOT WHAT I MEAN! ER–

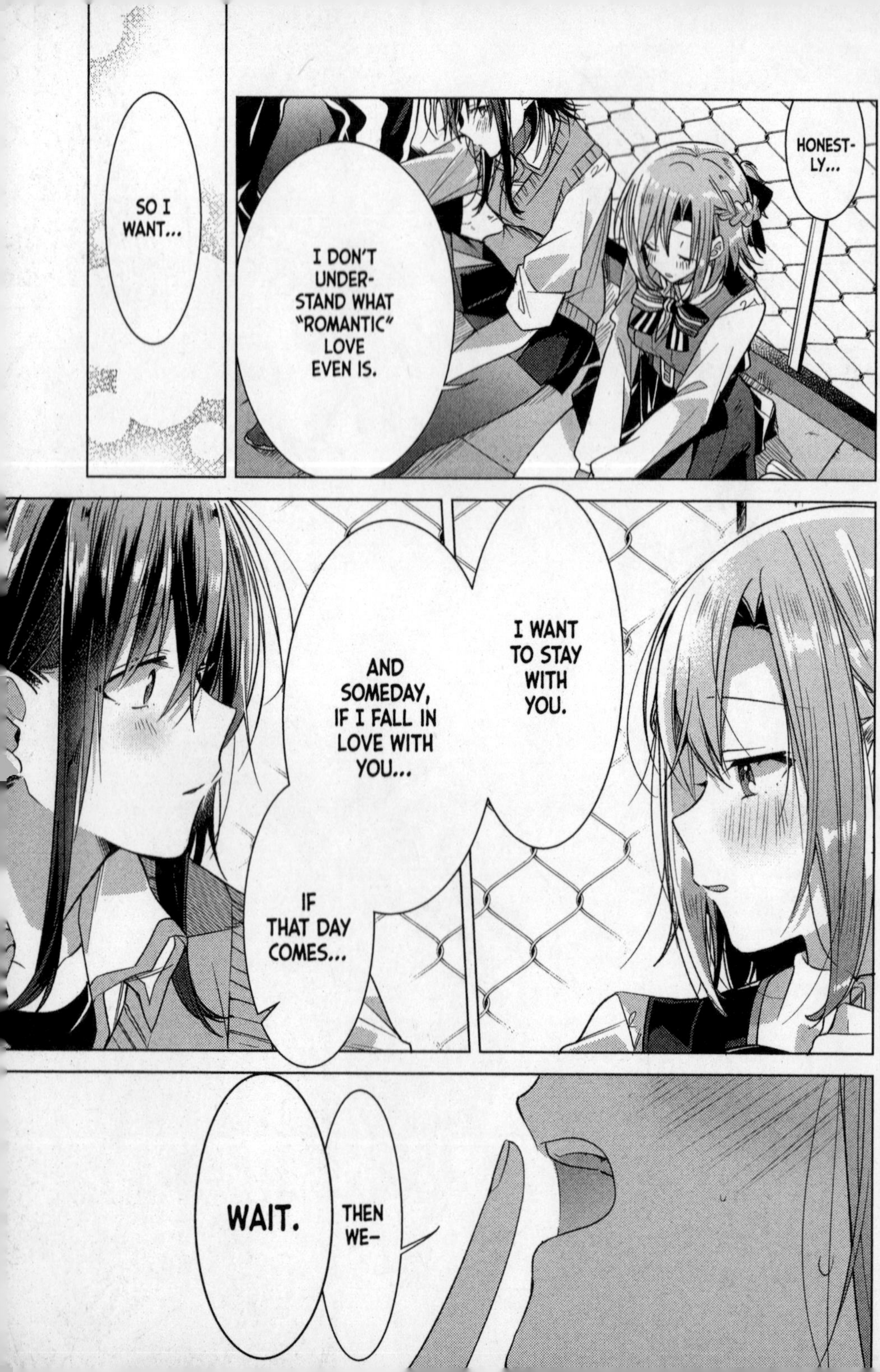
HONEST-LY...
I DON'T UNDER-STAND WHAT "ROMANTIC" LOVE EVEN IS.
SO I WANT...
I WANT TO STAY WITH YOU.
AND SOMEDAY, IF I FALL IN LOVE WITH YOU...
IF THAT DAY COMES...
THEN WE-
WAIT.

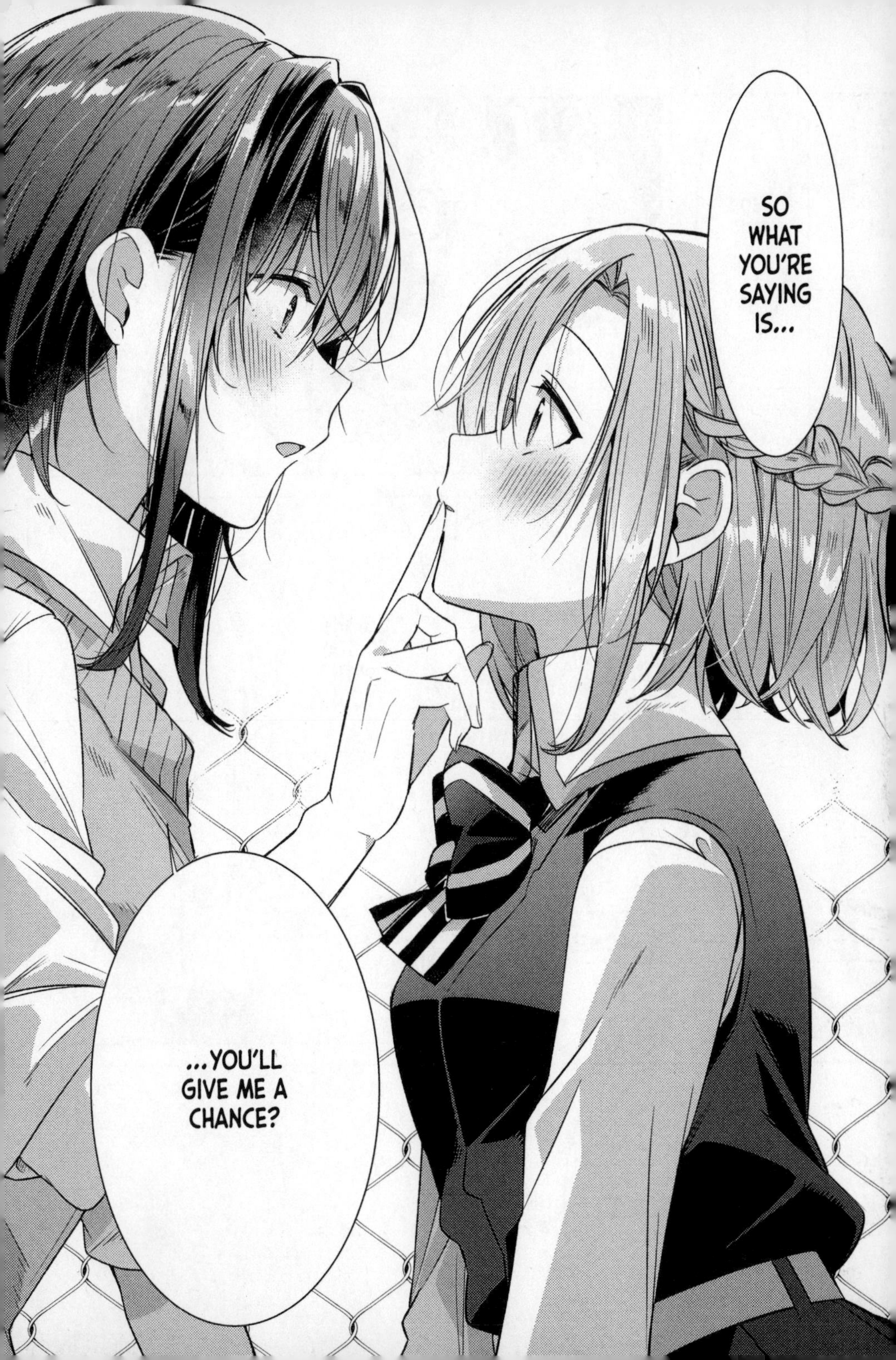
SO WHAT YOU'RE SAYING IS...
...YOU'LL GIVE ME A CHANCE?

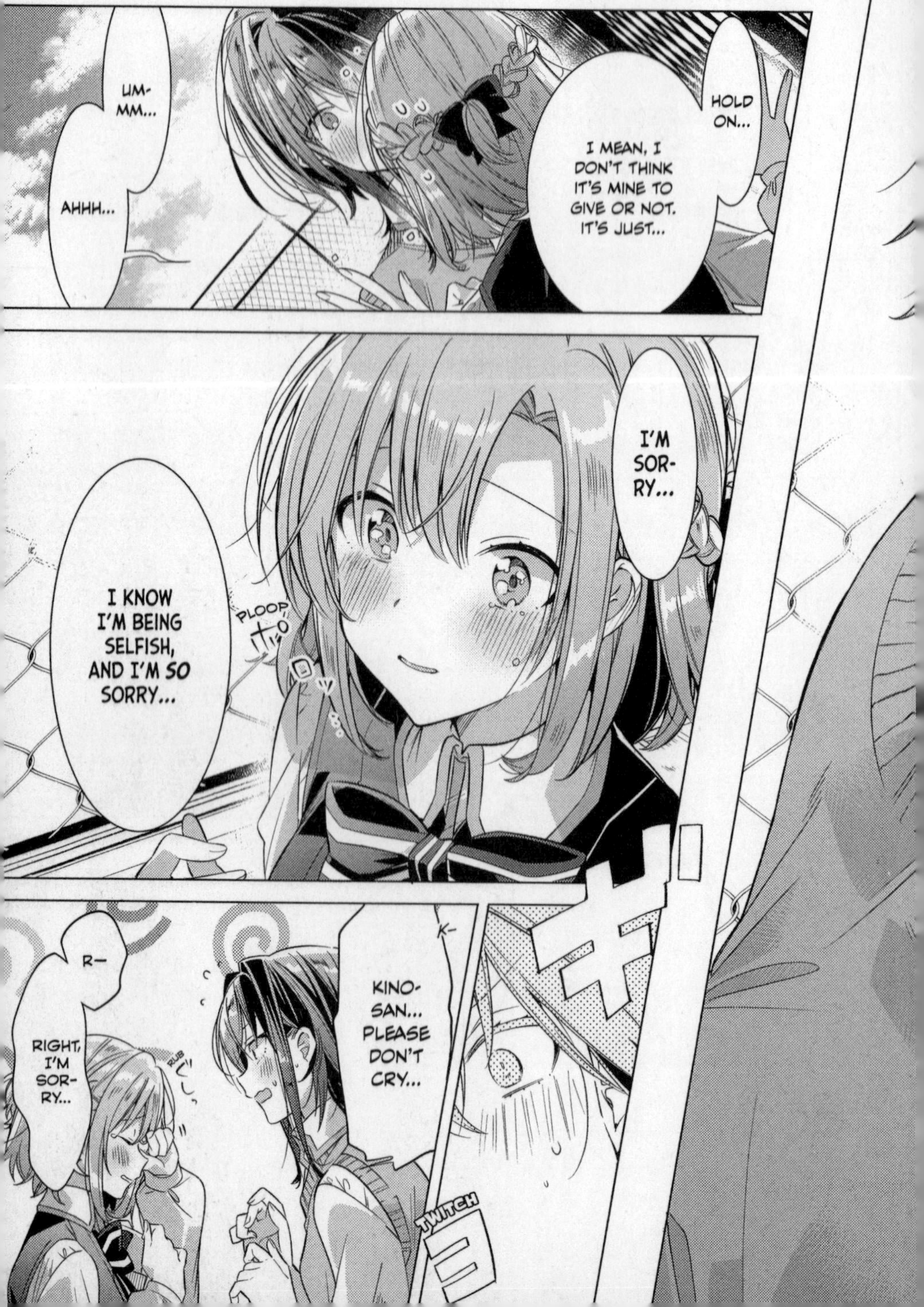
HOLD ON...
I MEAN, I DON'T THINK IT'S MINE TO GIVE OR NOT. IT'S JUST...
UMM-MM...
AHHH...
I'M SORRY...
PLOOP
I KNOW I'M BEING SELFISH, AND I'M SO SORRY...
TWITCH
K-
KINO-SAN... PLEASE DON'T CRY...
R—
RUB
RIGHT, I'M SORRY...

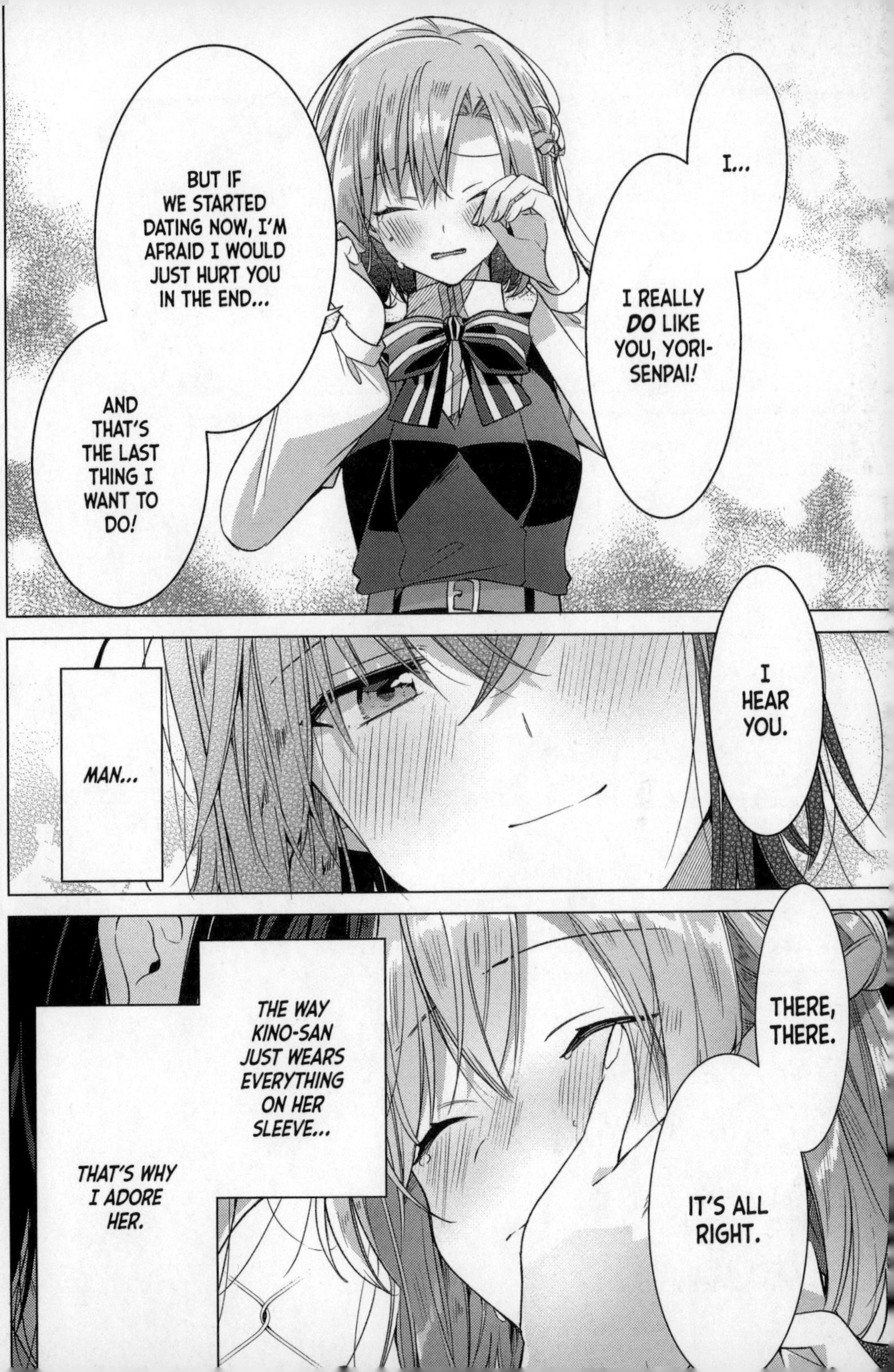
I...
I REALLY *DO* LIKE YOU, YORI-SENPAI!
BUT IF WE STARTED DATING NOW, I'M AFRAID I WOULD JUST HURT YOU IN THE END...
AND THAT'S THE LAST THING I WANT TO DO!
I HEAR YOU.
MAN...
THERE, THERE.
IT'S ALL RIGHT.
THE WAY KINO-SAN JUST WEARS EVERYTHING ON HER SLEEVE...
THAT'S WHY I ADORE HER.

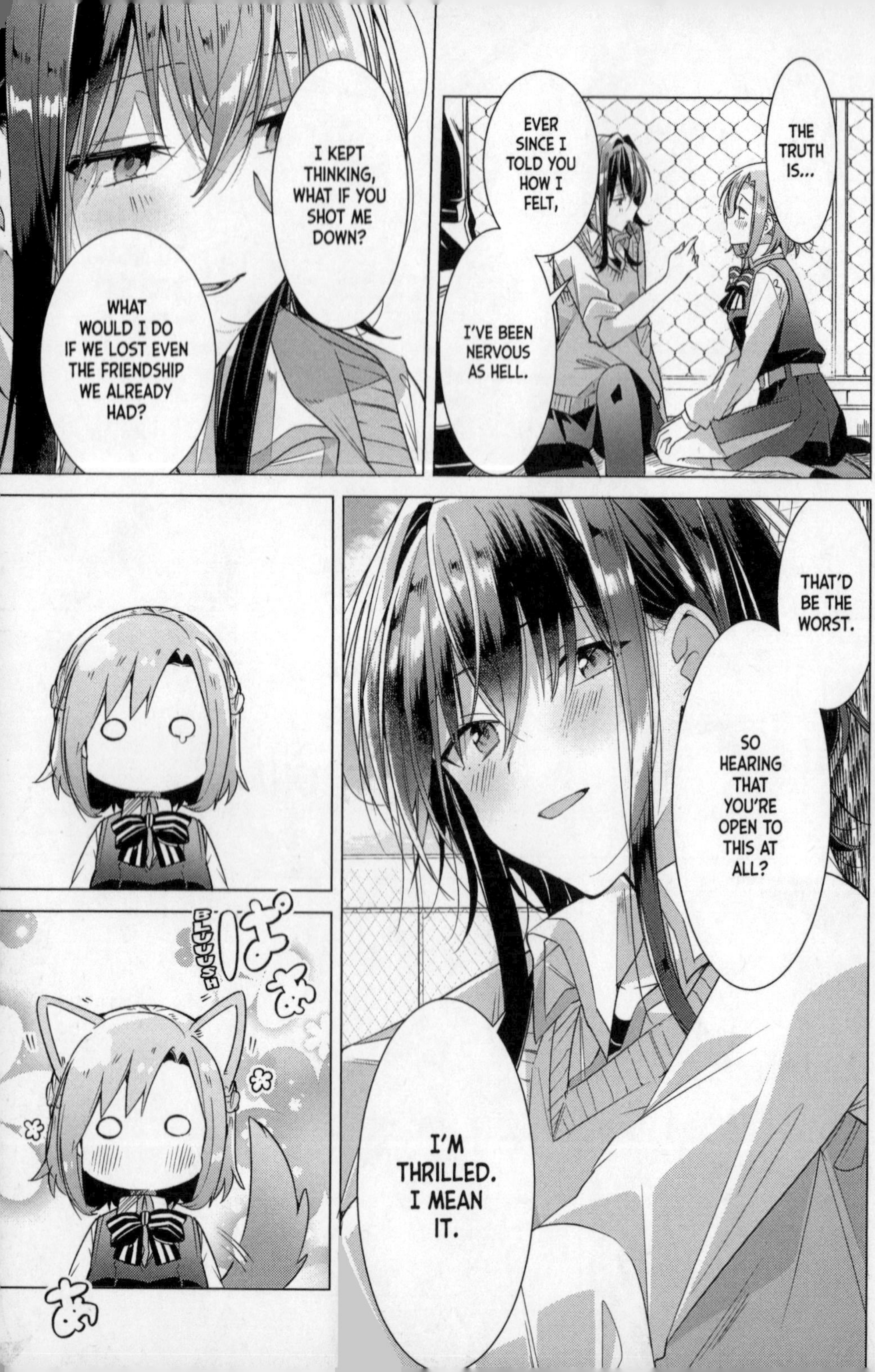
THE TRUTH IS...
EVER SINCE I TOLD YOU HOW I FELT,
I'VE BEEN NERVOUS AS HELL.
I KEPT THINKING, WHAT IF YOU SHOT ME DOWN?
WHAT WOULD I DO IF WE LOST EVEN THE FRIENDSHIP WE ALREADY HAD?
THAT'D BE THE WORST.
SO HEARING THAT YOU'RE OPEN TO THIS AT ALL?
I'M THRILLED. I MEAN IT.
BLUUUSH

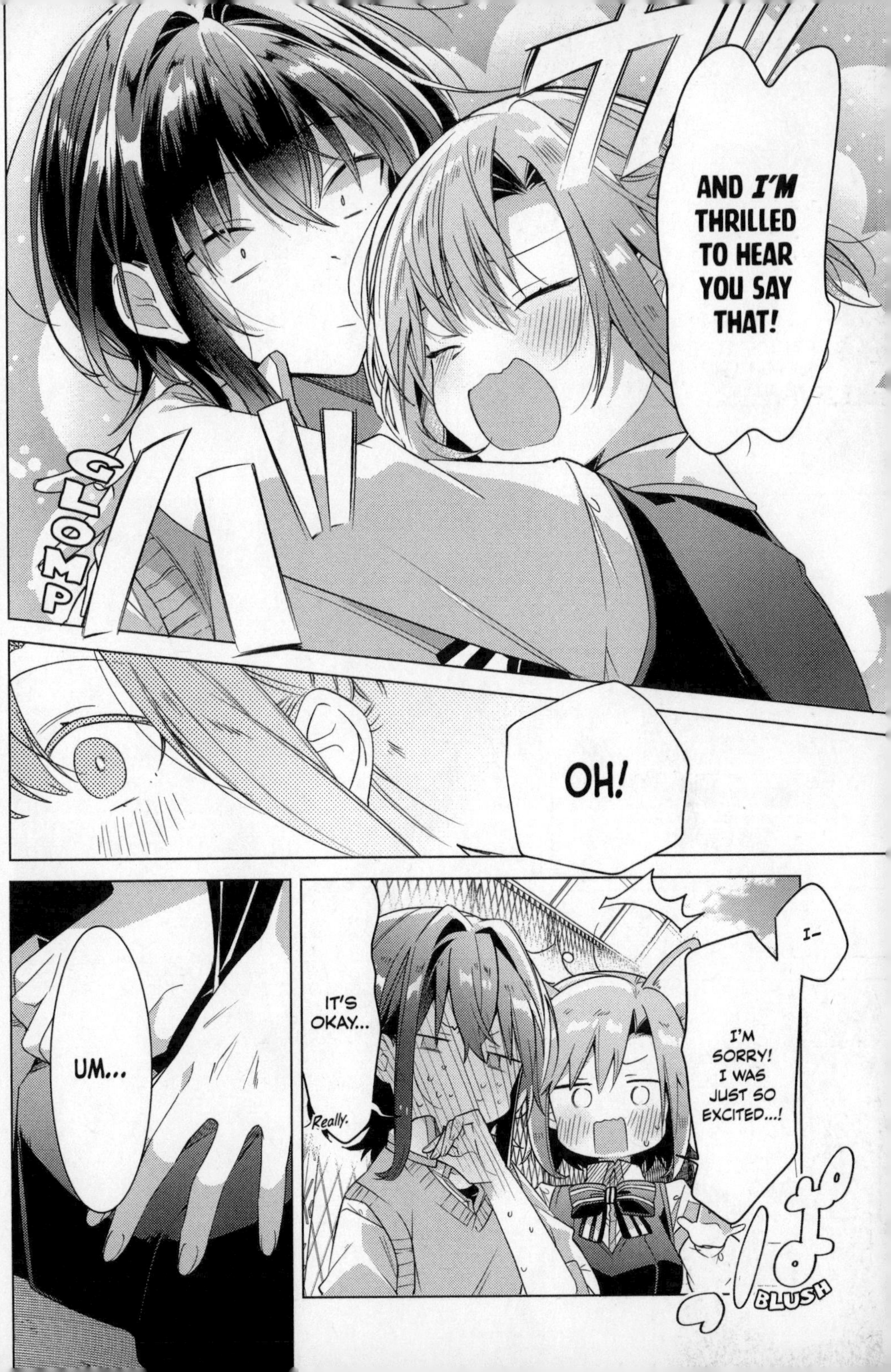
AND *I'M* THRILLED TO HEAR YOU SAY THAT!
GLOMP
OH!
I—
I'M SORRY! I WAS JUST SO EXCITED...!
IT'S OKAY...
Really.
BLUSH
UM...

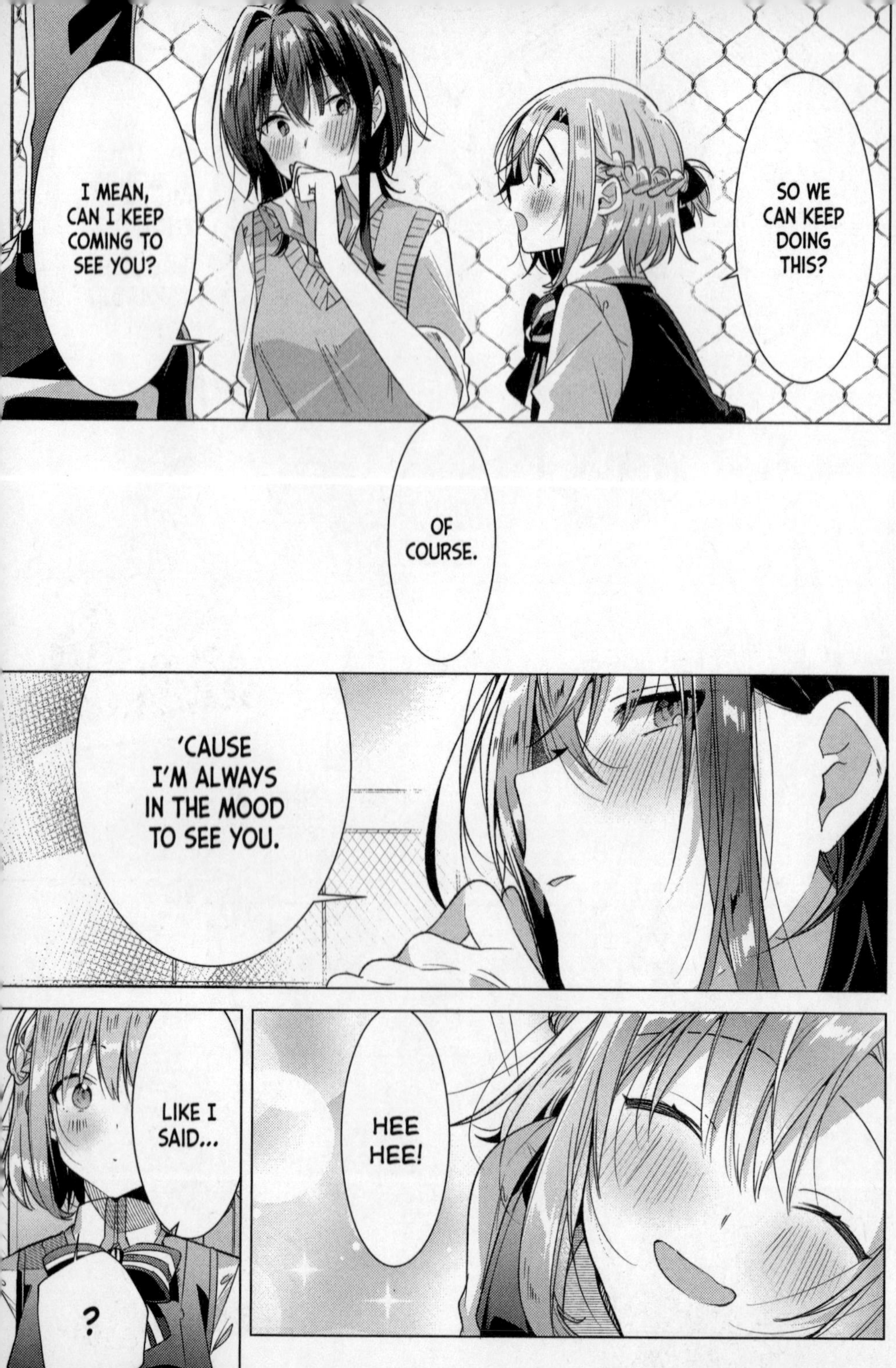
SO WE CAN KEEP DOING THIS?
I MEAN, CAN I KEEP COMING TO SEE YOU?
OF COURSE.
'CAUSE I'M ALWAYS IN THE MOOD TO SEE YOU.
HEE HEE!
LIKE I SAID...
?

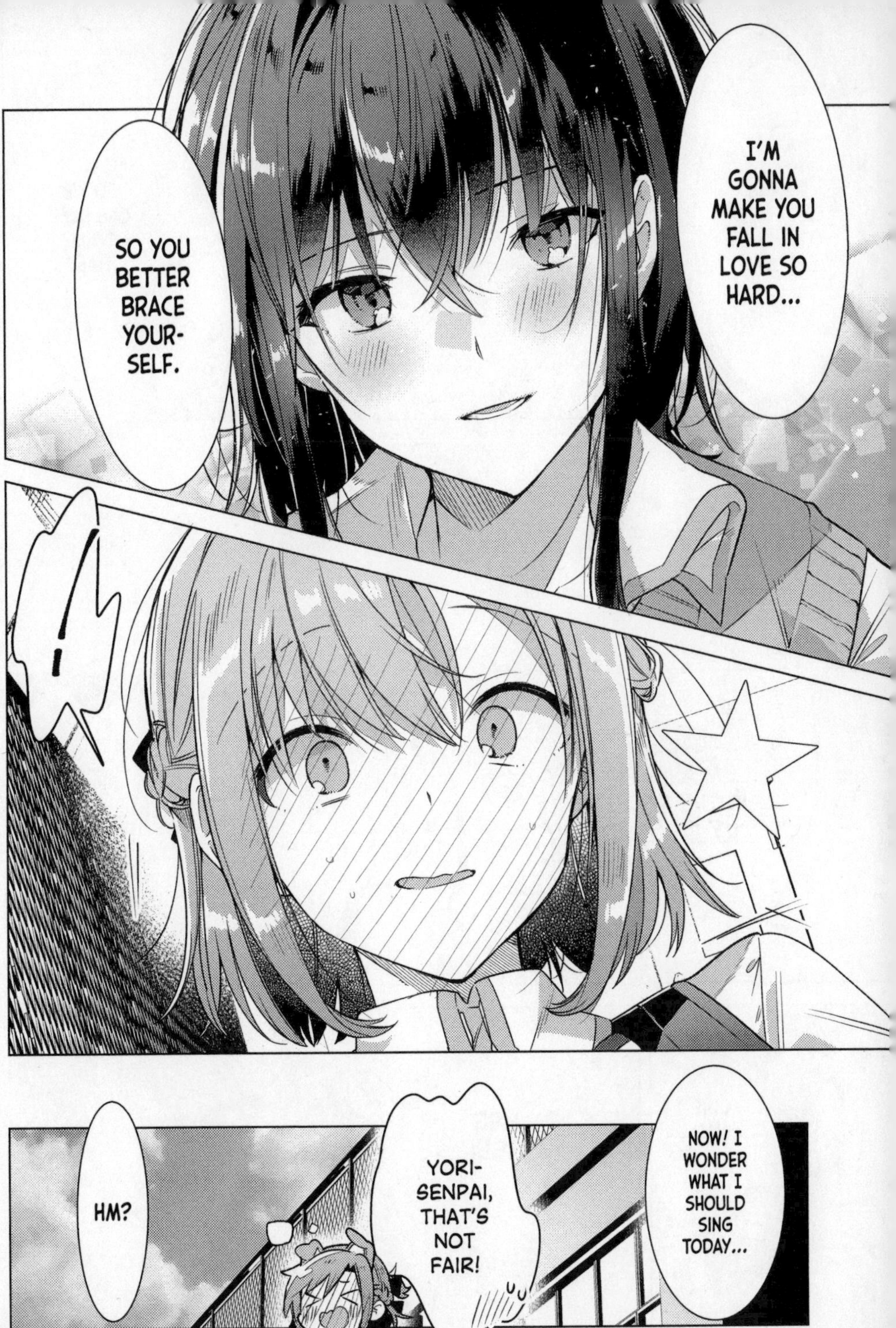
I'M GONNA MAKE YOU FALL IN LOVE SO HARD...
SO YOU BETTER BRACE YOURSELF.
!
NOW! I WONDER WHAT I SHOULD SING TODAY...
YORI-SENPAI, THAT'S NOT FAIR!
HM?

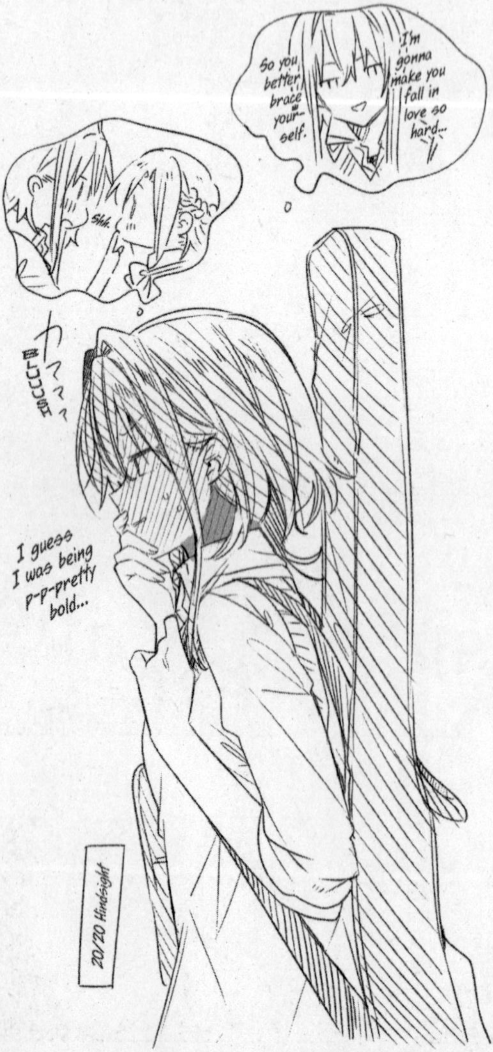
I'm gonna make you fall in love so hard...
So you better brace your-self.
Shh.
カァァァ
I guess I was being p-p-pretty bold...
20/20 Hindsight

Whisper Me
A Love Song

Eku
Takeshima

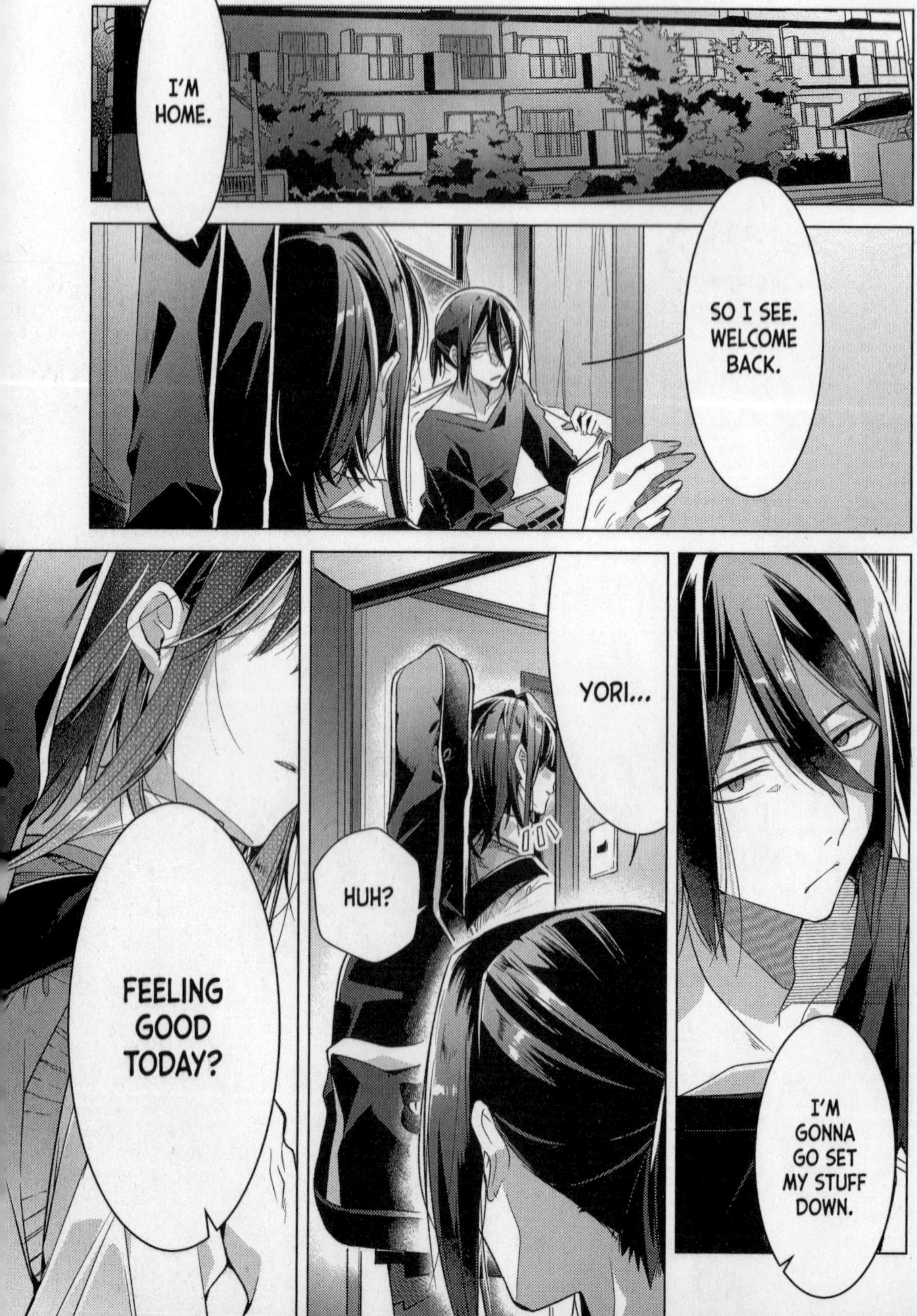
I'M HOME.
SO I SEE. WELCOME BACK.
I'M GONNA GO SET MY STUFF DOWN.
YORI...
HUH?
FEELING GOOD TODAY?

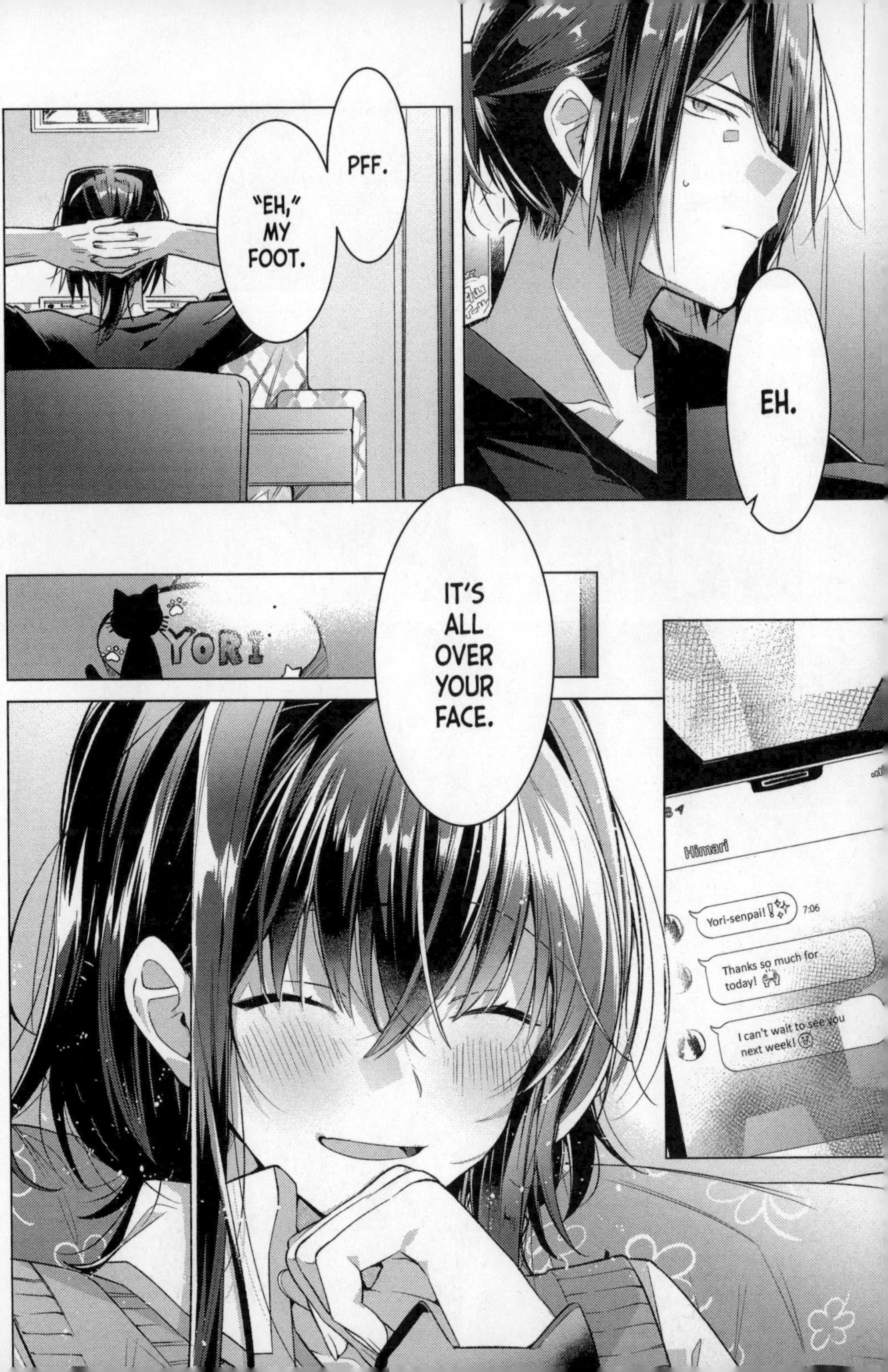
EH.
PFF.
"EH," MY FOOT.
IT'S ALL OVER YOUR FACE.
Himari
Yori-senpai!
7:06
Thanks so much for today!
I can't wait to see you next week!
YORI

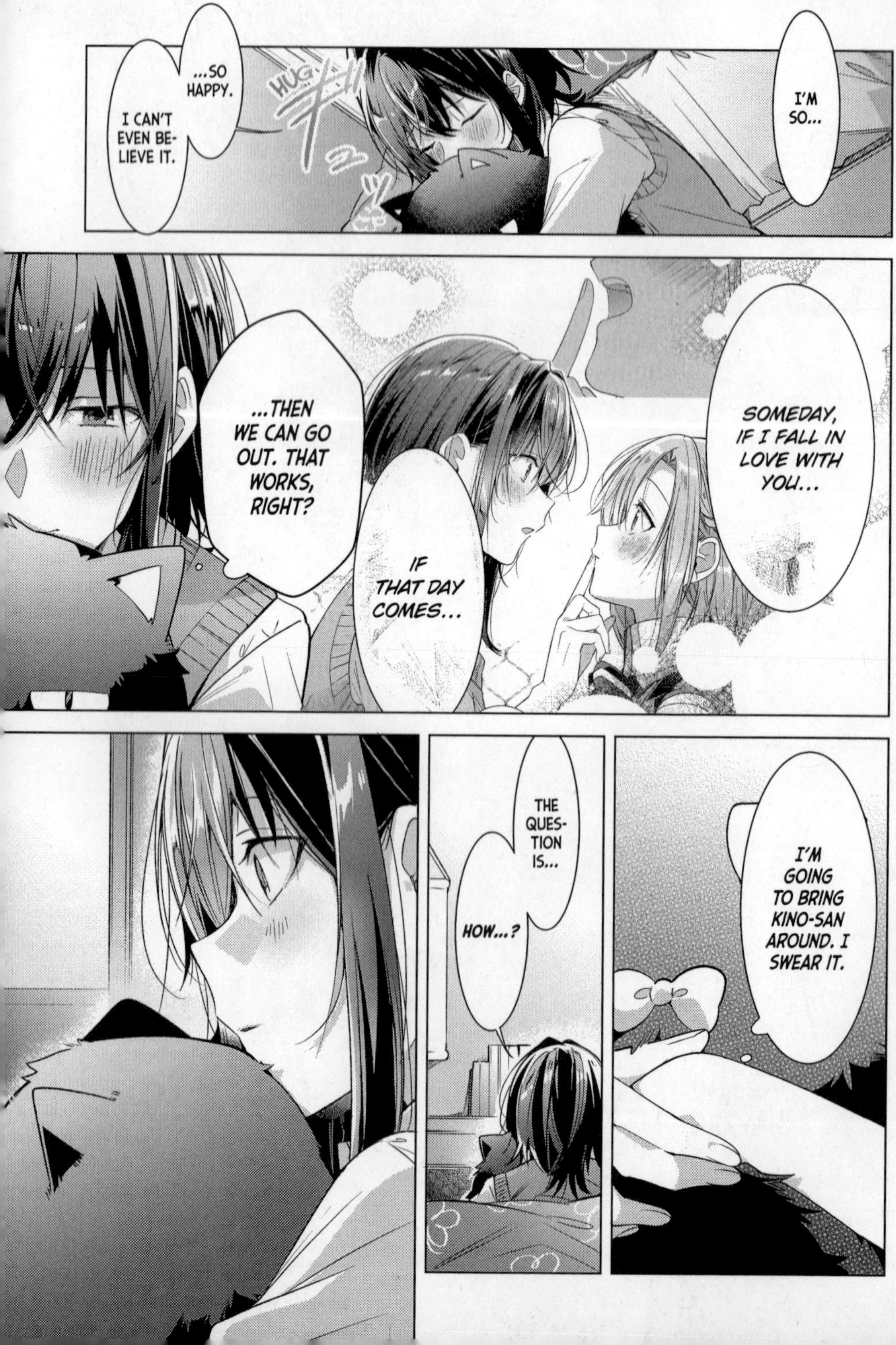
I'M SO...
...SO HAPPY.
HUG
I CAN'T EVEN BELIEVE IT.
SOMEDAY, IF I FALL IN LOVE WITH YOU...
IF THAT DAY COMES...
...THEN WE CAN GO OUT. THAT WORKS, RIGHT?
I'M GOING TO BRING KINO-SAN AROUND. I SWEAR IT.
THE QUESTION IS...
HOW...?

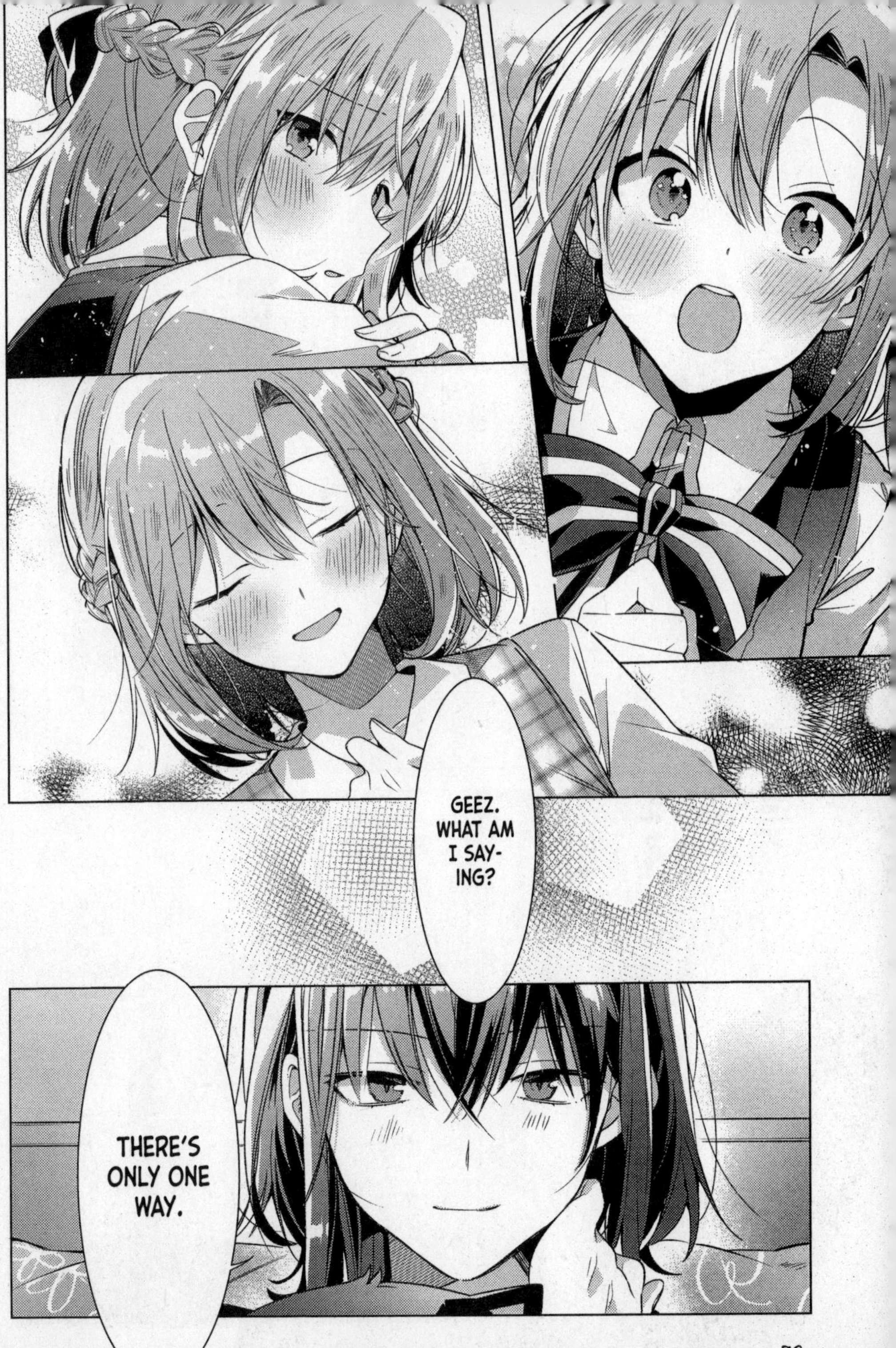
GEEZ. WHAT AM I SAYING?
THERE'S ONLY ONE WAY.

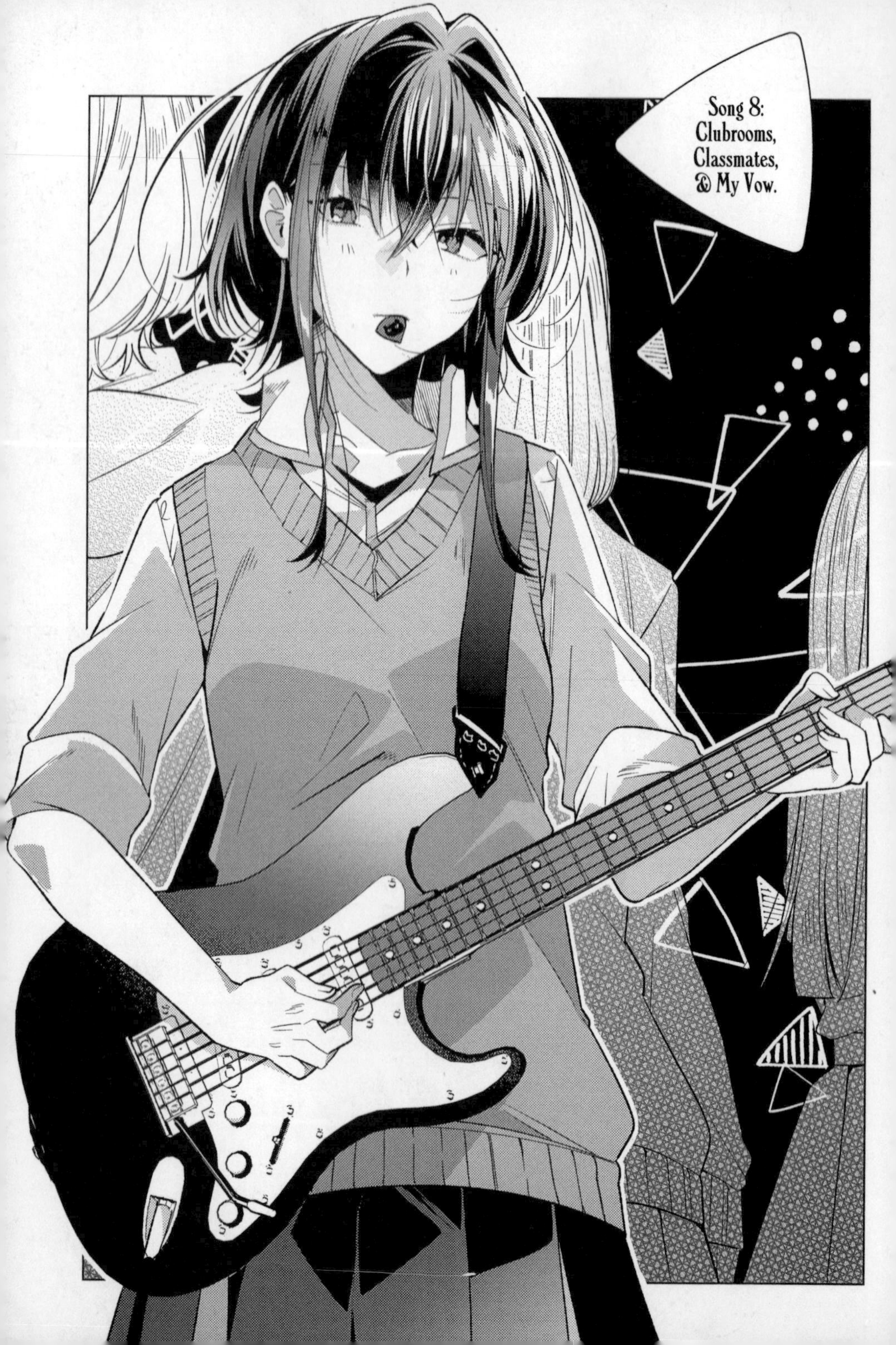
Song 8:
Clubrooms,
Classmates,
& My Vow.

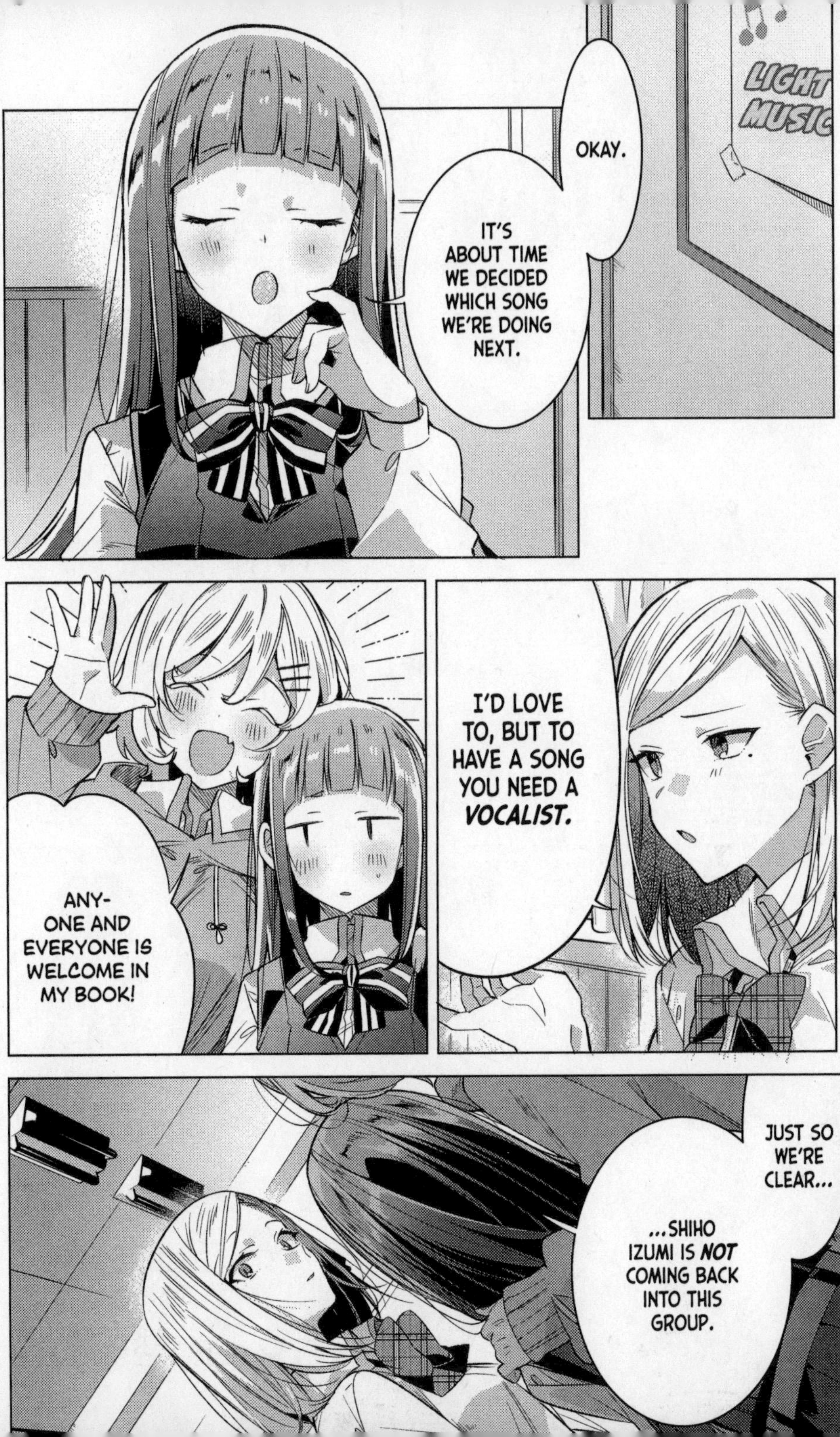
LIGHT MUSIC
OKAY.
IT'S ABOUT TIME WE DECIDED WHICH SONG WE'RE DOING NEXT.
I'D LOVE TO, BUT TO HAVE A SONG YOU NEED A *VOCALIST.*
ANY-ONE AND EVERYONE IS WELCOME IN MY BOOK!
JUST SO WE'RE CLEAR...
...SHIHO IZUMI IS *NOT* COMING BACK INTO THIS GROUP.

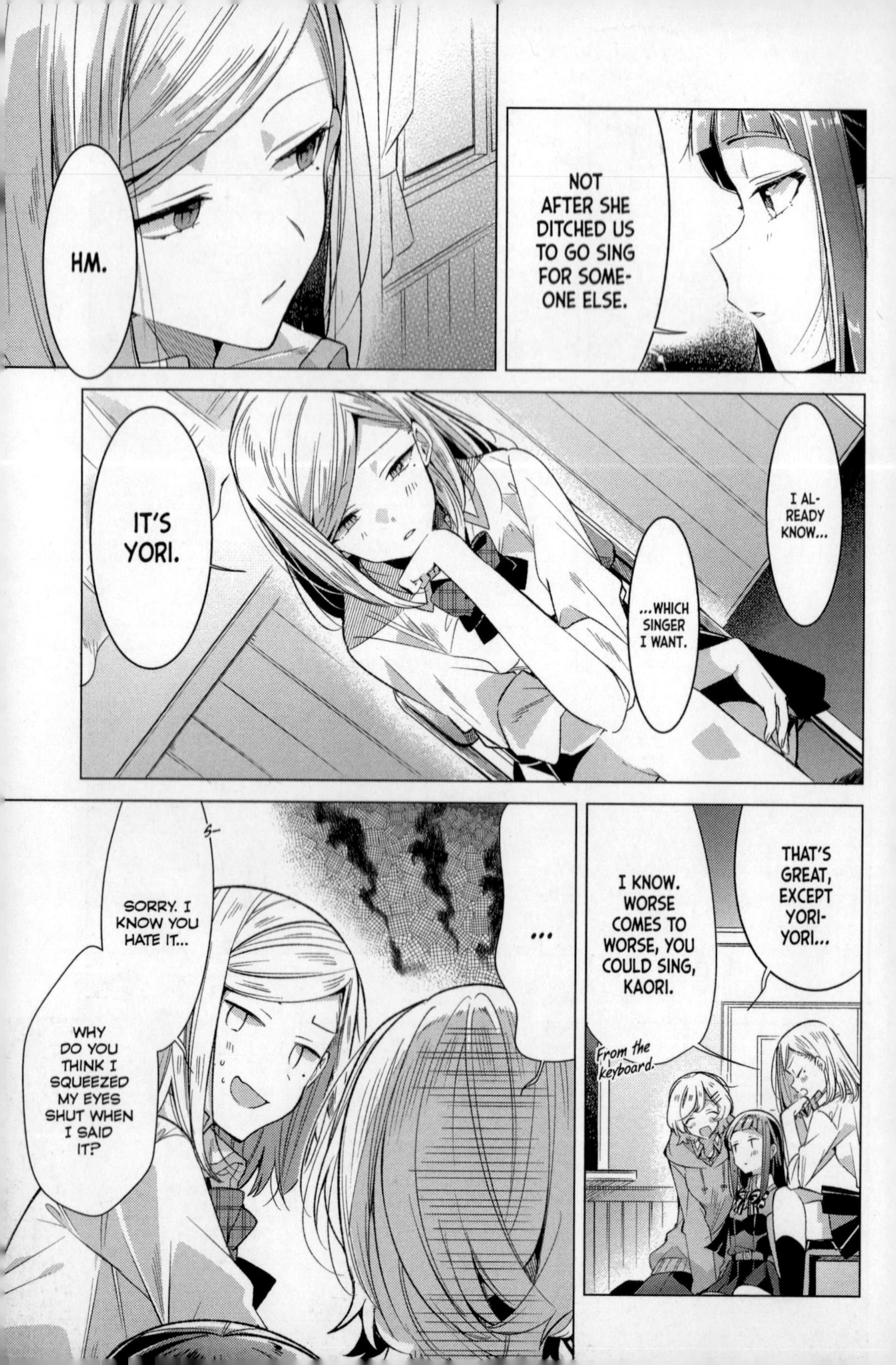
NOT AFTER SHE DITCHED US TO GO SING FOR SOMEONE ELSE.
HM.
I ALREADY KNOW...
...WHICH SINGER I WANT.
IT'S YORI.
THAT'S GREAT, EXCEPT YORIYORI...
I KNOW. WORSE COMES TO WORSE, YOU COULD SING, KAORI.
From the keyboard.
...
S—
SORRY. I KNOW YOU HATE IT...
WHY DO YOU THINK I SQUEEZED MY EYES SHUT WHEN I SAID IT?

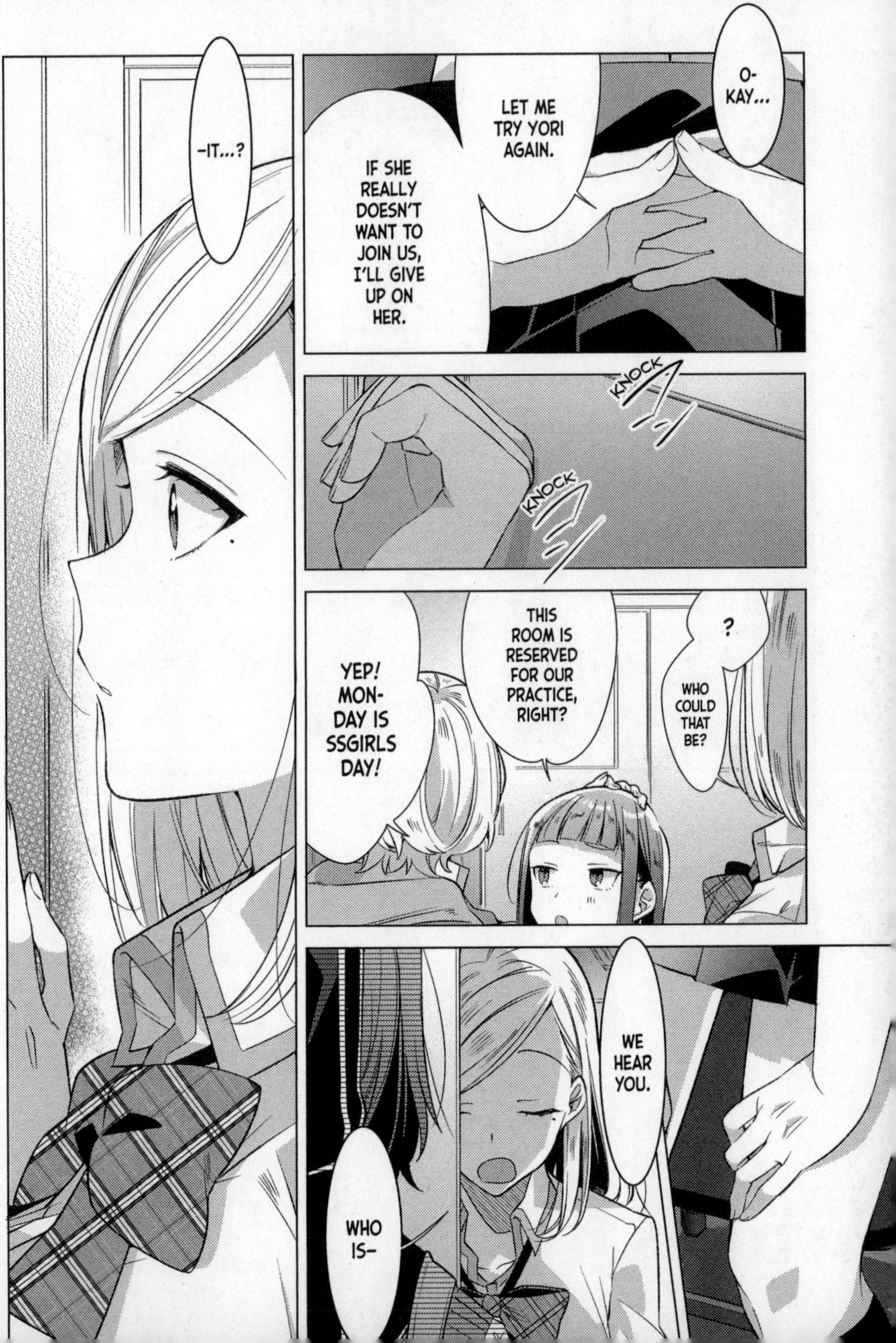
O-KAY...
LET ME TRY YORI AGAIN.
IF SHE REALLY DOESN'T WANT TO JOIN US, I'LL GIVE UP ON HER.
KNOCK
KNOCK
?
WHO COULD THAT BE?
THIS ROOM IS RESERVED FOR OUR PRACTICE, RIGHT?
YEP! MON-DAY IS SSGIRLS DAY!
WE HEAR YOU.
WHO IS-
-IT...?

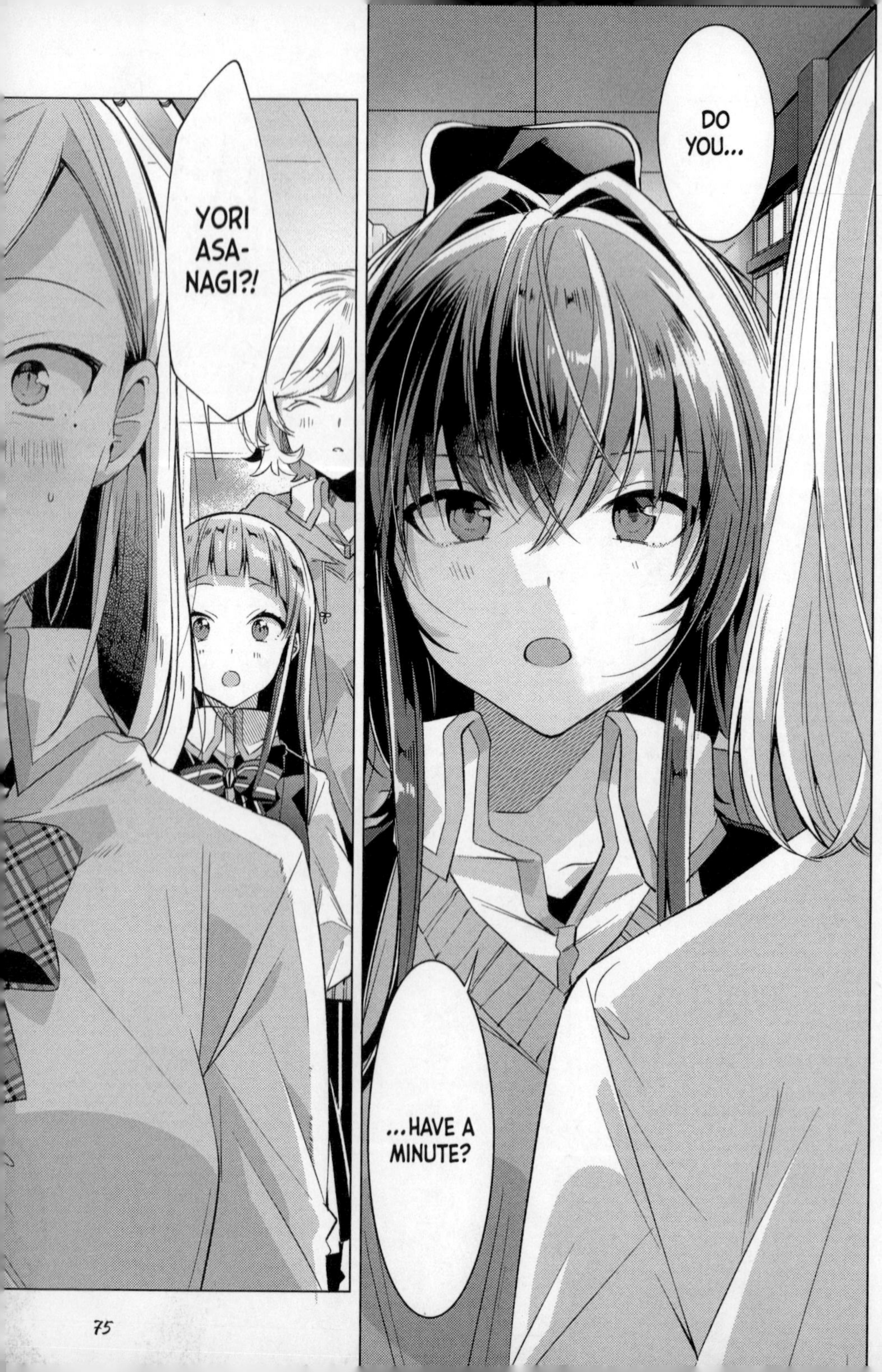
DO YOU...
...HAVE A MINUTE?
YORI ASA-NAGI?!

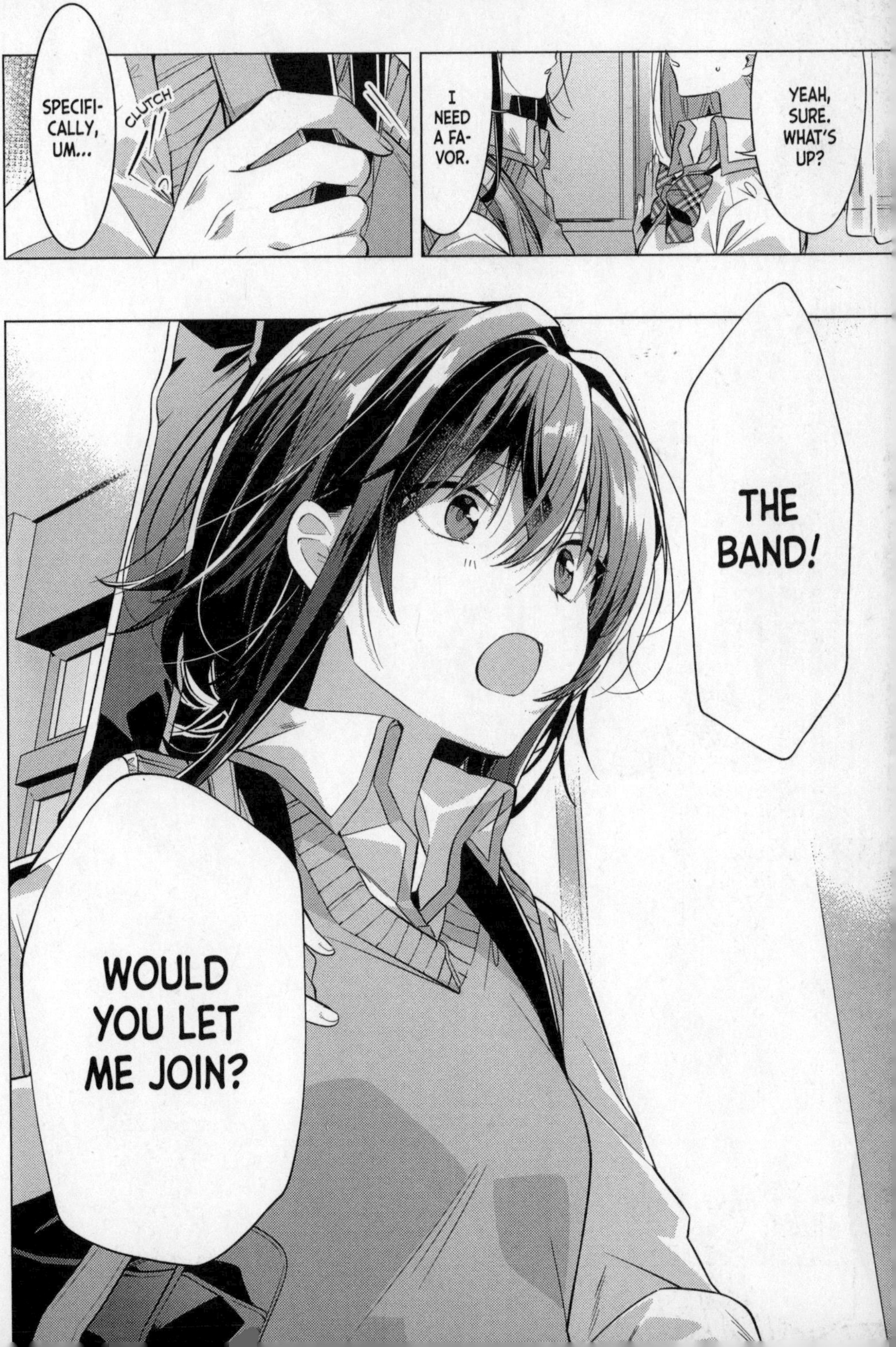
YEAH, SURE. WHAT'S UP?
I NEED A FA-VOR.
SPECIFI-CALLY, UM...
CLUTCH
THE BAND!
WOULD YOU LET ME JOIN?

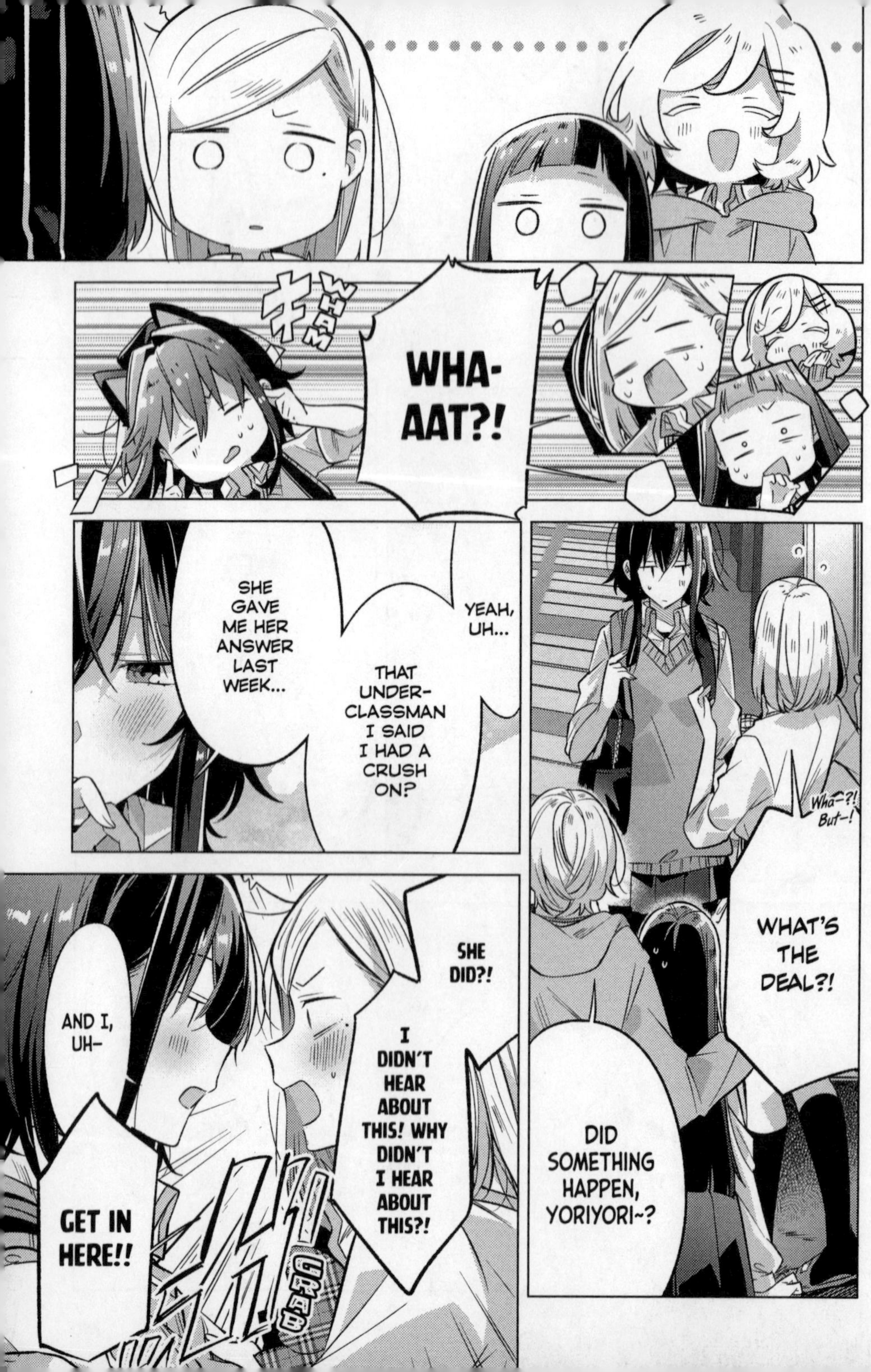
WHA-AAT?!
WHAM
Wha-?! But-!
WHAT'S THE DEAL?!
DID SOMETHING HAPPEN, YORIYORI~?
YEAH, UH...
THAT UNDER-CLASSMAN I SAID I HAD A CRUSH ON?
SHE GAVE ME HER ANSWER LAST WEEK...
SHE DID?!
I DIDN'T HEAR ABOUT THIS! WHY DIDN'T I HEAR ABOUT THIS?!
AND I, UH-
GET IN HERE!!
GRAB

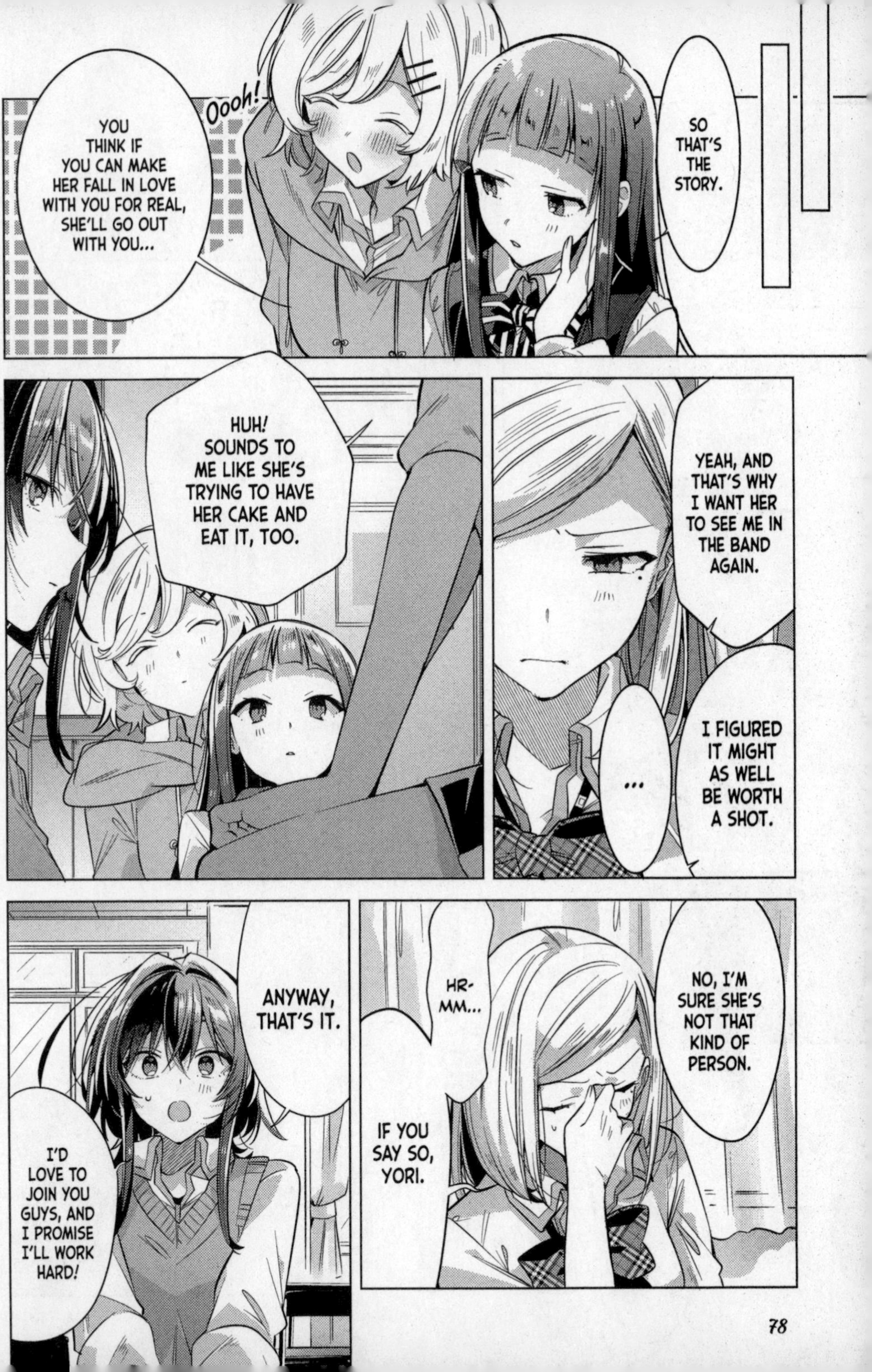
SO THAT'S THE STORY.
Oooh!
YOU THINK IF YOU CAN MAKE HER FALL IN LOVE WITH YOU FOR REAL, SHE'LL GO OUT WITH YOU...
YEAH, AND THAT'S WHY I WANT HER TO SEE ME IN THE BAND AGAIN.
I FIGURED IT MIGHT AS WELL BE WORTH A SHOT.
...
HUH! SOUNDS TO ME LIKE SHE'S TRYING TO HAVE HER CAKE AND EAT IT, TOO.
NO, I'M SURE SHE'S NOT THAT KIND OF PERSON.
HR-MM...
IF YOU SAY SO, YORI.
ANYWAY, THAT'S IT.
I'D LOVE TO JOIN YOU GUYS, AND I PROMISE I'LL WORK HARD!

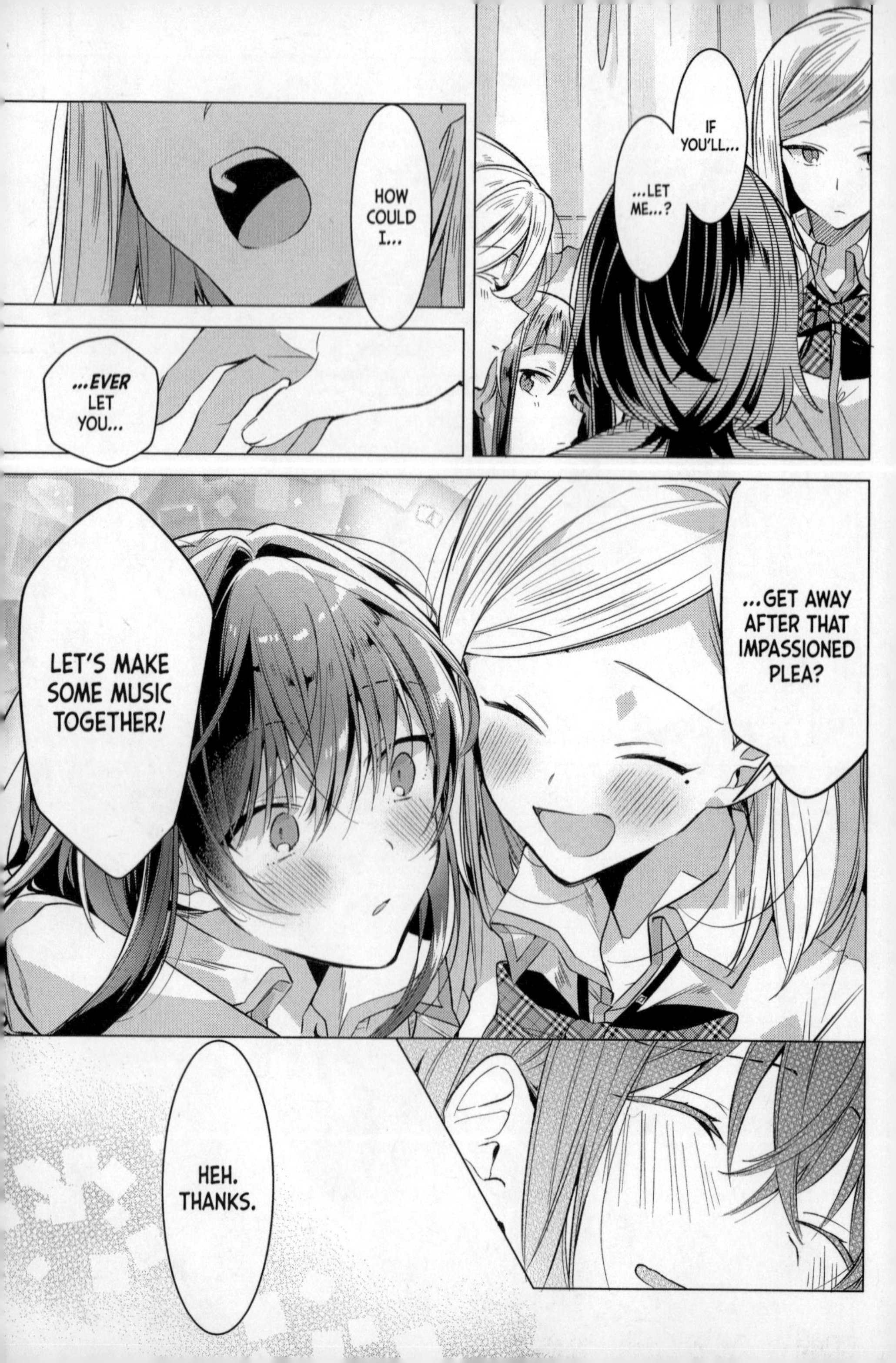

IF YOU'LL...
...LET ME...?
HOW COULD I...
...EVER LET YOU...
...GET AWAY AFTER THAT IMPASSIONED PLEA?
LET'S MAKE SOME MUSIC TOGETHER!
HEH. THANKS.

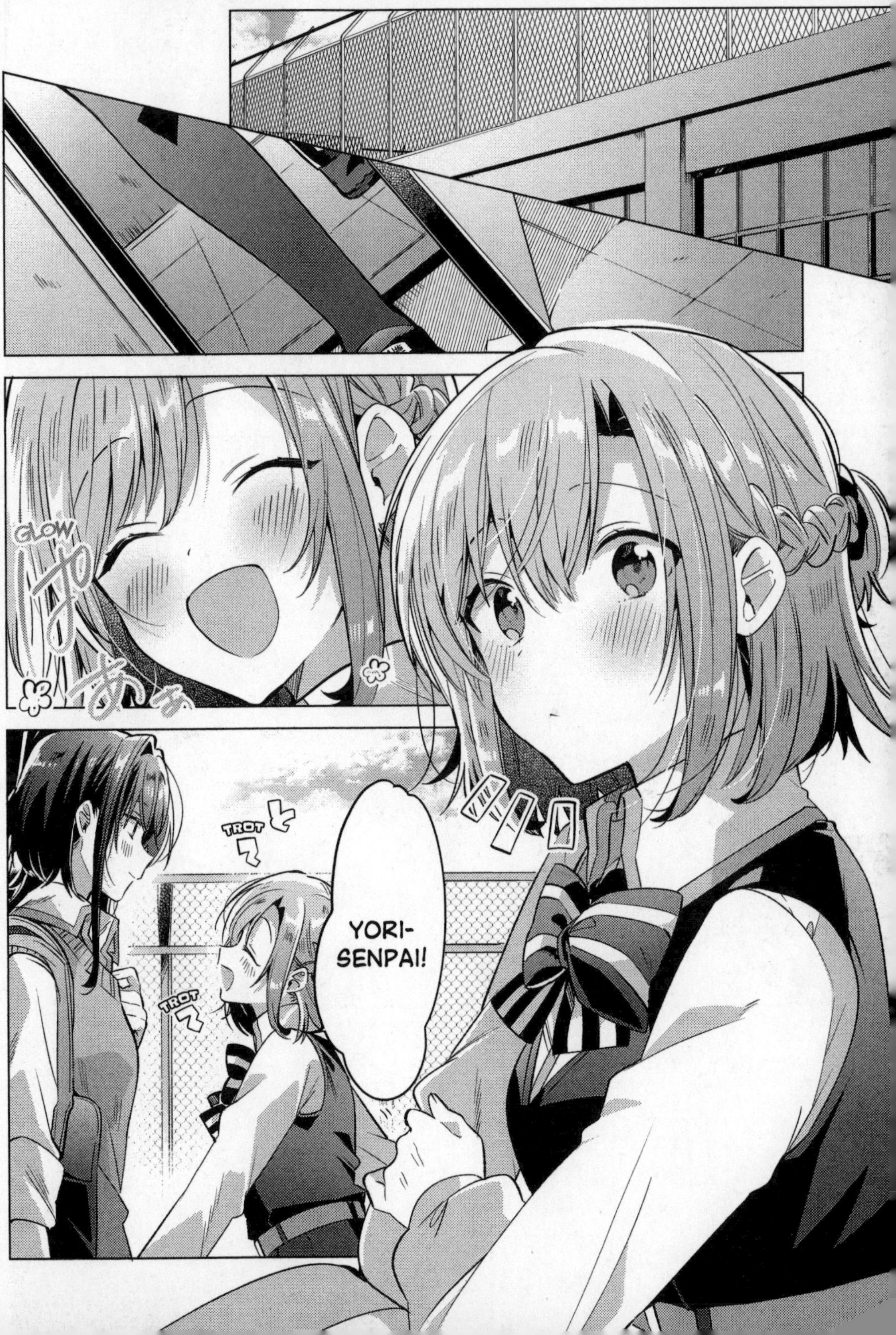
GLOW
TROT
TROT
YORI-SENPAI!

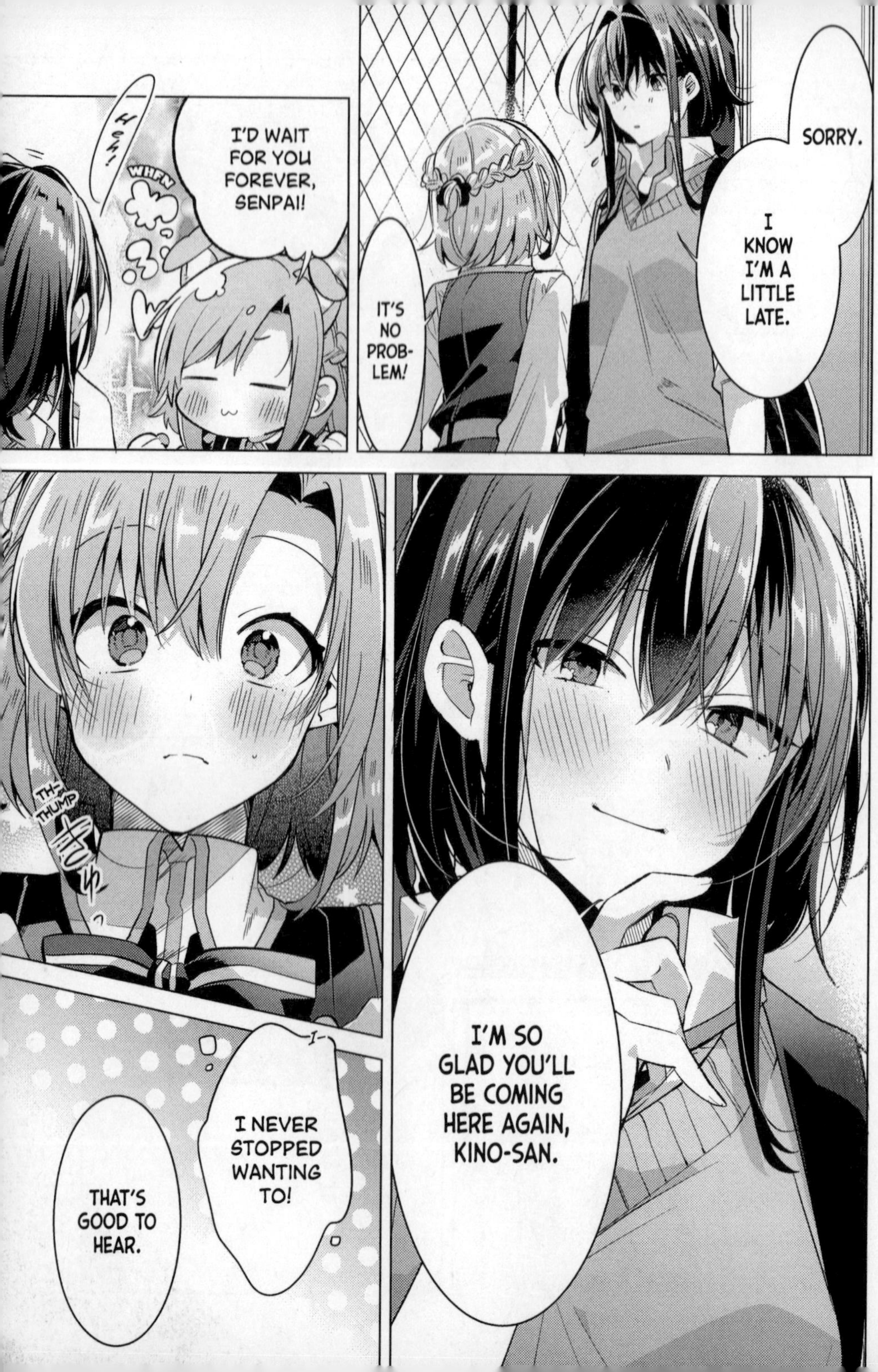
SORRY.
I KNOW I'M A LITTLE LATE.
IT'S NO PROBLEM!
I'D WAIT FOR YOU FOREVER, SENPAI!
Heh!
WHFN
I'M SO GLAD YOU'LL BE COMING HERE AGAIN, KINO-SAN.
TH-THUMP
I-
I NEVER STOPPED WANTING TO!
THAT'S GOOD TO HEAR.

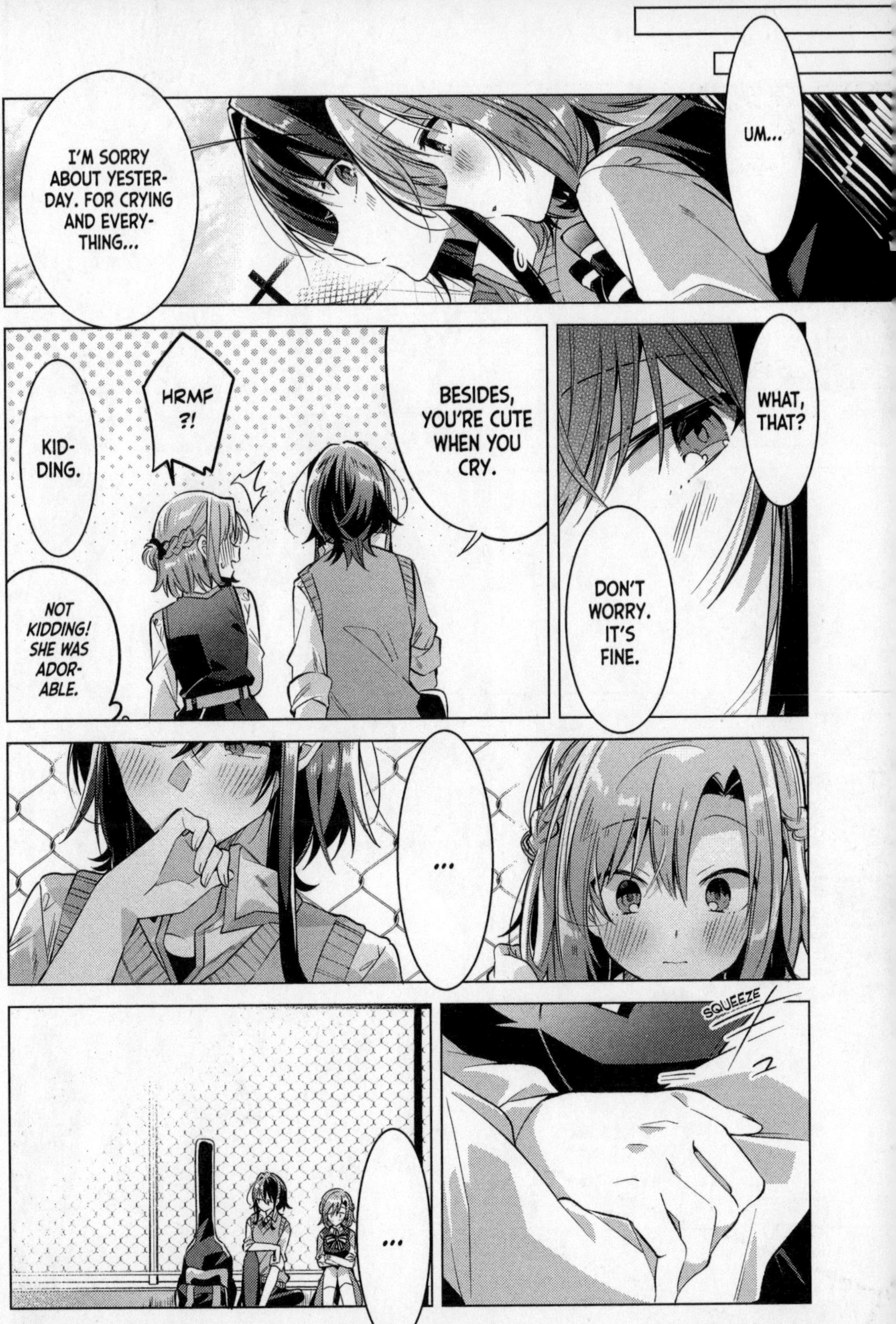
UM...
I'M SORRY ABOUT YESTER-DAY. FOR CRYING AND EVERY-THING...
WHAT, THAT?
DON'T WORRY. IT'S FINE.
BESIDES, YOU'RE CUTE WHEN YOU CRY.
HRMF ?!
KID-DING.
NOT KIDDING! SHE WAS ADOR-ABLE.
...
SQUEEZE
...

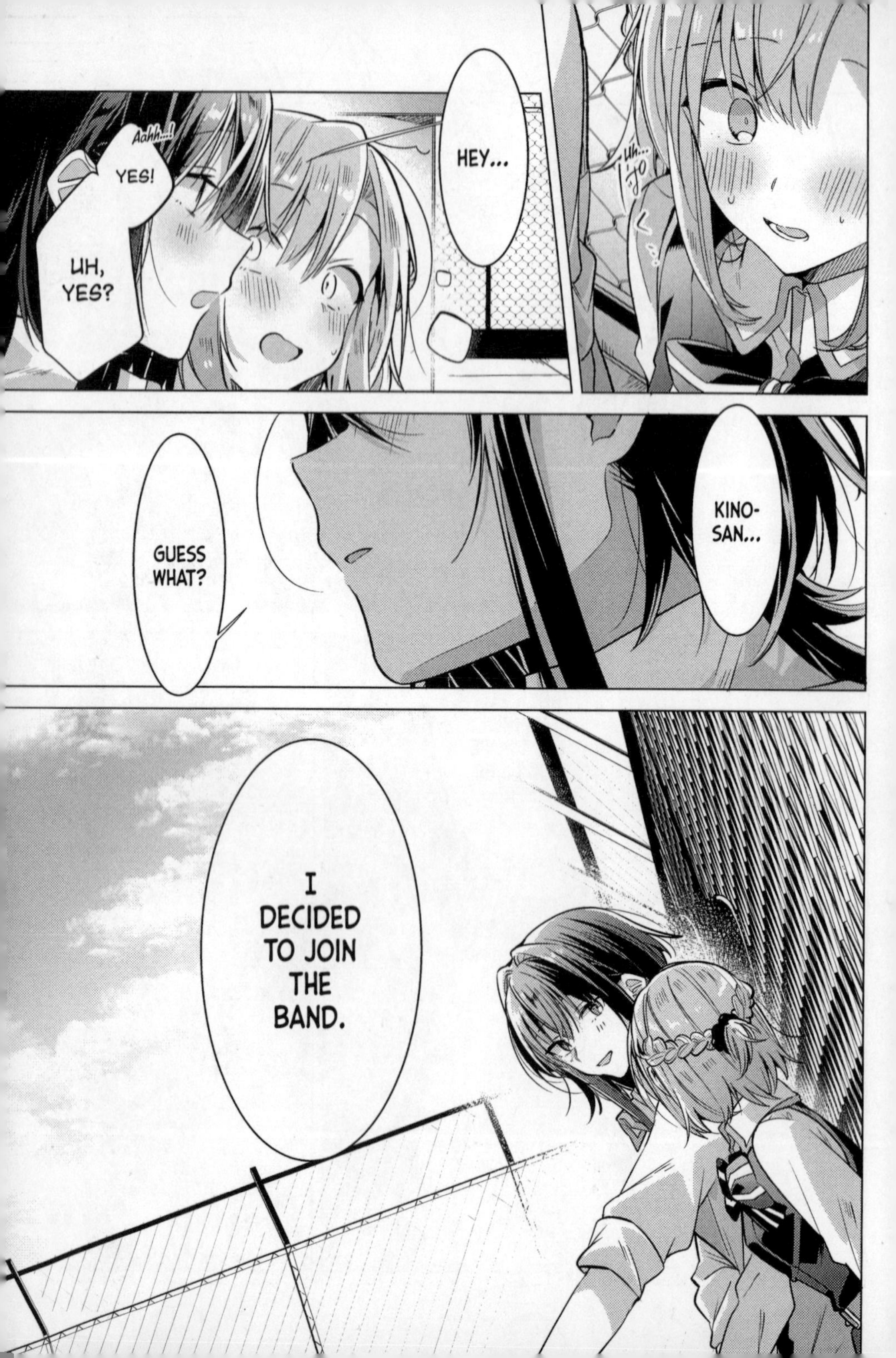
Uh...
HEY...
Aahh...!
YES!
UH, YES?
KINO-SAN...
GUESS WHAT?
I DECIDED TO JOIN THE BAND.

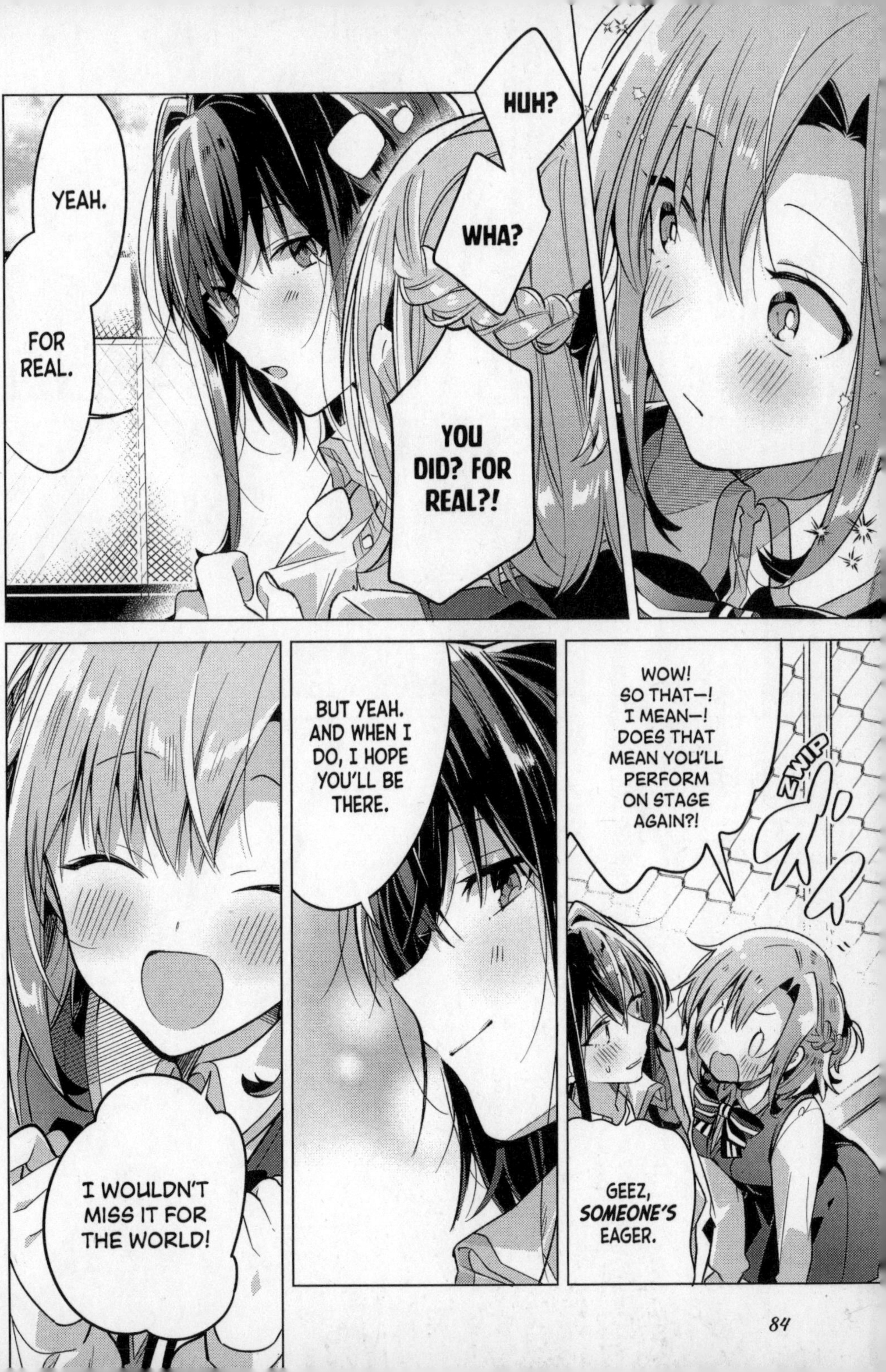
HUH?
WHA?
YOU DID? FOR REAL?!
YEAH.
FOR REAL.
WOW! SO THAT—! I MEAN—! DOES THAT MEAN YOU'LL PERFORM ON STAGE AGAIN?!
ZWIP
GEEZ, **SOMEONE'S** EAGER.
BUT YEAH. AND WHEN I DO, I HOPE YOU'LL BE THERE.
I WOULDN'T MISS IT FOR THE WORLD!

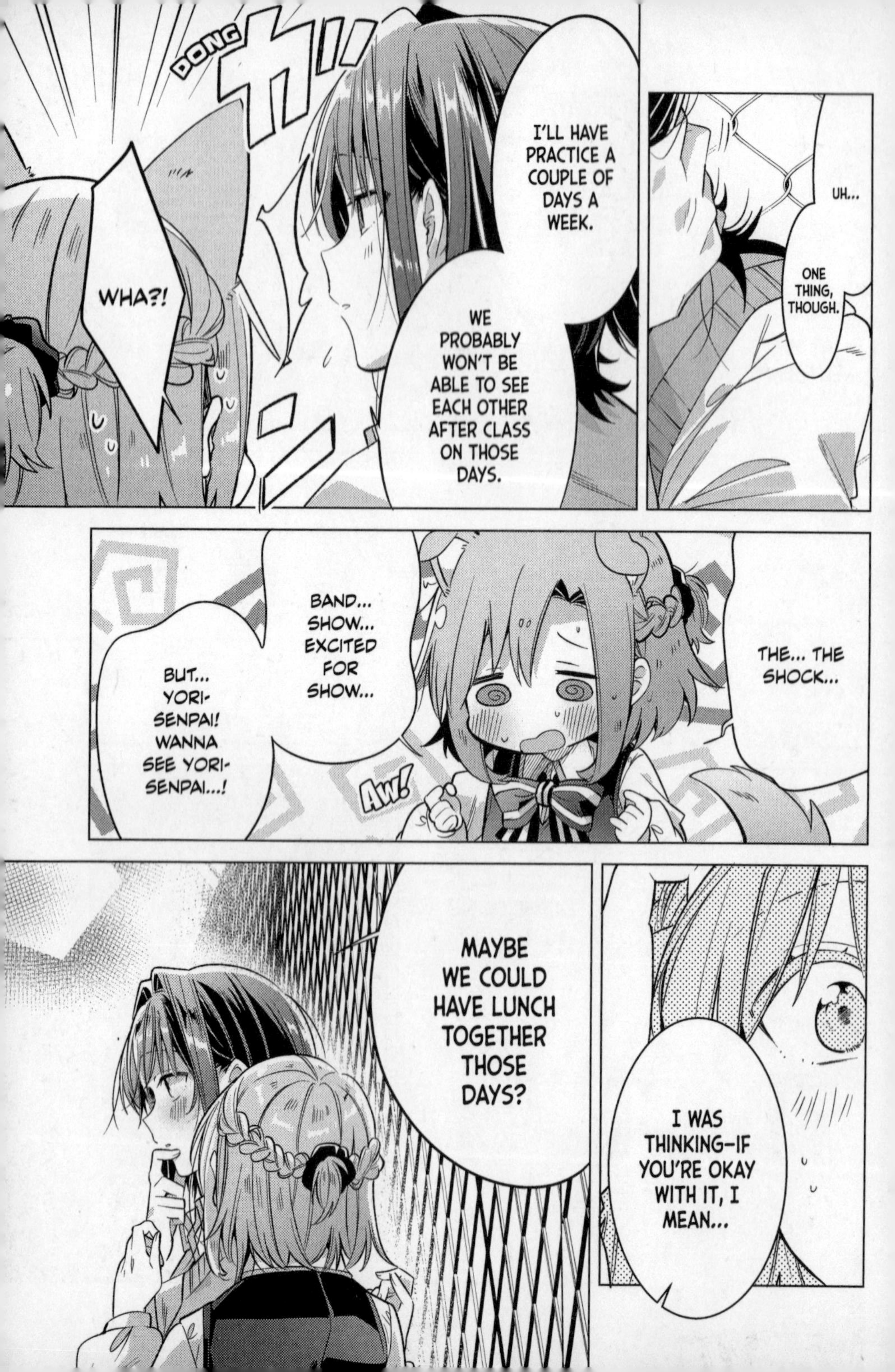
UH...
ONE THING, THOUGH.
I'LL HAVE PRACTICE A COUPLE OF DAYS A WEEK.
WE PROBABLY WON'T BE ABLE TO SEE EACH OTHER AFTER CLASS ON THOSE DAYS.
DONG
WHA?!
THE... THE SHOCK...
BAND... SHOW... EXCITED FOR SHOW...
BUT... YORI-SENPAI! WANNA SEE YORI-SENPAI...!
AW!
I WAS THINKING—IF YOU'RE OKAY WITH IT, I MEAN...
MAYBE WE COULD HAVE LUNCH TOGETHER THOSE DAYS?

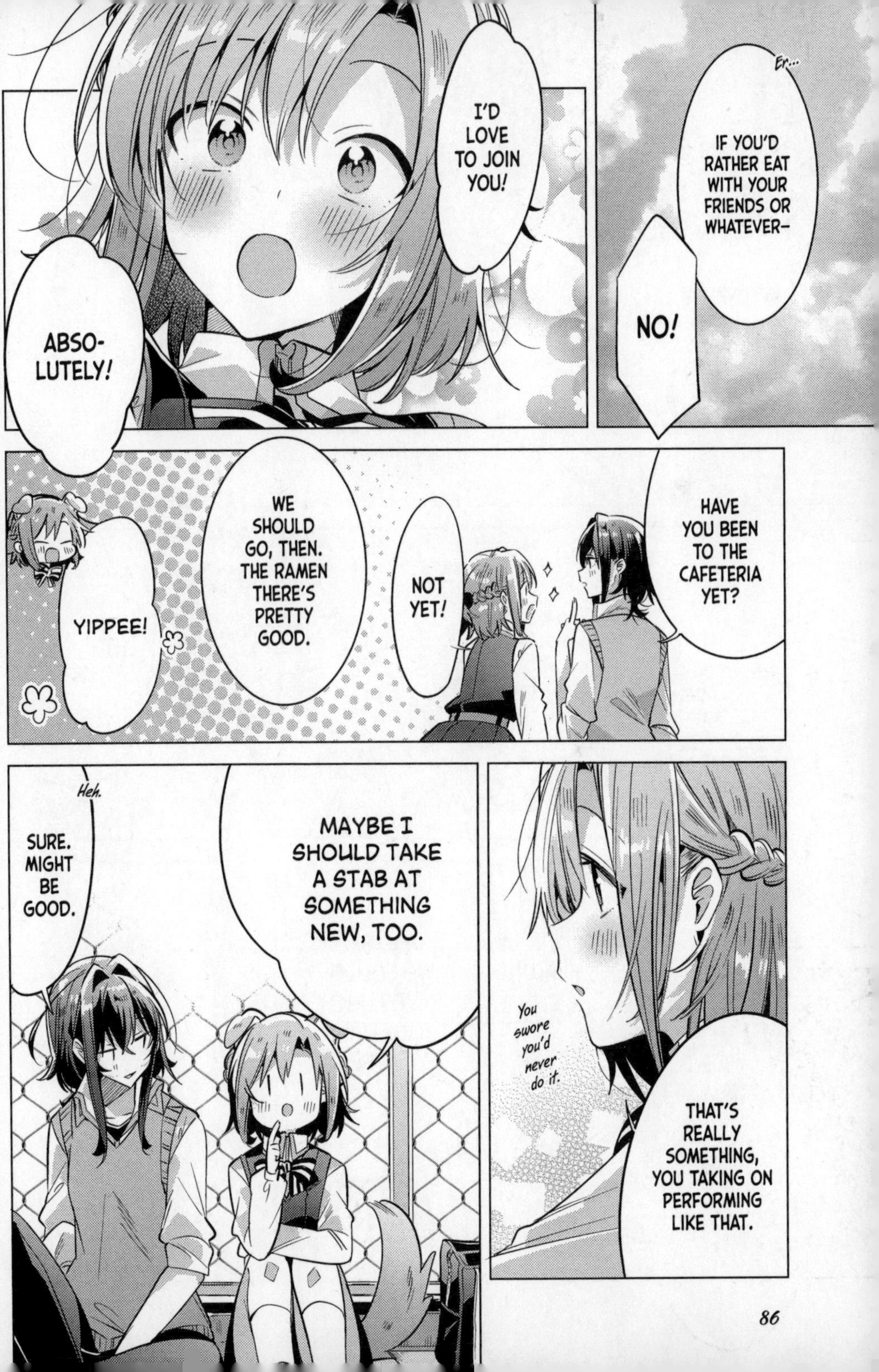
Er...
IF YOU'D RATHER EAT WITH YOUR FRIENDS OR WHATEVER—
NO!
I'D LOVE TO JOIN YOU!
ABSO-LUTELY!
HAVE YOU BEEN TO THE CAFETERIA YET?
NOT YET!
WE SHOULD GO, THEN. THE RAMEN THERE'S PRETTY GOOD.
YIPPEE!
THAT'S REALLY SOMETHING, YOU TAKING ON PERFORMING LIKE THAT.
You swore you'd never do it.
MAYBE I SHOULD TAKE A STAB AT SOMETHING NEW, TOO.
Heh.
SURE. MIGHT BE GOOD.

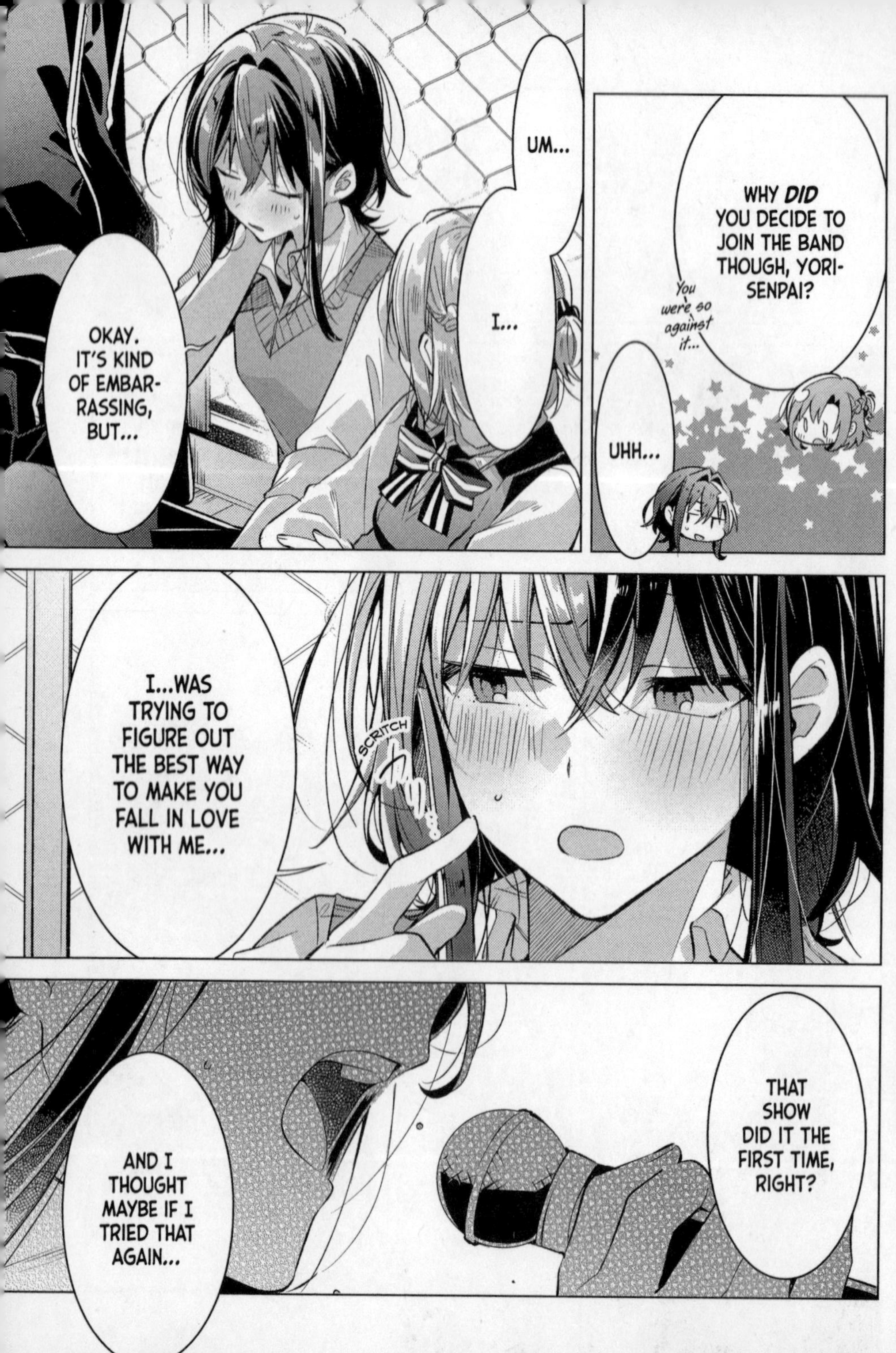
WHY *DID* YOU DECIDE TO JOIN THE BAND THOUGH, YORI-SENPAI?
You were so against it...
UHH...
UM...
I...
OKAY. IT'S KIND OF EMBARRASSING, BUT...
SCRITCH
I...WAS TRYING TO FIGURE OUT THE BEST WAY TO MAKE YOU FALL IN LOVE WITH ME...
THAT SHOW DID IT THE FIRST TIME, RIGHT?
AND I THOUGHT MAYBE IF I TRIED THAT AGAIN...

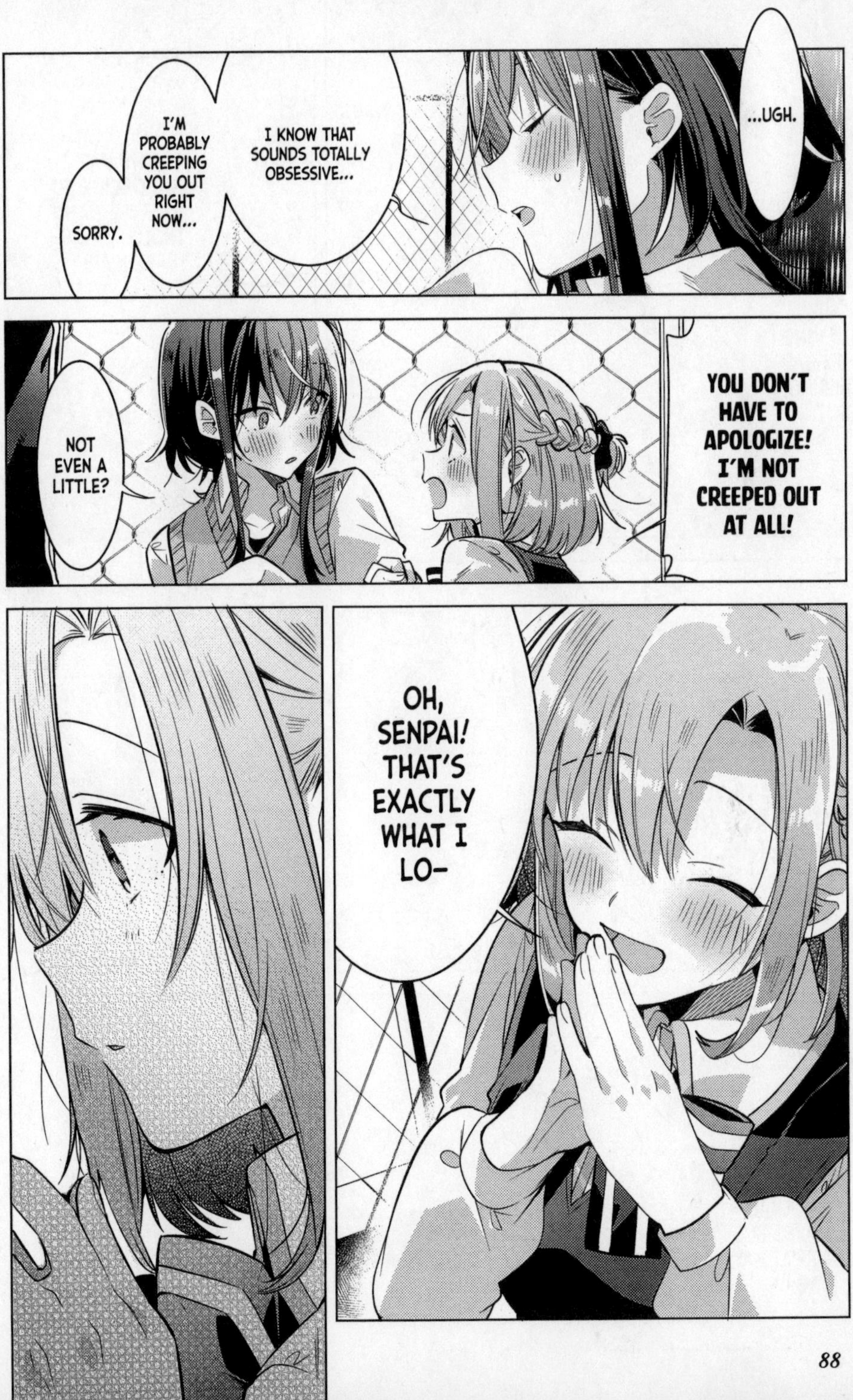
...UGH.
I KNOW THAT SOUNDS TOTALLY OBSESSIVE...
I'M PROBABLY CREEPING YOU OUT RIGHT NOW...
SORRY.
YOU DON'T HAVE TO APOLOGIZE! I'M NOT CREEPED OUT AT ALL!
NOT EVEN A LITTLE?
OH, SENPAI! THAT'S EXACTLY WHAT I LO-

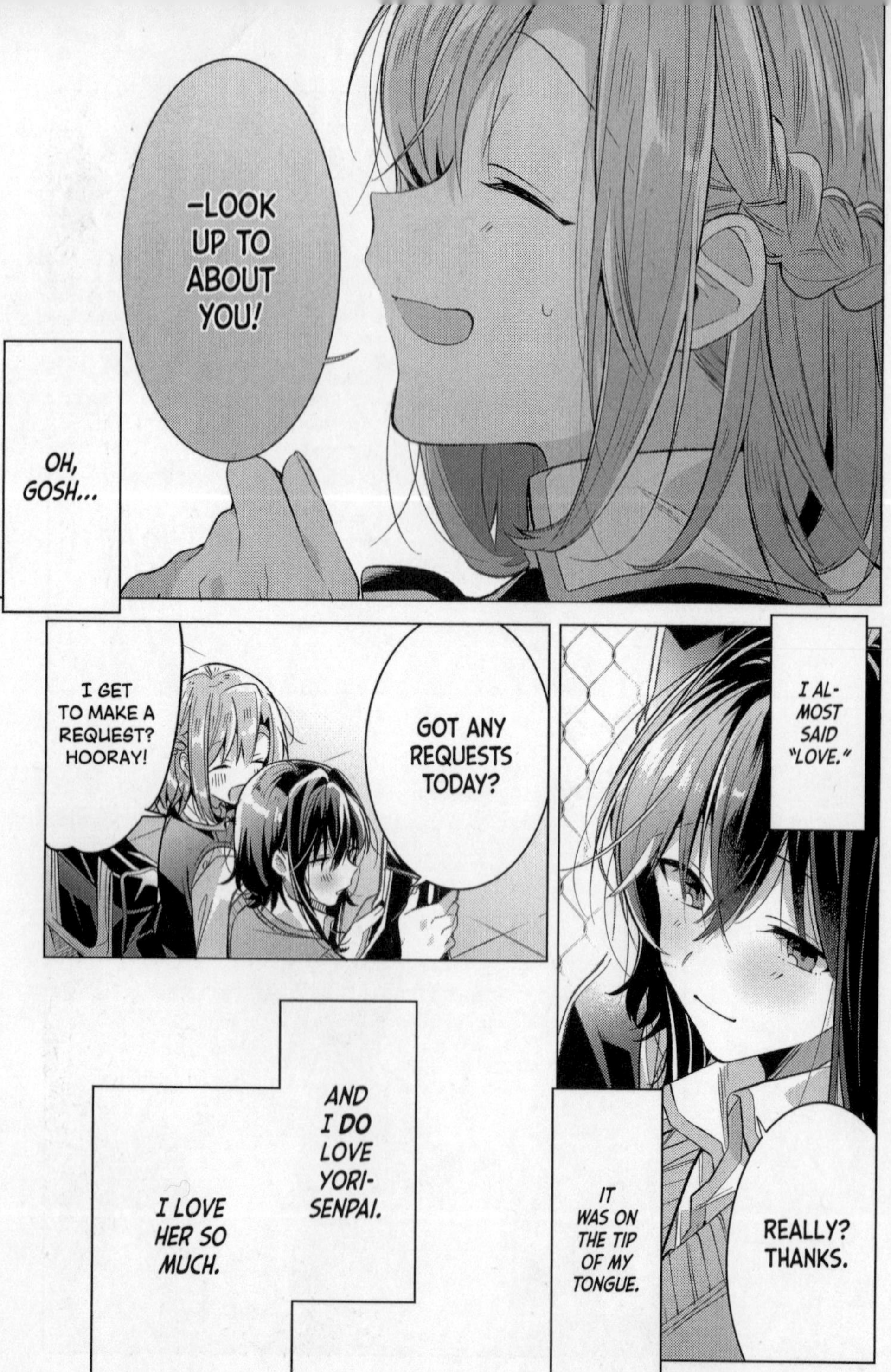
—LOOK UP TO ABOUT YOU!
OH, GOSH...
I AL-MOST SAID "LOVE."
REALLY? THANKS.
IT WAS ON THE TIP OF MY TONGUE.
GOT ANY REQUESTS TODAY?
I GET TO MAKE A REQUEST? HOORAY!
AND I DO LOVE YORI-SENPAI.
I LOVE HER SO MUCH.

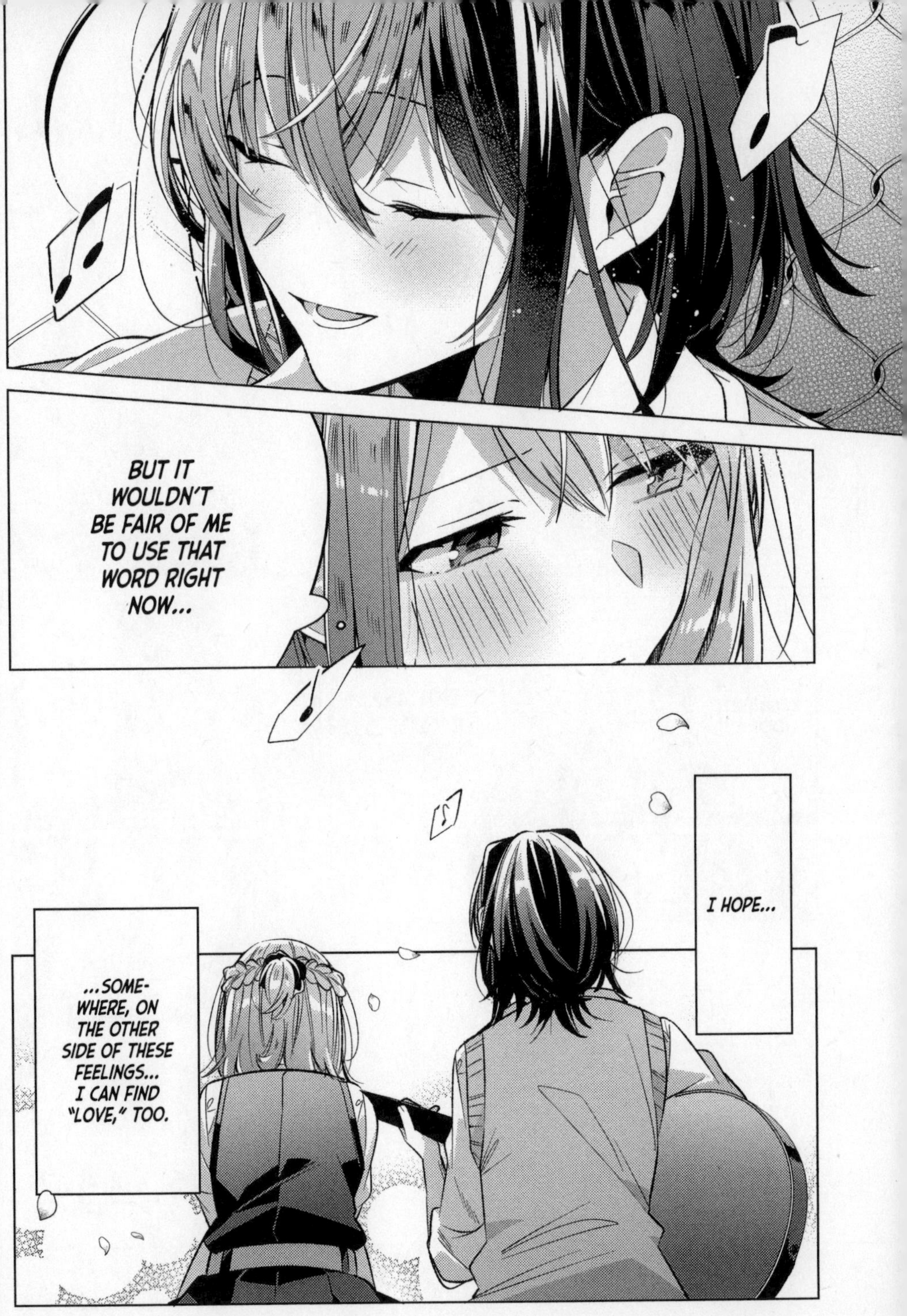
BUT IT WOULDN'T BE FAIR OF ME TO USE THAT WORD RIGHT NOW...
I HOPE...
...SOME-WHERE, ON THE OTHER SIDE OF THESE FEELINGS... I CAN FIND "LOVE," TOO.

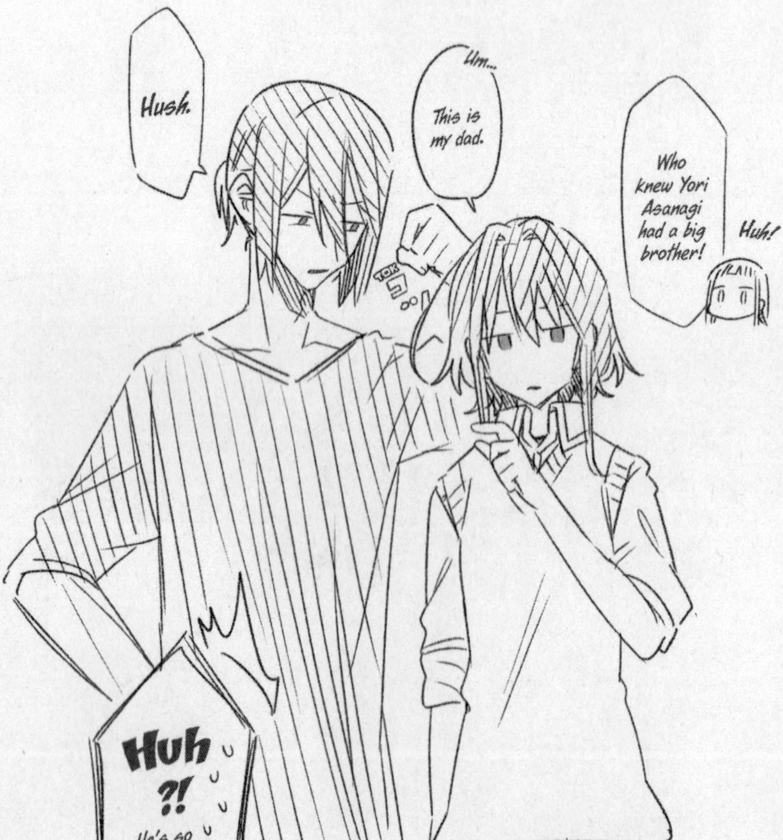
Huh!
Who knew Yori Asanagi had a big brother!
Um...
This is my dad.
Hush.
TOK
Huh?!
He's so young!

Whisper Me
A Love Song
Eku
Takeshima

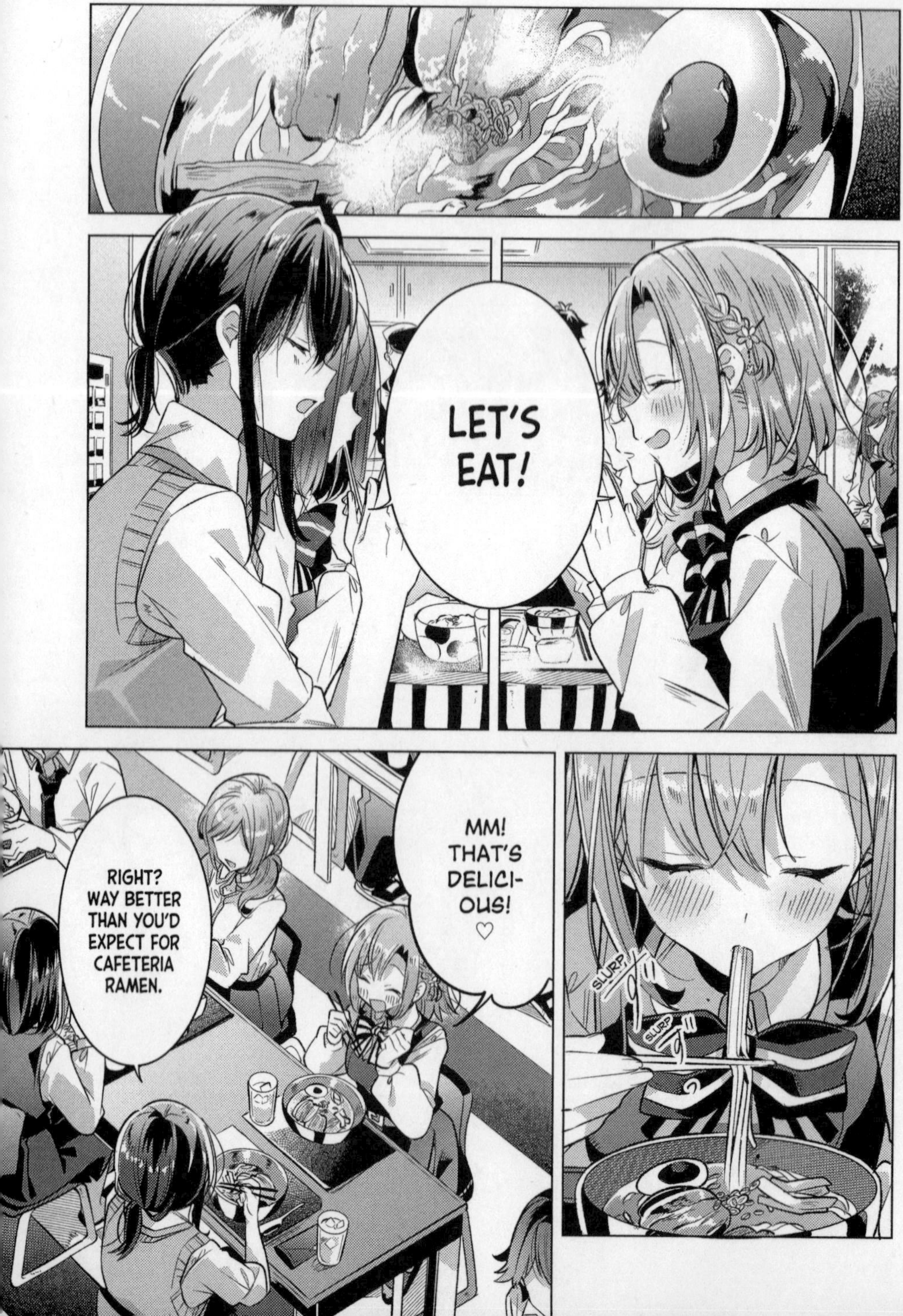
LET'S EAT!
SLURP
SLURP
MM! THAT'S DELICI-OUS! ♡
RIGHT? WAY BETTER THAN YOU'D EXPECT FOR CAFETERIA RAMEN.

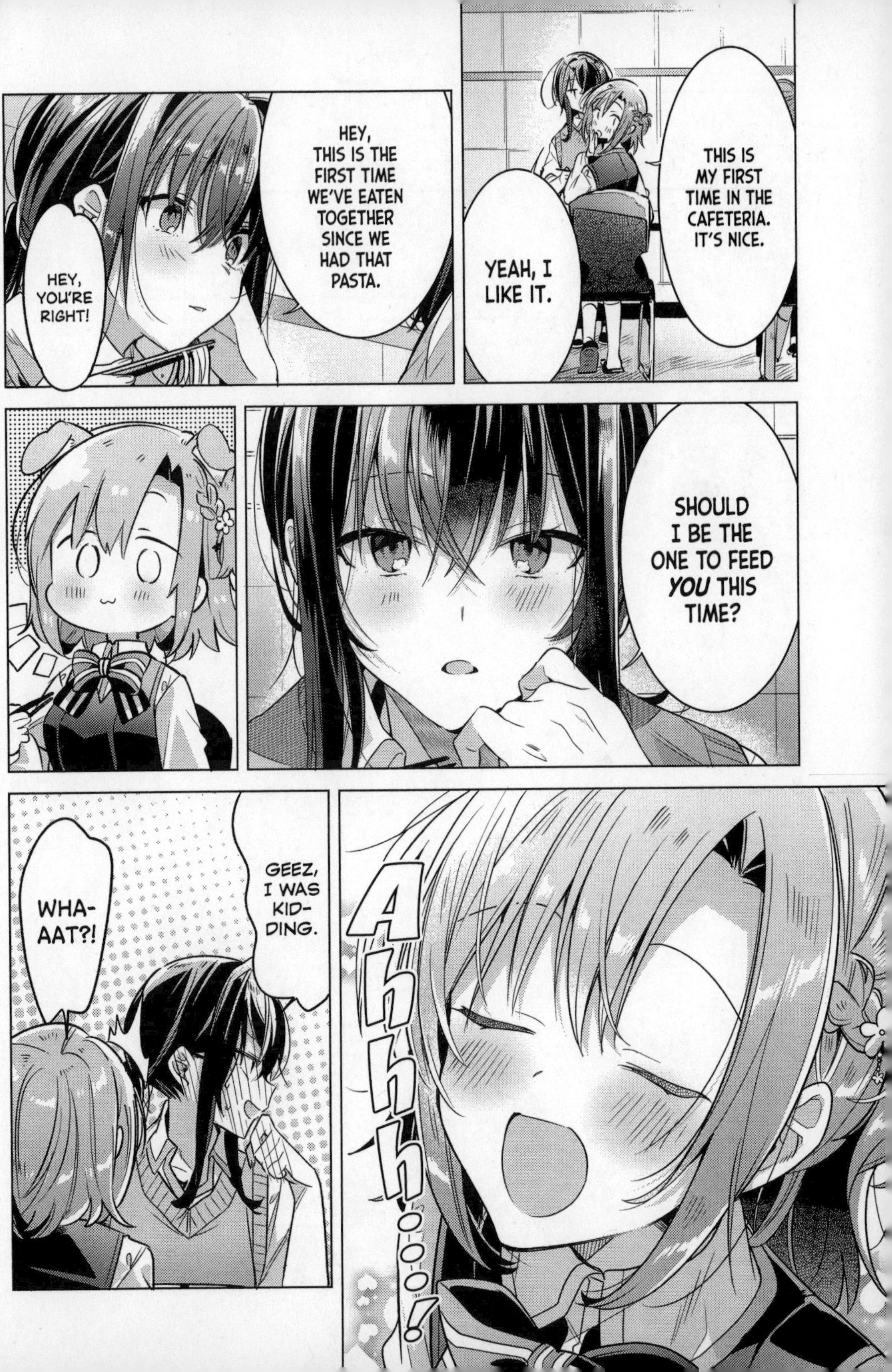
THIS IS MY FIRST TIME IN THE CAFETERIA. IT'S NICE.
YEAH, I LIKE IT.
HEY, THIS IS THE FIRST TIME WE'VE EATEN TOGETHER SINCE WE HAD THAT PASTA.
HEY, YOU'RE RIGHT!
SHOULD I BE THE ONE TO FEED *YOU* THIS TIME?
Ahhhh-o-o-o-o-!
GEEZ, I WAS KID-DING.
WHA-AAT?!

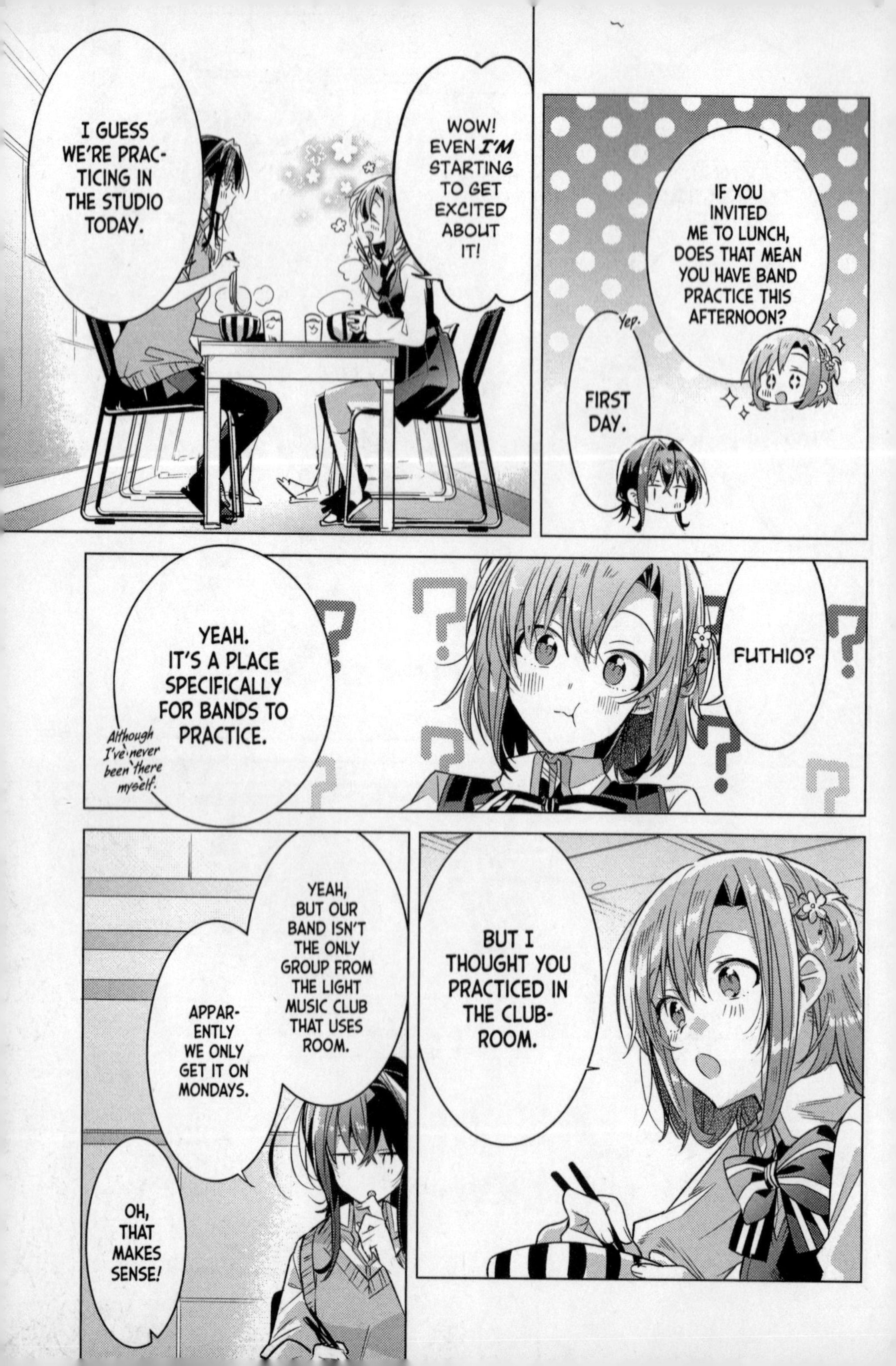
IF YOU INVITED ME TO LUNCH, DOES THAT MEAN YOU HAVE BAND PRACTICE THIS AFTERNOON?
Yep.
FIRST DAY.
WOW! EVEN *I'M* STARTING TO GET EXCITED ABOUT IT!
I GUESS WE'RE PRAC-TICING IN THE STUDIO TODAY.
FUTHIO?
YEAH. IT'S A PLACE SPECIFICALLY FOR BANDS TO PRACTICE.
Although I've never been there myself.
BUT I THOUGHT YOU PRACTICED IN THE CLUB-ROOM.
YEAH, BUT OUR BAND ISN'T THE ONLY GROUP FROM THE LIGHT MUSIC CLUB THAT USES ROOM.
APPAR-ENTLY WE ONLY GET IT ON MONDAYS.
OH, THAT MAKES SENSE!

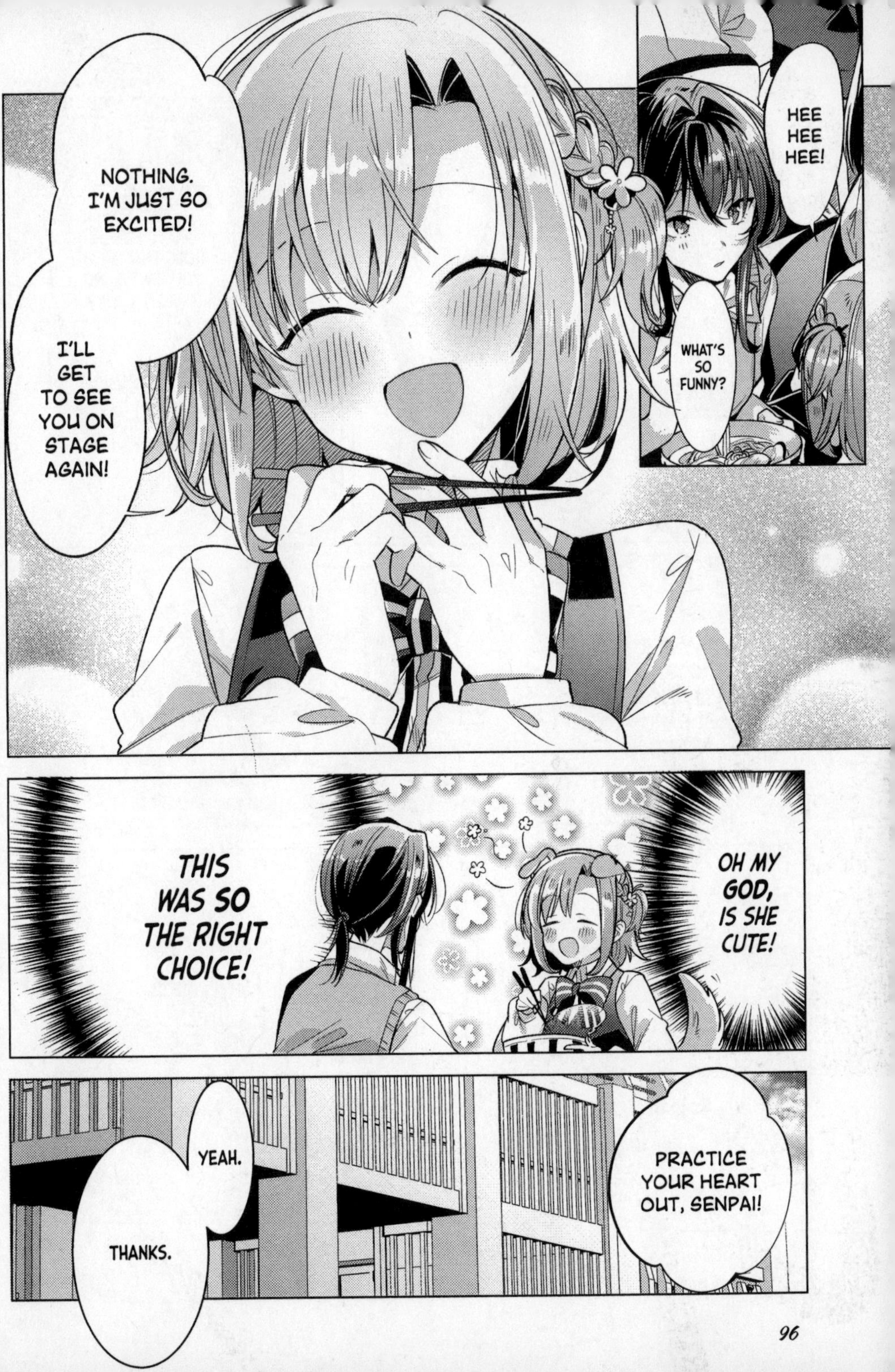
HEE HEE HEE!
WHAT'S SO FUNNY?
NOTHING. I'M JUST SO EXCITED!
I'LL GET TO SEE YOU ON STAGE AGAIN!
OH MY GOD, IS SHE CUTE!
THIS WAS SO THE RIGHT CHOICE!
PRACTICE YOUR HEART OUT, SENPAI!
YEAH.
THANKS.

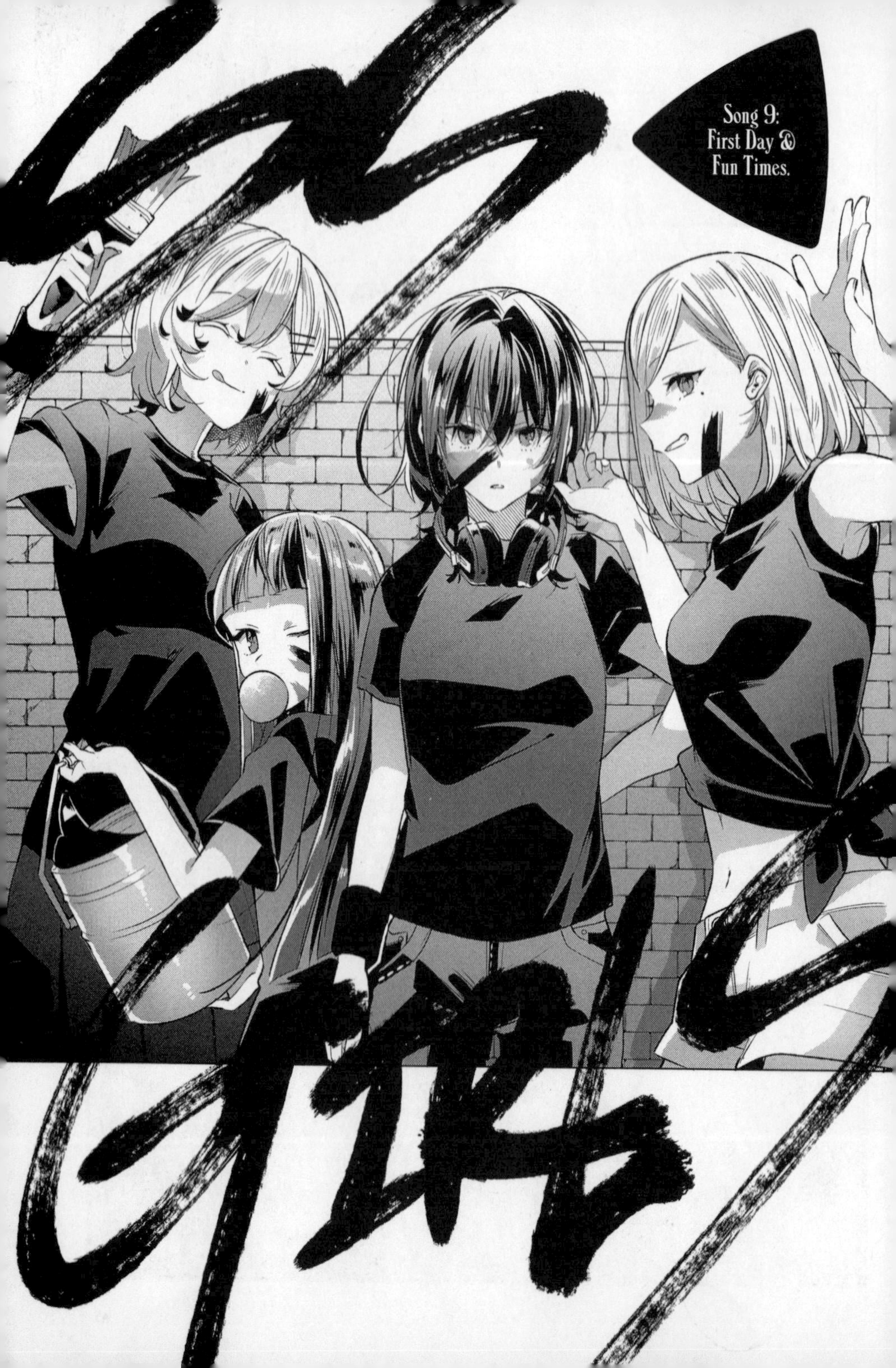
Song 9:
First Day &
Fun Times.

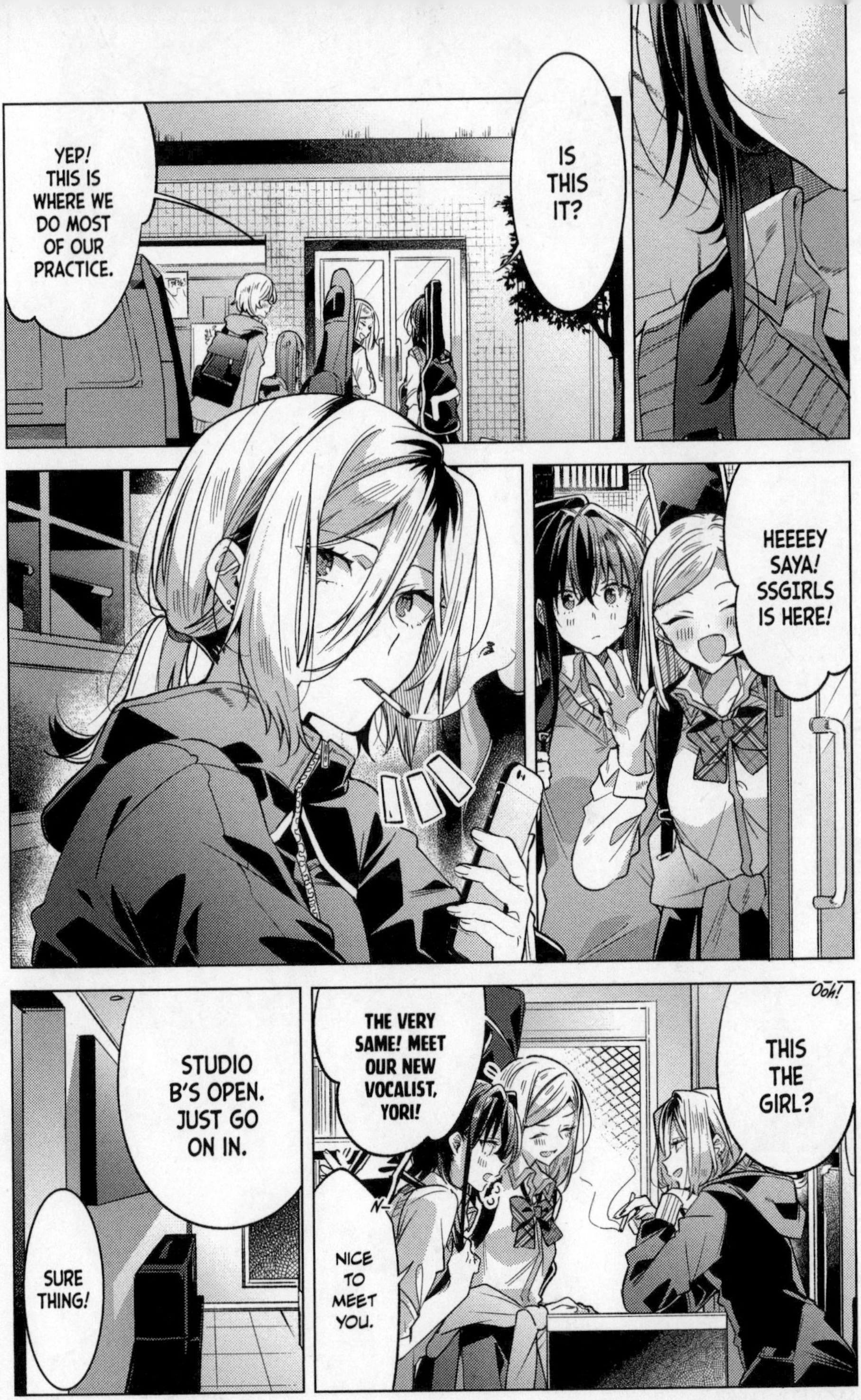
IS THIS IT?
YEP! THIS IS WHERE WE DO MOST OF OUR PRACTICE.
HEEEEY SAYA! SSGIRLS IS HERE!
Ooh!
THIS THE GIRL?
THE VERY SAME! MEET OUR NEW VOCALIST, YORI!
N—
NICE TO MEET YOU.
STUDIO B'S OPEN. JUST GO ON IN.
SURE THING!

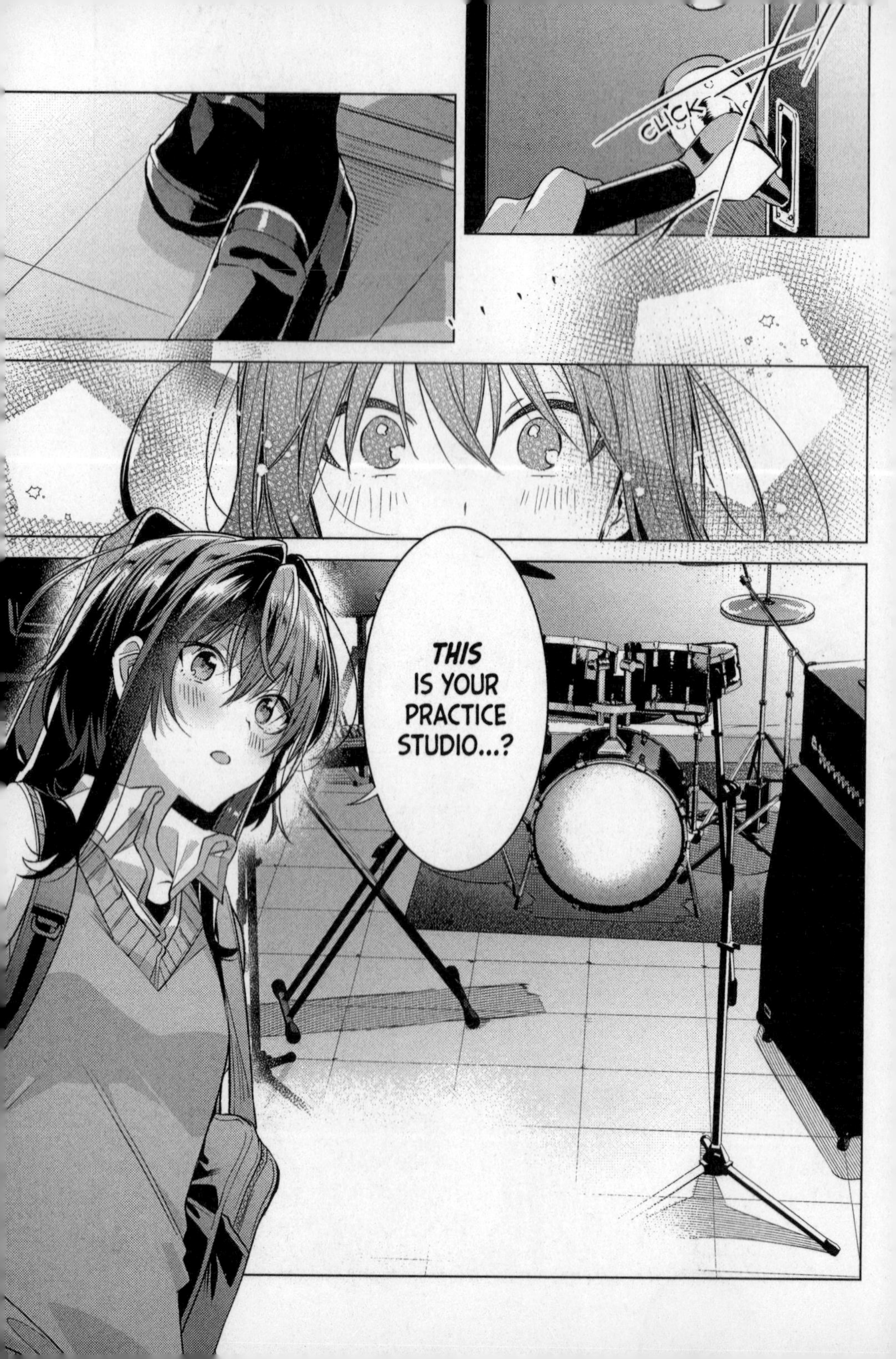
CLICK
THIS IS YOUR PRACTICE STUDIO...?

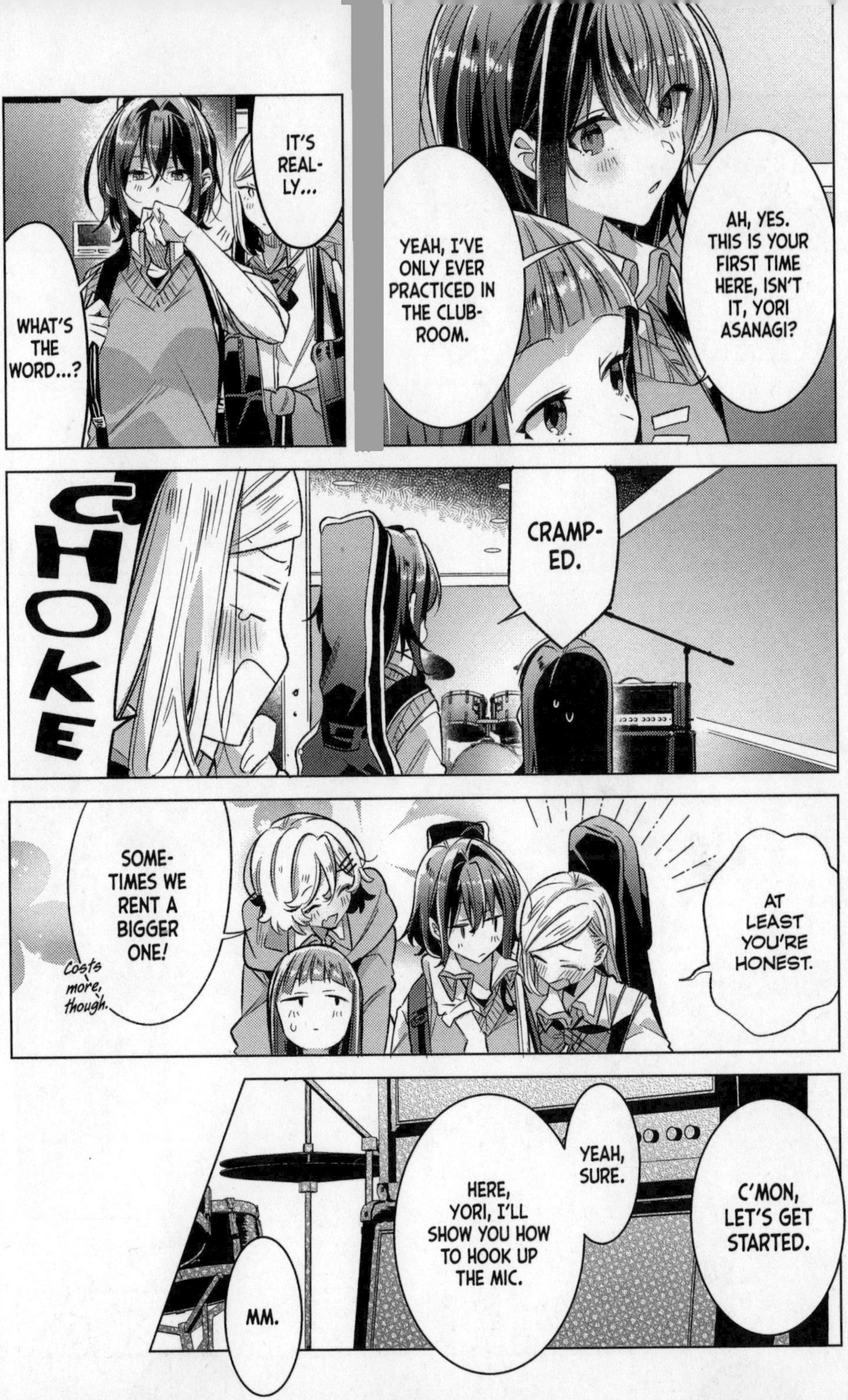
AH, YES. THIS IS YOUR FIRST TIME HERE, ISN'T IT, YORI ASANAGI?
YEAH, I'VE ONLY EVER PRACTICED IN THE CLUB-ROOM.
IT'S REAL-LY...
WHAT'S THE WORD...?
CRAMP-ED.
CHOKE
AT LEAST YOU'RE HONEST.
SOME-TIMES WE RENT A BIGGER ONE!
Costs more, though.
C'MON, LET'S GET STARTED.
YEAH, SURE.
HERE, YORI, I'LL SHOW YOU HOW TO HOOK UP THE MIC.
MM.

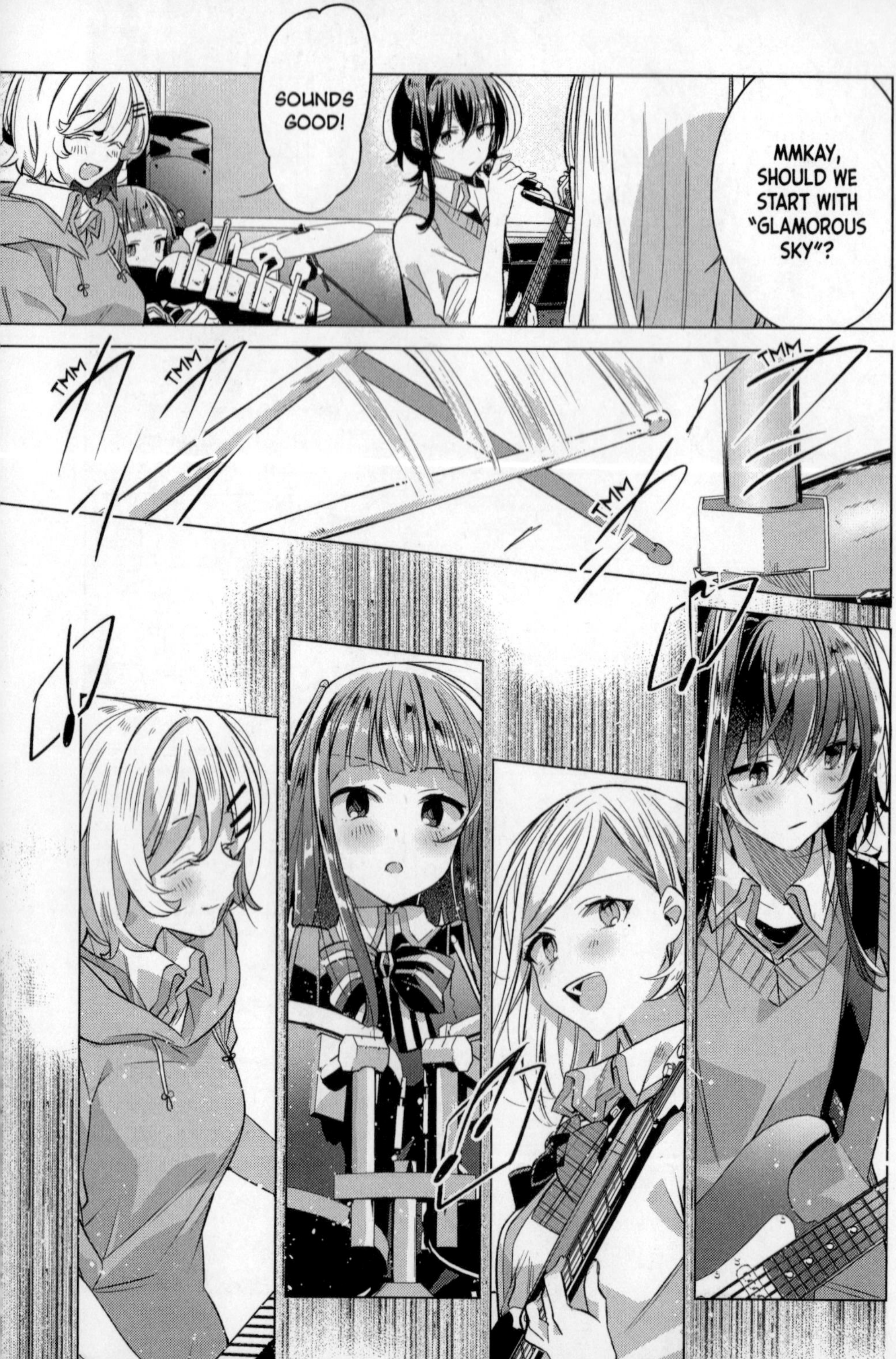
MMKAY, SHOULD WE START WITH "GLAMOROUS SKY"?
SOUNDS GOOD!
TMM
TMM
TMM
TMM

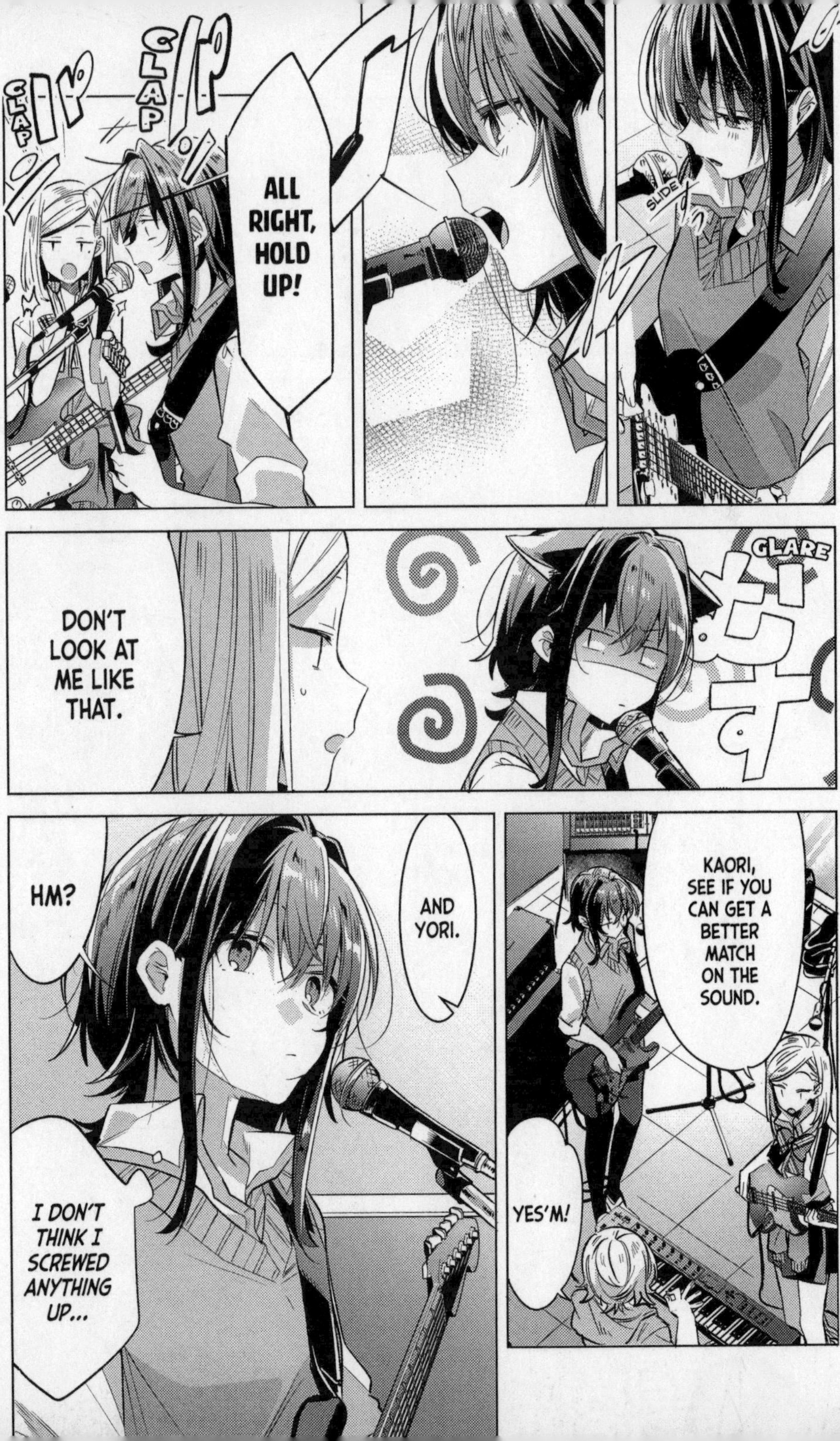
SLIDE
ALL RIGHT, HOLD UP!
CLAP
CLAP
GLARE
DON'T LOOK AT ME LIKE THAT.
KAORI, SEE IF YOU CAN GET A BETTER MATCH ON THE SOUND.
YES'M!
AND YORI.
HM?
I DON'T THINK I SCREWED ANYTHING UP...

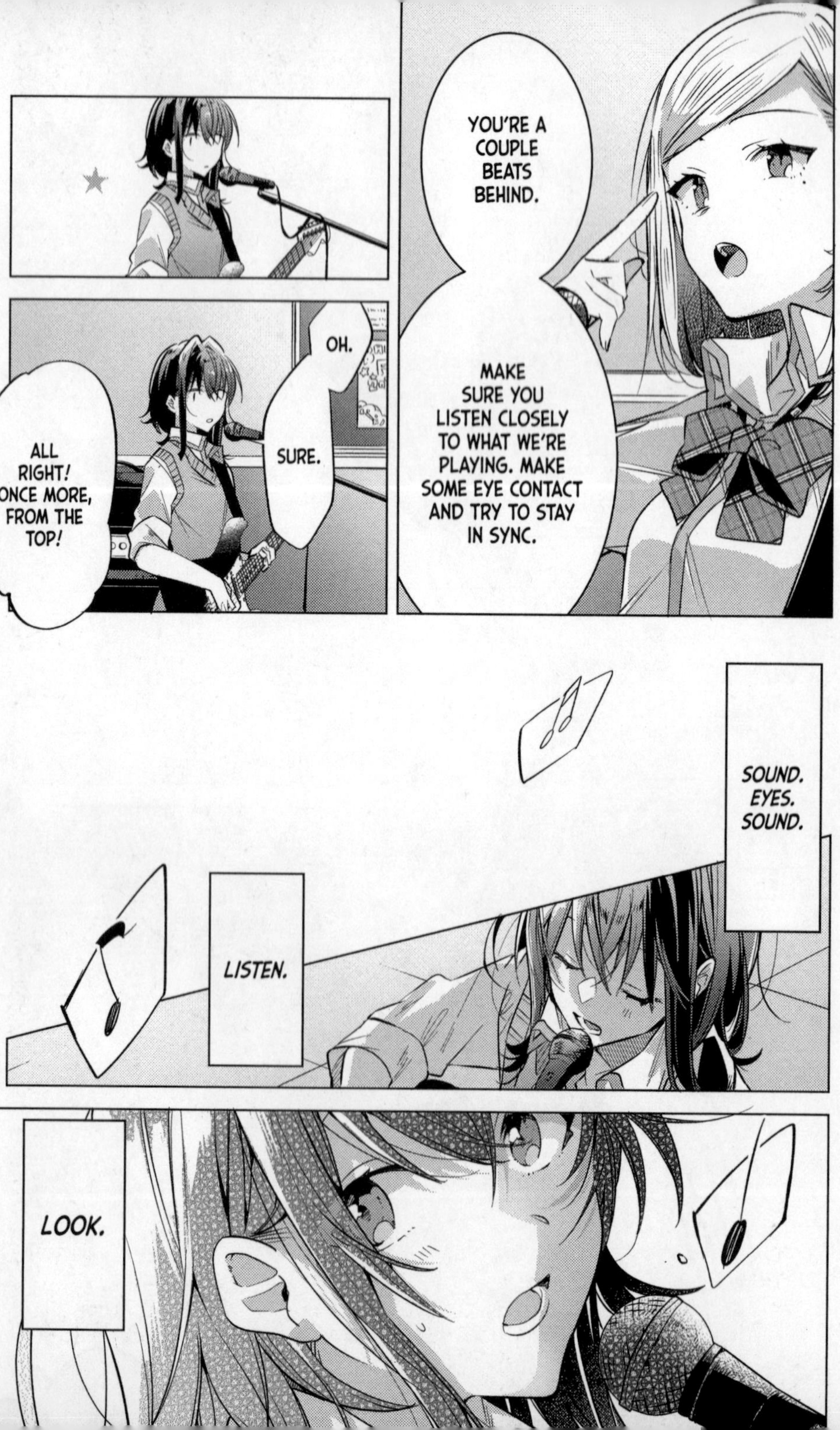
YOU'RE A COUPLE BEATS BEHIND.
MAKE SURE YOU LISTEN CLOSELY TO WHAT WE'RE PLAYING. MAKE SOME EYE CONTACT AND TRY TO STAY IN SYNC.
OH.
SURE.
ALL RIGHT! ONCE MORE, FROM THE TOP!
SOUND. EYES. SOUND.
LISTEN.
LOOK.

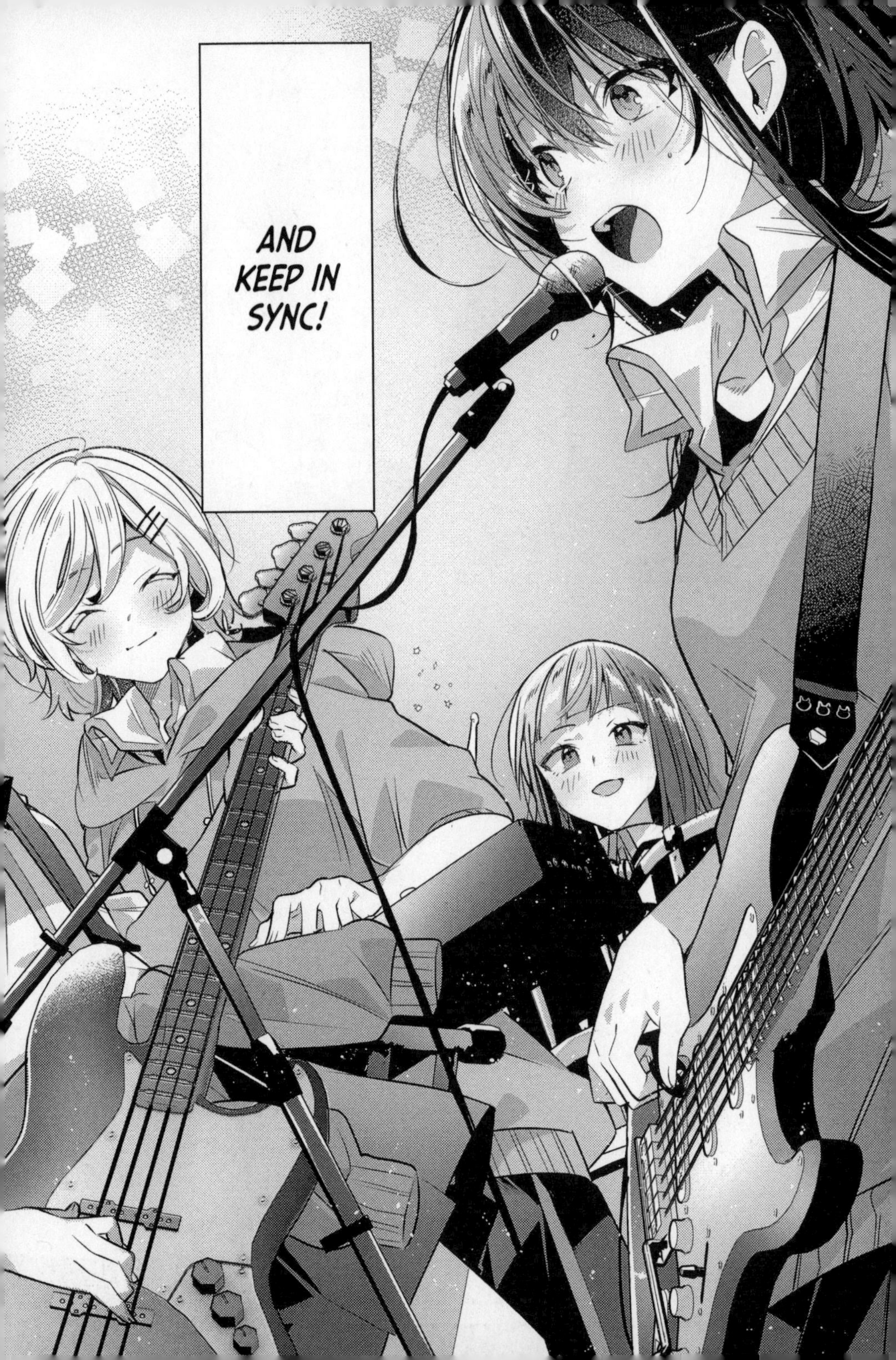
AND KEEP IN SYNC!

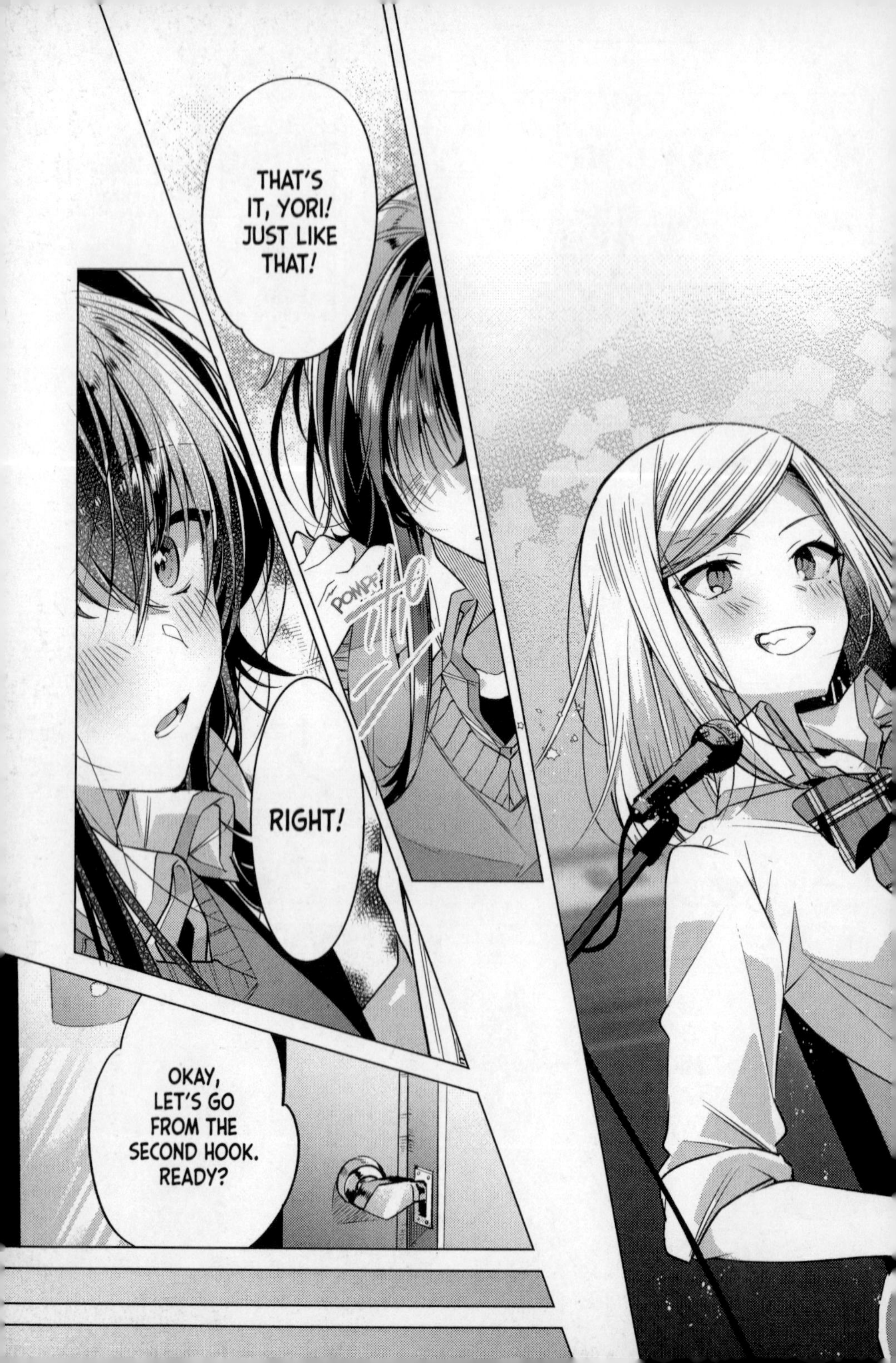
THAT'S IT, YORI! JUST LIKE THAT!
RIGHT!
OKAY, LET'S GO FROM THE SECOND HOOK. READY?

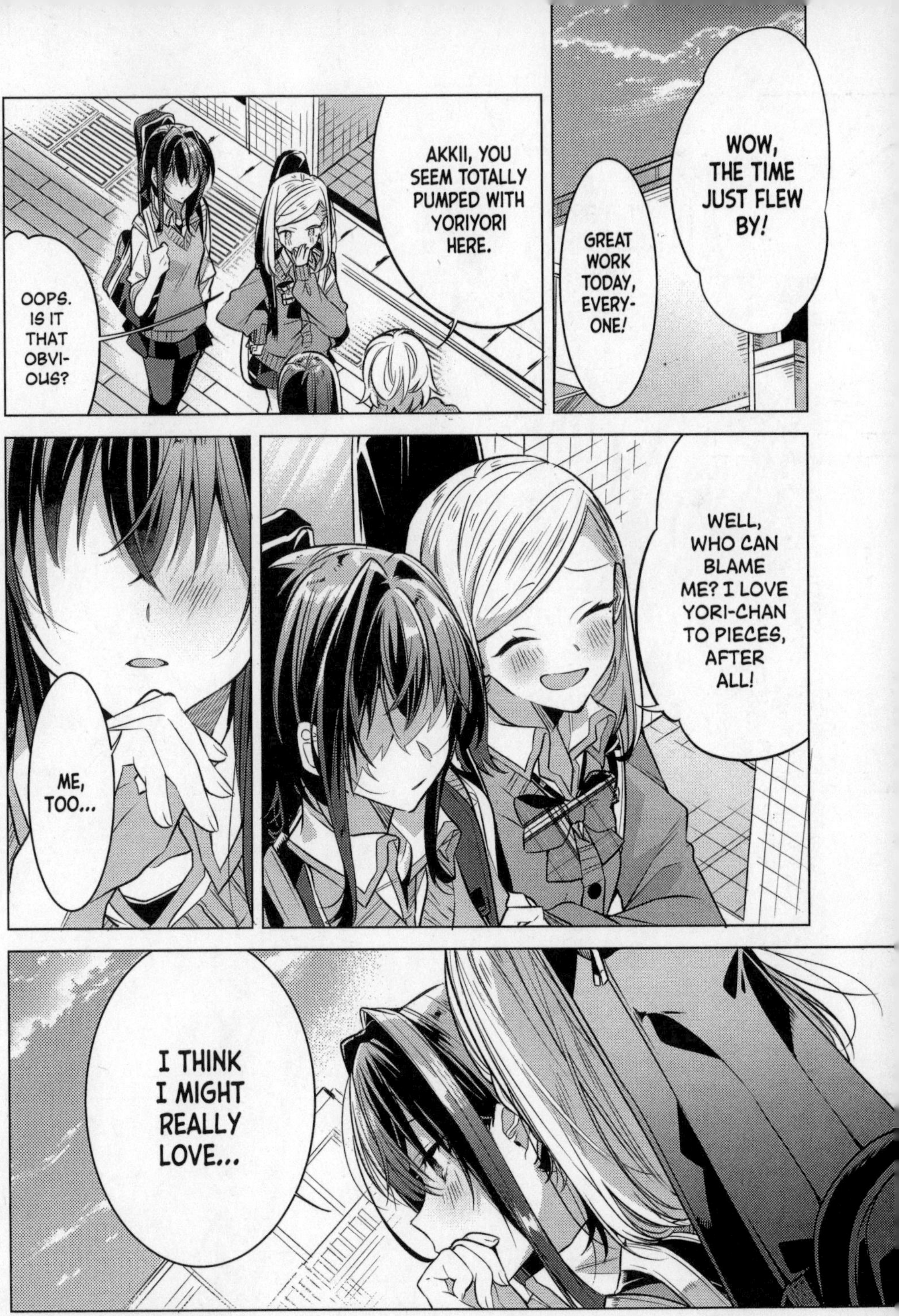
WOW, THE TIME JUST FLEW BY!
GREAT WORK TODAY, EVERYONE!
AKKII, YOU SEEM TOTALLY PUMPED WITH YORIYORI HERE.
OOPS. IS IT THAT OBVIOUS?
WELL, WHO CAN BLAME ME? I LOVE YORI-CHAN TO PIECES, AFTER ALL!
ME, TOO...
I THINK I MIGHT REALLY LOVE...

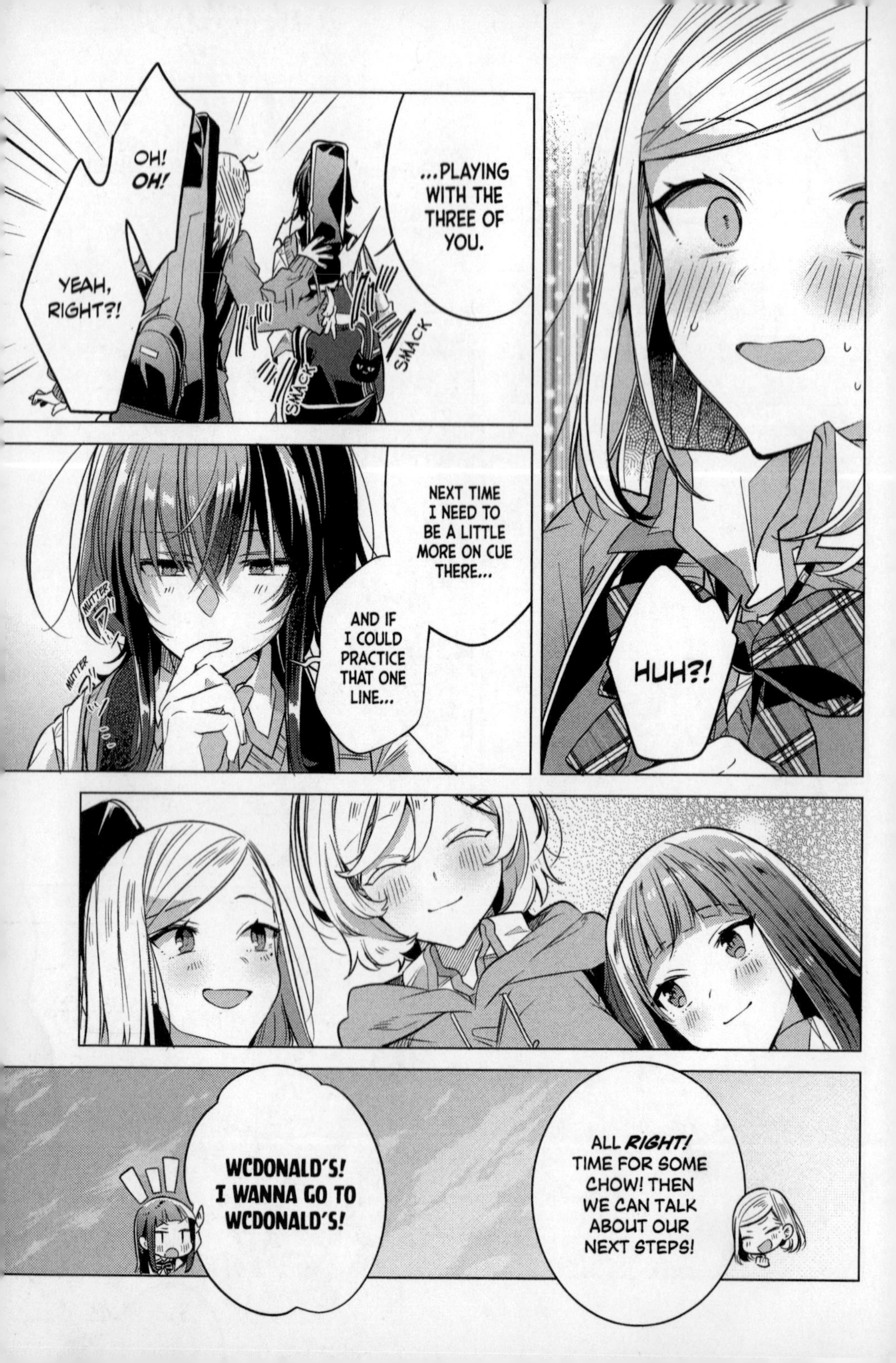
HUH?!
...PLAYING WITH THE THREE OF YOU.
OH! *OH!*
YEAH, RIGHT?!
SMACK
SMACK
NEXT TIME I NEED TO BE A LITTLE MORE ON CUE THERE...
AND IF I COULD PRACTICE THAT ONE LINE...
MUTTER
MUTTER
ALL *RIGHT!* TIME FOR SOME CHOW! THEN WE CAN TALK ABOUT OUR NEXT STEPS!
WCDONALD'S! I WANNA GO TO WCDONALD'S!

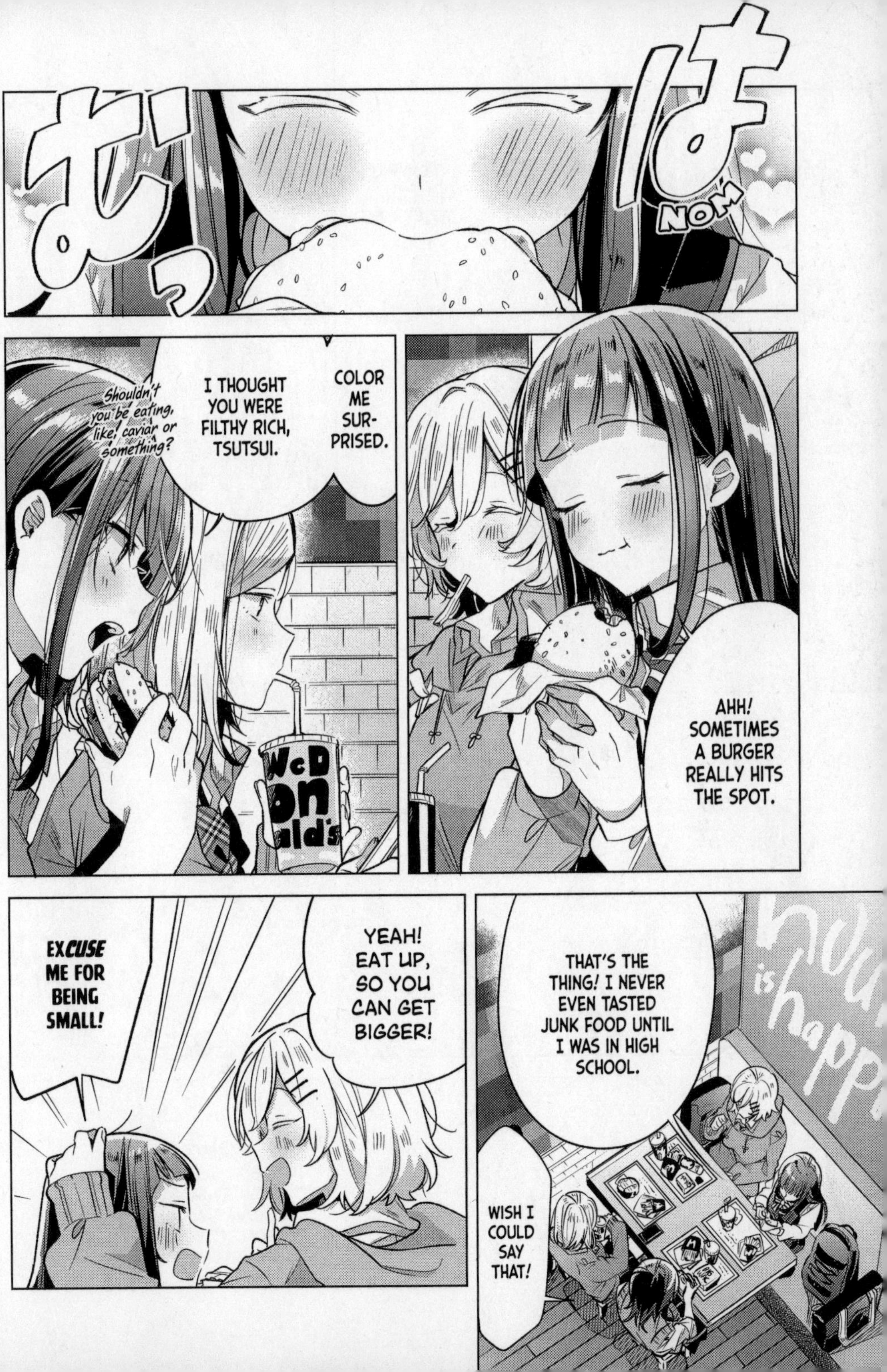
はむっ
NOM
AHH! SOMETIMES A BURGER REALLY HITS THE SPOT.
COLOR ME SURPRISED.
I THOUGHT YOU WERE FILTHY RICH, TSUTSUI.
Shouldn't you be eating, like, caviar or something?
THAT'S THE THING! I NEVER EVEN TASTED JUNK FOOD UNTIL I WAS IN HIGH SCHOOL.
WISH I COULD SAY THAT!
YEAH! EAT UP, SO YOU CAN GET BIGGER!
EXCUSE ME FOR BEING SMALL!

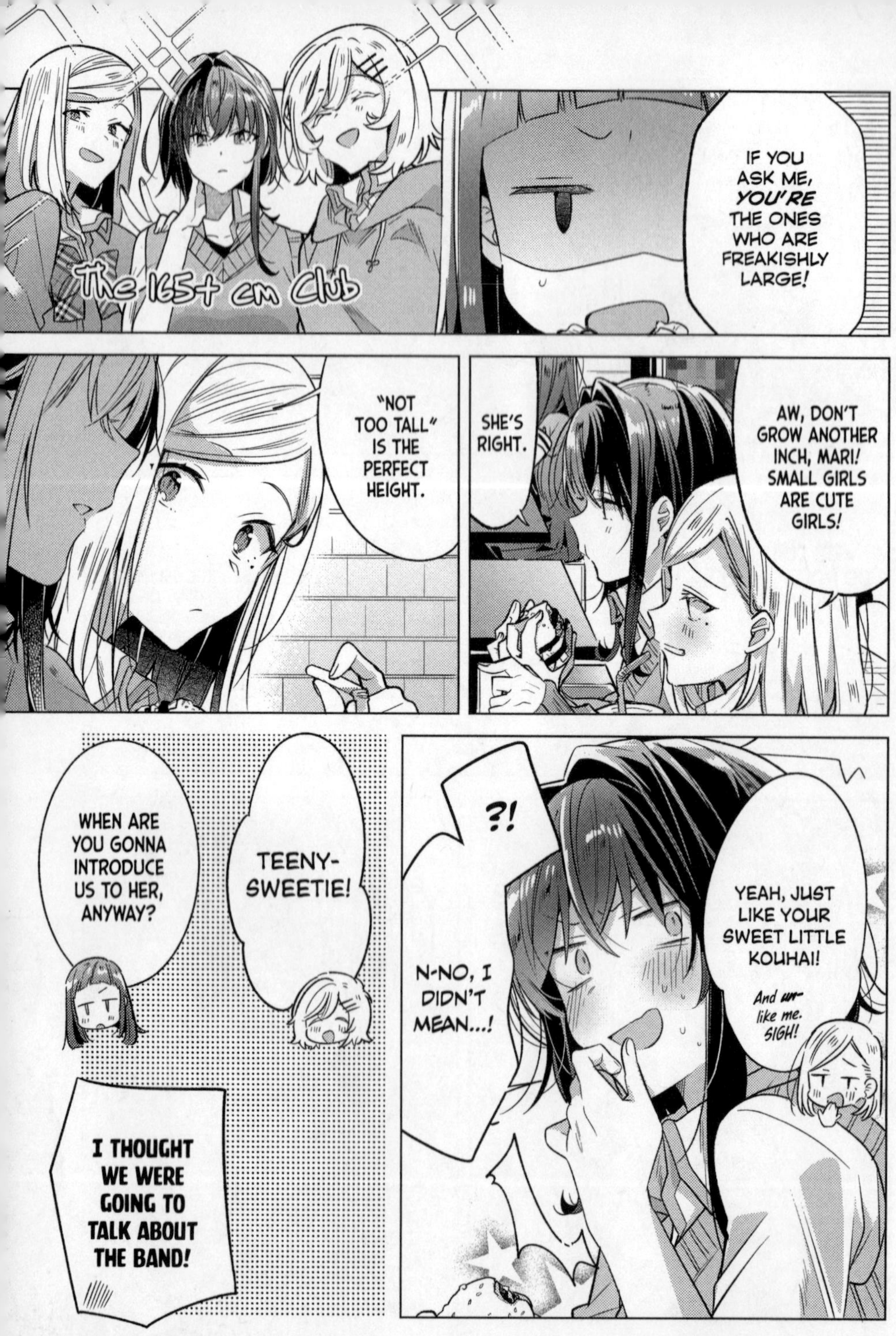
IF YOU ASK ME, *YOU'RE* THE ONES WHO ARE FREAKISHLY LARGE!
The 165+ cm Club
AW, DON'T GROW ANOTHER INCH, MARI! SMALL GIRLS ARE CUTE GIRLS!
SHE'S RIGHT.
"NOT TOO TALL" IS THE PERFECT HEIGHT.
YEAH, JUST LIKE YOUR SWEET LITTLE KOUHAI!
?!
And *un*-like me. SIGH!
N-NO, I DIDN'T MEAN...!
TEENY-SWEETIE!
WHEN ARE YOU GONNA INTRODUCE US TO HER, ANYWAY?
I THOUGHT WE WERE GOING TO TALK ABOUT THE BAND!

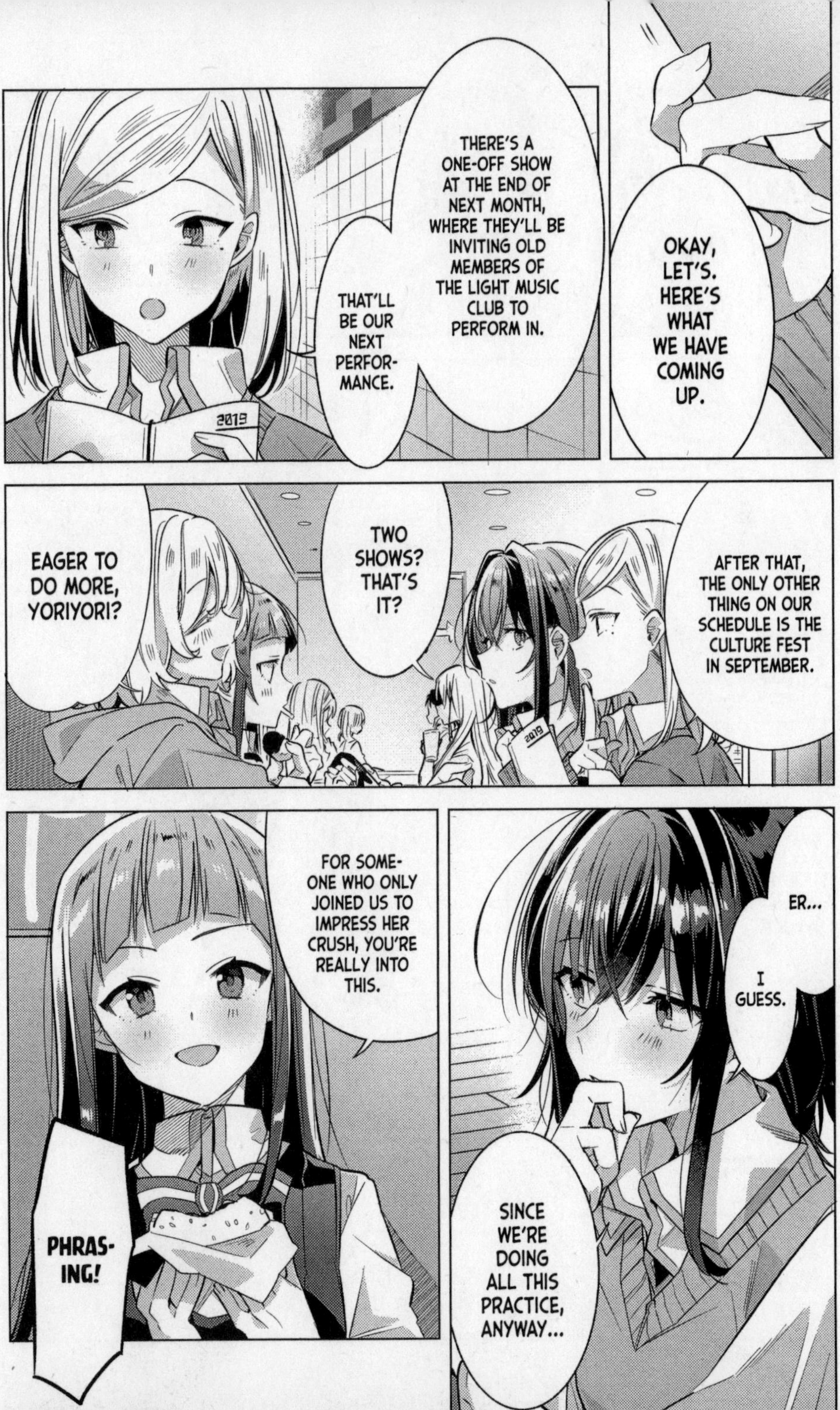
OKAY, LET'S. HERE'S WHAT WE HAVE COMING UP.
THERE'S A ONE-OFF SHOW AT THE END OF NEXT MONTH, WHERE THEY'LL BE INVITING OLD MEMBERS OF THE LIGHT MUSIC CLUB TO PERFORM IN.
THAT'LL BE OUR NEXT PERFOR-MANCE.
AFTER THAT, THE ONLY OTHER THING ON OUR SCHEDULE IS THE CULTURE FEST IN SEPTEMBER.
TWO SHOWS? THAT'S IT?
EAGER TO DO MORE, YORIYORI?
ER...
I GUESS.
SINCE WE'RE DOING ALL THIS PRACTICE, ANYWAY...
FOR SOME-ONE WHO ONLY JOINED US TO IMPRESS HER CRUSH, YOU'RE REALLY INTO THIS.
PHRAS-ING!

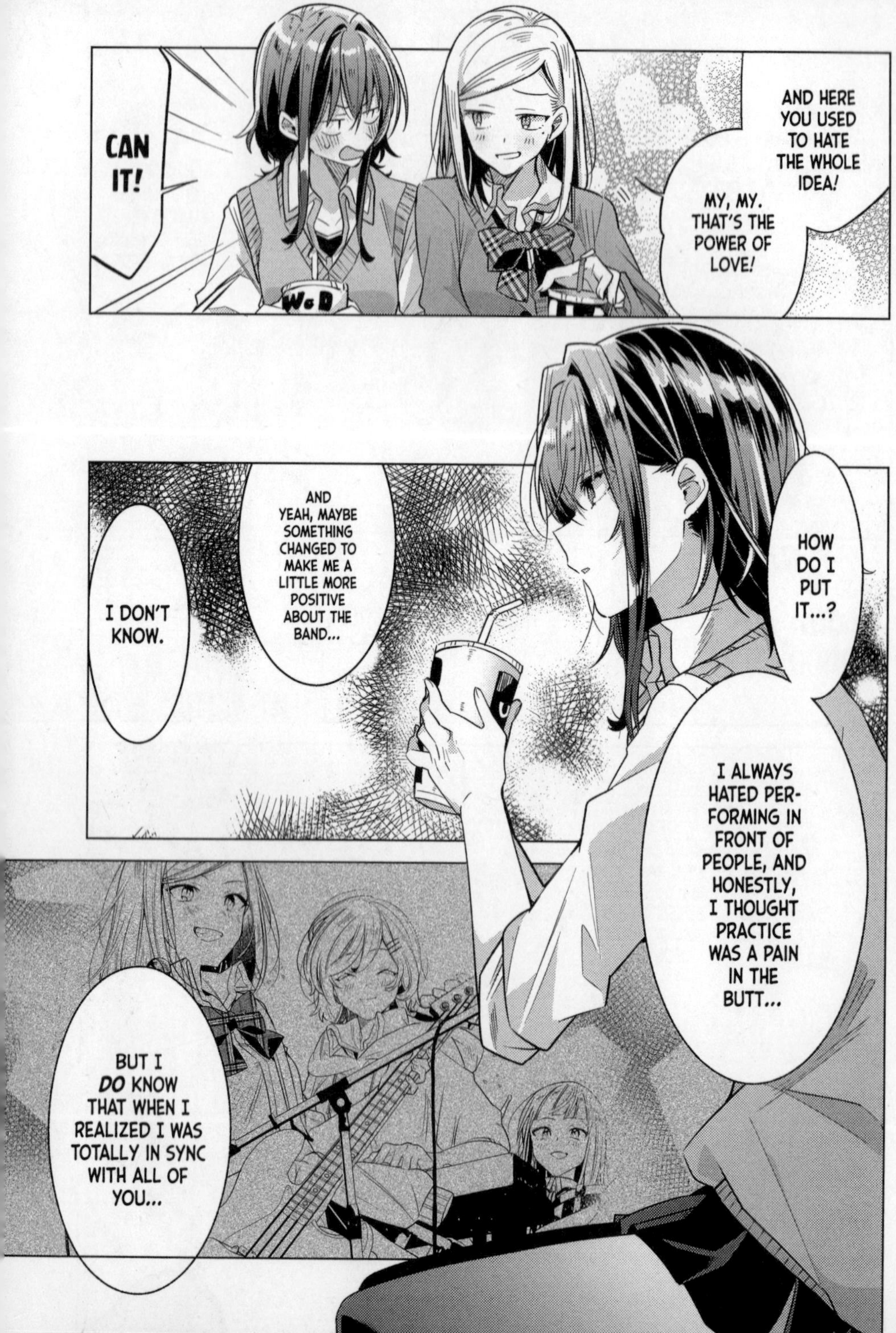
AND HERE YOU USED TO HATE THE WHOLE IDEA!
MY, MY. THAT'S THE POWER OF LOVE!
CAN IT!
HOW DO I PUT IT...?
AND YEAH, MAYBE SOMETHING CHANGED TO MAKE ME A LITTLE MORE POSITIVE ABOUT THE BAND...
I DON'T KNOW.
I ALWAYS HATED PER-FORMING IN FRONT OF PEOPLE, AND HONESTLY, I THOUGHT PRACTICE WAS A PAIN IN THE BUTT...
BUT I *DO* KNOW THAT WHEN I REALIZED I WAS TOTALLY IN SYNC WITH ALL OF YOU...

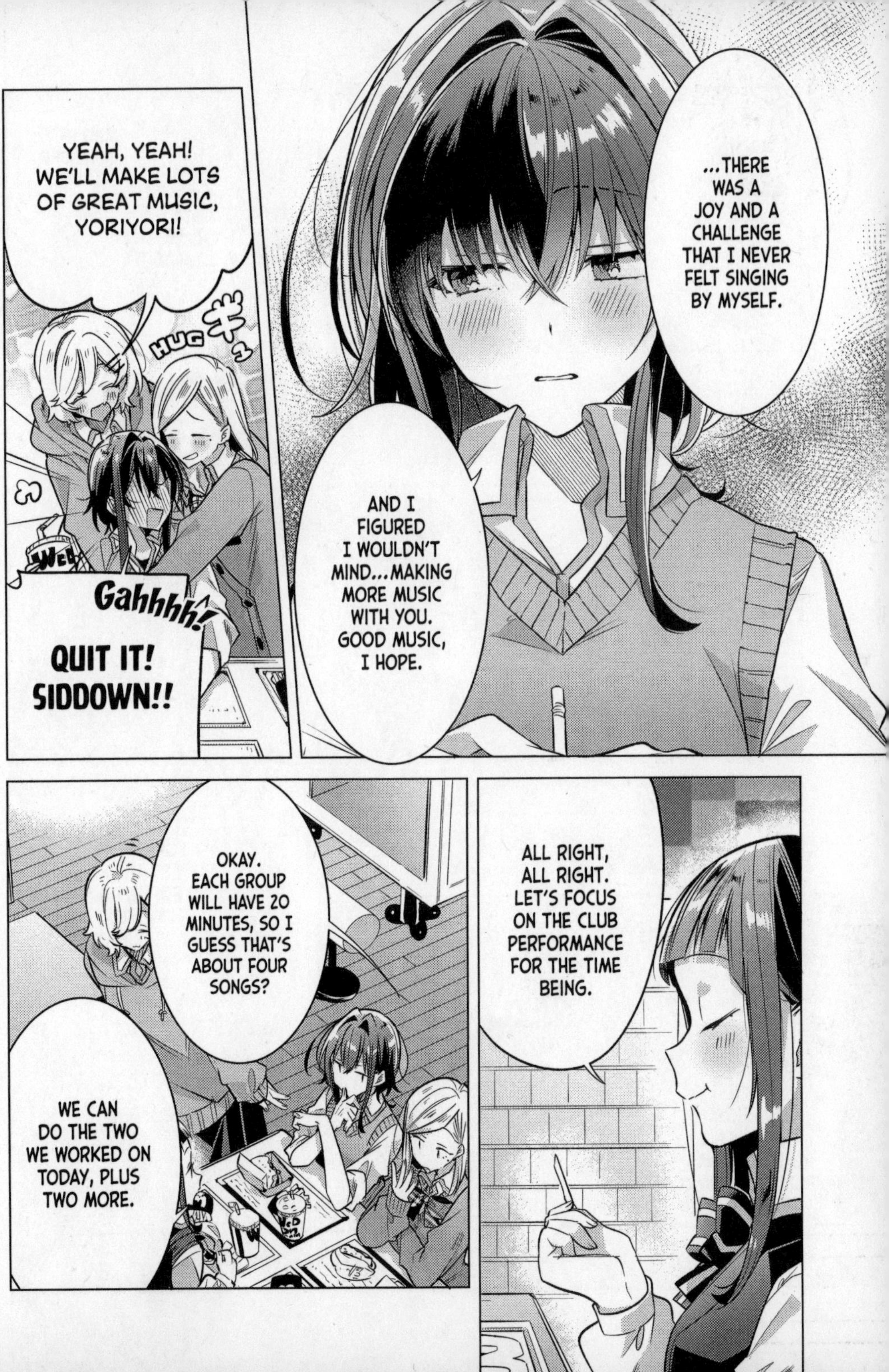
...THERE WAS A JOY AND A CHALLENGE THAT I NEVER FELT SINGING BY MYSELF.
AND I FIGURED I WOULDN'T MIND...MAKING MORE MUSIC WITH YOU. GOOD MUSIC, I HOPE.
YEAH, YEAH! WE'LL MAKE LOTS OF GREAT MUSIC, YORIYORI!
HUG
Gahhhh!
QUIT IT! SIDDOWN!!
ALL RIGHT, ALL RIGHT. LET'S FOCUS ON THE CLUB PERFORMANCE FOR THE TIME BEING.
OKAY. EACH GROUP WILL HAVE 20 MINUTES, SO I GUESS THAT'S ABOUT FOUR SONGS?
WE CAN DO THE TWO WE WORKED ON TODAY, PLUS TWO MORE.

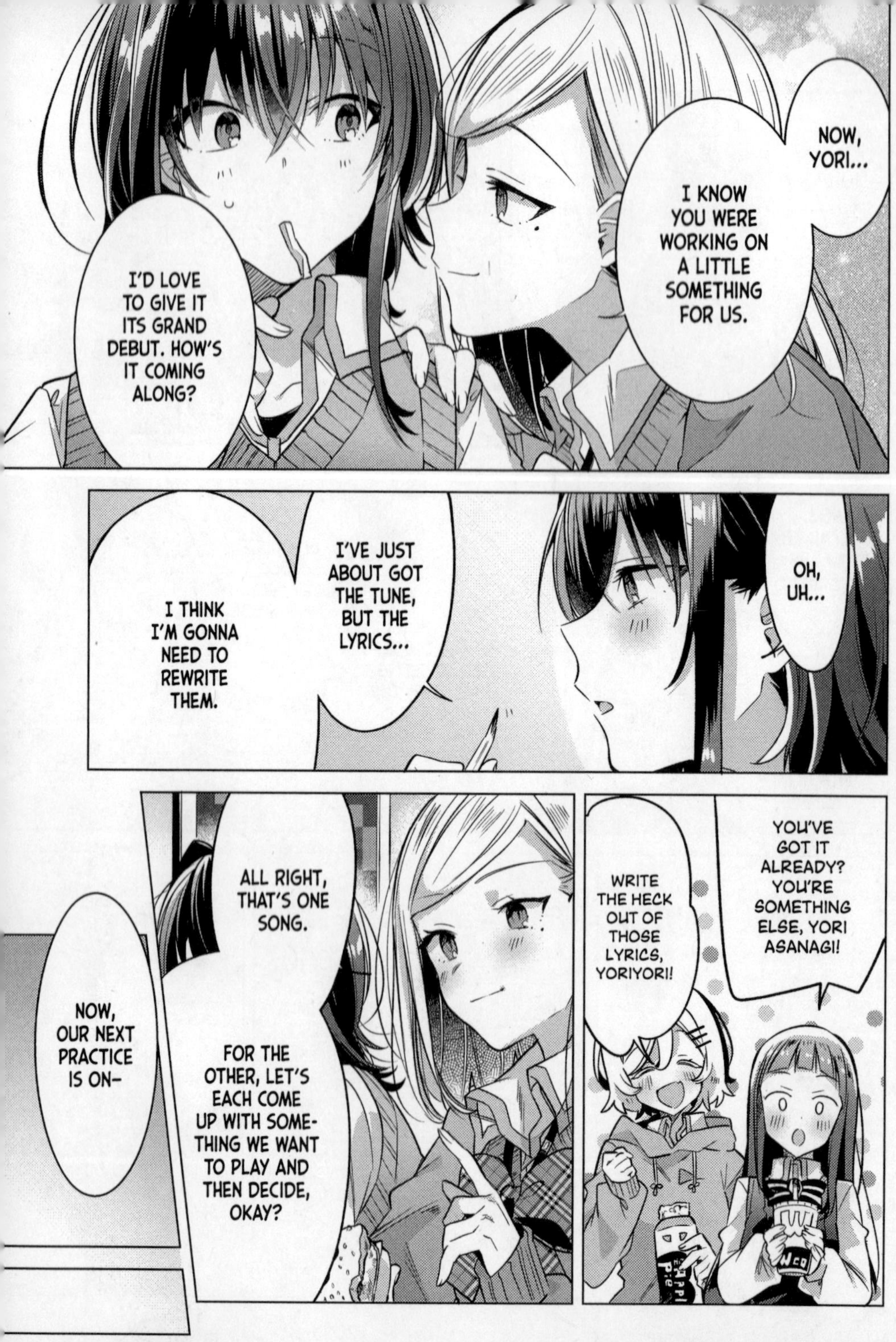
NOW, YORI...
I KNOW YOU WERE WORKING ON A LITTLE SOMETHING FOR US.
I'D LOVE TO GIVE IT ITS GRAND DEBUT. HOW'S IT COMING ALONG?
OH, UH...
I'VE JUST ABOUT GOT THE TUNE, BUT THE LYRICS...
I THINK I'M GONNA NEED TO REWRITE THEM.
YOU'VE GOT IT ALREADY? YOU'RE SOMETHING ELSE, YORI ASANAGI!
WRITE THE HECK OUT OF THOSE LYRICS, YORIYORI!
ALL RIGHT, THAT'S ONE SONG.
FOR THE OTHER, LET'S EACH COME UP WITH SOME-THING WE WANT TO PLAY AND THEN DECIDE, OKAY?
NOW, OUR NEXT PRACTICE IS ON–

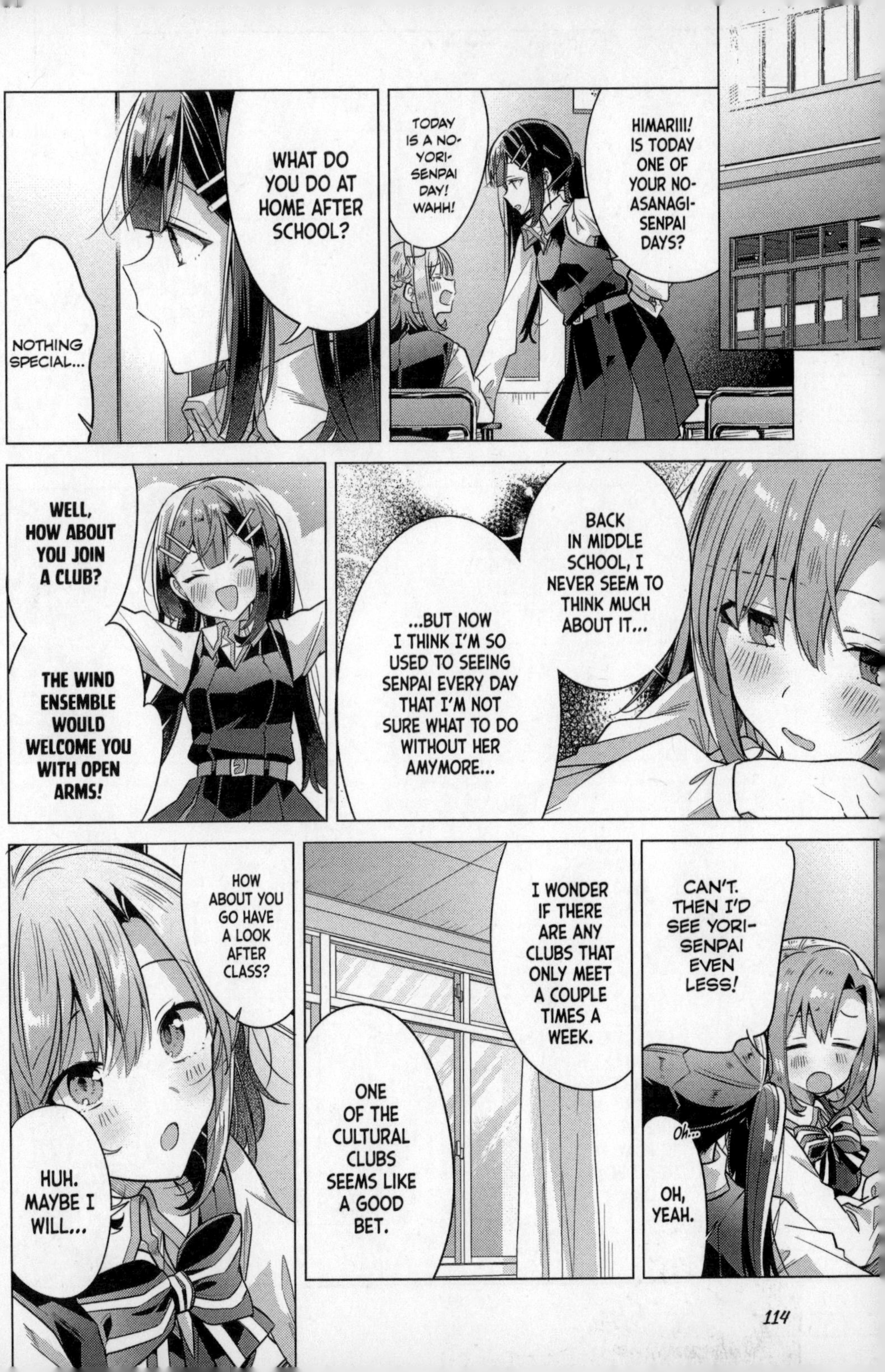
HIMARIII! IS TODAY ONE OF YOUR NO-ASANAGI-SENPAI DAYS?
TODAY IS A NO-YORI-SENPAI DAY! WAHH!
WHAT DO YOU DO AT HOME AFTER SCHOOL?
NOTHING SPECIAL...
BACK IN MIDDLE SCHOOL, I NEVER SEEM TO THINK MUCH ABOUT IT...
...BUT NOW I THINK I'M SO USED TO SEEING SENPAI EVERY DAY THAT I'M NOT SURE WHAT TO DO WITHOUT HER AMYMORE...
WELL, HOW ABOUT YOU JOIN A CLUB?
THE WIND ENSEMBLE WOULD WELCOME YOU WITH OPEN ARMS!
CAN'T. THEN I'D SEE YORI-SENPAI EVEN LESS!
Oh...
OH, YEAH.
I WONDER IF THERE ARE ANY CLUBS THAT ONLY MEET A COUPLE TIMES A WEEK.
ONE OF THE CULTURAL CLUBS SEEMS LIKE A GOOD BET.
HOW ABOUT YOU GO HAVE A LOOK AFTER CLASS?
HUH. MAYBE I WILL...

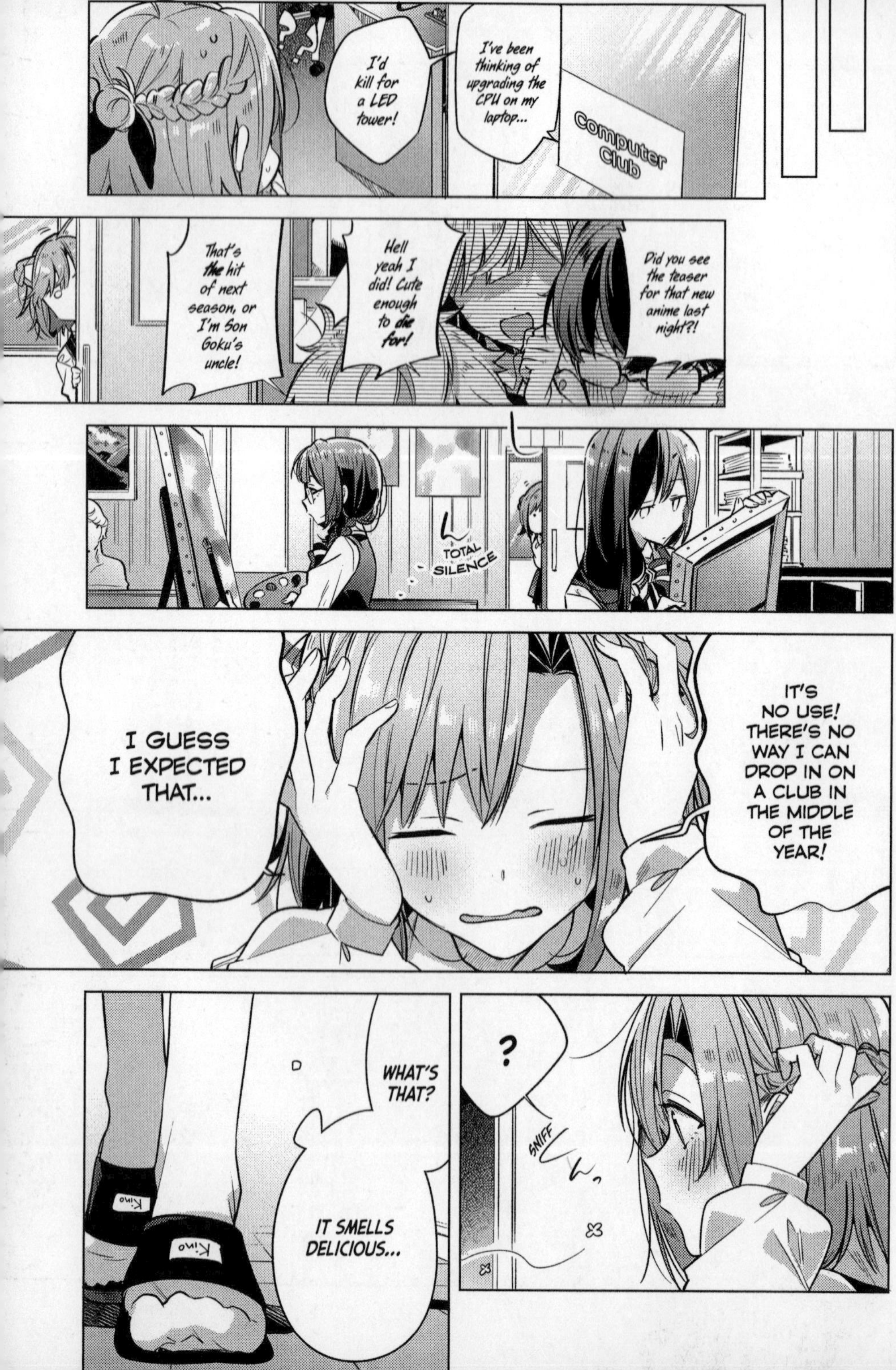

I've been thinking of upgrading the CPU on my laptop...
Computer Club
I'd kill for a LED tower!
Did you see the teaser for that new anime last night?!
Hell yeah I did! Cute enough to die for!
That's the hit of next season, or I'm Son Goku's uncle!
TOTAL SILENCE
IT'S NO USE! THERE'S NO WAY I CAN DROP IN ON A CLUB IN THE MIDDLE OF THE YEAR!
I GUESS I EXPECTED THAT...
?
SNIFF
WHAT'S THAT?
IT SMELLS DELICIOUS...
Kino
Kino

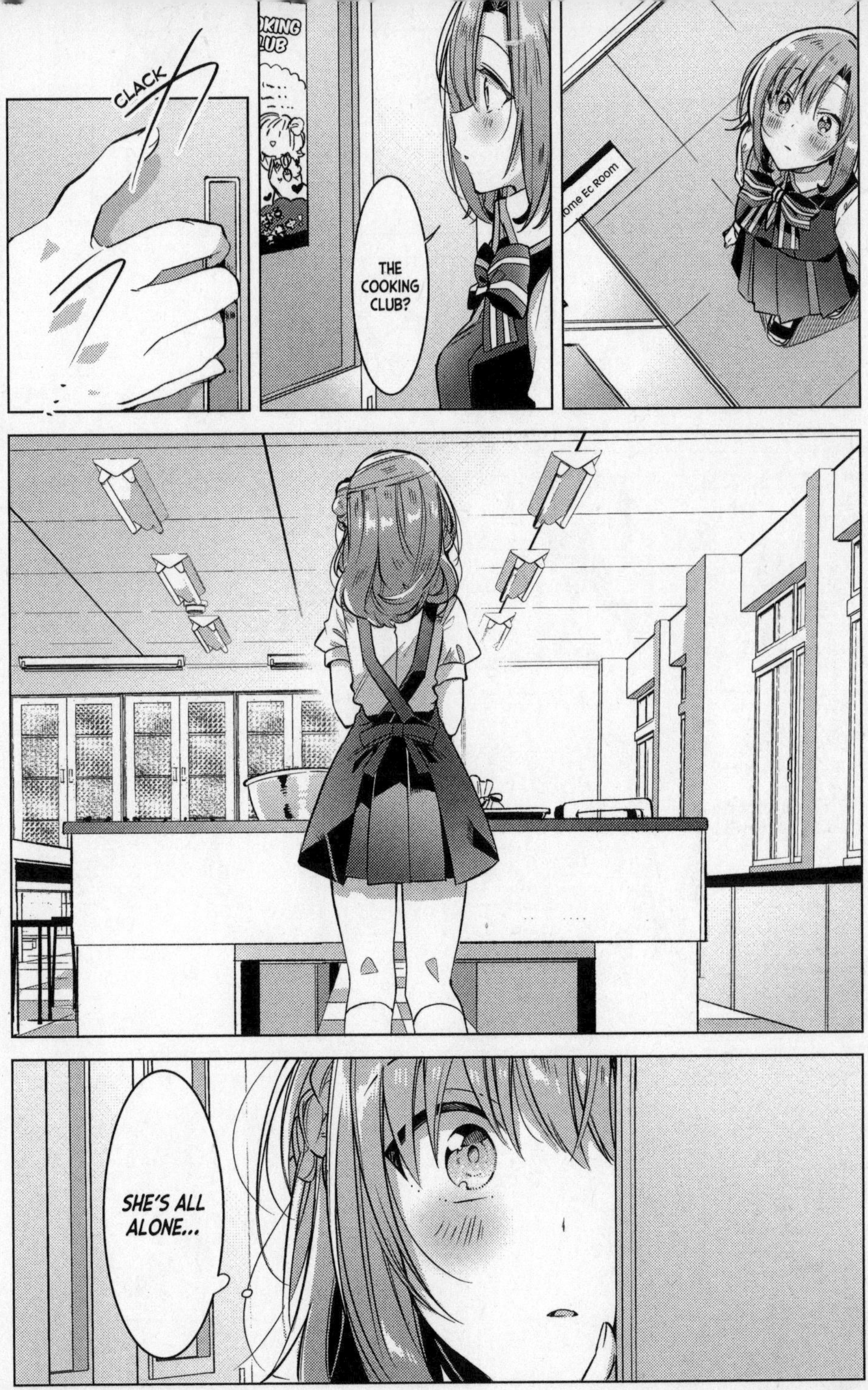
THE COOKING CLUB?
CLACK
SHE'S ALL ALONE...

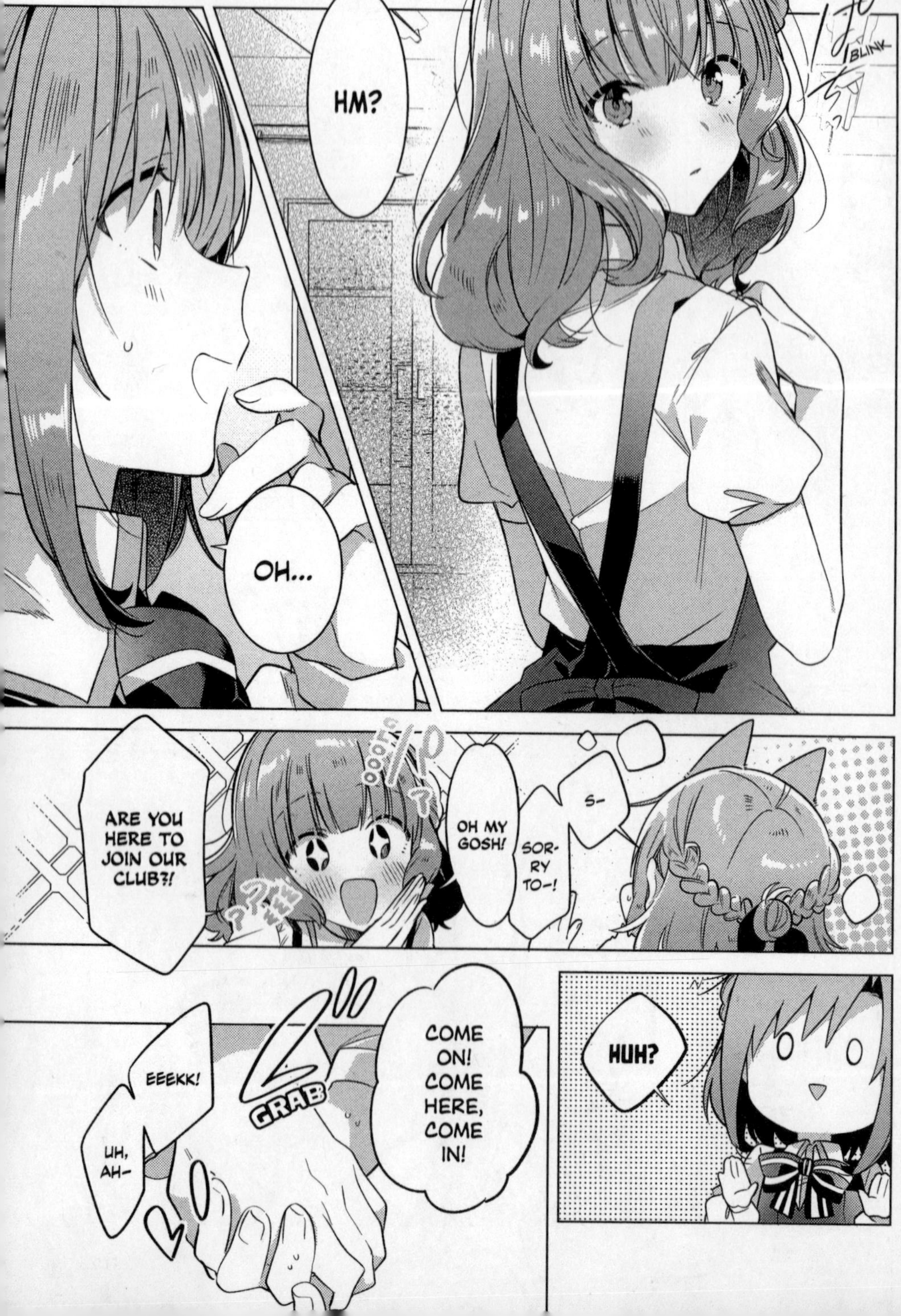
BLINK
HM?
OH...
S-
SOR-RY TO-!
OH MY GOSH!
ARE YOU HERE TO JOIN OUR CLUB?!
HUH?
COME ON! COME HERE, COME IN!
GRAB
EEEKK!
UH, AH-

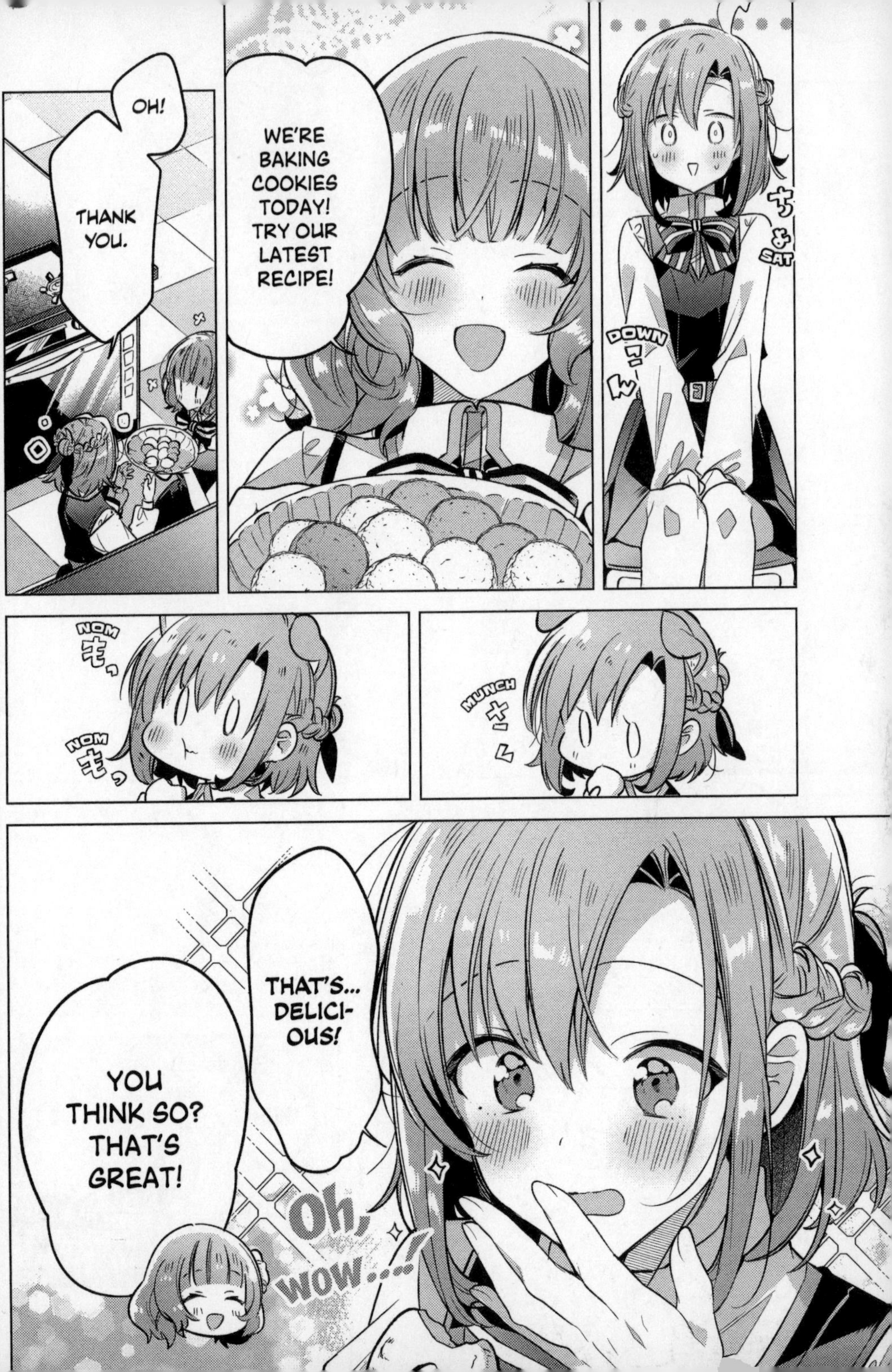
SAT
DOWN
WE'RE BAKING COOKIES TODAY! TRY OUR LATEST RECIPE!
OH!
THANK YOU.
MUNCH
NOM
NOM
THAT'S... DELICI-OUS!
YOU THINK SO? THAT'S GREAT!
Oh, wow...!

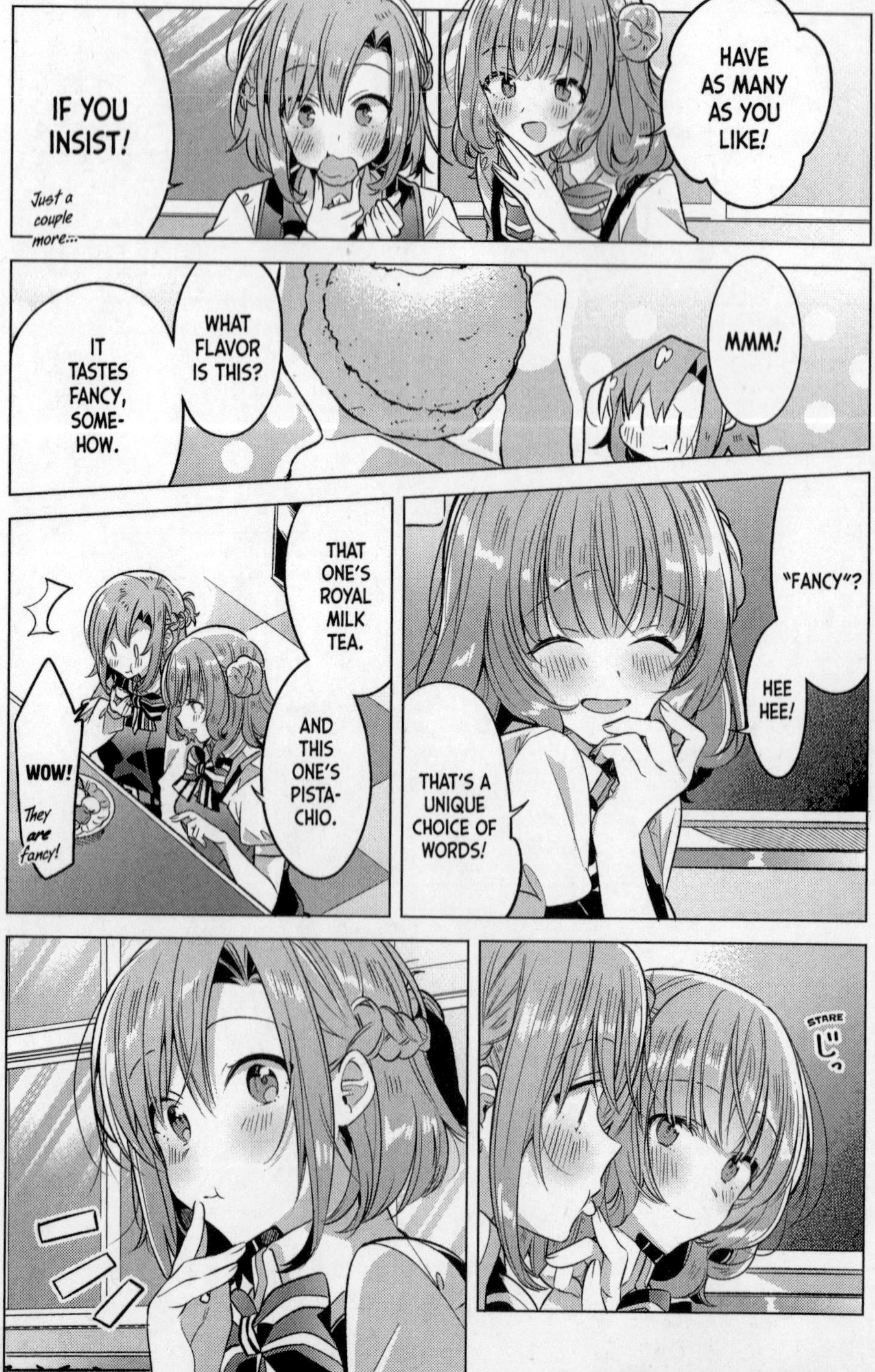
HAVE AS MANY AS YOU LIKE!
IF YOU INSIST!
Just a couple more...
MMM!
WHAT FLAVOR IS THIS?
IT TASTES FANCY, SOMEHOW.
"FANCY"?
HEE HEE!
THAT'S A UNIQUE CHOICE OF WORDS!
THAT ONE'S ROYAL MILK TEA.
AND THIS ONE'S PISTACHIO.
WOW!
They are fancy!
STARE

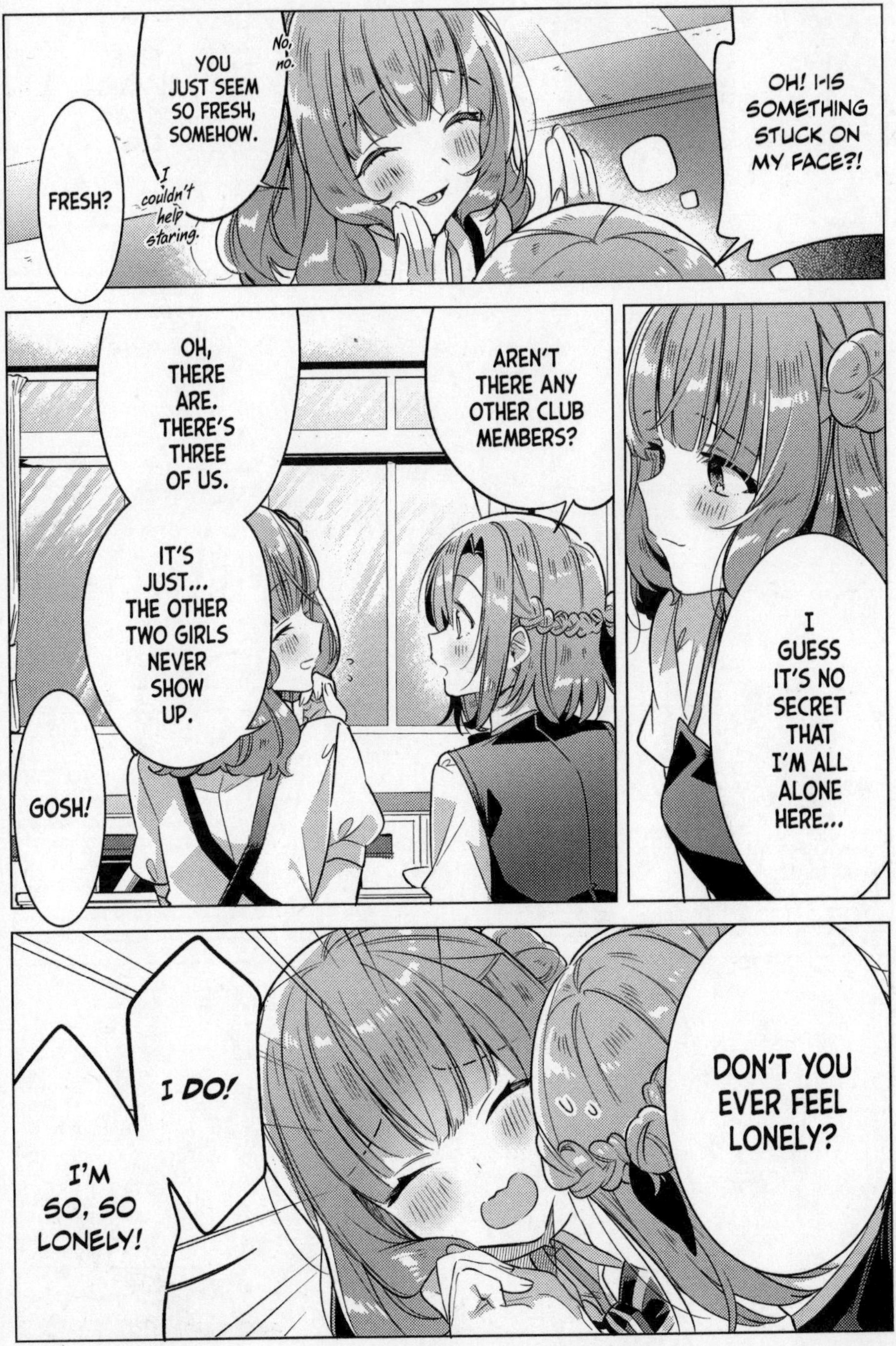
OH! I-IS SOMETHING STUCK ON MY FACE?!
No, no.
YOU JUST SEEM SO FRESH, SOMEHOW.
I couldn't help staring.
FRESH?
I GUESS IT'S NO SECRET THAT I'M ALL ALONE HERE...
AREN'T THERE ANY OTHER CLUB MEMBERS?
OH, THERE ARE. THERE'S THREE OF US.
IT'S JUST... THE OTHER TWO GIRLS NEVER SHOW UP.
GOSH!
DON'T YOU EVER FEEL LONELY?
I *DO!*
I'M SO, SO LONELY!

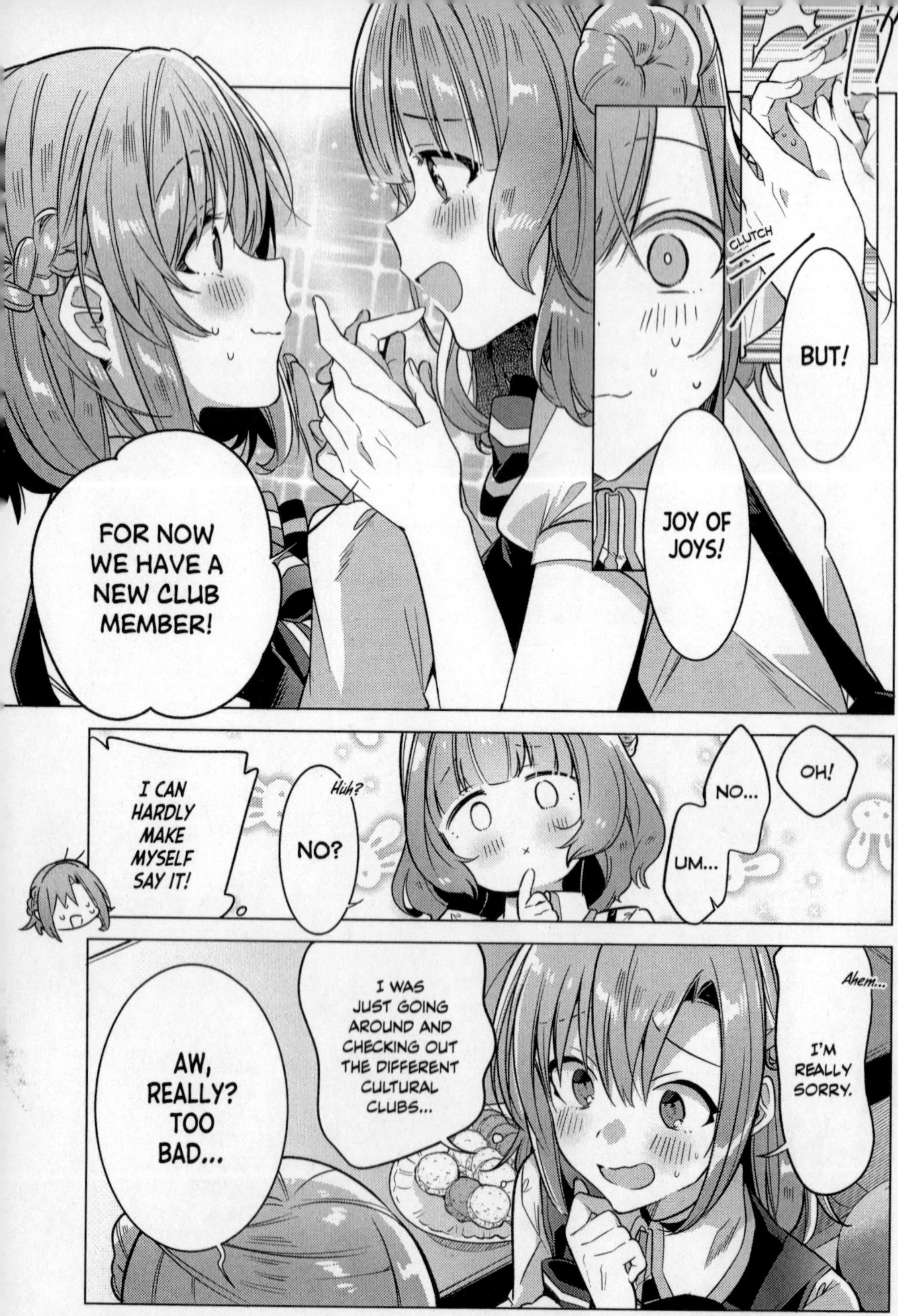
CLUTCH
BUT!
JOY OF JOYS!
FOR NOW WE HAVE A NEW CLUB MEMBER!
OH!
NO... UM...
Huh?
NO?
I CAN HARDLY MAKE MYSELF SAY IT!
Ahem...
I'M REALLY SORRY.
I WAS JUST GOING AROUND AND CHECKING OUT THE DIFFERENT CULTURAL CLUBS...
AW, REALLY? TOO BAD...

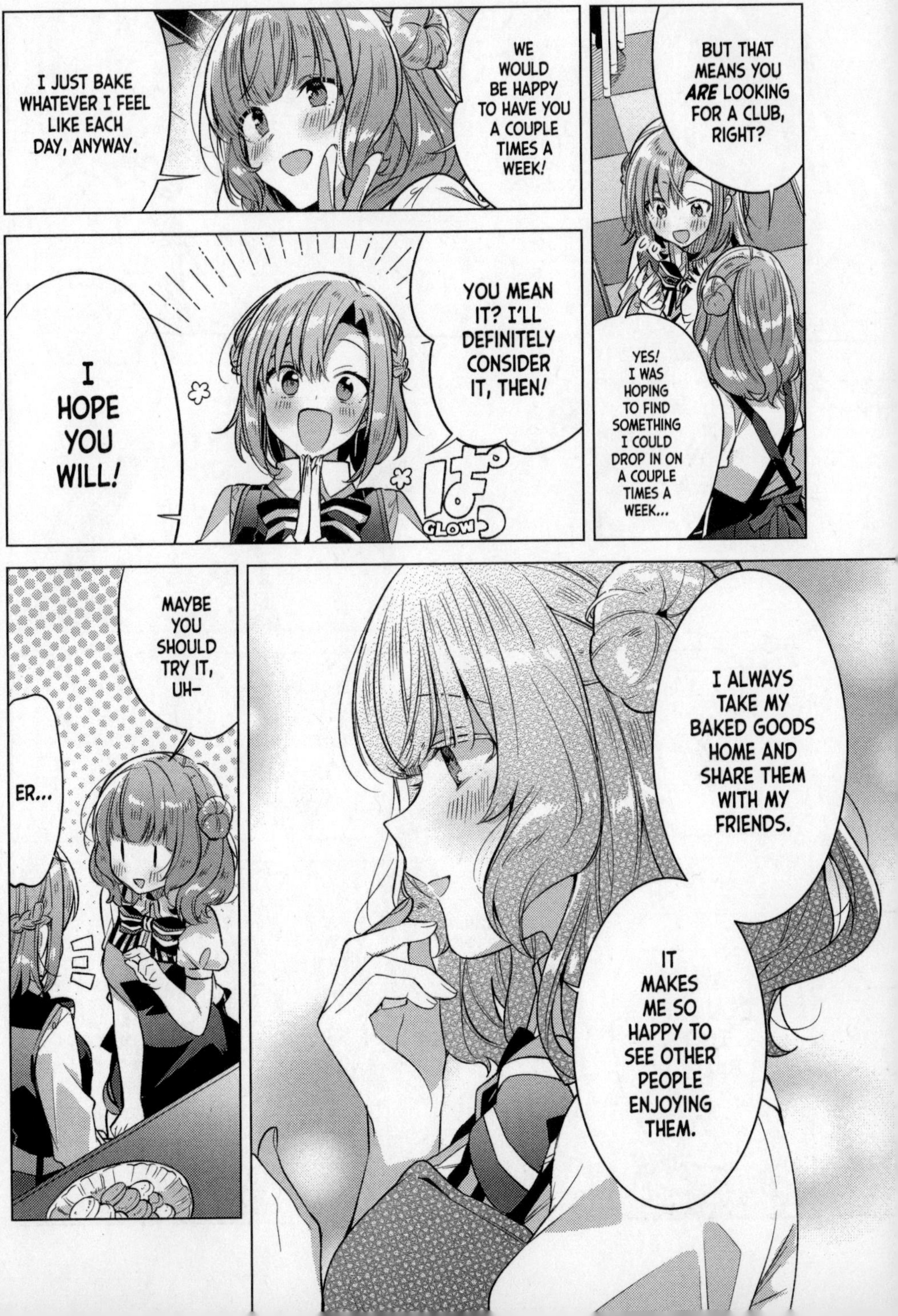
BUT THAT MEANS YOU ARE LOOKING FOR A CLUB, RIGHT?
YES! I WAS HOPING TO FIND SOMETHING I COULD DROP IN ON A COUPLE TIMES A WEEK...
WE WOULD BE HAPPY TO HAVE YOU A COUPLE TIMES A WEEK!
I JUST BAKE WHATEVER I FEEL LIKE EACH DAY, ANYWAY.
YOU MEAN IT? I'LL DEFINITELY CONSIDER IT, THEN!
ぱっ
GLOW
I HOPE YOU WILL!
I ALWAYS TAKE MY BAKED GOODS HOME AND SHARE THEM WITH MY FRIENDS.
IT MAKES ME SO HAPPY TO SEE OTHER PEOPLE ENJOYING THEM.
MAYBE YOU SHOULD TRY IT, UH-
ER...

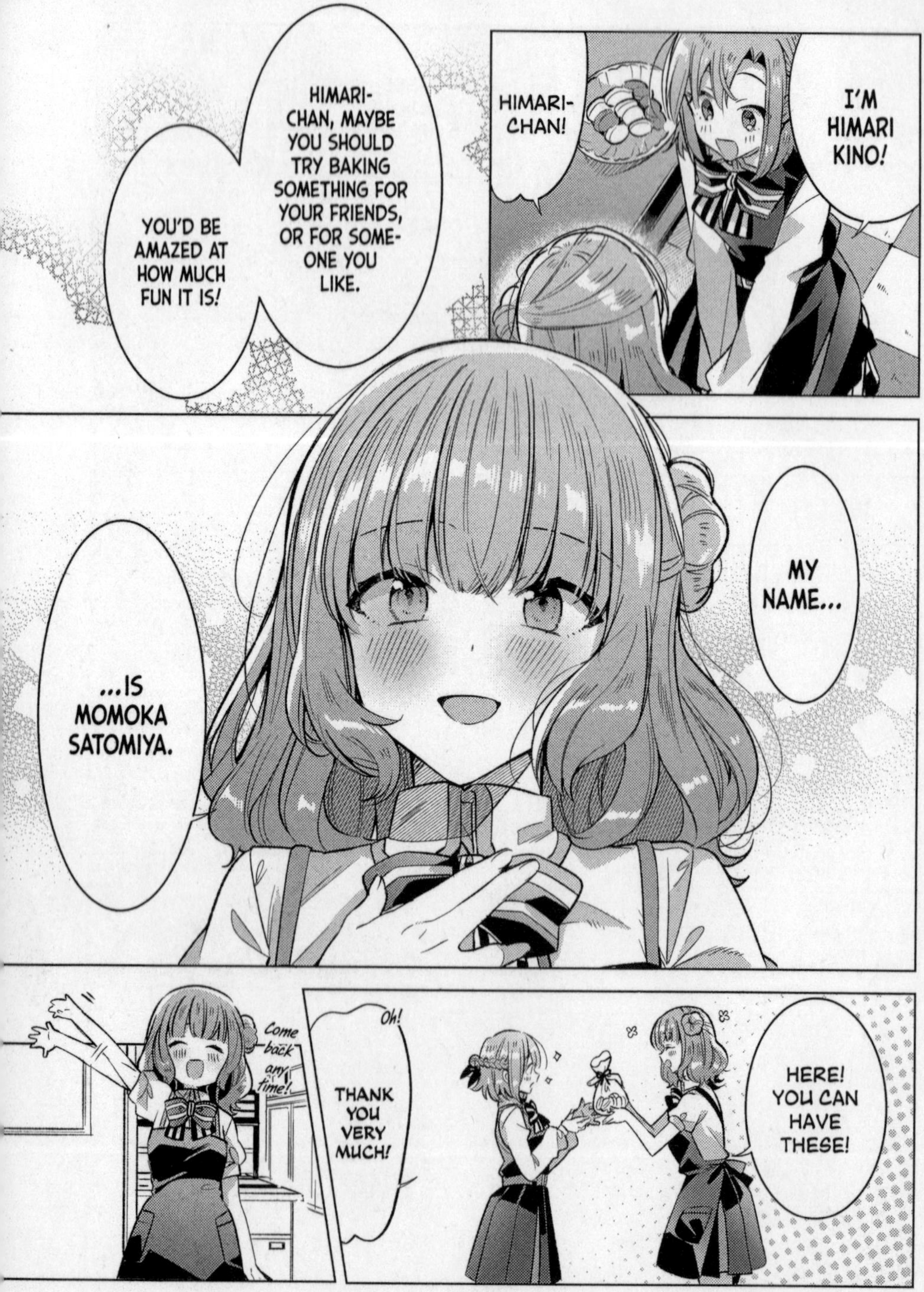
I'M HIMARI KINO!
HIMARI-CHAN!
HIMARI-CHAN, MAYBE YOU SHOULD TRY BAKING SOMETHING FOR YOUR FRIENDS, OR FOR SOME-ONE YOU LIKE.
YOU'D BE AMAZED AT HOW MUCH FUN IT IS!
MY NAME...
...IS MOMOKA SATOMIYA.
HERE! YOU CAN HAVE THESE!
Oh!
THANK YOU VERY MUCH!
Come back any time!

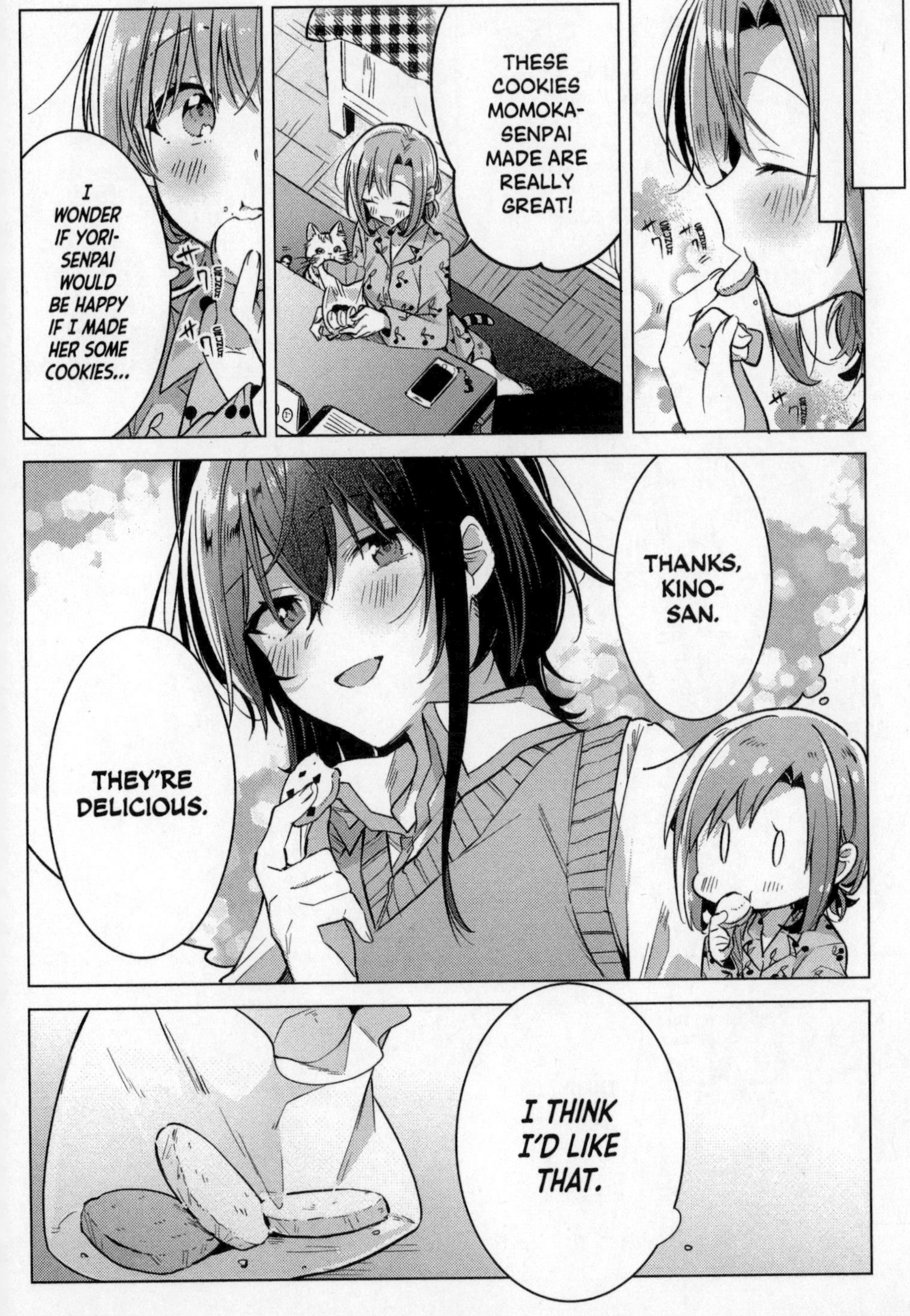
THESE COOKIES MOMOKA-SENPAI MADE ARE REALLY GREAT!
I WONDER IF YORI-SENPAI WOULD BE HAPPY IF I MADE HER SOME COOKIES...
THANKS, KINO-SAN.
THEY'RE DELICIOUS.
I THINK I'D LIKE THAT.

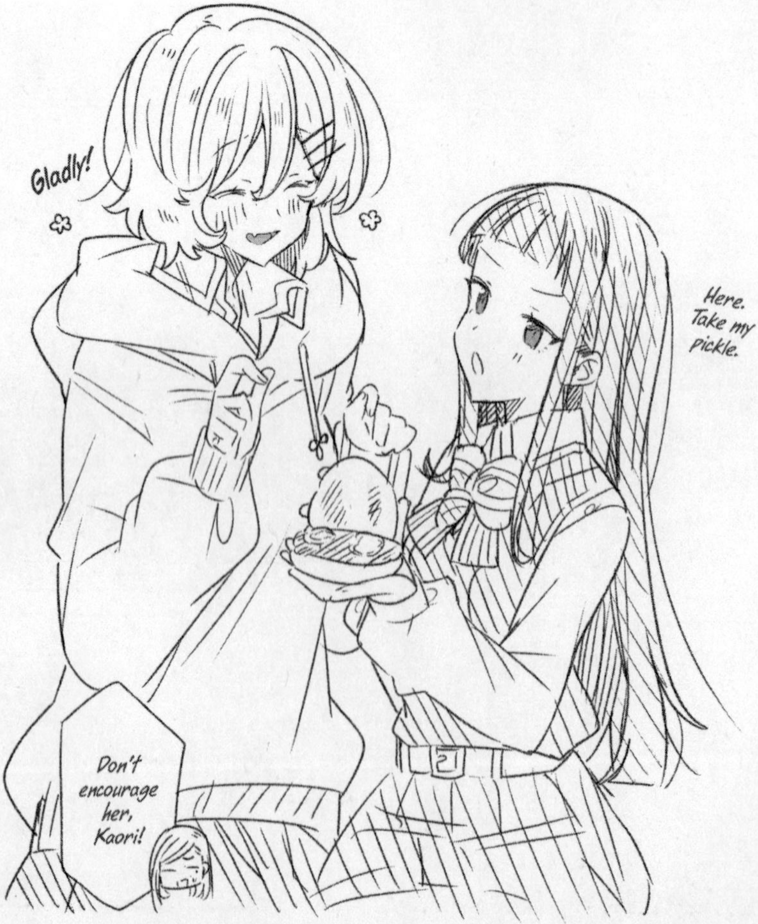
Here. Take my pickle.
Gladly!
Don't encourage her, Kaori!

Whisper Me
A Love Song
Eku
Takeshima

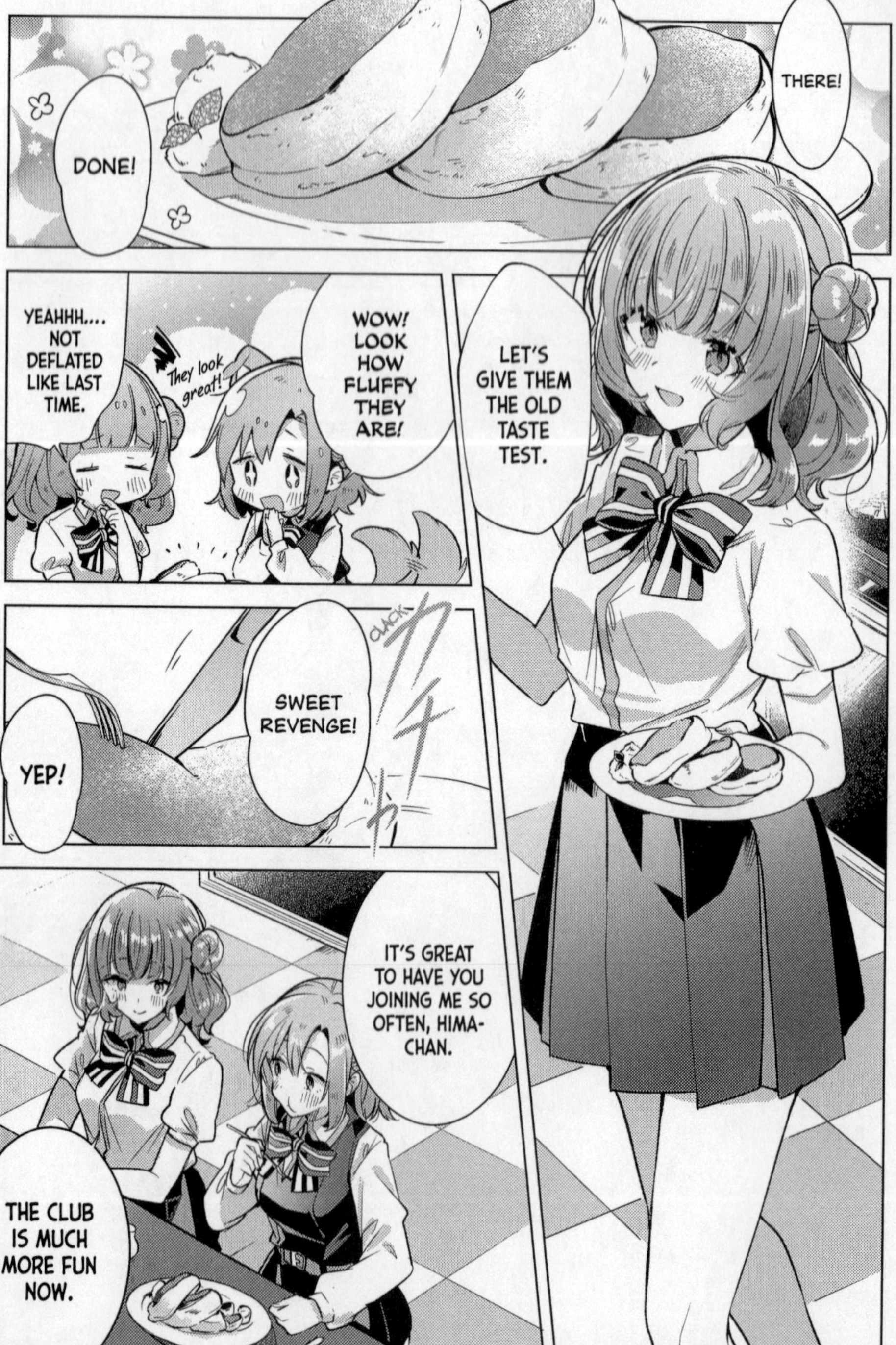
THERE!
DONE!
LET'S GIVE THEM THE OLD TASTE TEST.
WOW! LOOK HOW FLUFFY THEY ARE!
They look great!
YEAHHH.... NOT DEFLATED LIKE LAST TIME.
CLACK
SWEET REVENGE!
YEP!
IT'S GREAT TO HAVE YOU JOINING ME SO OFTEN, HIMA-CHAN.
THE CLUB IS MUCH MORE FUN NOW.

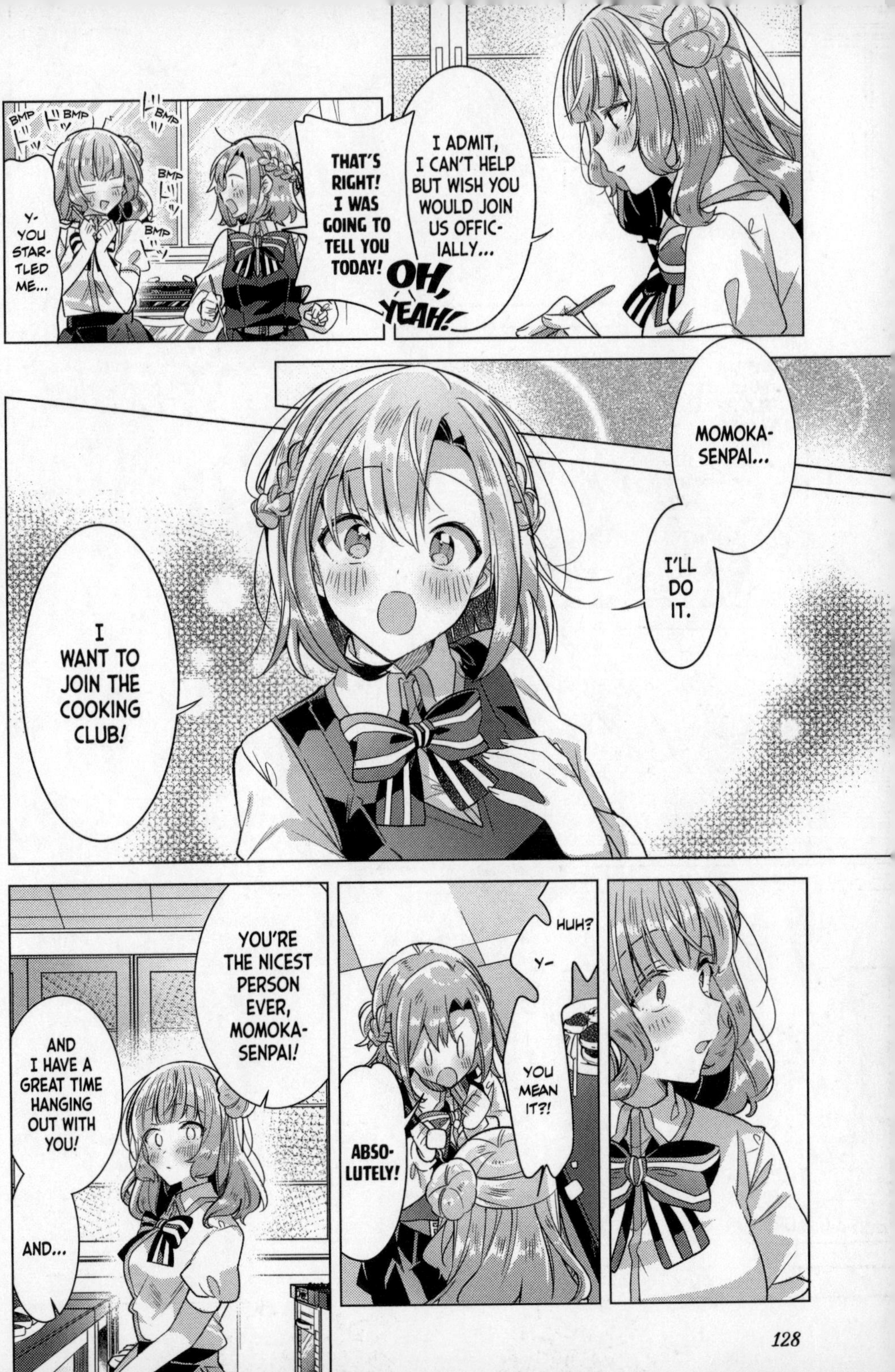

I ADMIT, I CAN'T HELP BUT WISH YOU WOULD JOIN US OFFICIALLY...
OH, YEAH!
THAT'S RIGHT! I WAS GOING TO TELL YOU TODAY!
BMP BMP BMP BMP BMP
Y-YOU STARTLED ME...
MOMOKA-SENPAI...
I'LL DO IT.
I WANT TO JOIN THE COOKING CLUB!
HUH?
Y-
YOU MEAN IT?!
ABSOLUTELY!
YOU'RE THE NICEST PERSON EVER, MOMOKA-SENPAI!
AND I HAVE A GREAT TIME HANGING OUT WITH YOU!
AND...

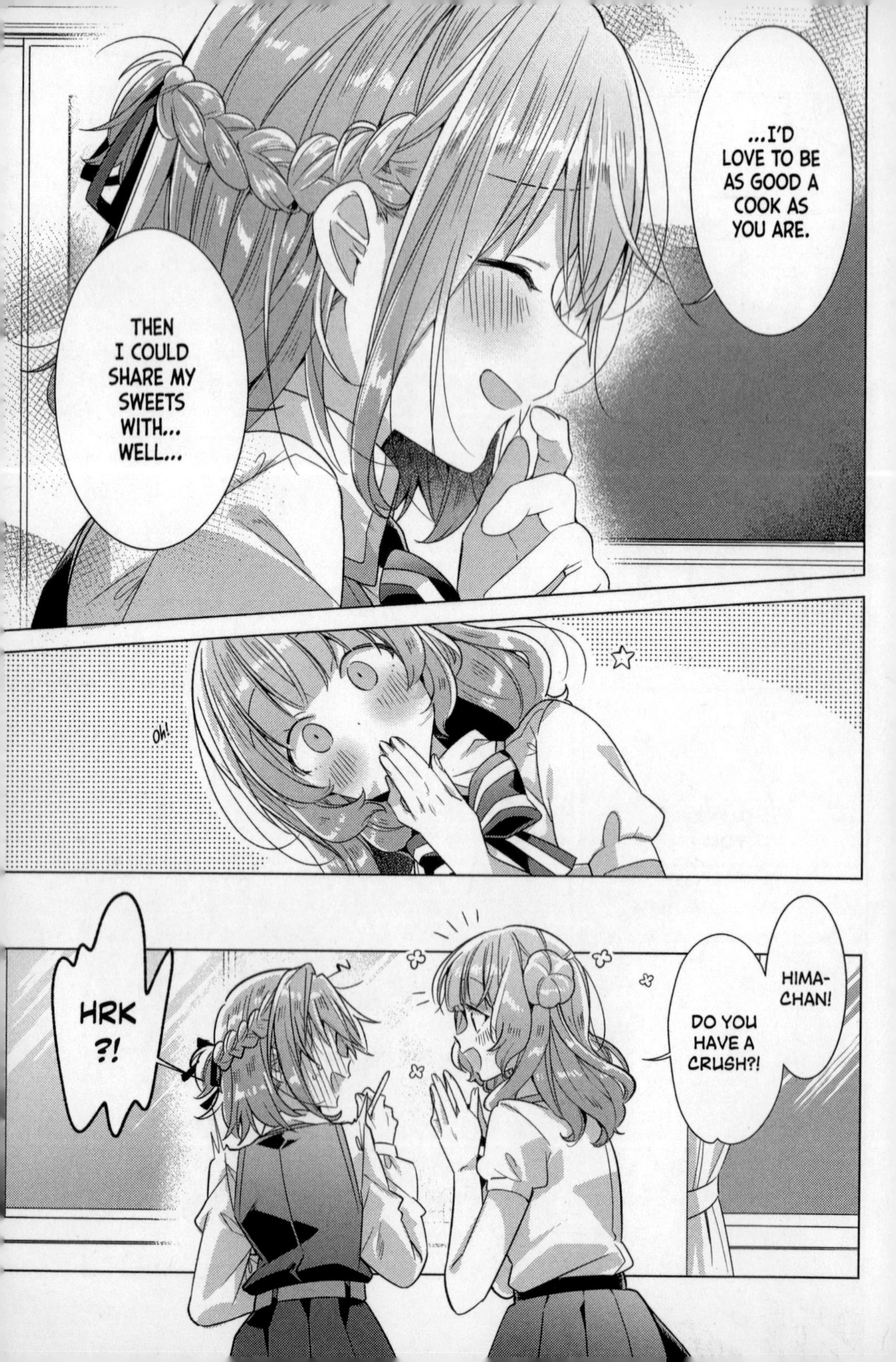
...I'D LOVE TO BE AS GOOD A COOK AS YOU ARE.
THEN I COULD SHARE MY SWEETS WITH... WELL...
OH!
HIMA-CHAN!
DO YOU HAVE A CRUSH?!
HRK ?!

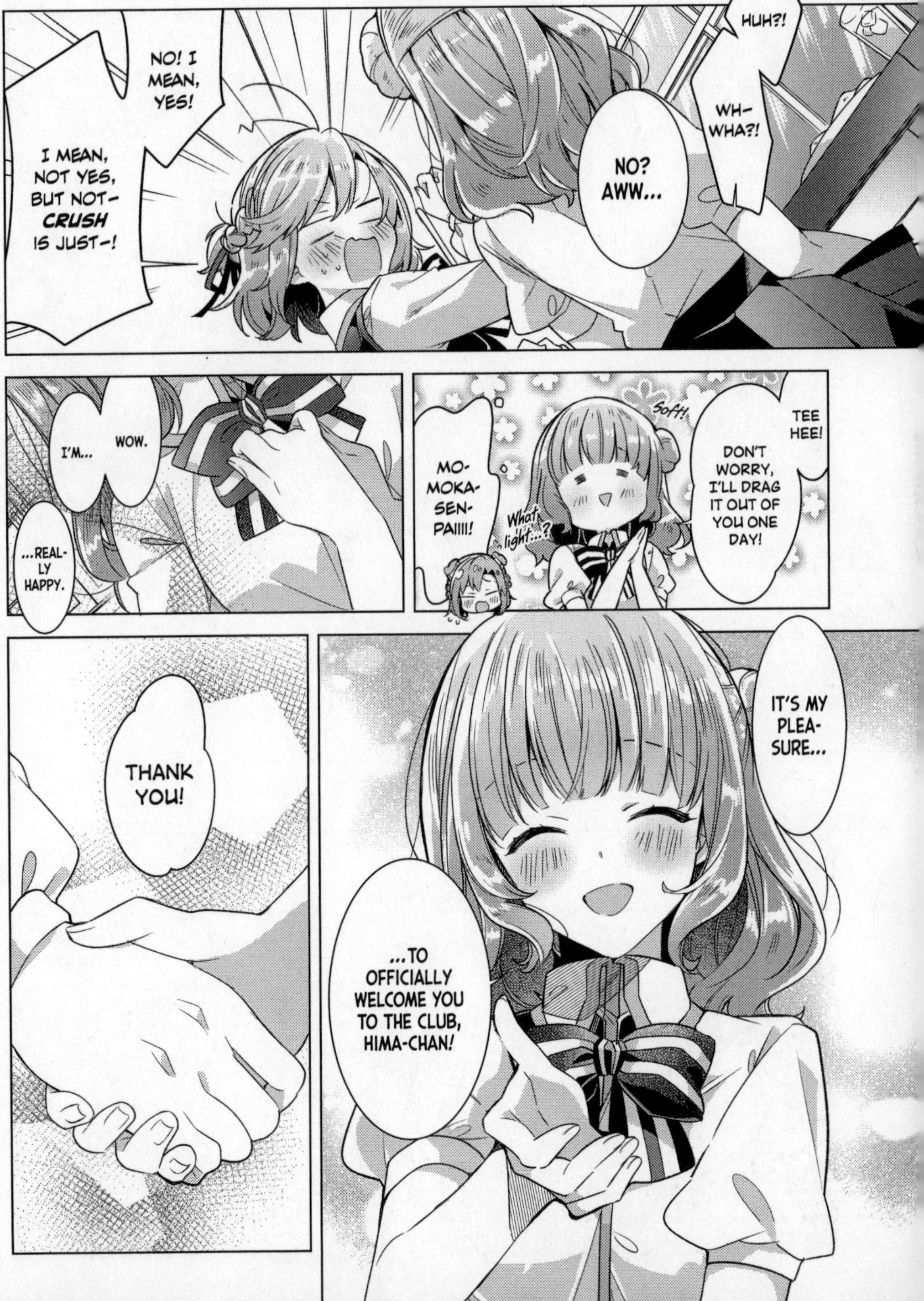
HUH?!
WH- WHA?!
NO? AWW...
NO! I MEAN, YES!
I MEAN, NOT YES, BUT NOT-*CRUSH* IS JUST-!
TEE HEE!
DON'T WORRY, I'LL DRAG IT OUT OF YOU ONE DAY!
Soft!
MO-MOKA-SEN-PAIIII!
What light...?
WOW.
I'M...
...REAL-LY HAPPY.
IT'S MY PLEA-SURE...
...TO OFFICIALLY WELCOME YOU TO THE CLUB, HIMA-CHAN!
THANK YOU!

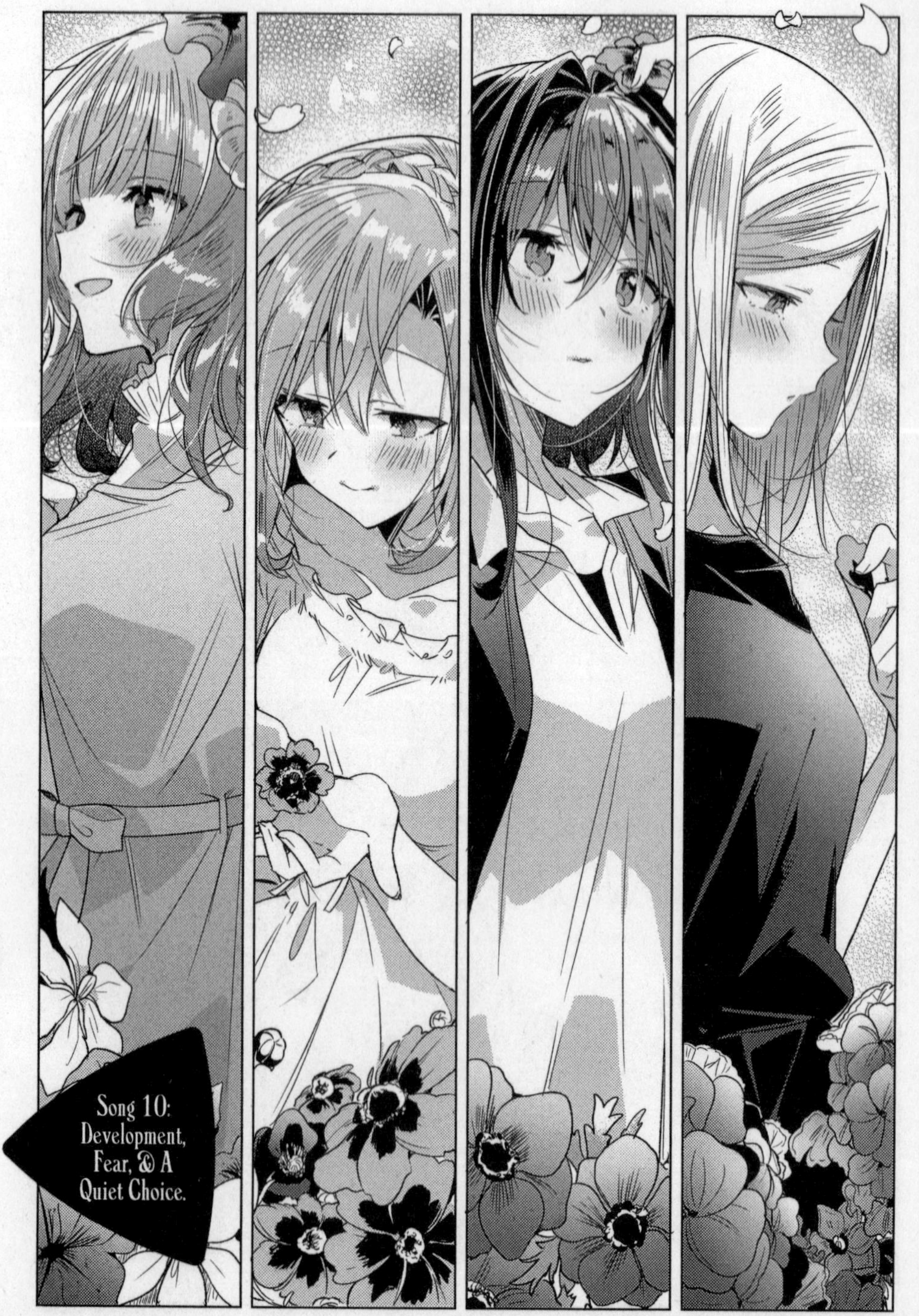
Song 10:
Development,
Fear, & A
Quiet Choice.

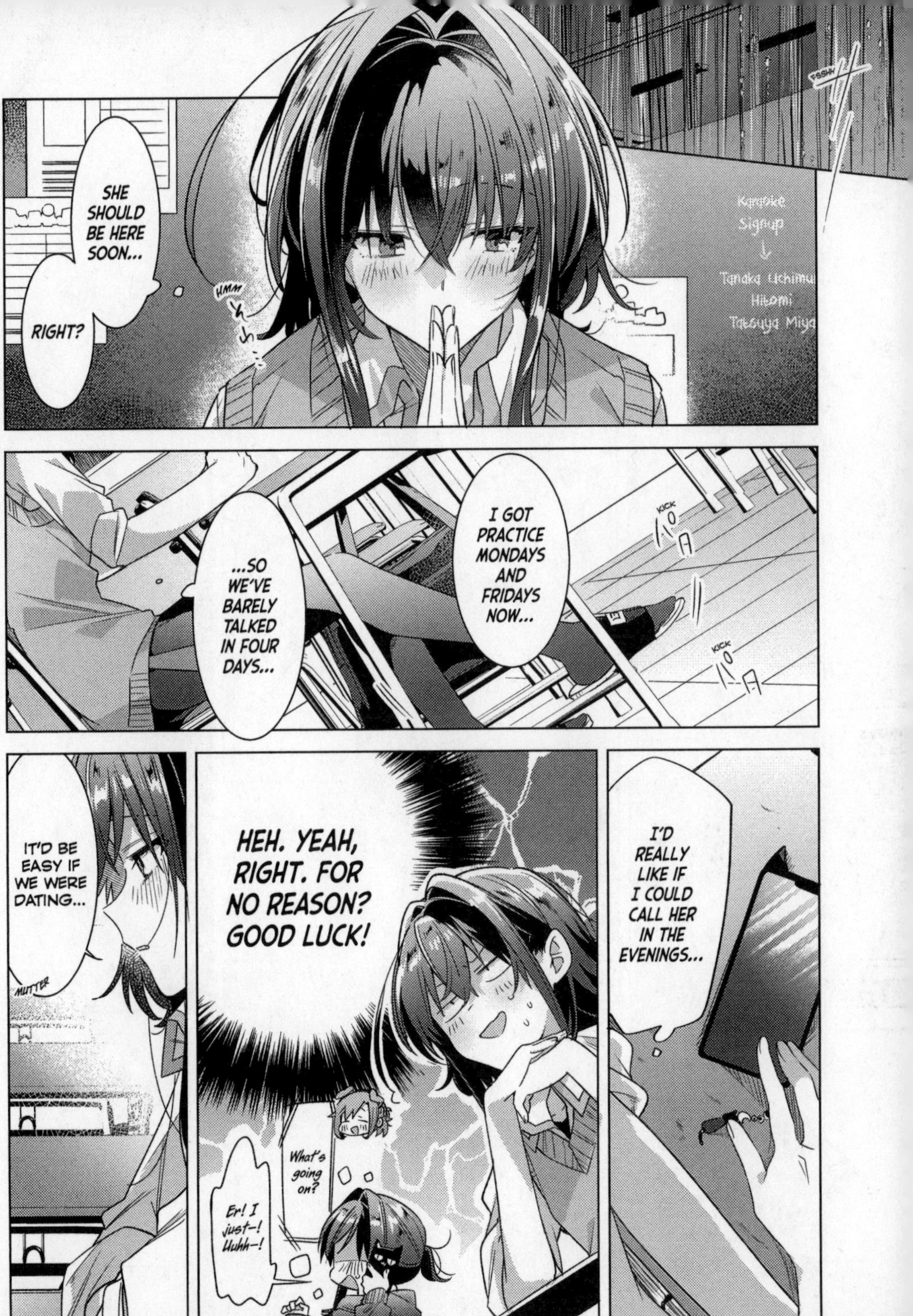
FSSHH
Karaoke
Signup
Hitomi
HMM
SHE SHOULD BE HERE SOON...
RIGHT?
KICK
KICK
I GOT PRACTICE MONDAYS AND FRIDAYS NOW...
...SO WE'VE BARELY TALKED IN FOUR DAYS...
I'D REALLY LIKE IF I COULD CALL HER IN THE EVENINGS...
HEH. YEAH, RIGHT. FOR NO REASON? GOOD LUCK!
What's going on?
Er! I just-! Uhh-!
IT'D BE EASY IF WE WERE DATING...
MUTTER

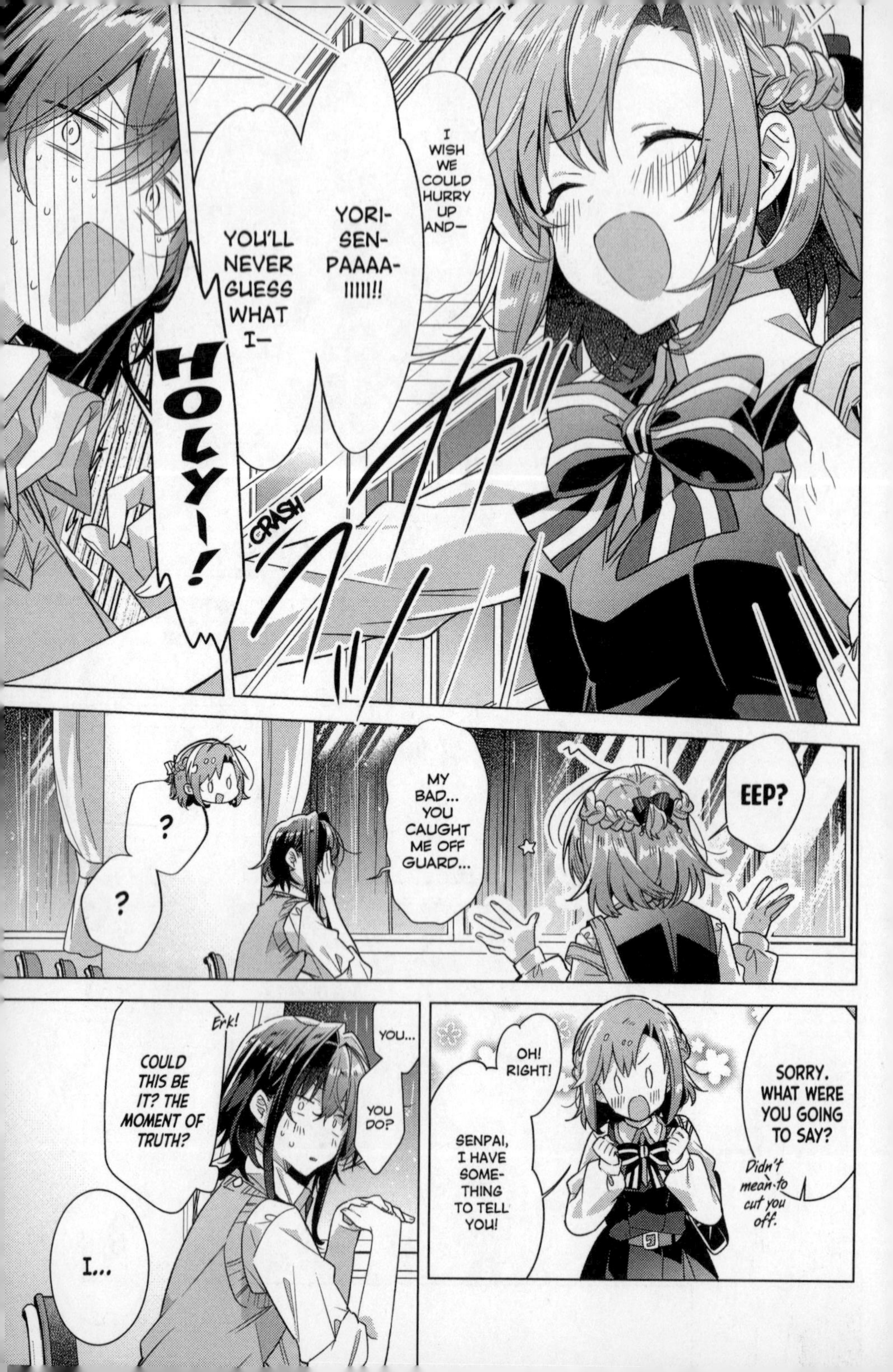
I WISH WE COULD HURRY UP AND—
YORI-SEN-PAAAA-!!!!!!!
YOU'LL NEVER GUESS WHAT I—
HOLY—!
CRASH
EEP?
MY BAD... YOU CAUGHT ME OFF GUARD...
?
?
SORRY. WHAT WERE YOU GOING TO SAY?
Didn't mean to cut you off.
OH! RIGHT!
SENPAI, I HAVE SOME-THING TO TELL YOU!
YOU...
Erk!
YOU DO?
COULD THIS BE IT? THE MOMENT OF TRUTH?
I...

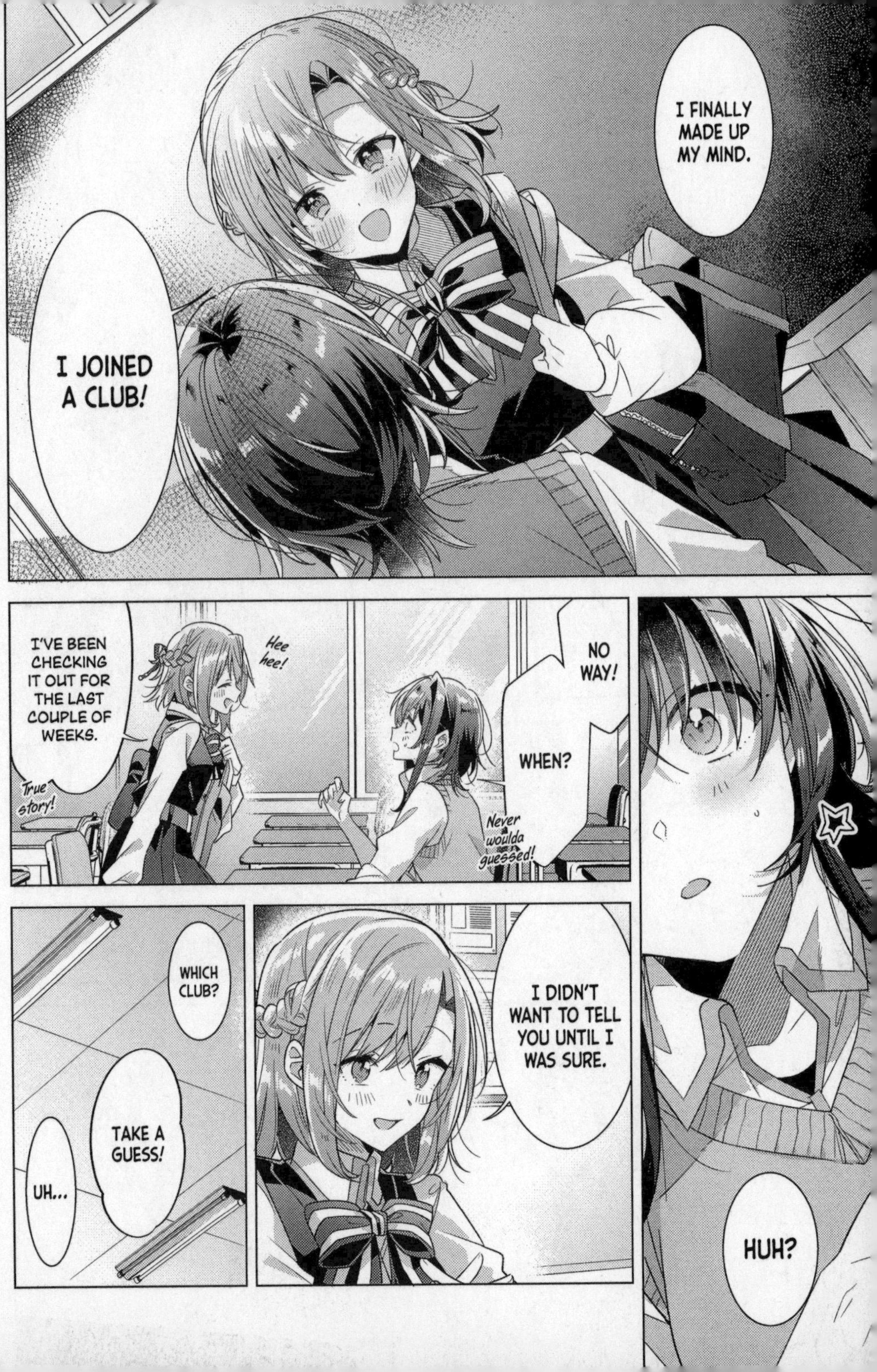
I FINALLY MADE UP MY MIND.
I JOINED A CLUB!
HUH?
NO WAY!
WHEN?
Never woulda guessed!
Hee hee!
I'VE BEEN CHECKING IT OUT FOR THE LAST COUPLE OF WEEKS.
True story!
I DIDN'T WANT TO TELL YOU UNTIL I WAS SURE.
WHICH CLUB?
TAKE A GUESS!
UH...

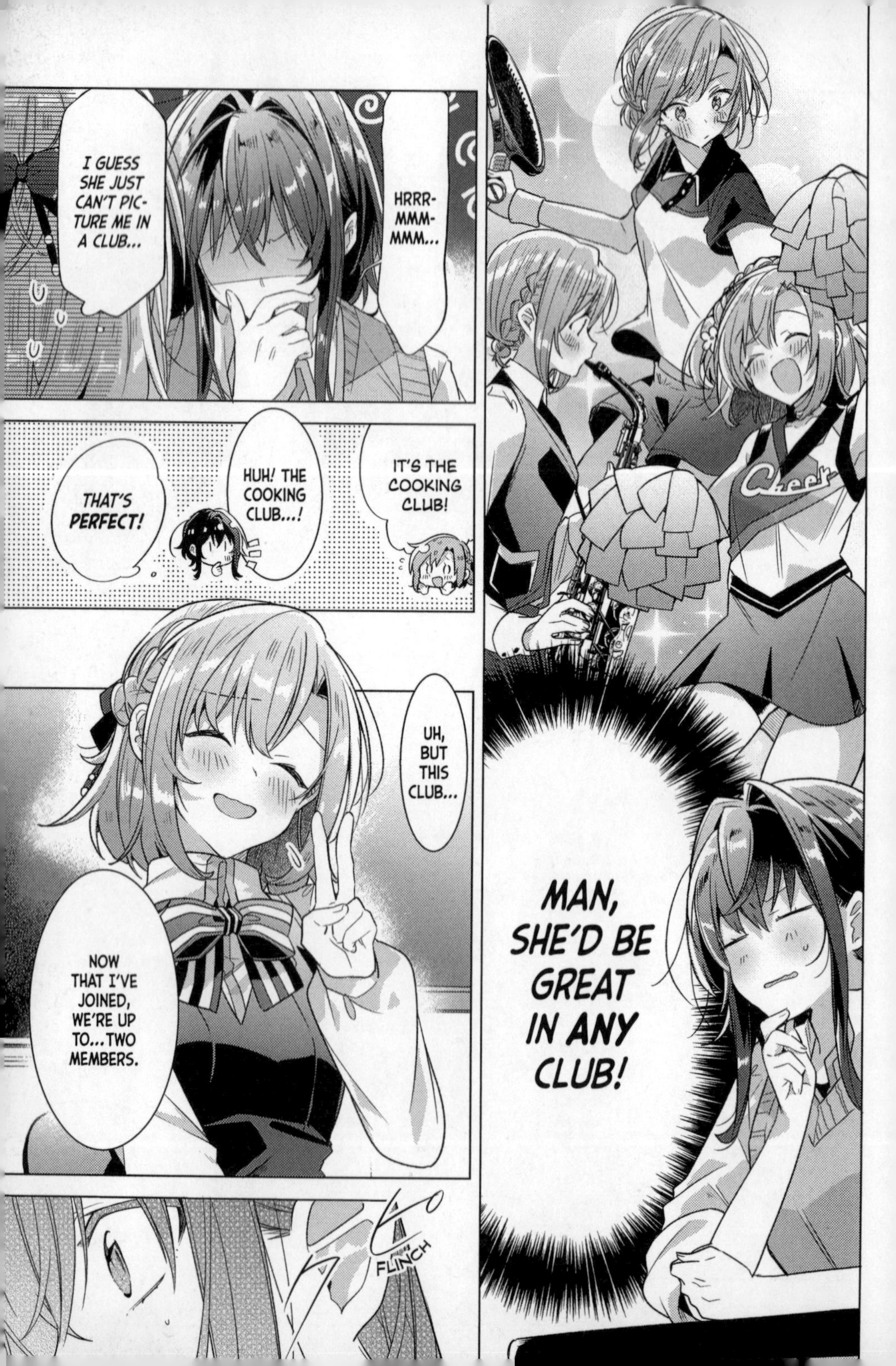
MAN, SHE'D BE GREAT IN ANY CLUB!
HRRR-MMM-MMM...
I GUESS SHE JUST CAN'T PICTURE ME IN A CLUB...
IT'S THE COOKING CLUB!
HUH! THE COOKING CLUB...!
THAT'S PERFECT!
UH, BUT THIS CLUB...
NOW THAT I'VE JOINED, WE'RE UP TO...TWO MEMBERS.
FLINCH

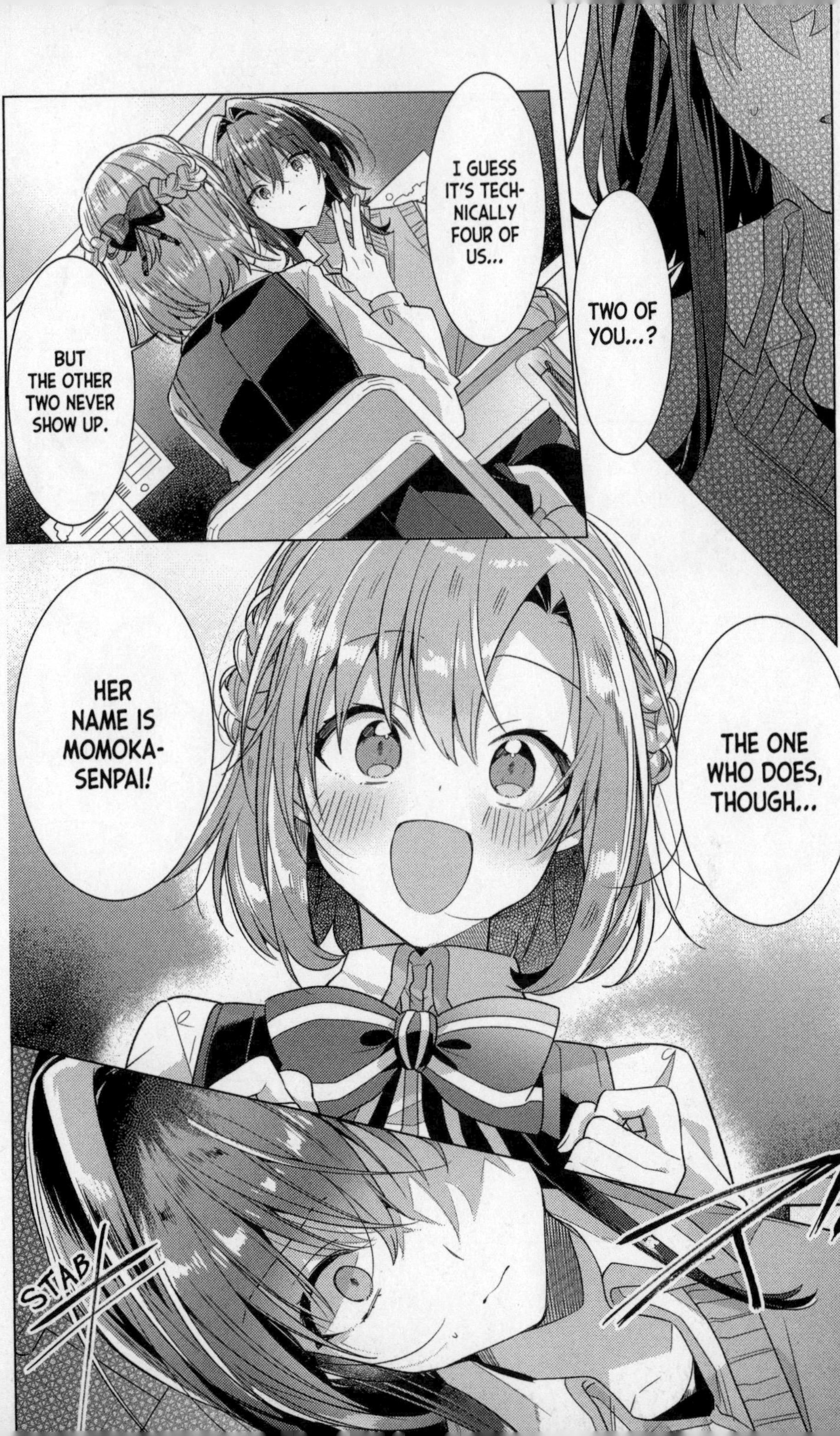
TWO OF YOU...?
I GUESS IT'S TECHNICALLY FOUR OF US...
BUT THE OTHER TWO NEVER SHOW UP.
THE ONE WHO DOES, THOUGH...
HER NAME IS MOMOKA-SENPAI!
STAB

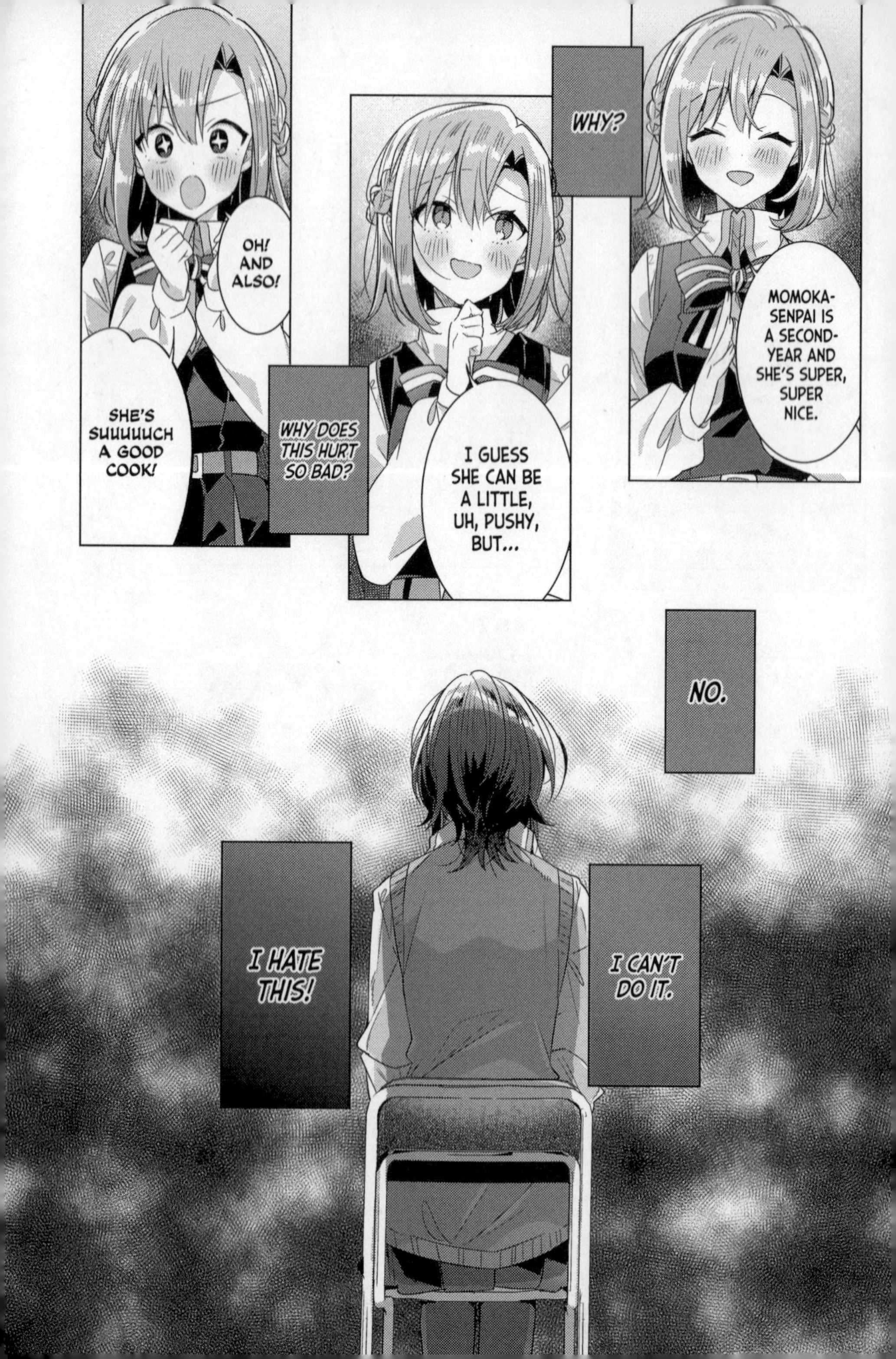
MOMOKA-SENPAI IS A SECOND-YEAR AND SHE'S SUPER, SUPER NICE.
WHY?
I GUESS SHE CAN BE A LITTLE, UH, PUSHY, BUT...
WHY DOES THIS HURT SO BAD?
OH! AND ALSO!
SHE'S SUUUUUCH A GOOD COOK!
NO.
I CAN'T DO IT.
I HATE THIS!

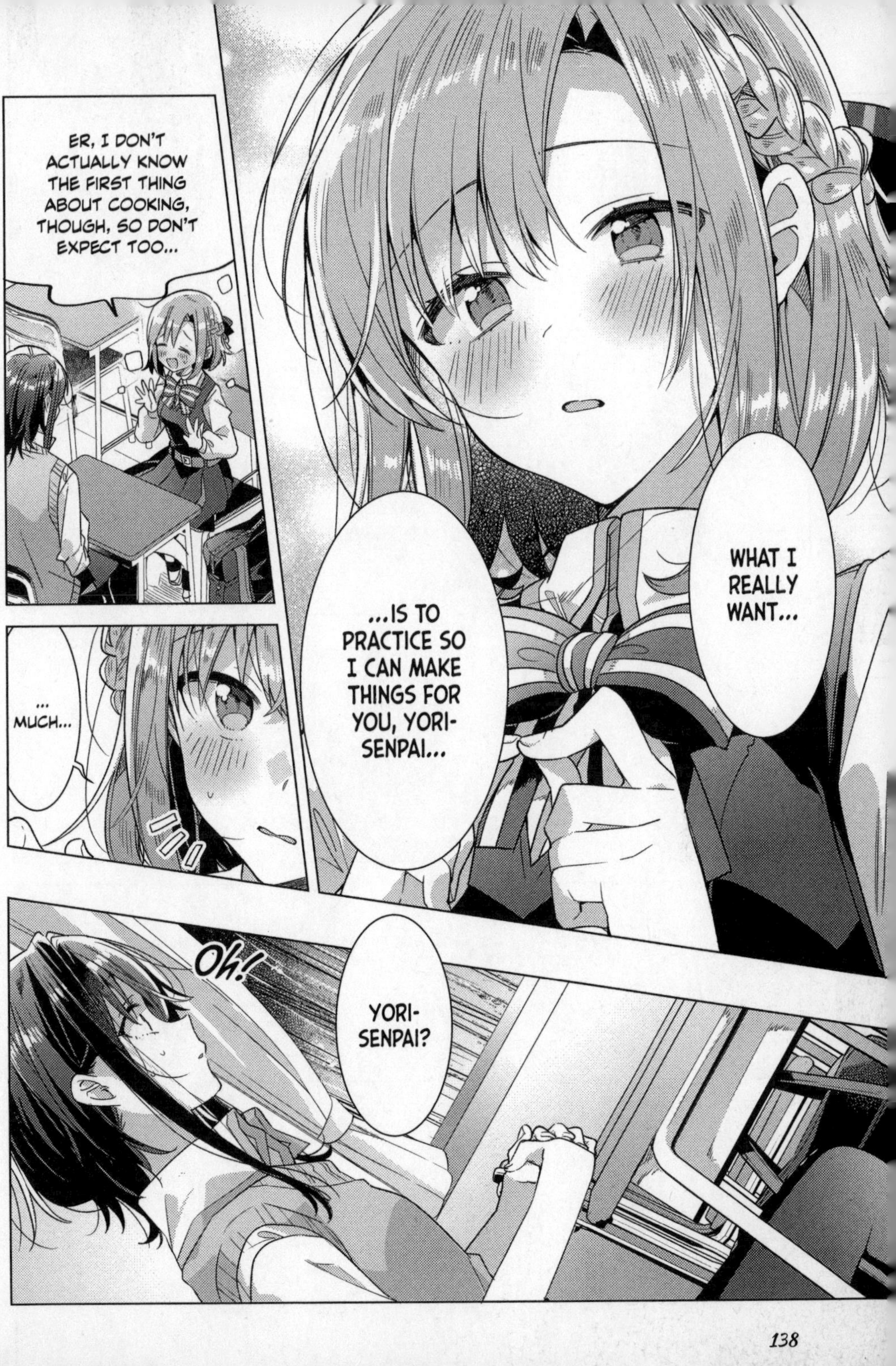
WHAT I REALLY WANT...
...IS TO PRACTICE SO I CAN MAKE THINGS FOR YOU, YORI-SENPAI...
ER, I DON'T ACTUALLY KNOW THE FIRST THING ABOUT COOKING, THOUGH, SO DON'T EXPECT TOO...
... MUCH...
YORI-SENPAI?
Oh!

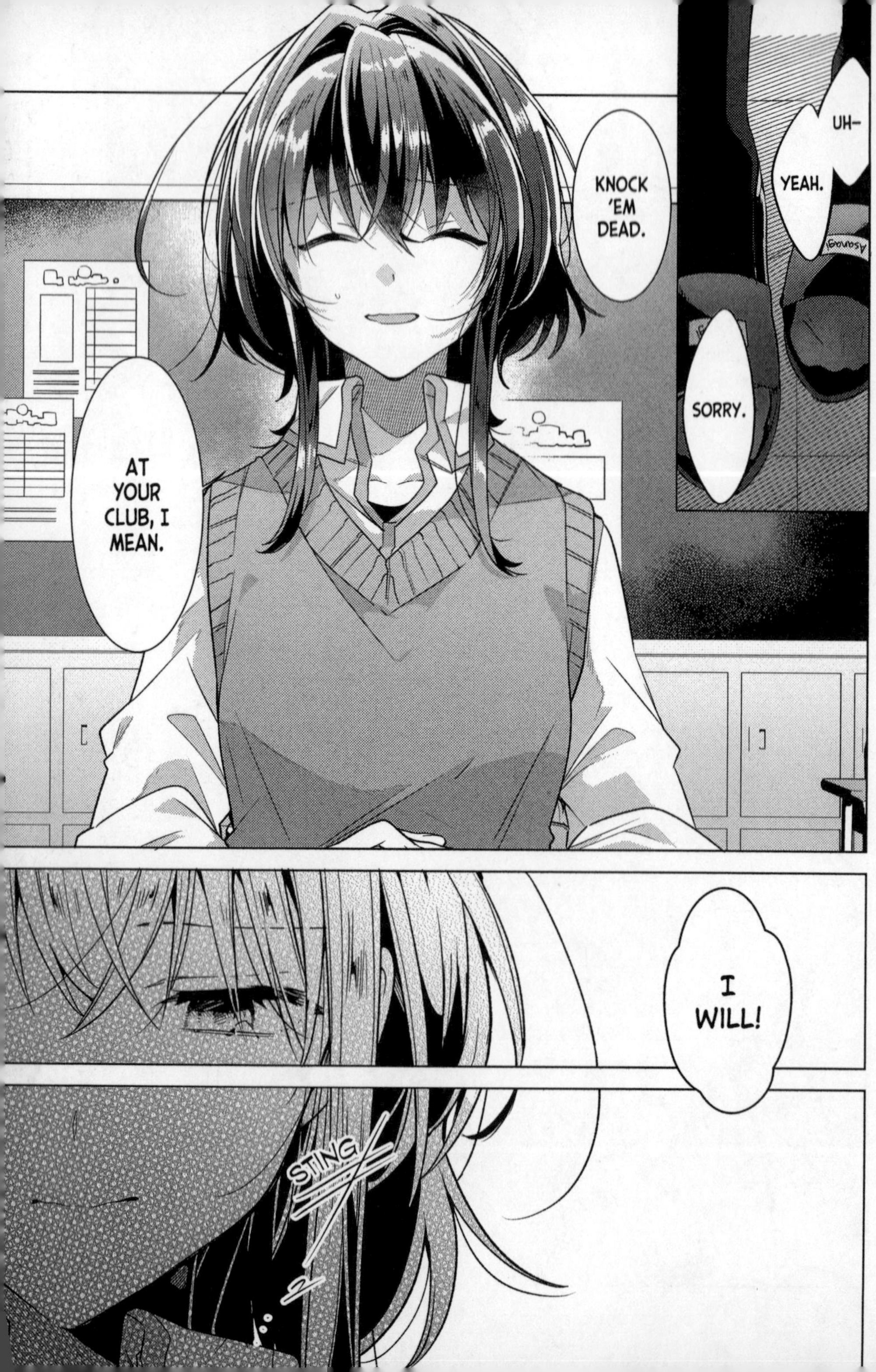
UH–
YEAH.
SORRY.
KNOCK 'EM DEAD.
AT YOUR CLUB, I MEAN.
I WILL!
STING

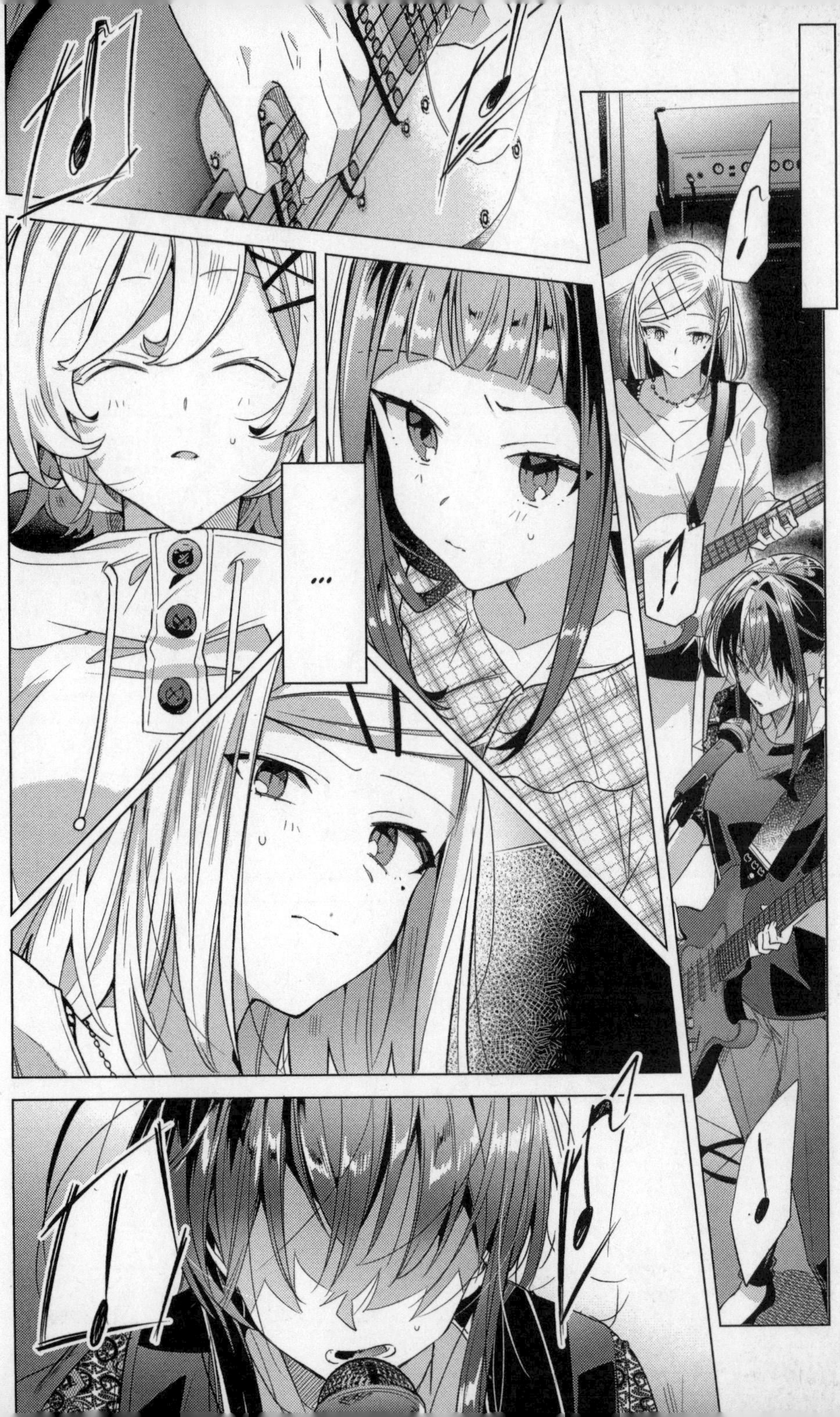
...

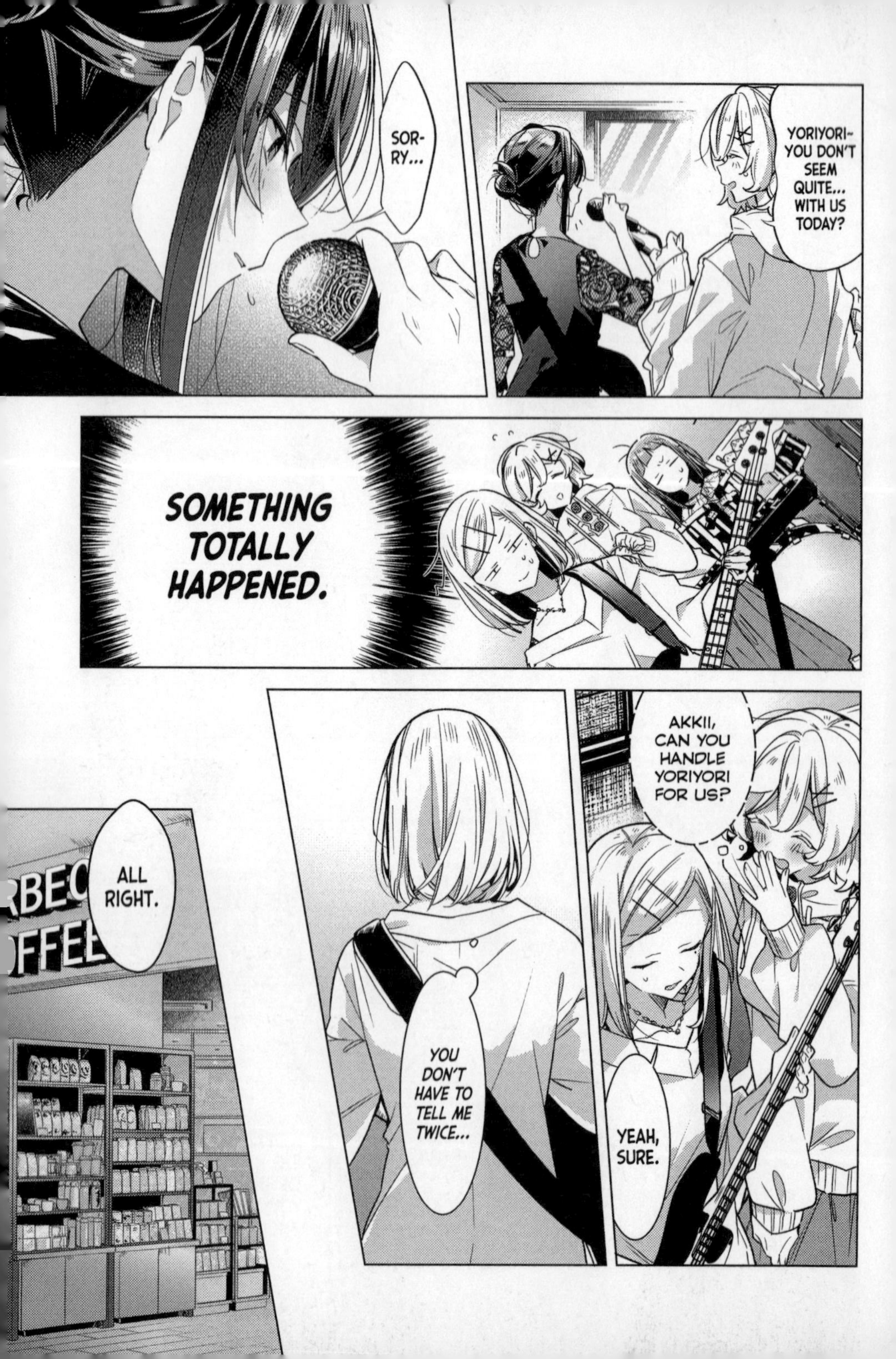

YORIYORI~ YOU DON'T SEEM QUITE... WITH US TODAY?
SORRY...
SOMETHING TOTALLY HAPPENED.
AKKII, CAN YOU HANDLE YORIYORI FOR US?
YEAH, SURE.
YOU DON'T HAVE TO TELL ME TWICE...
ALL RIGHT.

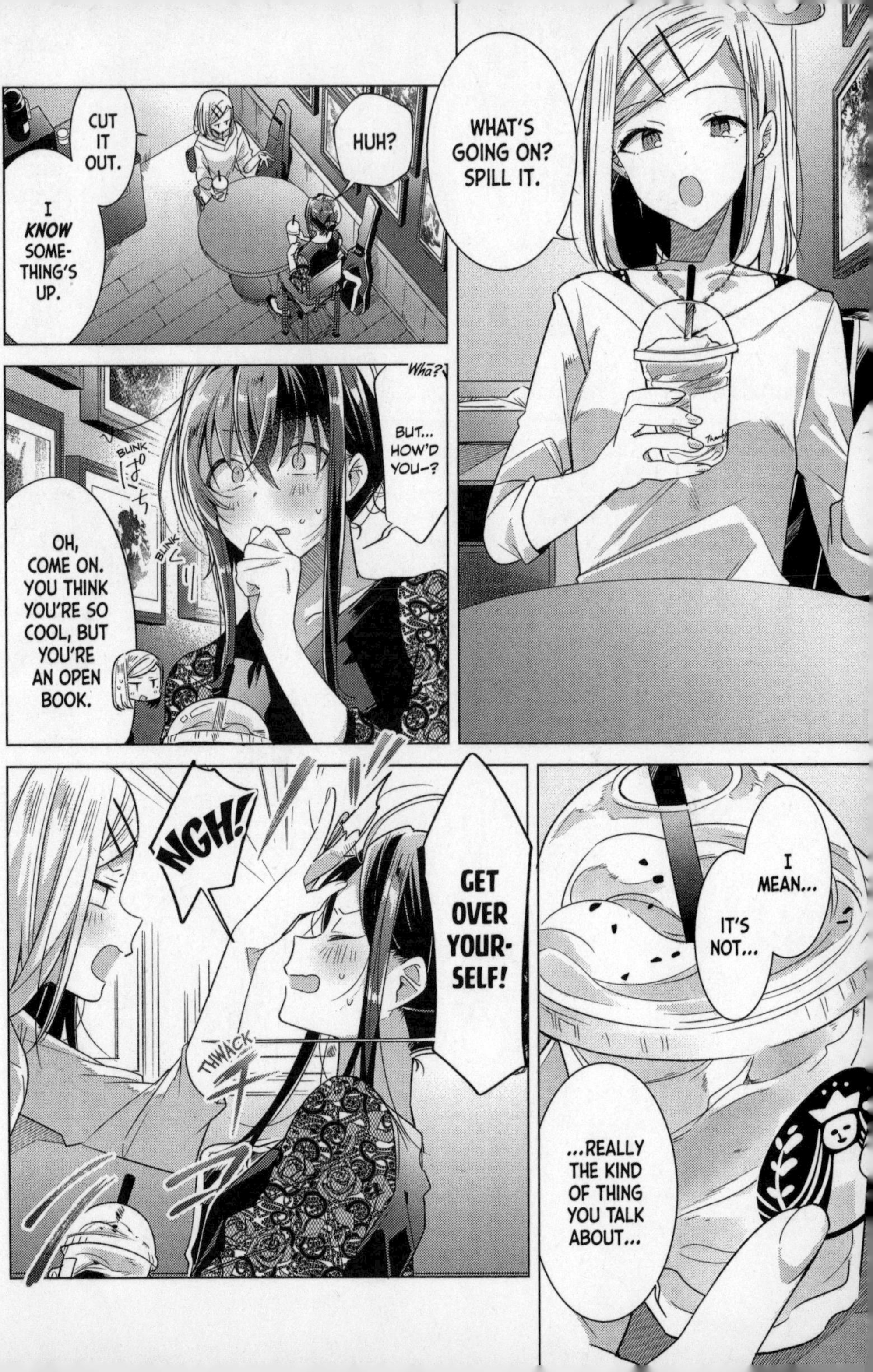
WHAT'S GOING ON? SPILL IT.
HUH?
CUT IT OUT.
I *KNOW* SOMETHING'S UP.
Wha?
BUT... HOW'D YOU-?
BLINK ぱち
BLINK くり
OH, COME ON. YOU THINK YOU'RE SO COOL, BUT YOU'RE AN OPEN BOOK.
I MEAN...
IT'S NOT...
...REALLY THE KIND OF THING YOU TALK ABOUT...
GET OVER YOURSELF!
NGH!
THWACK

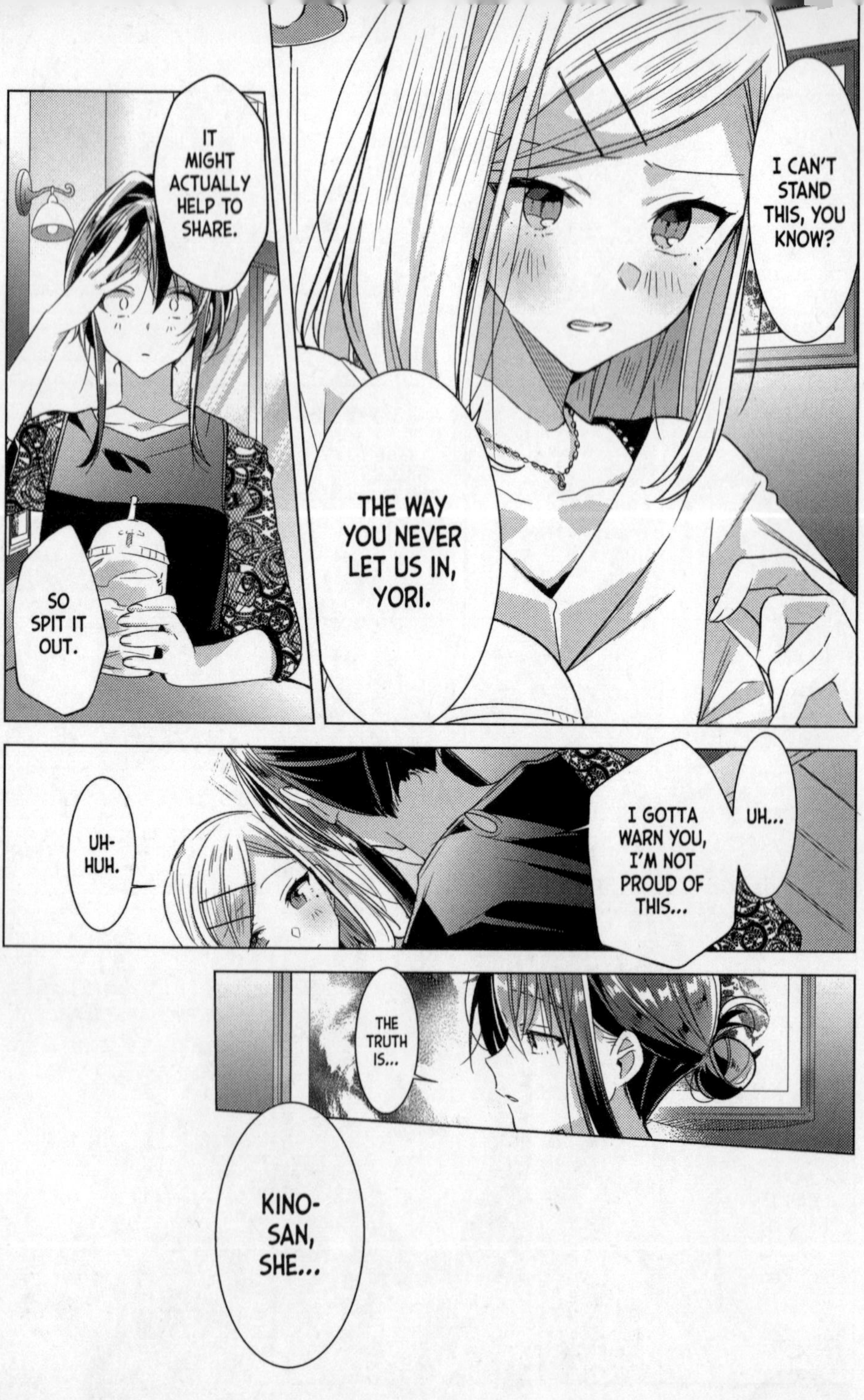
I CAN'T STAND THIS, YOU KNOW?
THE WAY YOU NEVER LET US IN, YORI.
IT MIGHT ACTUALLY HELP TO SHARE.
SO SPIT IT OUT.
UH...
I GOTTA WARN YOU, I'M NOT PROUD OF THIS...
UH-HUH.
THE TRUTH IS...
KINO-SAN, SHE...

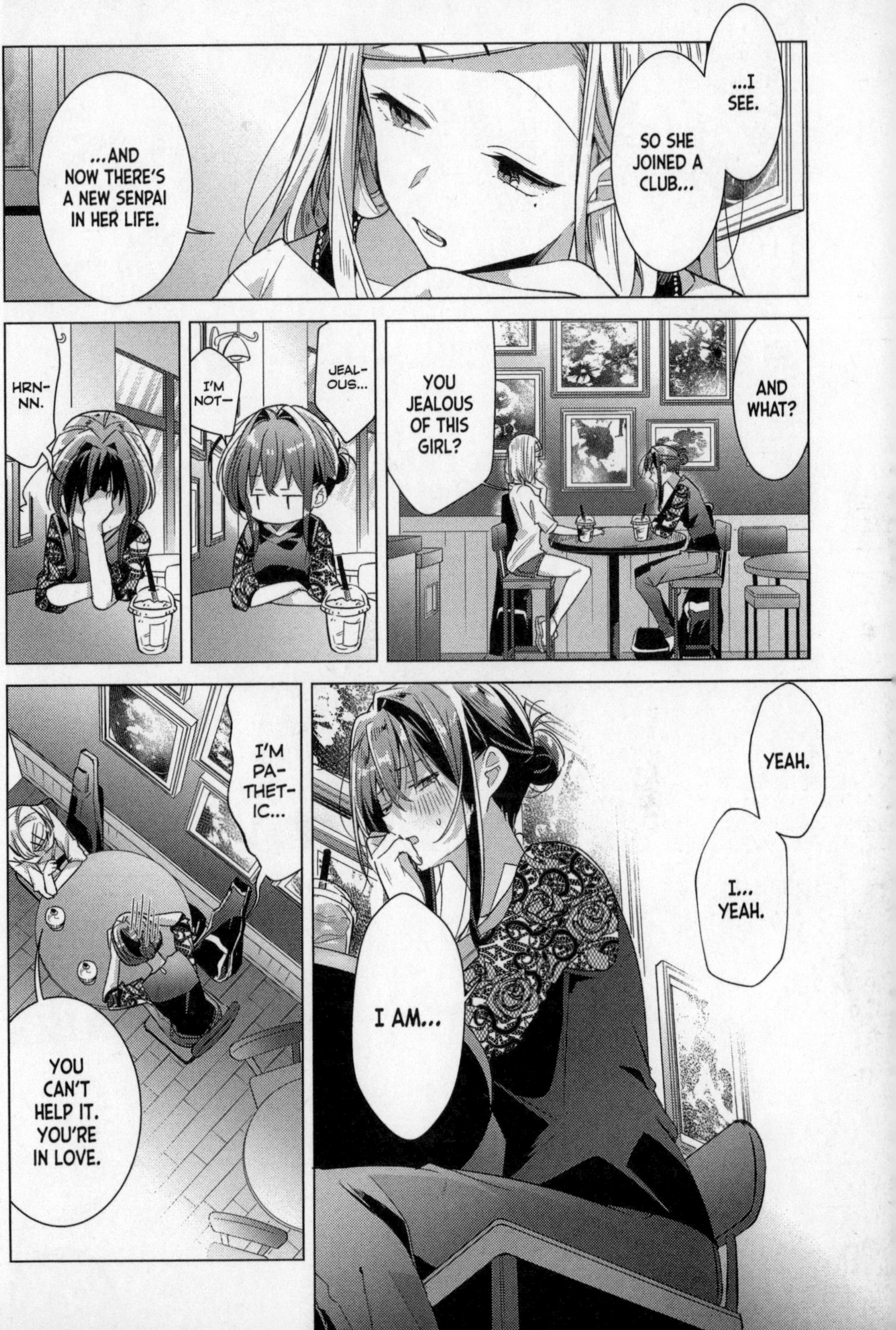
...I SEE.
SO SHE JOINED A CLUB...
...AND NOW THERE'S A NEW SENPAI IN HER LIFE.
AND WHAT?
YOU JEALOUS OF THIS GIRL?
JEAL-OUS...
I'M NOT—
HRN-NN.
YEAH.
I... YEAH.
I AM...
I'M PA-THET-IC...
YOU CAN'T HELP IT. YOU'RE IN LOVE.

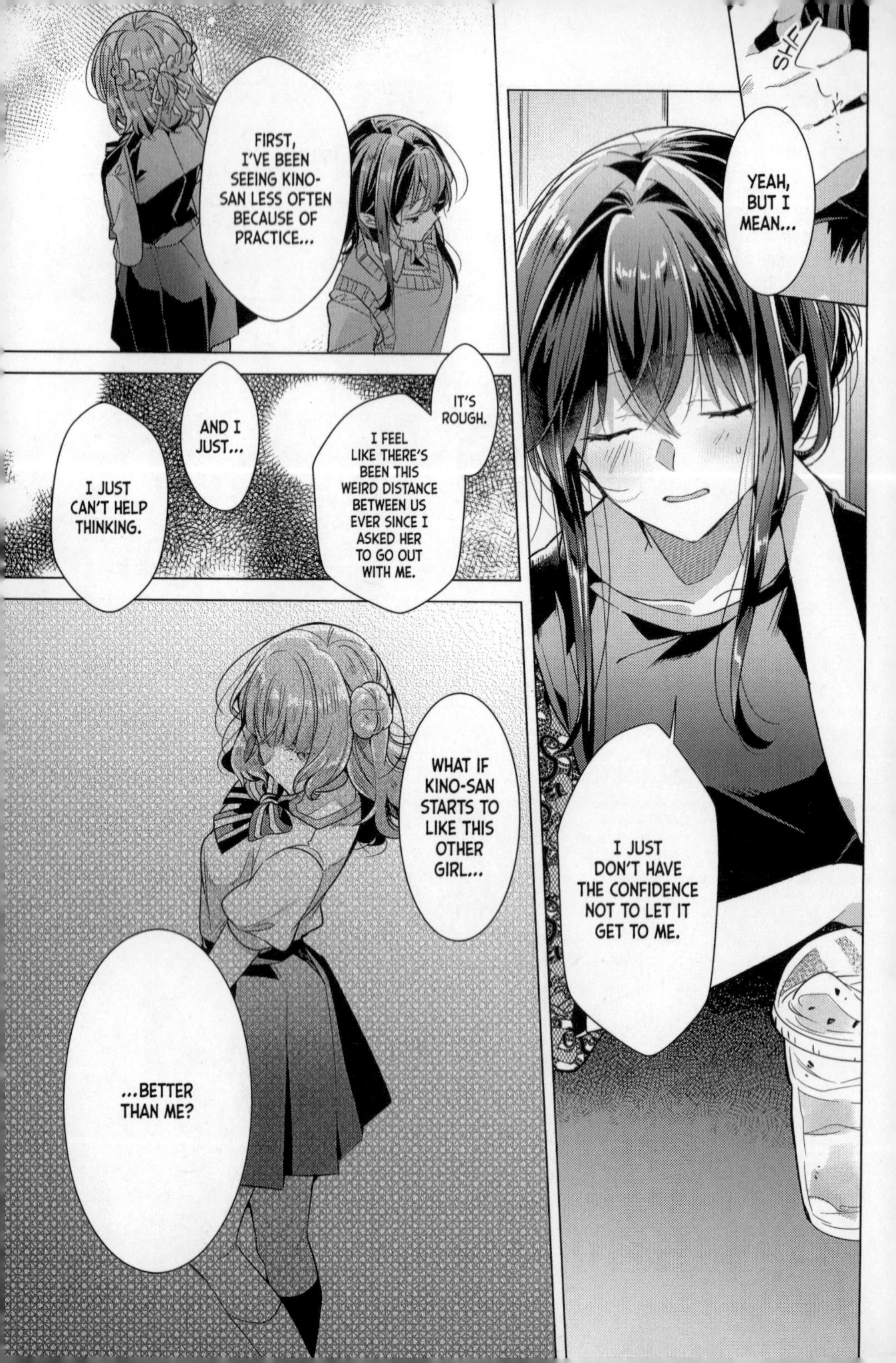
SHF
YEAH, BUT I MEAN...
I JUST DON'T HAVE THE CONFIDENCE NOT TO LET IT GET TO ME.
FIRST, I'VE BEEN SEEING KINO-SAN LESS OFTEN BECAUSE OF PRACTICE...
IT'S ROUGH.
I FEEL LIKE THERE'S BEEN THIS WEIRD DISTANCE BETWEEN US EVER SINCE I ASKED HER TO GO OUT WITH ME.
AND I JUST...
I JUST CAN'T HELP THINKING.
WHAT IF KINO-SAN STARTS TO LIKE THIS OTHER GIRL...
...BETTER THAN ME?

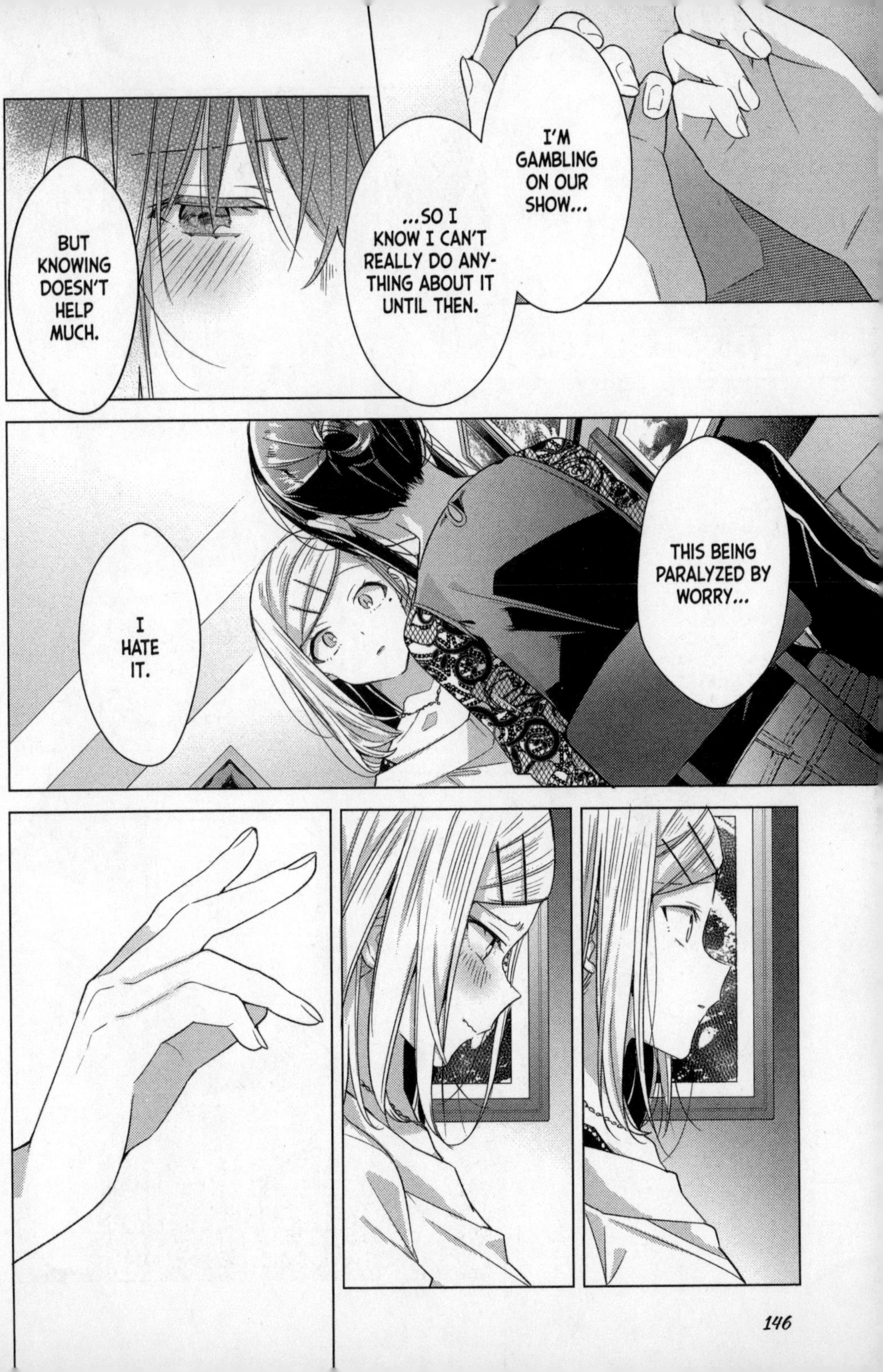
I'M GAMBLING ON OUR SHOW...
...SO I KNOW I CAN'T REALLY DO ANY-THING ABOUT IT UNTIL THEN.
BUT KNOWING DOESN'T HELP MUCH.
THIS BEING PARALYZED BY WORRY...
I HATE IT.

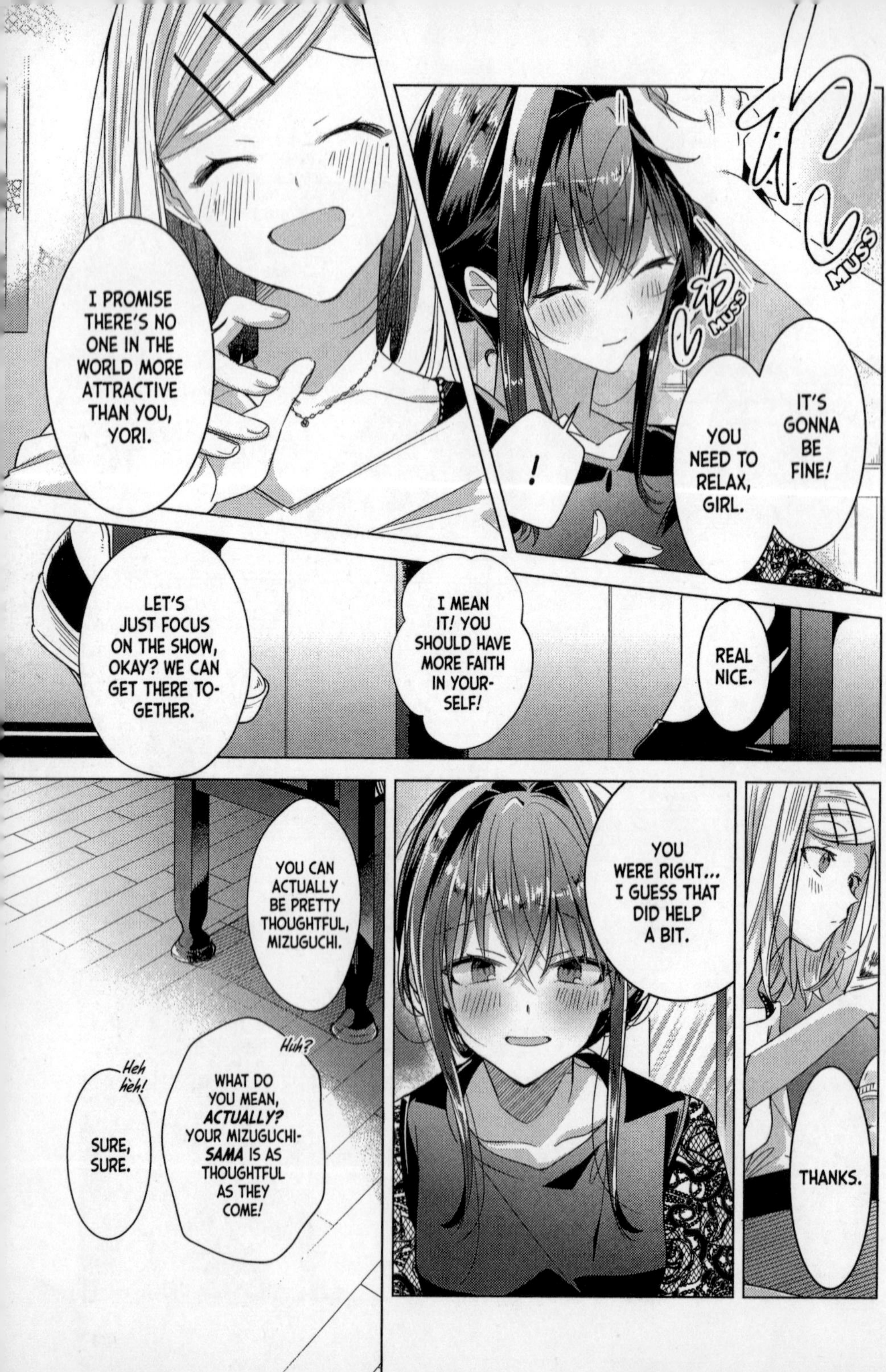
MUSS
MUSS
IT'S GONNA BE FINE!
YOU NEED TO RELAX, GIRL.
!
I PROMISE THERE'S NO ONE IN THE WORLD MORE ATTRACTIVE THAN YOU, YORI.
REAL NICE.
I MEAN IT! YOU SHOULD HAVE MORE FAITH IN YOURSELF!
LET'S JUST FOCUS ON THE SHOW, OKAY? WE CAN GET THERE TOGETHER.
THANKS.
YOU WERE RIGHT... I GUESS THAT DID HELP A BIT.
YOU CAN ACTUALLY BE PRETTY THOUGHTFUL, MIZUGUCHI.
Huh?
WHAT DO YOU MEAN, *ACTUALLY?* YOUR MIZUGUCHI-*SAMA* IS AS THOUGHTFUL AS THEY COME!
Heh heh!
SURE, SURE.

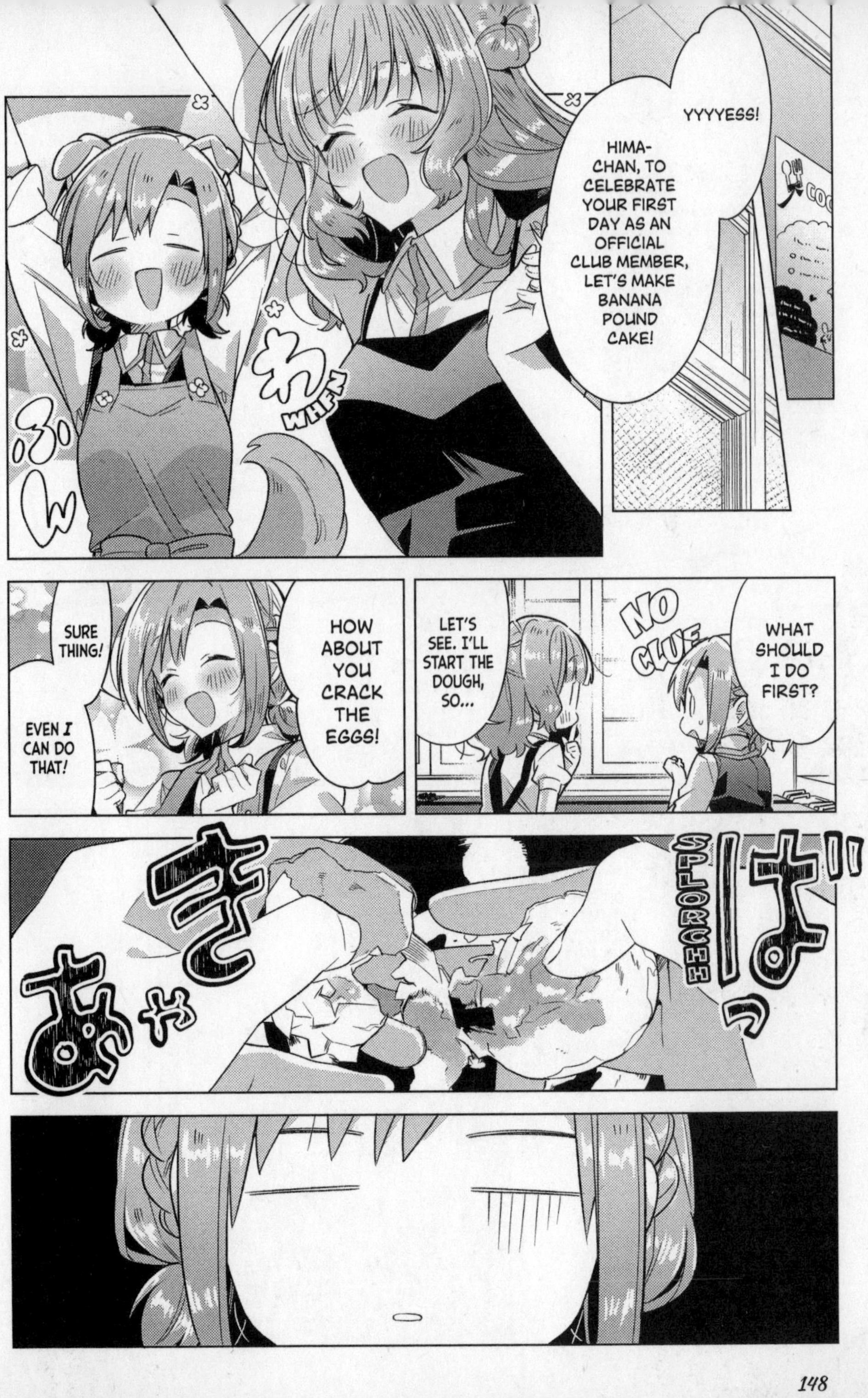
YYYYESS!
HIMA-CHAN, TO CELEBRATE YOUR FIRST DAY AS AN OFFICIAL CLUB MEMBER, LET'S MAKE BANANA POUND CAKE!
WHFZ
WHAT SHOULD I DO FIRST?
NO CLUE
LET'S SEE. I'LL START THE DOUGH, SO...
HOW ABOUT YOU CRACK THE EGGS!
SURE THING!
EVEN I CAN DO THAT!
SPLORCHH

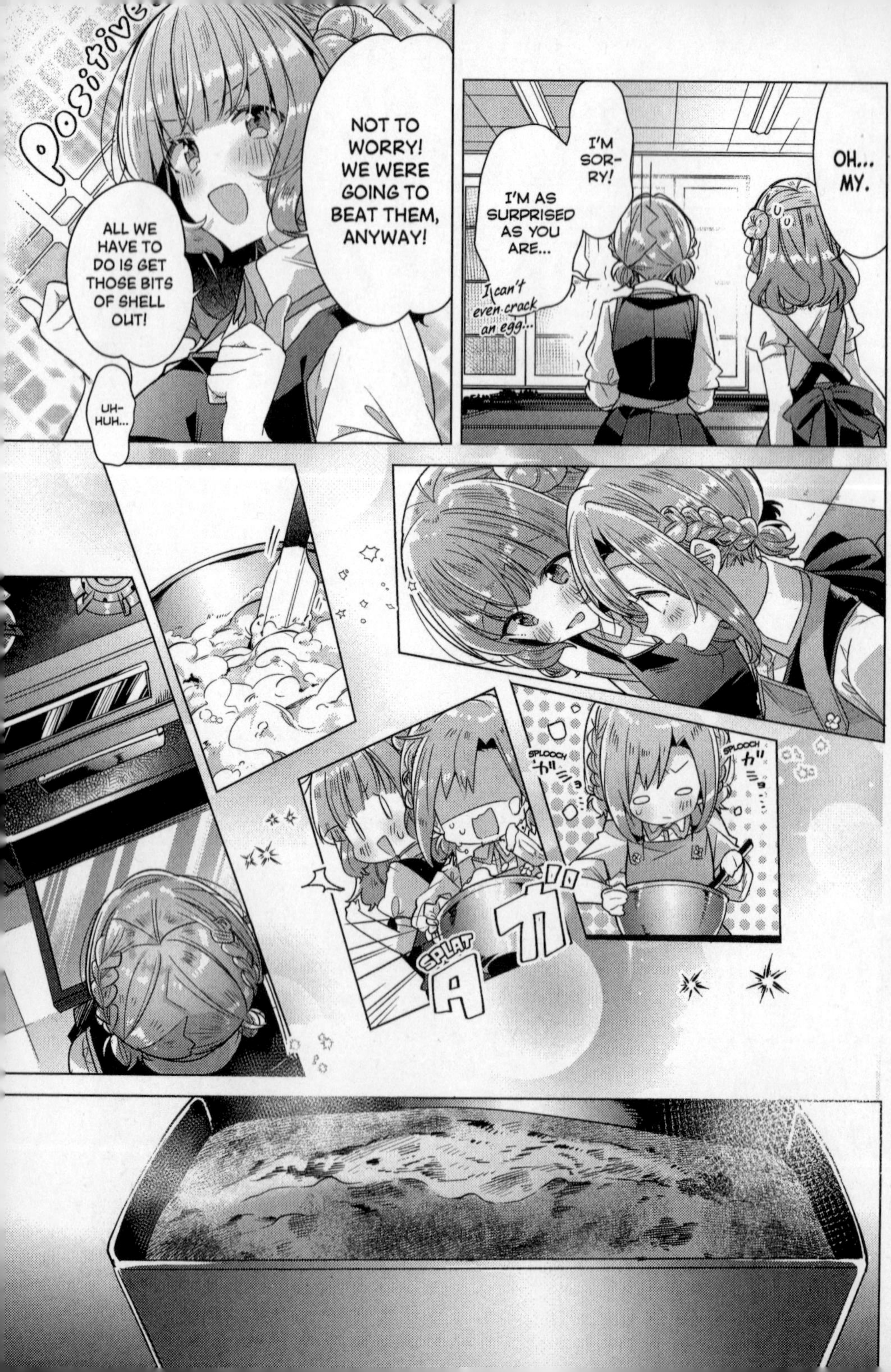
OH... MY.
I'M SORRY!
I'M AS SURPRISED AS YOU ARE...
I can't even crack an egg...
NOT TO WORRY! WE WERE GOING TO BEAT THEM, ANYWAY!
Positive
ALL WE HAVE TO DO IS GET THOSE BITS OF SHELL OUT!
UH-HUH...
SPLOOCH
SPLOOCH
SPLAT
ガ

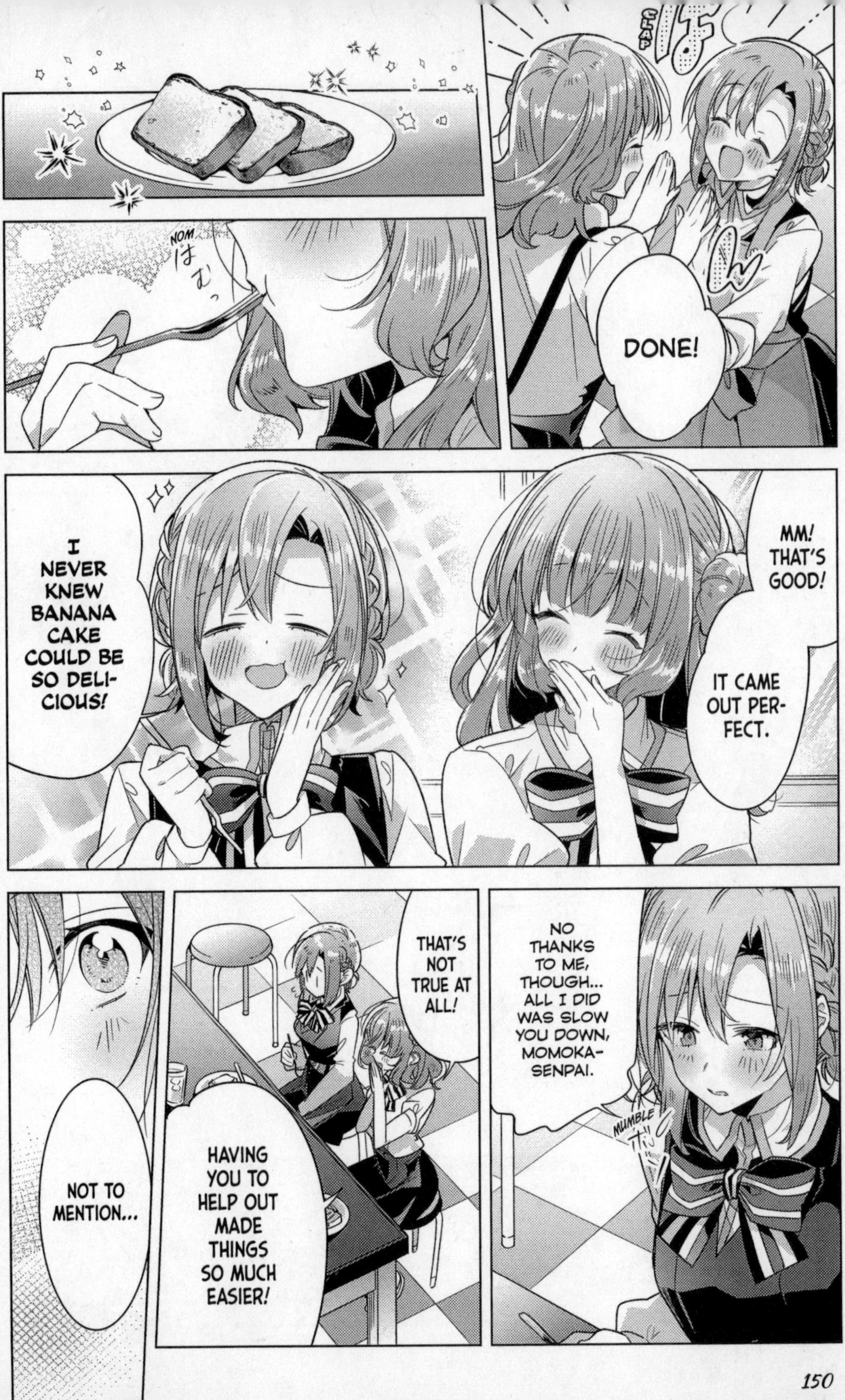
CLAP
ぱ
DONE!
NOM
はむっ
MM! THAT'S GOOD!
IT CAME OUT PERFECT.
I NEVER KNEW BANANA CAKE COULD BE SO DELICIOUS!
NO THANKS TO ME, THOUGH... ALL I DID WAS SLOW YOU DOWN, MOMOKA-SENPAI.
MUMBLE
THAT'S NOT TRUE AT ALL!
HAVING YOU TO HELP OUT MADE THINGS SO MUCH EASIER!
NOT TO MENTION...

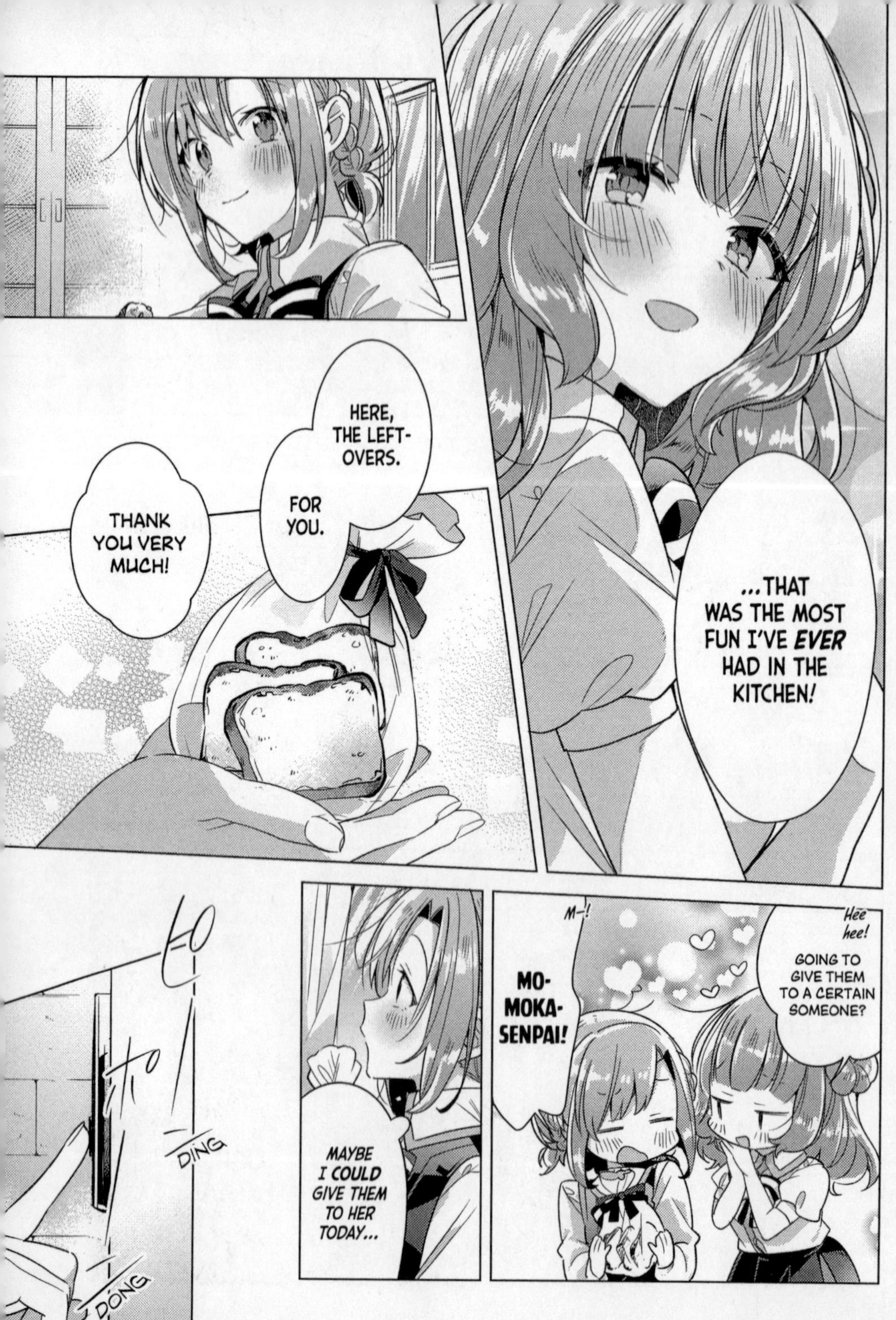
...THAT WAS THE MOST FUN I'VE *EVER* HAD IN THE KITCHEN!
HERE, THE LEFT-OVERS.
FOR YOU.
THANK YOU VERY MUCH!
Hee hee!
GOING TO GIVE THEM TO A CERTAIN SOMEONE?
M-!
MO-MOKA-SENPAI!
MAYBE I COULD GIVE THEM TO HER TODAY...
DING
DONG

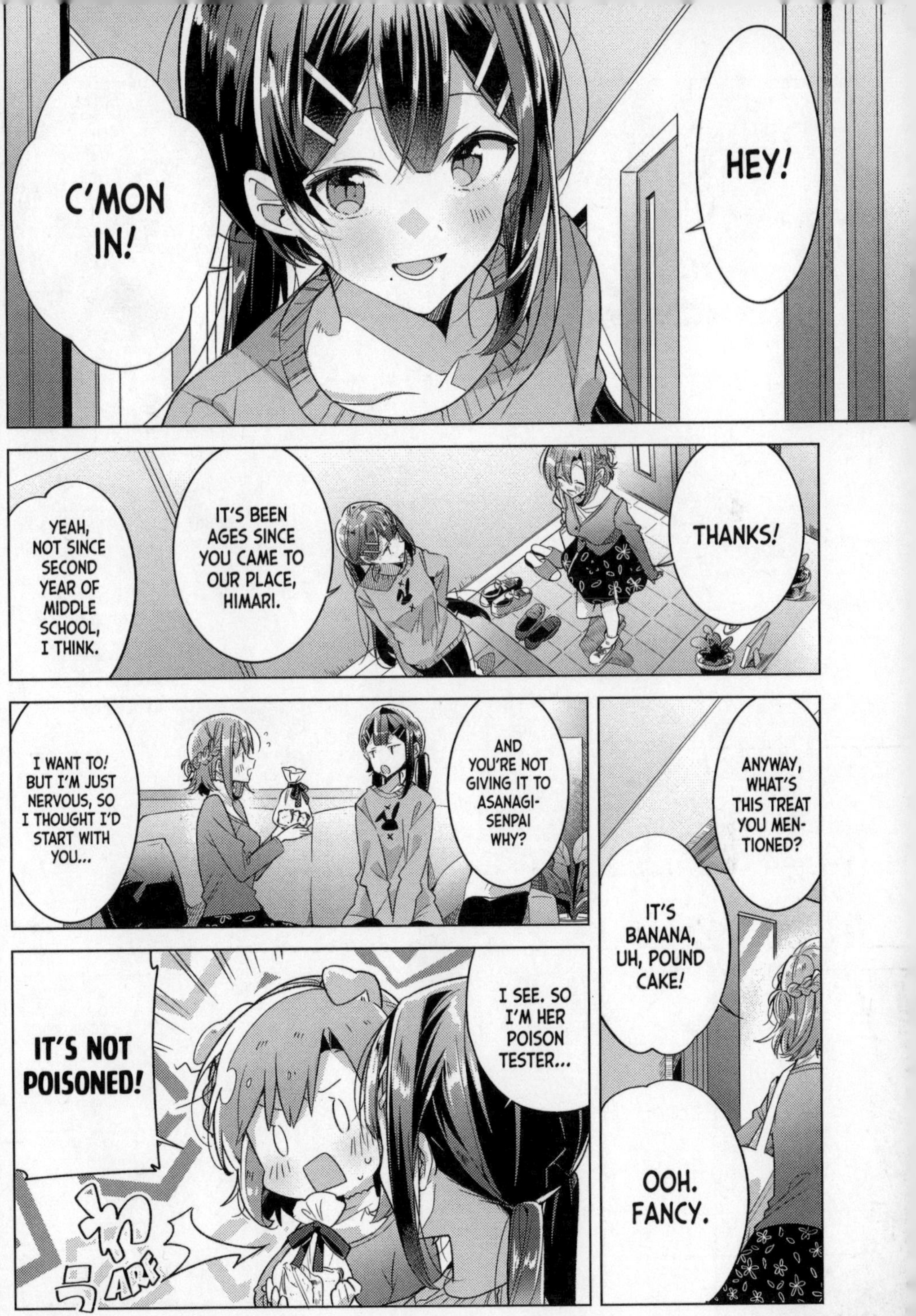
HEY!
C'MON IN!
THANKS!
IT'S BEEN AGES SINCE YOU CAME TO OUR PLACE, HIMARI.
YEAH, NOT SINCE SECOND YEAR OF MIDDLE SCHOOL, I THINK.
ANYWAY, WHAT'S THIS TREAT YOU MEN-TIONED?
IT'S BANANA, UH, POUND CAKE!
OOH. FANCY.
AND YOU'RE NOT GIVING IT TO ASANAGI-SENPAI WHY?
I WANT TO! BUT I'M JUST NERVOUS, SO I THOUGHT I'D START WITH YOU...
I SEE. SO I'M HER POISON TESTER...
IT'S NOT POISONED!
わう
ARF

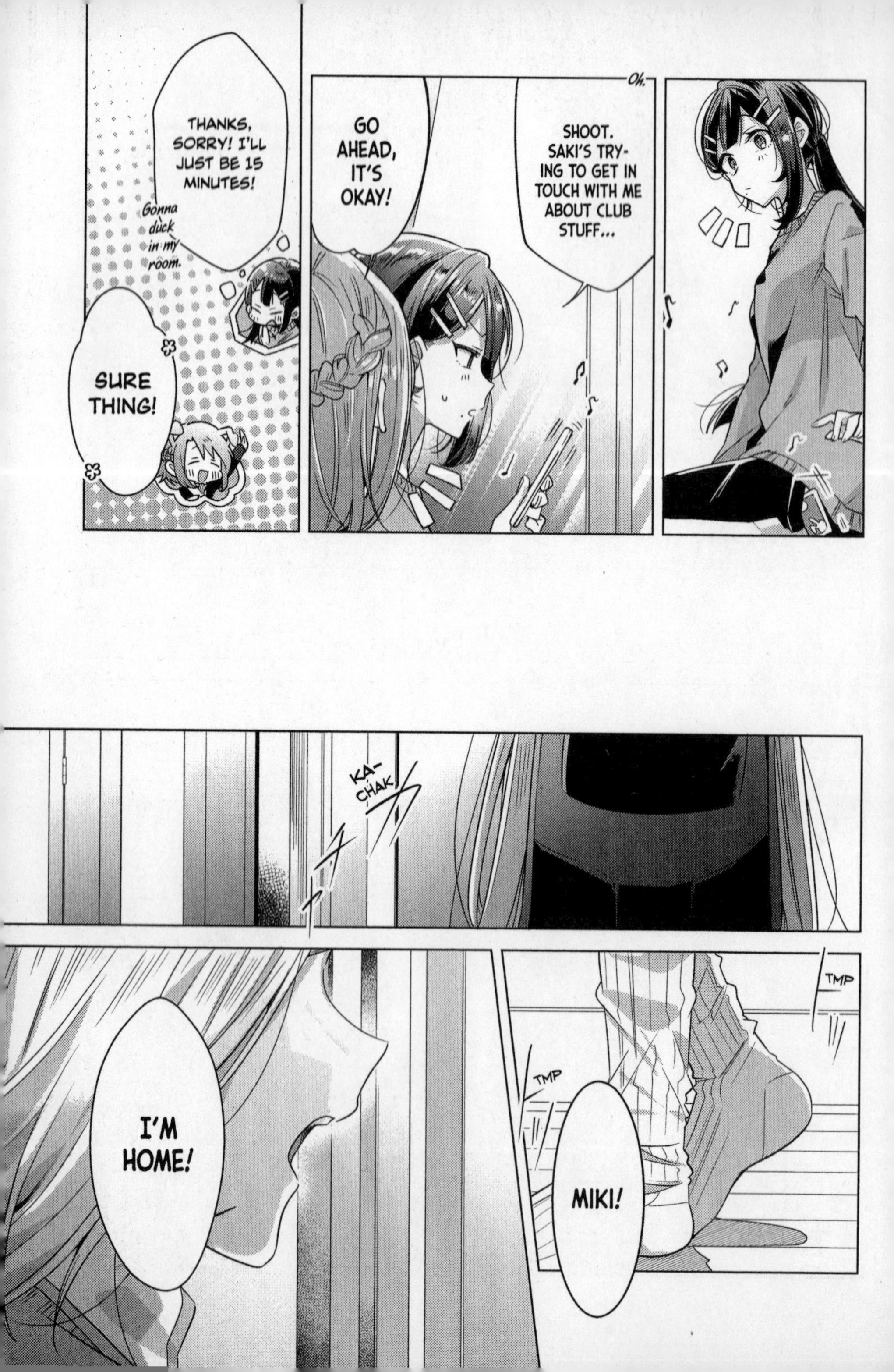
Oh.
SHOOT. SAKI'S TRY-ING TO GET IN TOUCH WITH ME ABOUT CLUB STUFF...
GO AHEAD, IT'S OKAY!
THANKS, SORRY! I'LL JUST BE 15 MINUTES!
Gonna duck in my room.
SURE THING!
KA-CHAK
TMP
TMP
MIKI!
I'M HOME!

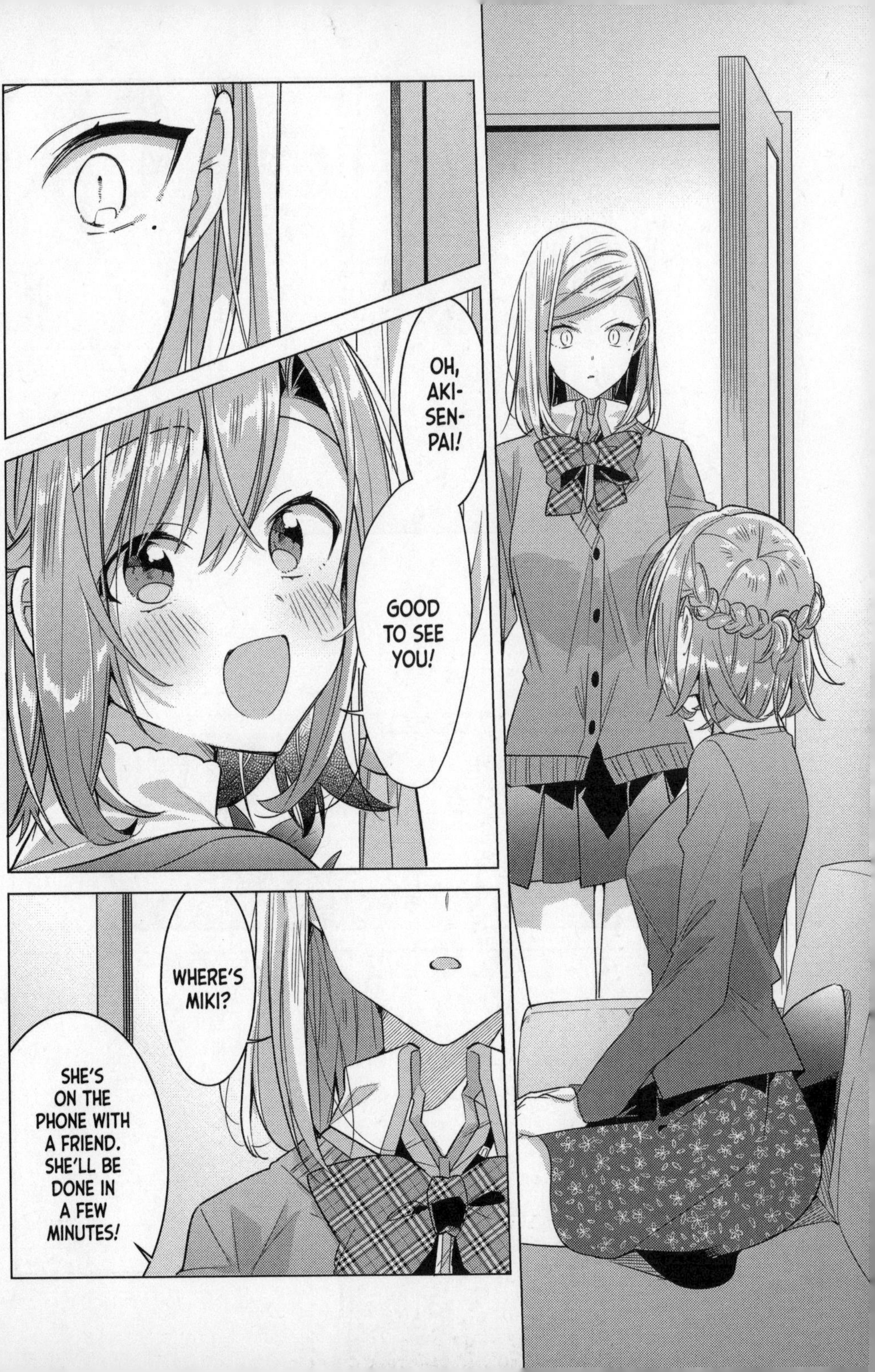
OH, AKI-SEN-PAI!
GOOD TO SEE YOU!
WHERE'S MIKI?
SHE'S ON THE PHONE WITH A FRIEND. SHE'LL BE DONE IN A FEW MINUTES!

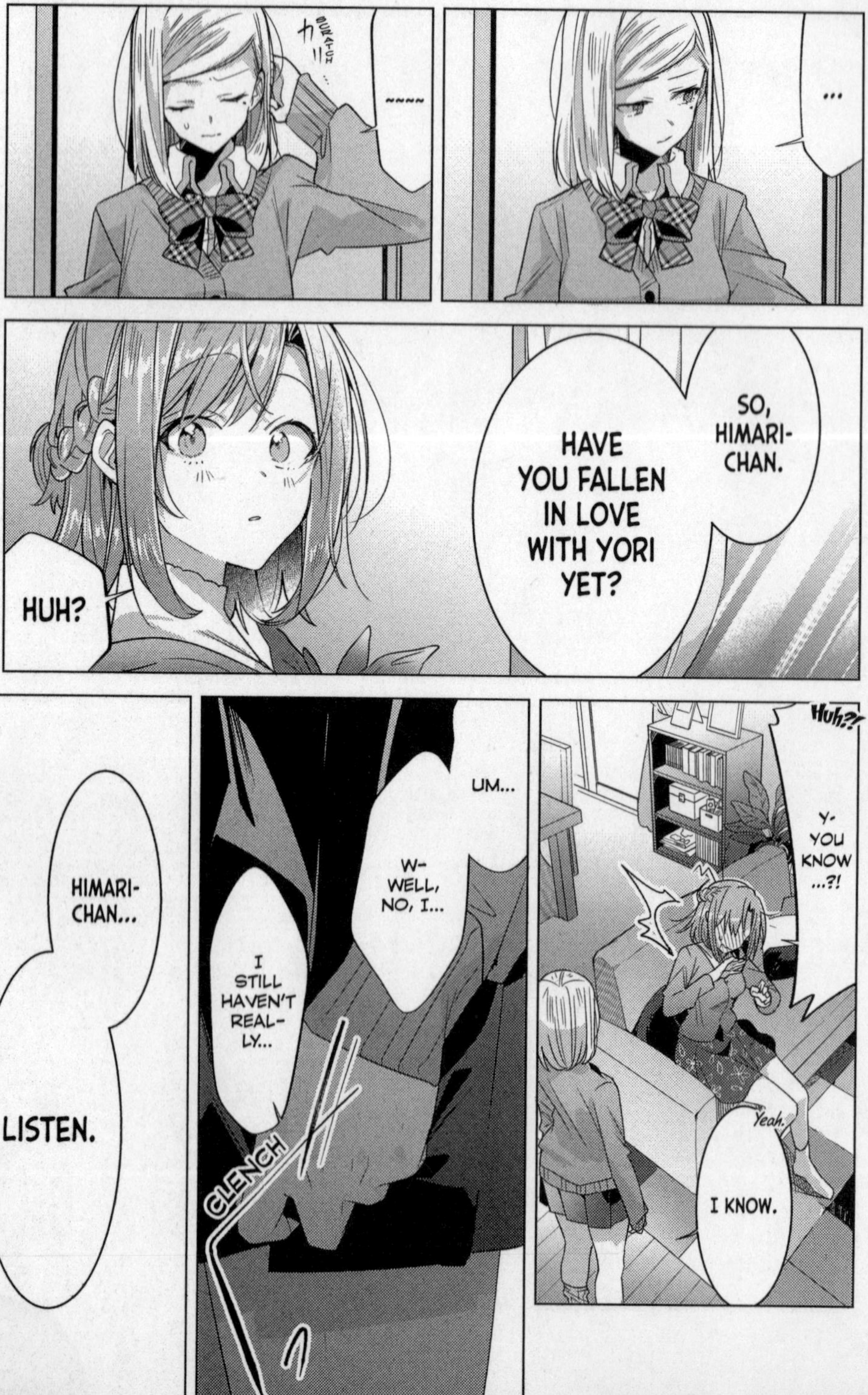
...
SCRATCH
~~~~
SO, HIMARI-CHAN.
HAVE YOU FALLEN IN LOVE WITH YORI YET?
HUH?
Huh?!
Y-YOU KNOW...?!
Yeah.
I KNOW.
UM...
W-WELL, NO, I...
I STILL HAVEN'T REALLY...
CLENCH
HIMARI-CHAN...
LISTEN.
~~~~

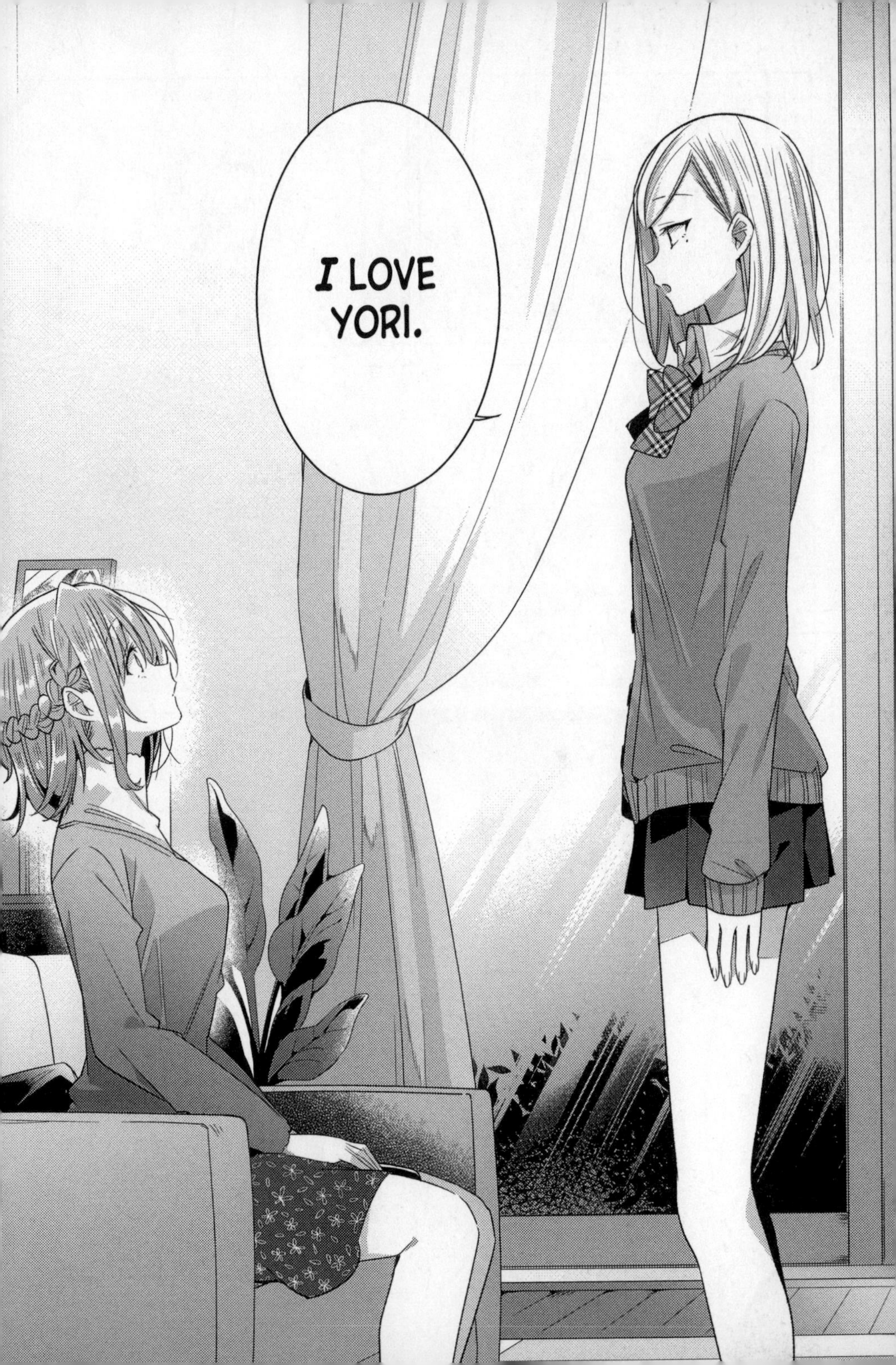
I LOVE YORI.

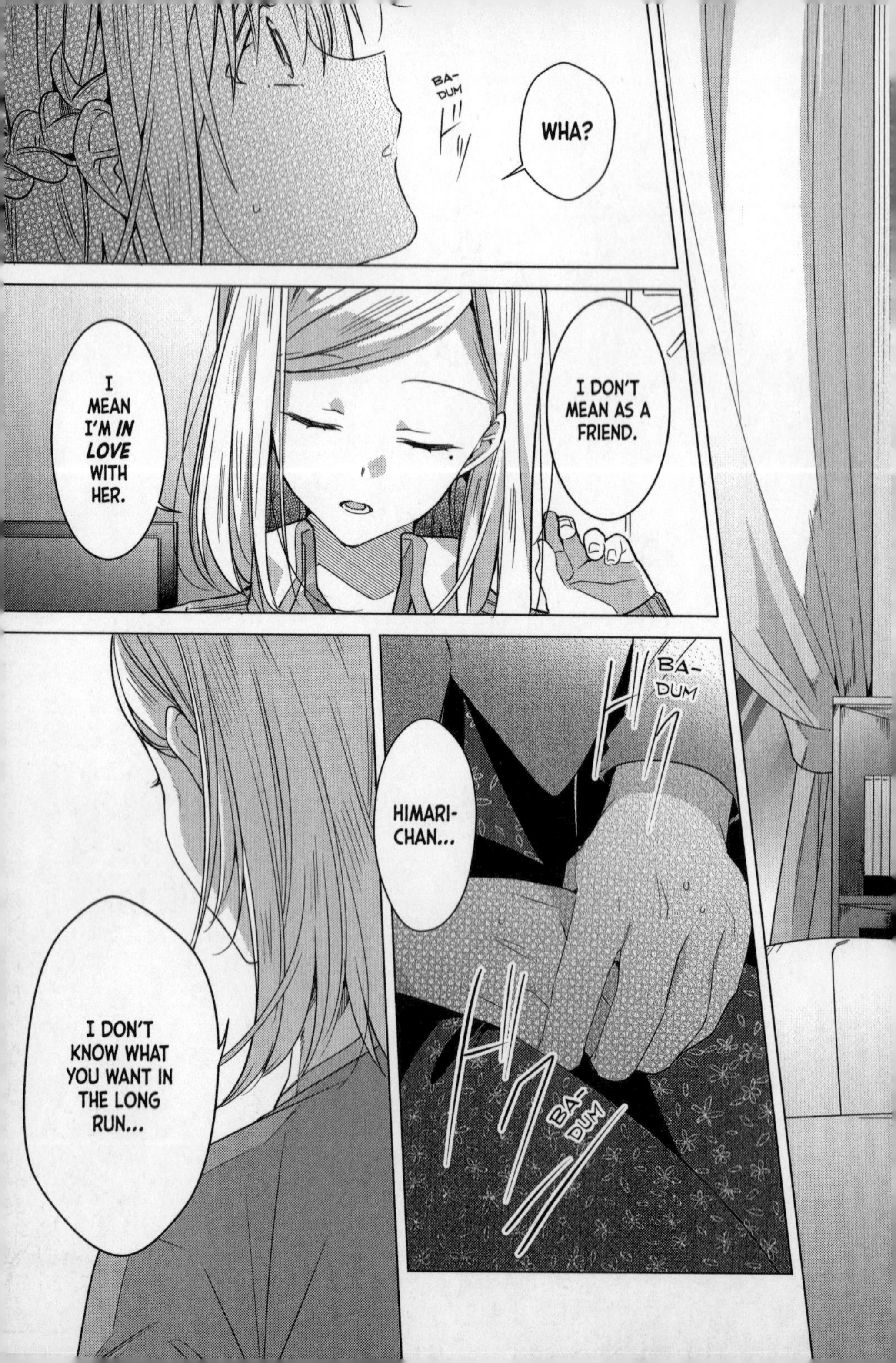
BA-DUM
WHA?
I DON'T MEAN AS A FRIEND.
I MEAN I'M *IN LOVE* WITH HER.
BA-DUM
HIMARI-CHAN...
BA-DUM
I DON'T KNOW WHAT YOU WANT IN THE LONG RUN...

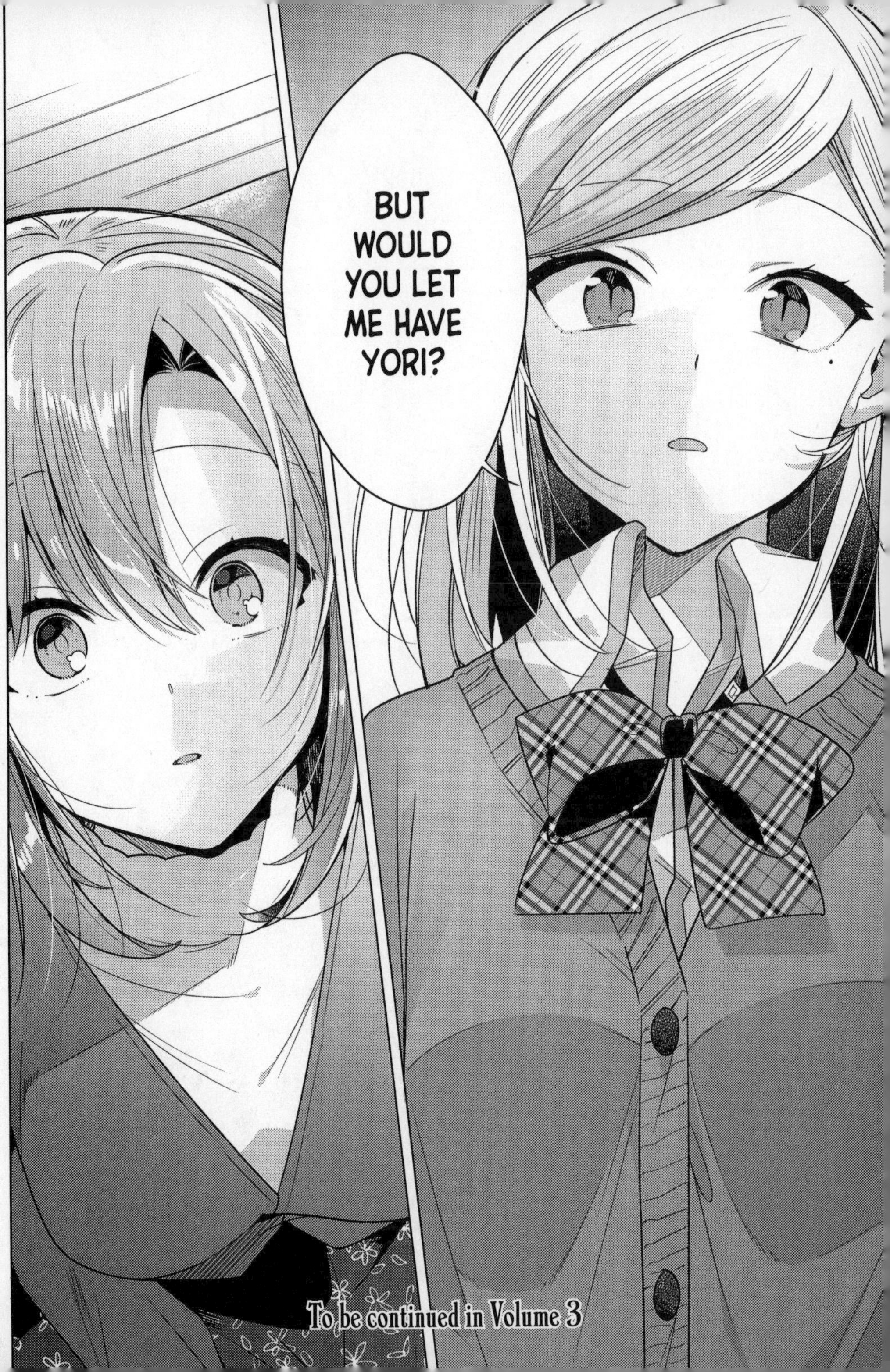
BUT WOULD YOU LET ME HAVE YORI?
To be continued in Volume 3

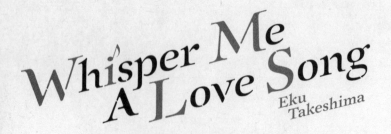

Whisper Me
A Love Song
Eku
Takeshima

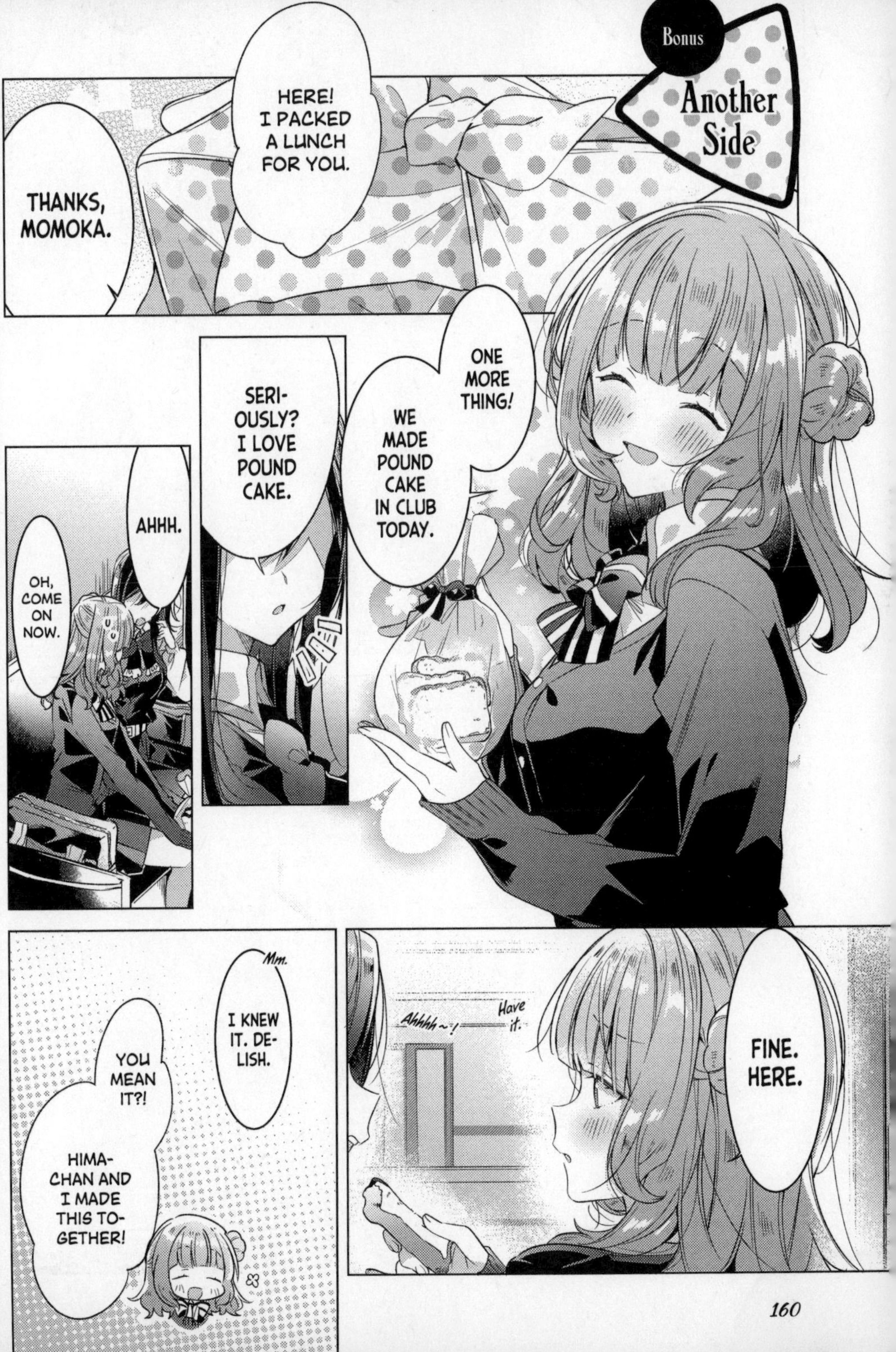
Bonus
Another Side
HERE! I PACKED A LUNCH FOR YOU.
THANKS, MOMOKA.
ONE MORE THING!
WE MADE POUND CAKE IN CLUB TODAY.
SERI-OUSLY? I LOVE POUND CAKE.
AHHH.
OH, COME ON NOW.
FINE. HERE.
Have it.
Ahhhh~!
Mm.
I KNEW IT. DE-LISH.
YOU MEAN IT?!
HIMA-CHAN AND I MADE THIS TO-GETHER!

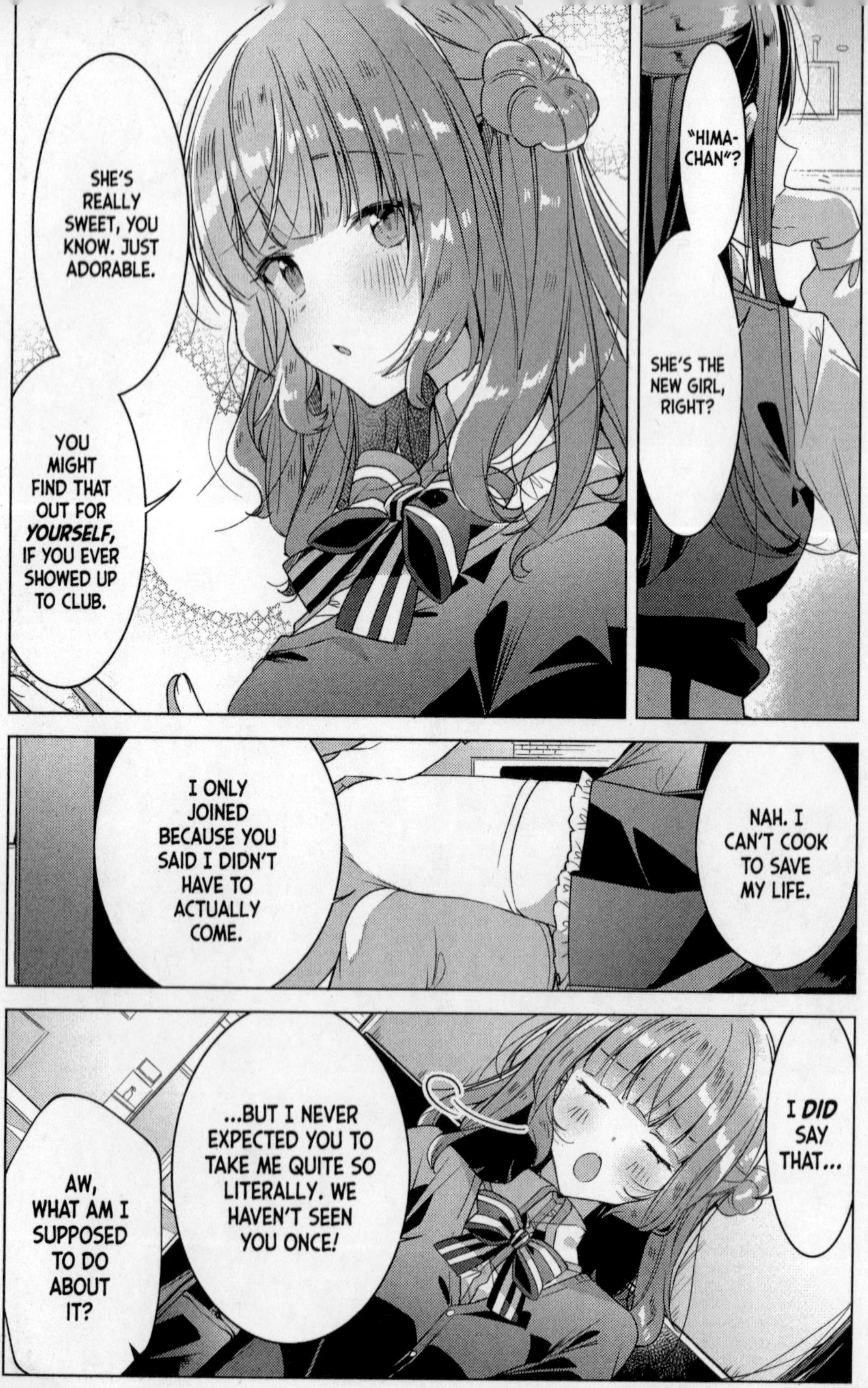
"HIMA-CHAN"?
SHE'S THE NEW GIRL, RIGHT?
SHE'S REALLY SWEET, YOU KNOW. JUST ADORABLE.
YOU MIGHT FIND THAT OUT FOR ***YOURSELF,*** IF YOU EVER SHOWED UP TO CLUB.
NAH. I CAN'T COOK TO SAVE MY LIFE.
I ONLY JOINED BECAUSE YOU SAID I DIDN'T HAVE TO ACTUALLY COME.
I ***DID*** SAY THAT...
...BUT I NEVER EXPECTED YOU TO TAKE ME QUITE SO LITERALLY. WE HAVEN'T SEEN YOU ONCE!
AW, WHAT AM I SUPPOSED TO DO ABOUT IT?

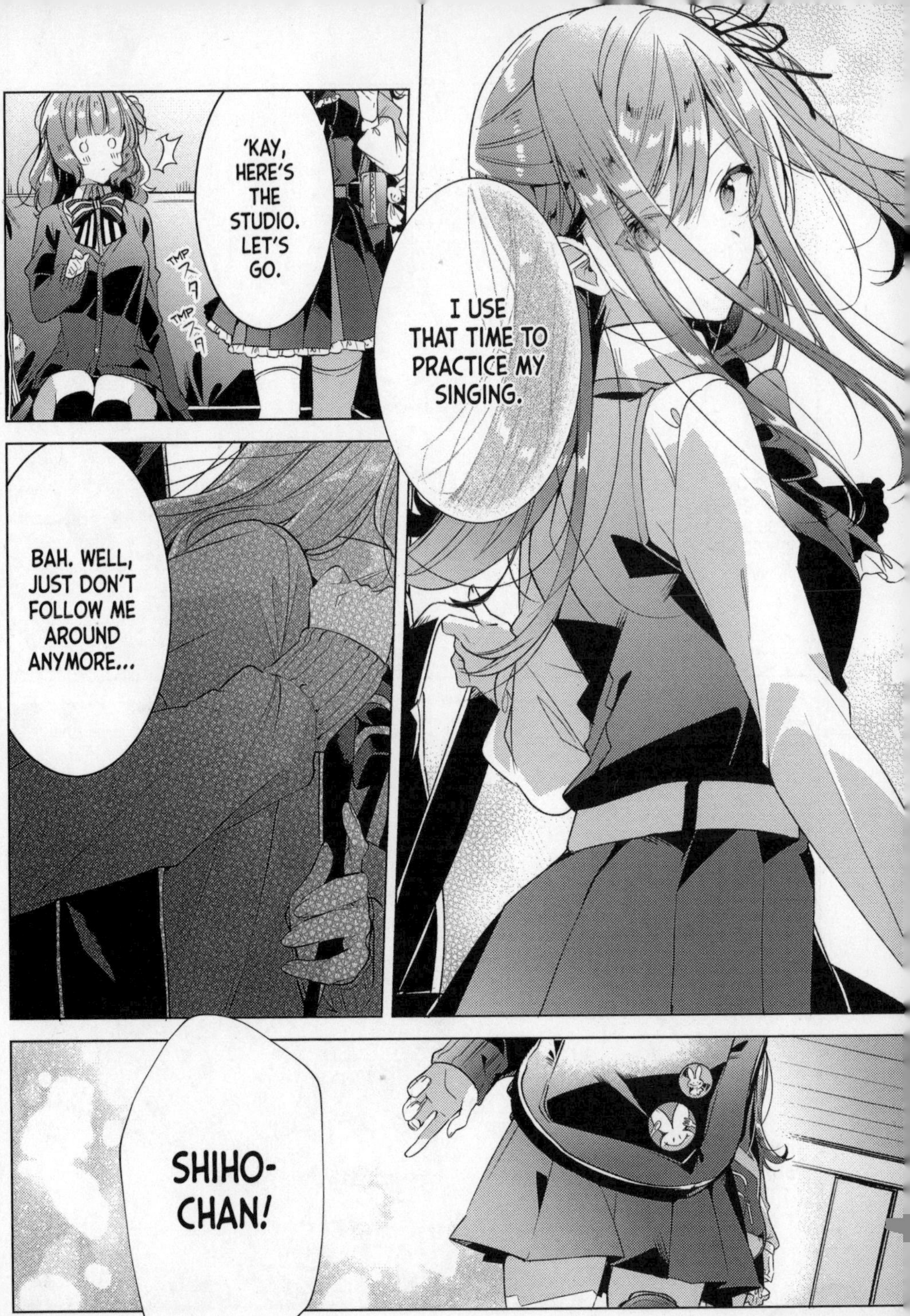

I USE THAT TIME TO PRACTICE MY SINGING.
'KAY, HERE'S THE STUDIO. LET'S GO.
TMP スタ
TMP スタ
BAH. WELL, JUST DON'T FOLLOW ME AROUND ANYMORE...
SHIHO-CHAN!

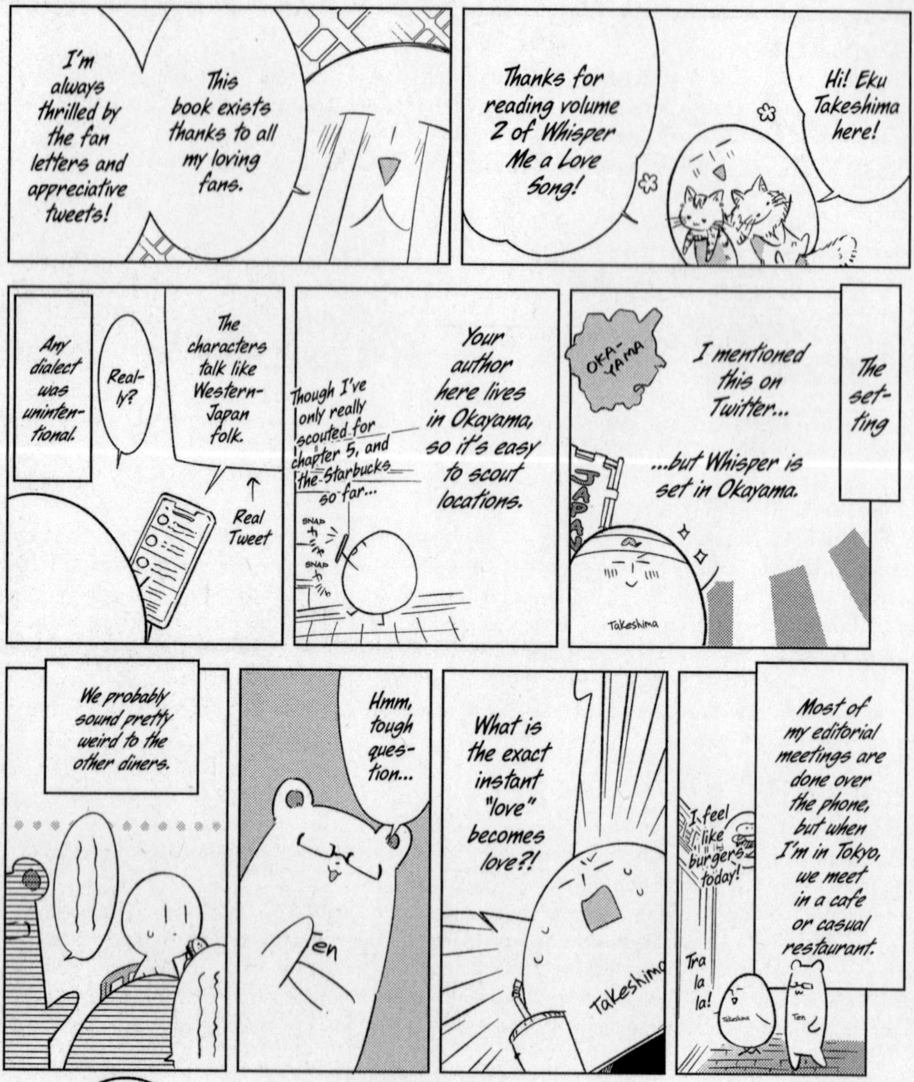
Hi! Eku Takeshima here!
Thanks for reading volume 2 of Whisper Me a Love Song!
This book exists thanks to all my loving fans.
I'm always thrilled by the fan letters and appreciative tweets!
The setting
I mentioned this on Twitter...
OKA-YAMA
...but Whisper is set in Okayama.
Takeshima
Your author here lives in Okayama, so it's easy to scout locations.
Though I've only really scouted for chapter 5, and the Starbucks so far...
SNAP
SNAP
The characters talk like Western-Japan folk.
Real Tweet
Really?
Any dialect was unintentional.
Most of my editorial meetings are done over the phone, but when I'm in Tokyo, we meet in a cafe or casual restaurant.
I feel like burgers today!
Tra la la!
Takeshima
Ten
What is the exact instant "love" becomes love?!
Takeshima
Hmm, tough question...
Ten
We probably sound pretty weird to the other diners.

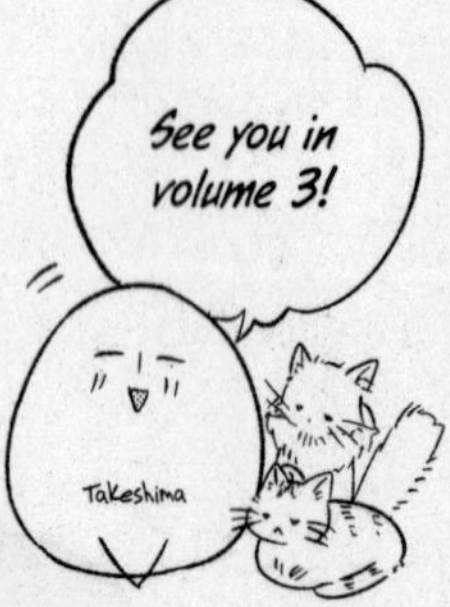
See you in volume 3!
Takeshima

SPECIAL THANKS

Editor – Ten-san

Design – SALIDAS-sama

All my assistants

And—
everyone who picked up this book!
Thank you all so much!

TRANSLATION NOTES

Friday Night Movie, page 8
Miki asks Himari if she saw last week's *kin-ro*, short for *"kinyoubi roodshoo"* ("Friday road show," "road show" being a term that went out of use long ago in the US but remains standard in Japan to refer chiefly to a movie's theatrical release, though in this case means its being shown on television), or Friday night movie. Nippon TV (NTV) broadcasts a movie of the week each Friday evening, ranging from popular domestic offerings to Hollywood blockbusters.

Away From Your Family, page 42
In Japanese, Himari's mother says that *"shucchou"* must be difficult for her husband. *Shucchou* means a business trip, of any length, so it's possible Himari's dad is only gone for a few days. However, in many companies and government organizations in Japan, workers are shuffled from one post or department to another on a regular basis (a process known as *jinji idou* or "personnel transfer"), and can sometimes be sent on long-term assignment to a distant location within Japan or even overseas with minimal notice. They typically complete the assignments alone, with their families staying behind. If this is the kind of *shucchou* Himari's dad is on, it could be quite a while before he gets that home-cooked meal.

I Love You So Much, page 42
Non-Japanese speakers wondering how to say "I love you" in Japanese often stumble on the expression *aishiteiru*. This phrase literally uses the character/word for "love" *(ai)*, plus the verb *suru* ("to do"; *shite iru* is the present progressive form, indicating an ongoing state of affairs). However, *ai shite iru* is actually an uncommon expression in Japanese. It's extremely direct, and is therefore seen as very forceful, not always a desirable quality in communication in Japanese. Instead, expressing affection in Japanese often involves phrases like *suki* (I like/love you), *daisuki* (I adore you), or other words or actions that convey the idea indirectly. Even between married partners, an actual *"Aishiteiru"* isn't very typical, so it helps convey how sweet Himari's parents are on each other.

SLURP, page 93
Ramen is served piping hot, and the only way to eat it without scorching yourself is to suck it into your mouth. This helps pass air over the noodles and cool them just enough to make them edible. It also tends to produce a noisy slurping sound, which isn't considered rude in Japan the way it is in some other cultures. Yori describes the cafeteria ramen as "better than you'd expect," which is a fair assessment. Ramen in Japan is a bit like hamburgers in a place like the US: you can find it virtually anywhere, but its very ubiquity generates a sliding scale of quality. Ramen can range from what feels like nothing more than mouthfuls of salt and grease to a sublime combination of noodles, broth, and other ingredients bursting with *umami*. Cafeteria ramen, let us say, doesn't tend to be on the high end of this spectrum.

Culture Fest, page 110
The *bunka-sai*, or culture festival, is a common ritual in Japanese schools, a day or two each year when the school holds an open house and students put on all kinds of events, performances, and installations such as food stalls or haunted houses.

Cultural Clubs, page 114
Miki refers to the *bunka-bu* (*bunka*, "culture," and *bu*, club or clubs). This isn't the name of a specific club, but is a generic term for just about any club that isn't an athletic or sports team.

The Other Two Girls Never Show Up, page 120
In Japanese, Momoka describes the other two club members with the standard but evocative expression *yuurei buin,* or "ghost club members."

C'mon In, page 152
Japanese homes typically have a *genkan,* a small area right in front of the door floored with tile, linoleum, or some other durable material that can withstand having shoes on it. Anyone entering the house removes their shoes in the *genkan* – going into a Japanese house with your shoes on is a major faux pas. (In the second panel on page 154, you can also see how some of the family members have left their shoes facing outward, so they're easy to slip on when the person leaves.) The *genkan* is typically built slightly lower than the actual floor of the house, so a visitor to the home is invited not to "come in" but to "come up" (*"agatte,"* from the verb *agaru*), which is what Miki says in the first panel on this page. A visitor entering a house says *"O-jama shimasu,"* literally meaning "I humbly intrude." (This is Himari's response in the second panel.)

Okayama, page 163
Located on the western half of Japan's main island, Okayama is situated midway between the cities of Hiroshima (farther west) and Kobe (to the east). Okayama is the name of both the prefecture (pictured in panel three on page 165) and its capital city.

Takeshima

For volume 2, I fretted almost as much as my characters about what "love" is. I hope you'll come along to see what they discover!

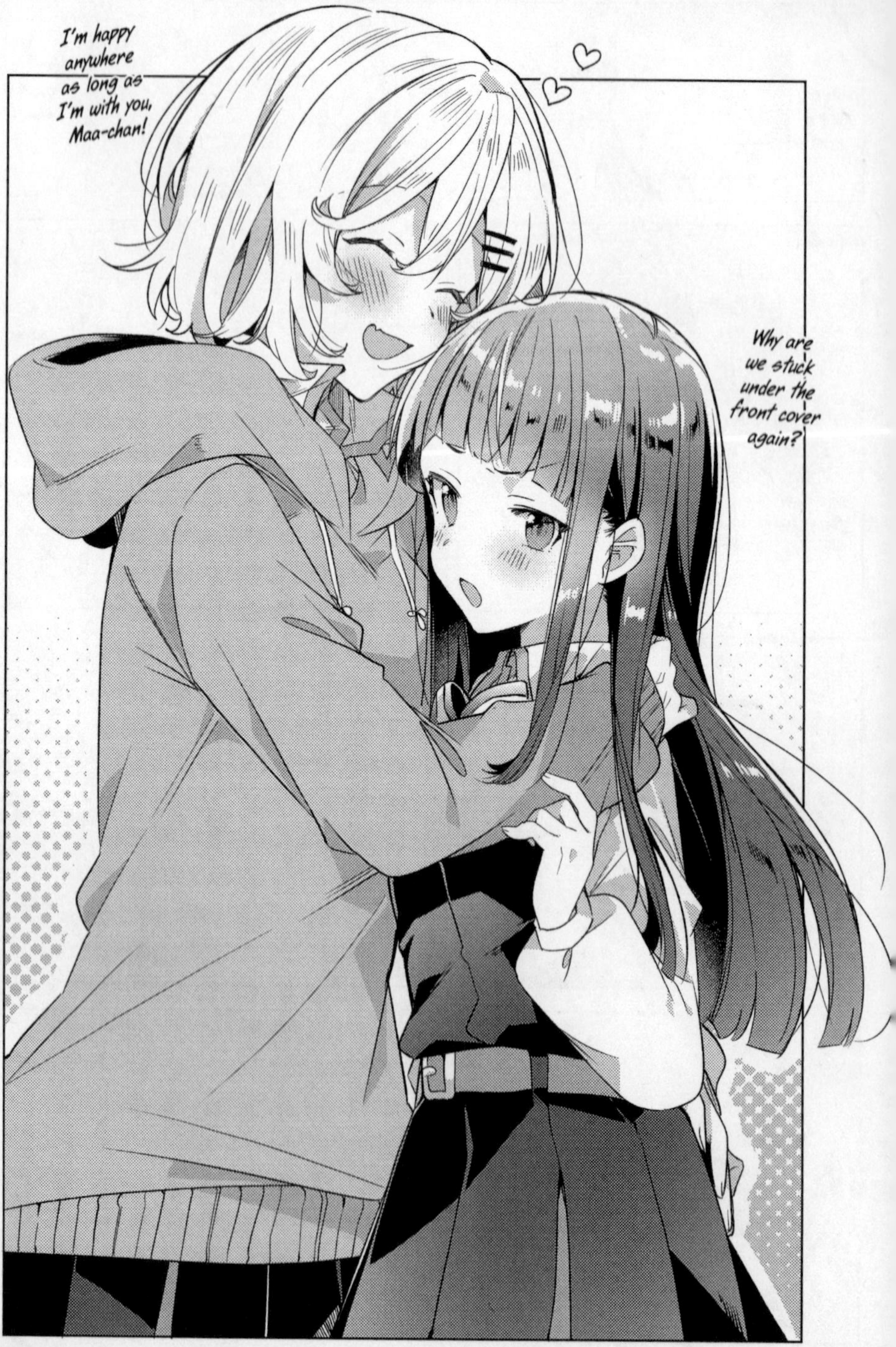
Why are we stuck under the front cover again?
I'm happy anywhere as long as I'm with you, Maa-chan!

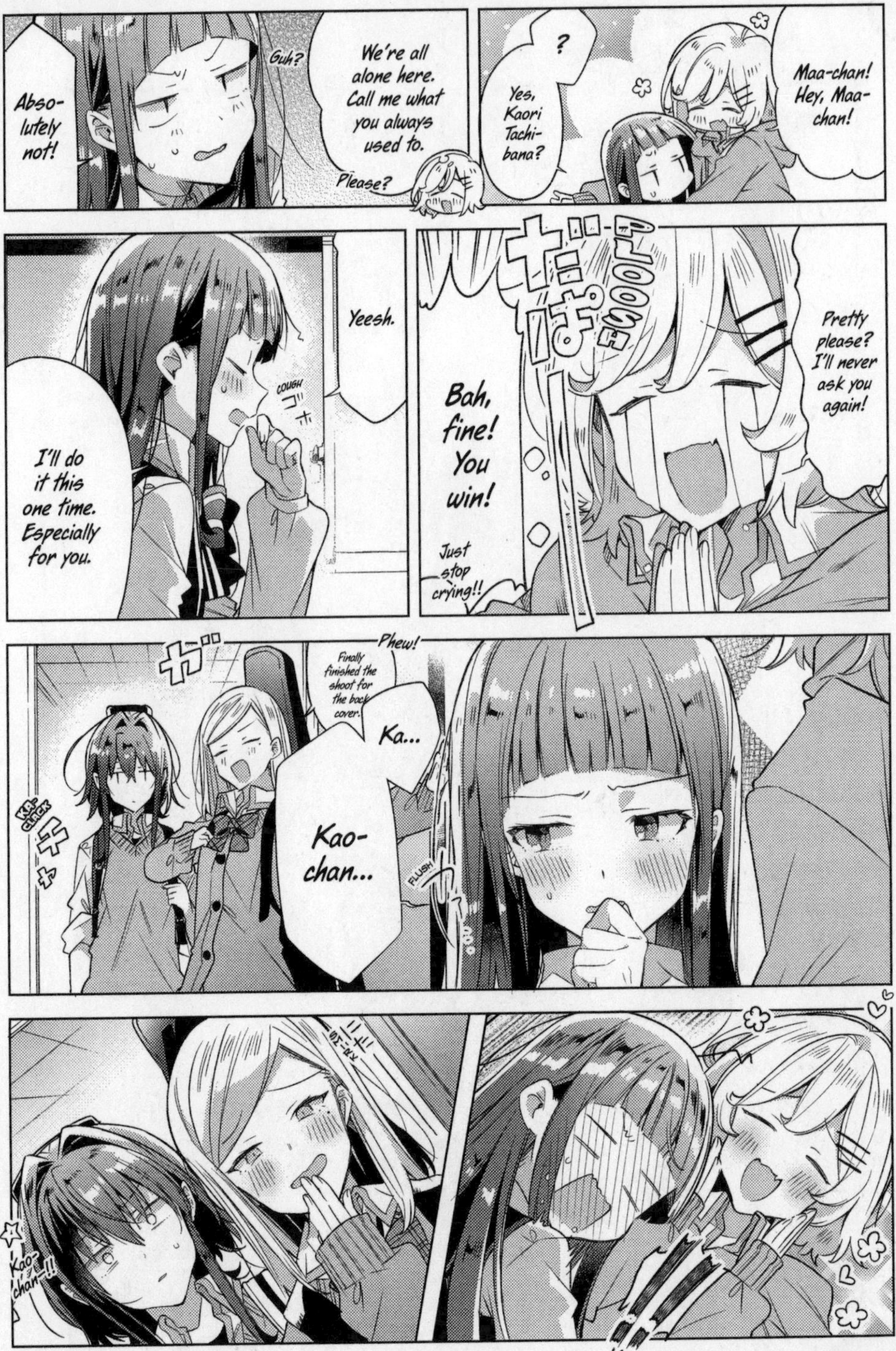
Maa-chan! Hey, Maa-chan!
?
Yes, Kaori Tachibana?
We're all alone here. Call me what you always used to.
Please?
Guh?
Abso-lutely not!
Pretty please? I'll never ask you again!
PLOOSH
Bah, fine! You win!
Just stop crying!!
Yeesh.
COUGH
I'll do it this one time. Especially for you.
Ka...
Kao-chan...
FLUSH
Phew!
Finally finished the shoot for the back cover.
KA-CLICK
Kao-chan--!!

Yuri Is My Job!

miman

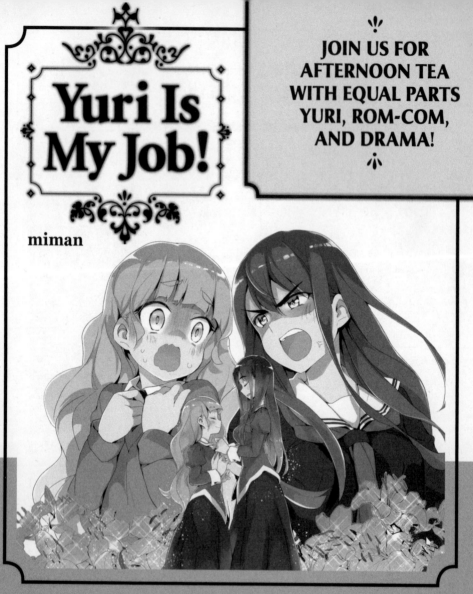

JOIN US FOR AFTERNOON TEA WITH EQUAL PARTS YURI, ROM-COM, AND DRAMA!

Hime is a picture-perfect high school princess, so when she accidentally injures a café manager named Mai, she's willing to cover some shifts to keep her façade intact. To Hime's surprise, the café is themed after a private school where the all-female staff always puts on their best act for their loyal customers. However, under the guidance of the most graceful girl there, Hime can't help but blush and blunder! Beneath all the frills and laughter, Hime feels tension brewing as she finds out more about her new job and her budding feelings...

KC KODANSHA COMICS

"A quirky, fun comedy series... If you're a yuri fan, or perhaps interested in getting into it but not sure where to start, this book is worth picking up."
— Anime UK News

A SMART, NEW ROMANTIC COMEDY FOR FANS OF *SHORTCAKE CAKE* AND *TERRACE HOUSE*!

KC
KODANSHA
COMICS

A romance manga starring high school girl Meeko, who learns to live on her own in a boarding house whose living room is home to the odd (but handsome) Matsunaga-san. She begins to adjust to her new life away from her parents, but Meeko soon learns that no matter how far away from home she is, she's still a young girl at heart — especially when she finds herself falling for Matsunaga-san.

PERFECT WORLD

Rie Aruga

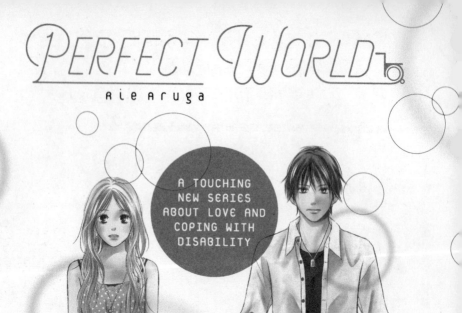

A TOUCHING NEW SERIES ABOUT LOVE AND COPING WITH DISABILITY

An office party reunites Tsugumi with her high school crush Itsuki. He's realized his dream of becoming an architect, but along the way, he experienced a spinal injury that put him in a wheelchair. Now Tsugumi's rekindled feelings will butt up against prejudices she never considered — and Itsuki will have to decide if he's ready to let someone into his heart...

"Depicts with great delicacy and courage the difficulties some with disabilities experience getting involved in romantic relationships... Rie Aruga refuses to romanticize, pushing her heroine to face the reality of disability. She invites her readers to the same tasks of empathy, knowledge and recognition."
—Slate.fr

"An important entry [in manga romance]... The emotional core of both plot and characters indicates thoughtfulness... [Aruga's] research is readily apparent in the text and artwork, making this feel like a real story."
—Anime News Network

KC KODANSHA COMICS

Knight of the ICE

Yayoi Ogawa

Knight of the Ice ©Yayoi Ogawa/Kodansha Ltd.

SKATING THRILLS AND ICY CHILLS WITH THIS NEW TINGLY ROMANCE SERIES!

A rom-com on ice, perfect for fans of *Princess Jellyfish* and *Wotakoi*. Kokoro is the talk of the figure-skating world, winning trophies and hearts. But little do they know... he's actually a huge nerd! From the beloved creator of *You're My Pet* (*Tramps Like Us*).

Chitose is a serious young woman, working for the health magazine *SASSO*. Or at least, she would be, if she wasn't constantly getting distracted by her childhood friend, international figure skating star Kokoro Kijinami! In the public eye and on the ice, Kokoro is a gallant, flawless knight, but behind his glittery costumes and breathtaking spins lies a secret: He's actually a hopelessly romantic otaku, who can only land his quad jumps when Chitose is on hand to recite a spell from his favorite magical girl anime!

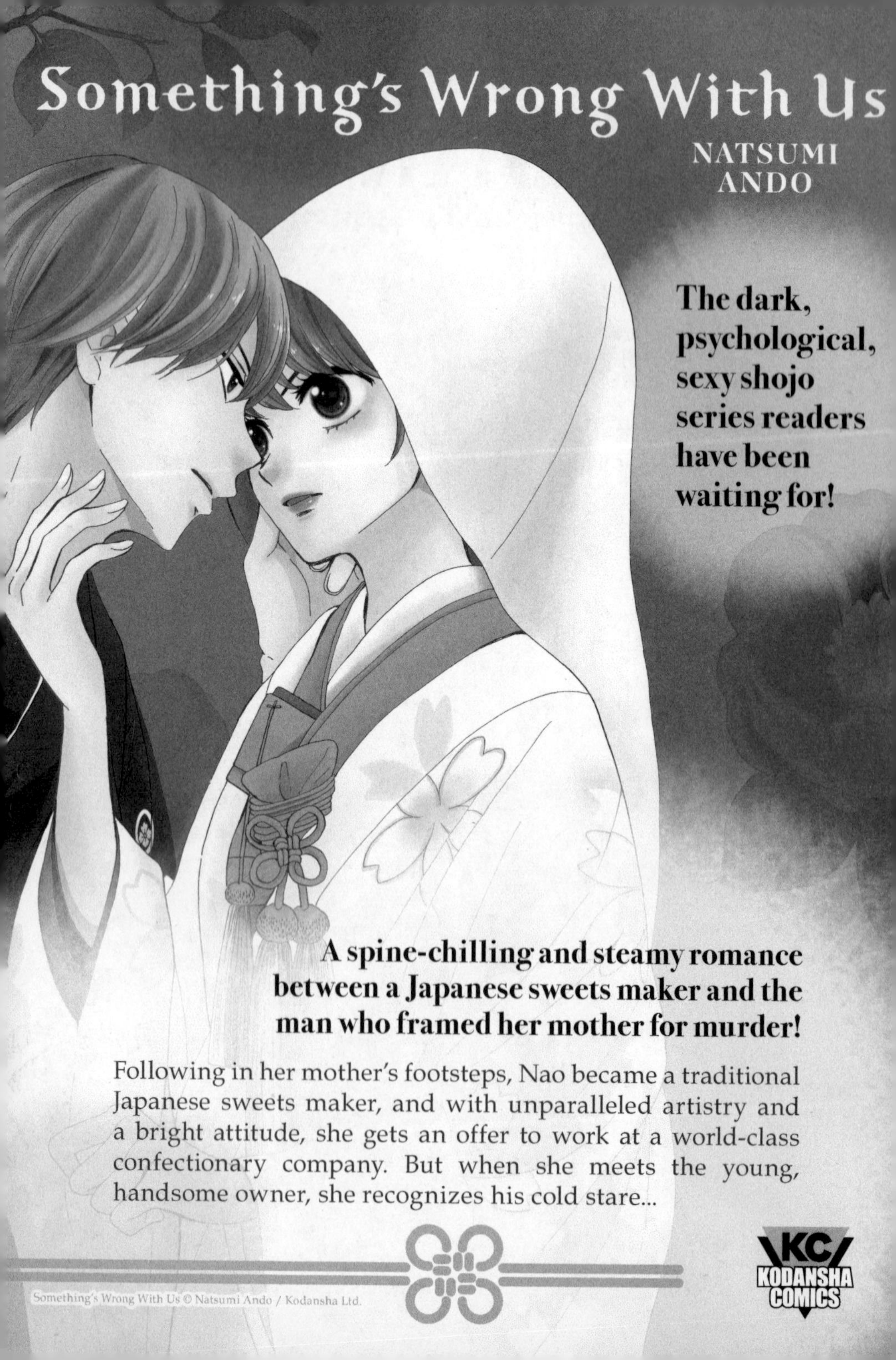
Something's Wrong With Us
NATSUMI ANDO
The dark, psychological, sexy shojo series readers have been waiting for!
A spine-chilling and steamy romance between a Japanese sweets maker and the man who framed her mother for murder!
Following in her mother's footsteps, Nao became a traditional Japanese sweets maker, and with unparalleled artistry and a bright attitude, she gets an offer to work at a world-class confectionary company. But when she meets the young, handsome owner, she recognizes his cold stare...
Something's Wrong With Us © Natsumi Ando / Kodansha Ltd.
KC
KODANSHA COMICS

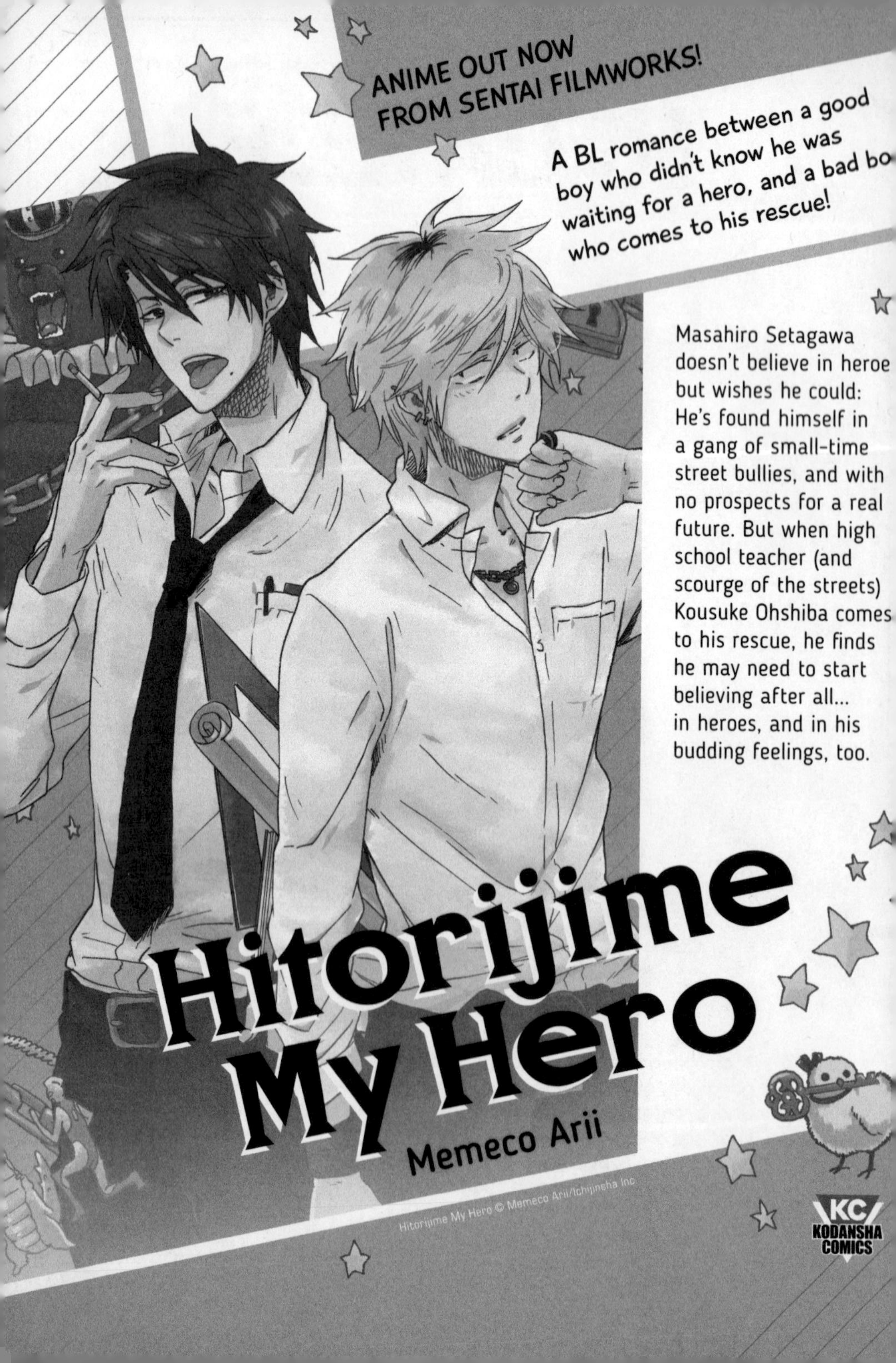
ANIME OUT NOW
FROM SENTAI FILMWORKS!
A BL romance between a good boy who didn't know he was waiting for a hero, and a bad bo who comes to his rescue!
Masahiro Setagawa doesn't believe in heroe but wishes he could: He's found himself in a gang of small-time street bullies, and with no prospects for a real future. But when high school teacher (and scourge of the streets) Kousuke Ohshiba comes to his rescue, he finds he may need to start believing after all... in heroes, and in his budding feelings, too.
Hitorijime My Hero
Memeco Arii
Hitorijime My Hero © Memeco Arii/Ichijinsha Inc
KC KODANSHA COMICS

One of CLAMP's biggest hits returns in this definitive, premium, hardcover 20th anniversary collector's edition!

"A wonderfully entertaining story that would be a great installment in anybody's manga collection."
— Anime News Network

"CLAMP is an all-female manga-creating team whose feminine touch shows in this entertaining, sci-fi soap opera."
— Publishers Weekly

Poor college student Hideki is down on his luck. All he wants is a good job, a girlfriend, and his very own "persocom"—the latest and greatest in humanoid computer technology. Hideki's luck changes one night when he finds Chi—a persocom thrown out in a pile of trash. But Hideki soon discovers that there's much more to his cute new persocom than meets the eye.

KC
KODANSHA
COMICS

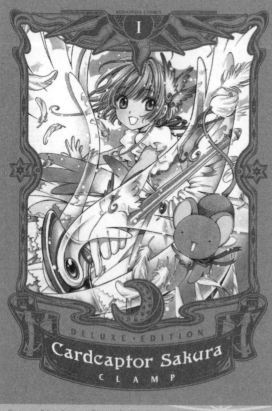

A Kodansha Comics Trade Paperback Original
Whisper Me a Love Song 2 copyright © 2020 Eku Takeshima
English translation copyright © 2020 Eku Takeshima

Published in the United States by Kodansha Comics, an imprint of Kodansha USA Publishing, LLC, New York.

Publication rights for this English edition arranged through Kodansha Ltd., Tokyo.

First published in Japan in 2020 by Ichijinsha Inc., Tokyo as *Sayasaku you ni koi wo utau*, volume 2.

ISBN 978-1-64651-146-4

Original cover design by SALIDAS

Printed in the United States of America.

www.kodanshacomics.com

9 8 7 6 5 4 3 2 1
Translation: Kevin Steinbach
Lettering: Jennifer Skarupa
Editing: Tiff Ferentini
Kodansha Comics edition cover design: Matt Akuginow

Publisher: Kiichiro Sugawara

Director of publishing services: Ben Applegate
Associate director of operations: Stephen Pakula
Publishing services managing editor: Noelle Webster
Assistant production manager: Emi Lotto, Angela Zurlo
Logo and character art ©Kodansha USA Publishing, LLC

THE SWEET SCENT OF LOVE IS IN THE AIR! FOR FANS OF OFFBEAT ROMANCES LIKE *WOTAKOI*

Sweat and Soap © Kintetsu Yamada / Kodansha Ltd.

In an office romance, there's a fine line between sexy and awkward... and that line is where Asako — a woman who sweats copiously — meets Koutarou — a perfume developer who can't get enough of Asako's, er, scent. Don't miss a romcom manga like no other!

In love, there are no save points.

NOW AN ANIME!

ヲタクに恋は難しい

WOTAKOI:
LOVE IS HARD FOR OTAKU
by FUJITA

Narumi has had it rough: Every boyfriend she's had dumped her once they found out she was an otaku, so she's gone to great lengths to hide it. At her new job, she bumps into Hirotaka, her childhood friend and fellow otaku. When Hirotaka almost gets her secret outed at work, she comes up with a plan to keep him quiet. But he comes up with a counter-proposal: Why doesn't she just date him instead?